A Cross-Cultural Examination of Women in Higher Education and the Workplace

Reem A. Abu-Lughod
Royal University for Women, Bahrain & School of Social Sciences and Education, California State University, Bakersfield, USA

A volume in the Advances in Higher Education and Professional Development (AHEPD) Book Series

Published in the United States of America by
    IGI Global
    Information Science Reference (an imprint of IGI Global)
    701 E. Chocolate Avenue
    Hershey PA, USA 17033
    Tel: 717-533-8845
    Fax: 717-533-8661
    E-mail: cust@igi-global.com
    Web site: http://www.igi-global.com

Copyright © 2024 by IGI Global. All rights reserved. No part of this publication may be reproduced, stored or distributed in any form or by any means, electronic or mechanical, including photocopying, without written permission from the publisher.
Product or company names used in this set are for identification purposes only. Inclusion of the names of the products or companies does not indicate a claim of ownership by IGI Global of the trademark or registered trademark.

                Library of Congress Cataloging-in-Publication Data

Names: Abu-Lughod, Reem, 1978- editor.
Title: A cross-cultural examination of women in higher education and the
   workplace / edited by Reem Abu-Lughod.
Description: Hershey, PA : Information Science Reference, [2024] | Includes
   bibliographical references and index. | Summary: "As such, this book
   will examine the marginalization of women in higher education and the
   workplace. It will also shed light on some of the factors that may have
   contributed to this marginalization, including culture, socio-economic
   factors, race and ethnicity, and the perception of the role of women in
   society"-- Provided by publisher.
Identifiers: LCCN 2024002260 (print) | LCCN 2024002261 (ebook) | ISBN
   9798369301029 (h/c) | ISBN 9798369301036 (s/c) | ISBN 9798369301043
   (ebook)
Subjects: LCSH: Women in higher education--Cross-cultural studies. | Sexism
   in higher education--Cross-cultural studies.
Classification: LCC LC1567 .C76 2024 (print) | LCC LC1567 (ebook) | DDC
   378.0082--dc23/eng/20240212
LC record available at https://lccn.loc.gov/2024002260
LC ebook record available at https://lccn.loc.gov/2024002261

This book is published in the IGI Global book series Advances in Higher Education and Professional Development (AHEPD) (ISSN: 2327-6983; eISSN: 2327-6991)

British Cataloguing in Publication Data
A Cataloguing in Publication record for this book is available from the British Library.
All work contributed to this book is new, previously-unpublished material.
The views expressed in this book are those of the authors, but not necessarily of the publisher.
For electronic access to this publication, please contact: eresources@igi-global.com.

Advances in Higher Education and Professional Development (AHEPD) Book Series

Jared Keengwe
University of North Dakota, USA

ISSN:2327-6983
EISSN:2327-6991

MISSION

As world economies continue to shift and change in response to global financial situations, job markets have begun to demand a more highly-skilled workforce. In many industries a college degree is the minimum requirement and further educational development is expected to advance. With these current trends in mind, the **Advances in Higher Education & Professional Development (AHEPD) Book Series** provides an outlet for researchers and academics to publish their research in these areas and to distribute these works to practitioners and other researchers.

AHEPD encompasses all research dealing with higher education pedagogy, development, and curriculum design, as well as all areas of professional development, regardless of focus.

COVERAGE

- Adult Education
- Assessment in Higher Education
- Career Training
- Coaching and Mentoring
- Continuing Professional Development
- Governance in Higher Education
- Higher Education Policy
- Pedagogy of Teaching Higher Education
- Vocational Education

IGI Global is currently accepting manuscripts for publication within this series. To submit a proposal for a volume in this series, please contact our Acquisition Editors at Acquisitions@igi-global.com or visit: http://www.igi-global.com/publish/.

The Advances in Higher Education and Professional Development (AHEPD) Book Series (ISSN 2327-6983) is published by IGI Global, 701 E. Chocolate Avenue, Hershey, PA 17033-1240, USA, www.igi-global.com. This series is composed of titles available for purchase individually; each title is edited to be contextually exclusive from any other title within the series. For pricing and ordering information please visit http://www.igi-global.com/book-series/advances-higher-education-professional-development/73681. Postmaster: Send all address changes to above address. Copyright © 2024 IGI Global. All rights, including translation in other languages reserved by the publisher. No part of this series may be reproduced or used in any form or by any means – graphics, electronic, or mechanical, including photocopying, recording, taping, or information and retrieval systems – without written permission from the publisher, except for non commercial, educational use, including classroom teaching purposes. The views expressed in this series are those of the authors, but not necessarily of IGI Global.

Titles in this Series

For a list of additional titles in this series, please visit:
http://www.igi-global.com/book-series/advances-higher-education-professional-development/73681

Global Perspectives on Decolonizing Postgraduate Education
Mishack Thiza Gumbo (University of South Africa, South Africa) Michael Gaotlhobogwe (University of Botswana, Botswana) Constantino Pedzisai (Chinhoyi University of Technology, Zimbabwe) Zingiswa Mybert Monica Jojo (Rhodes University, South Africa) and Christopher B. Knaus (University of Washington, Tacoma, USA & University of South Africa, South Africa)
Information Science Reference • © 2024 • 339pp • H/C (ISBN: 9798369312896) • US $230.00

Emerging Research in Agricultural Teacher Education
R. Kirby Barrick (University of Florida, USA (Retired)) and Andrew C. Thoron (Abraham Baldwin Agricultural College, USA)
Information Science Reference • © 2024 • 426pp • H/C (ISBN: 9798369327661) • US $245.00

Engaging Higher Education Teachers and Students With Transnational Leadership
Gareth Richard Morris (University of Nottingham, Ningbo, China) and Shayna Kozuch (University of Nottingham, Ningbo, China)
Information Science Reference • © 2024 • 306pp • H/C (ISBN: 9798369361009) • US $245.00

Preparing Students From the Academic World to Career Paths A Comprehensive Guide
Cassandra Sligh Conway (South Carolina State University, USA) and Andy Jiahao Liu (University of Arizona, USA)
Information Science Reference • © 2024 • 334pp • H/C (ISBN: 9781799879992) • US $215.00

Empowering Teams in Higher Education Strategies for Success
Tashieka Simone Burris-Melville (University of Technology, Jamaica) Shalieka Tiffia Burris (University of Technology, Jamaica) and Kristin Bledsoe (Trevecca Nazarene University, USA)
Information Science Reference • © 2024 • 392pp • H/C (ISBN: 9798369315200) • US $235.00

701 East Chocolate Avenue, Hershey, PA 17033, USA
Tel: 717-533-8845 x100 • Fax: 717-533-8661
E-Mail: cust@igi-global.com • www.igi-global.com

Table of Contents

Foreword xiv

Preface xvi

Introduction xxiii

Chapter 1
One Stride at a Time: Women Breaking Through the Glass Ceiling in the MENA Region 1
    Reem Ali Abu-Lughod, Royal University for Women, Bahrain & School of Social Sciences and Education, California State University, Bakersfield, USA

Chapter 2
Post-Pandemic Agents and Culture Vultures: Women in Higher Education 18
    Catherine Hayes, University of Sunderland, UK

Chapter 3
Profess*Her: The Revelatory Power of the Black Female Professor 43
    Catherine Saunders, Howard University, USA

Chapter 4
Black Women Professors' ART for Well-Being in Teacher Education 60
    Rosalynne Elisabeth Duff, Georgia State University, USA

Chapter 5
A Social-Ecological Model for Racially Diverse Women in Higher Education: Organizational Support and Affirmative Action 87
    Lolita L. Kincade, SUNY Plattsburgh, USA

Chapter 6
Women in the Academy: Challenges, Barriers, Promising Practices, and
Policies 113
    Sandy White Watson, University of Louisiana at Monroe, USA

Chapter 7
Advocating for Quota System as a Model for Women's Participation in
Political Affairs in Southern Africa: The case of Zimbabwe 137
    Menard Musendekwa, Reformed Church University, Zimbabwe

Chapter 8
Hispanic Women Professors in Higher Education in the US 151
    Antonio Daniel Juan Rubio, Universidad de Granada, Spain
    Jimmy Hernandez, Hispanic Association of Colleges and Universities,
        USA

Chapter 9
The Western Gaze and African Feminism: Twin Peaks in the Global Higher
Education Workforce 177
    Catherine Hayes, University of Sunderland, UK

Chapter 10
Examining Women Leaders' Role in Broadening Participation in STEM at
HBCUs 197
    Kimarie Engerman, Center for the Advancement of STEM Leadership,
        University of the Virgin Islands, US Virgin Islands
    Angelicque Tucker Blackmon, Center for the Advancement of STEM
        Leadership, University of the Virgin Islands, US Virgin Islands
    Camille A. McKayle, Center for the Advancement of STEM Leadership,
        University of the Virgin Islands, US Virgin Islands
    Elizabeth Jaeger, Center for the Advancement of STEM Leadership,
        University of the Virgin Islands, US Virgin Islands

Chapter 11
Micro-Enterprises, Performance Factors, and the Role of Gender 214
    Chelo Durante, Cebu Technological University, Philippines
    Michel Plaisent, Université du Québec à Montréal, Canada
    Cataldo Zuccaro, Université du Québec à Montréal, Canada
    Jean-Pierre Gueyie, Université du Québec à Montréal, Canada
    Prosper Bernard, Université du Québec à Montréal, Canada

Chapter 12
Inclusive Practices in Higher Education and Workplaces Strategies for
Empowering Women 237
  Mustafa Kayyali, HE Higher Education Ranking, Syria

Conclusion 263

Compilation of References 265

About the Contributors 307

Index 313

Detailed Table of Contents

Foreword xiv

Preface xvi

Introduction xxiii

Chapter 1
One Stride at a Time: Women Breaking Through the Glass Ceiling in the
MENA Region 1
  *Reem Ali Abu-Lughod, Royal University for Women, Bahrain & School
      of Social Sciences and Education, California State University,
      Bakersfield, USA*

Gender inequalities are a worldwide phenomenon hindering women's progress in higher education and the workforce. To fully grasp the current manifestations of this problem, it is crucial to examine the reasons behind it and shed light on the changes in policies that have moved toward overcoming it. This chapter focuses on women in the Middle East and North Africa (MENA) region; it specifically explores the roles of women in pursuing higher education and employment, as the two are intertwined in the complexity of advancing women in different disciplines and professions. The chapter also highlights how traditional and patriarchal societies in the MENA region place an unconscious bias on women, placing an expectation on them to be homemakers and caretakers for their families. Finally, the chapter presents how, despite more work to be done, the MENA region has advanced in promoting more women in higher education and the workforce but that a call for more collaboration in the region is needed.

Chapter 2
Post-Pandemic Agents and Culture Vultures: Women in Higher Education 18
  Catherine Hayes, University of Sunderland, UK

The marginalization of women across the 21st century workforces remains a fundamental issue for address in terms of global economies where factors contributing to inequality and inequity pervade. This chapter illuminates the agency of women in the context of higher education institutions where the COVID-19 pandemic provided an opportunity for them to undertake skills and outperform their male counterparts, in situations which up until that point history had maintained as the preserve of men. The existential crisis facing higher education institutions (HEIs) as a direct consequence of 2020 has served as a lens through which other facets of ambiguity and contingency also influence meta-thinking concerning their strategic governance and operationalization of policies in practice. Just how representative these women leaders were of those working across diverse leadership contexts and settings is also something that remains open to scrutiny, and this chapter explores debates of the agency of women in leadership roles.

Chapter 3
Profess*Her: The Revelatory Power of the Black Female Professor 43
   Catherine Saunders, Howard University, USA

The twentieth and twenty-first century has conveyed a notable increase in the number of Black women joining the professoriate. While triumphant, Black female presence has yielded significant professional and personal hardships for the Black woman. These hardships, often undervalued or dismissed by the institution, silences stories of mistreatment to maintain the illusion of diversity and inclusion. My chapter makes a notable departure from scholarly dialogue on the Black female professor that conceptualizes her trajectory through the looking glass of what Patricia Hill Collins called controlling images in Black Feminist Thought (2000). Instead, my project highlights the unique position of the Black female professor in the academy through a concept I call Profess*Her. The term references the unique, revelatory power of the Black female professor that exposes what is and what must change in order to stride toward true freedom as actualized and encouraged by the academic institution.

Chapter 4
Black Women Professors' ART for Well-Being in Teacher Education 60
   Rosalynne Elisabeth Duff, Georgia State University, USA

Within the academy, Black Women professors have cultivated theories and practices for well-being, utilizing memoirs for theorization and social movements. However, their theories and practices should be more valued within the literature on holistic or healing pedagogies or teacher education (Muhammad et al., 2020). Teacher education is in a crisis with reports of high demands and stress levels with low autonomy and pay (Doan et al., 2023). This is an exploratory study of six Black Women professors' healing theories and practices produced through the genre of memoirs. Therefore, this chapter aims to inform professors, teacher educators, and educational leaders about Black Women's healing practices as creative expressions of their activism, research, and teaching (ART) (Tyson, 2001) and ways of well-being. In this way, it aims to move Black Women's healing theories and ways of knowing from the margins to the center of knowledge production in the context of teacher education.

Chapter 5
A Social-Ecological Model for Racially Diverse Women in Higher
Education: Organizational Support and Affirmative Action 87
    Lolita L. Kincade, SUNY Plattsburgh, USA

Systemic and structural inequities have created barriers to the success of women of color in higher education. In the U.S., racially diverse women are underrepresented among faculty and senior leaders, and they experience complex challenges because of their intersectional identities. This chapter builds on a Social-Ecological Model of Support (SEM), designed to guide the development of effective interventions through social environments. There is a focus on the organizational level, which promotes practices and policies that advance diversity and opportunity for racially diverse women in higher education roles. An examination of race and gender-based affirmative action and its effects, to include increased representation of White women as higher education faculty and senior leaders is provided. Also outlined are recommendations to strengthen affirmative action programs in ways that promote diversity, mitigating issues of gendered racism and intersectional discrimination, which compromise recruitment, retention, and advancement of racially diverse women in higher education settings.

Chapter 6
Women in the Academy: Challenges, Barriers, Promising Practices, and
Policies 113
    Sandy White Watson, University of Louisiana at Monroe, USA

In this chapter, the author examines the state of women in higher education, including a discussion of roadblocks and deterrents. The author reveals deterrents/roadblocks in common recruitment practices, retainment requirements, and advancement policies. She then focuses on initiatives designed to mitigate those deterrents that act to transform institutions, starting with research and evaluation, identifying and forming pipeline initiatives designed to encourage women to apply for positions in higher education. These initiatives are classified as structures (such as childcare facilities, lactation centers, family resource centers, etc.), pipeline initiatives (equity advisors, ombudspersons/offices, etc.), programs/initiatives (peer networking, mentoring, etc.), policies (tenure clock extensions, etc.), and climate initiatives (addressing unconscious bias, bystander interventions, etc.).

Chapter 7
Advocating for Quota System as a Model for Women's Participation in
Political Affairs in Southern Africa: The case of Zimbabwe 137
    Menard Musendekwa, Reformed Church University, Zimbabwe

Despite the advent of gender-based policies and initiatives that have tended to dominate the participatory discourse both nationally and internationally, the literature on women and gender emphasises the slow pace of transition and development (Mapuva 2013). Severe decline of women participation in political affairs in Zimbabwe since 2008 may be indicators that women are continually drifting into the margins as far as politics is concerned. This research proposes that advocacy full implementation of Quota System (QS) may increase women participation in political affairs .The research is a historical reflection of advocacy towards women participation in political affairs in Zimbabwe as the case for Southern Africa.

Chapter 8
Hispanic Women Professors in Higher Education in the US 151
    Antonio Daniel Juan Rubio, Universidad de Granada, Spain
    Jimmy Hernandez, Hispanic Association of Colleges and Universities,
      USA

Although the Hispanic population has become the largest minority group in the United States, this fact has not been reflected in their presence as tenured or non-tenured professors at the country's colleges and universities. And this is especially aggravated in the case of Hispanic females. The decreasing number of Hispanic female professors in Higher Education in the United States foretells this delicate situation. A major concern associated with the Hispanics' lack of involvement in higher education is the seeming lack of awareness among the general population that such a problem exists. Therefore, the objective of this chapter is to examine some specific outstanding and representative cases. Hispanic women professors continue to remain underrepresented in faculty and leadership position in the country.

Chapter 9
The Western Gaze and African Feminism: Twin Peaks in the Global Higher
Education Workforce 177
    Catherine Hayes, University of Sunderland, UK

This chapter serves as a mechanism of recognizing and acknowledging the illegitimacy of historic and traditional western approaches to narratives of African feminist epistemology. These approaches have engendered lenses of perspective which are irrefutably skewed by colonialism and whose address is warranted in ensuring both a means of learning about the end of an era and the prospect of a more authentically framed future framed, shaped, and determined from within African culture and context by those. To undertake this acknowledgement and recognition is one of the first and much belated to framing steps in ensuring that the articulation of truth lies best with those whose lived truths they are, rather than any tokenistic perceptions of them, consequently articulated through Western lenses of perspective.

Chapter 10
Examining Women Leaders' Role in Broadening Participation in STEM at HBCUs 197
 Kimarie Engerman, Center for the Advancement of STEM Leadership,
  University of the Virgin Islands, US Virgin Islands
 Angelicque Tucker Blackmon, Center for the Advancement of STEM
  Leadership, University of the Virgin Islands, US Virgin Islands
 Camille A. McKayle, Center for the Advancement of STEM Leadership,
  University of the Virgin Islands, US Virgin Islands
 Elizabeth Jaeger, Center for the Advancement of STEM Leadership,
  University of the Virgin Islands, US Virgin Islands

This research examines women academic leaders' role in broadening participation in science technology, engineering, and mathematics (STEM) disciplines at Historically Black Colleges and Universities (HBCUs). HBCUs produce a high percentage of Black STEM graduates which contributes to the nation's diverse STEM workforce. Additionally, women are known to be transformative leaders. Interpretative phenomenological analysis (IPA) was used in this study to understand the academic women leaders' role. A semi-structured interview was administered to obtain information on the women's leadership style or characteristics, STEM success as a leader, and the relationship between women's leadership and STEM success at their respective institution. The study findings have implications for institutions to capitalize on the significant role women leaders play in the success of students, faculty, and the institution overall.

Chapter 11
Micro-Enterprises, Performance Factors, and the Role of Gender 214
 Chelo Durante, Cebu Technological University, Philippines
 Michel Plaisent, Université du Québec à Montréal, Canada
 Cataldo Zuccaro, Université du Québec à Montréal, Canada
 Jean-Pierre Gueyie, Université du Québec à Montréal, Canada
 Prosper Bernard, Université du Québec à Montréal, Canada

Life in developing countries often relies on informal economy and micro-enterprises, often created and managed by women. Their performance has been studied in the literature of management and world development and factors of success have been suggested among which the access to micro-financing organizations, being member of network, having an innovative spirit and accepting the related risk and being able to overcome hostile business conditions. The difficulties are reported as being worst for women who suffers from stereotypes about their abilities and negative cultural factors. This chapter reports on a cross-sectional study among 200 entrepreneurs and test those hypothesis.

Chapter 12
Inclusive Practices in Higher Education and Workplaces Strategies for
Empowering Women..237
   Mustafa Kayyali, HE Higher Education Ranking, Syria

This book chapter addresses the shifting landscape of inclusive practices in both higher education and workplace contexts, with a specific focus on strategies targeted at empowering women. It looks into the multiple facets of gender equality, covering the historical context of gender inequality, contemporary issues encountered by women, cross-cultural viewpoints, success stories, and best practices. The chapter underlines the crucial importance of intersectionality and mental health support in establishing an inclusive and equal environment for women. By studying and praising these inclusive traditions, this chapter strives to provide a thorough knowledge of the challenging journey towards gender equality and the empowerment of women in many cultural contexts.

Conclusion 263

Compilation of References 265

About the Contributors 307

Index 313

Foreword

When a university name is heard, most people experience an emotional response. The response can be one of thrill, excitement, or nostalgia. Conversely, it can also be one of tragedy, rejection, or sadness. Some visuals, such as school colors, mascots, logos, fight songs, and rivalries, come to mind. Memorable areas of the campus, such as a fountain, a statue, a famous building, and a quad area, might also be associated with the university. Friendships that were made during university study are also a noteworthy occurrence. Thinking about the times that one shared with loved ones and family legacy might also be an unforgettable connection that an individual has with their alma mater.

An excellent, supportive professor who provides advice and leadership and has effective pedagogical practices can also be remembered fondly. I flashback to when I was sitting in a creative writing class, working on what I thought was my best piece yet. When it was my turn to stand before the class and read it aloud, the professor had his usual look of disdain on his face. Although his reaction was not what I was seeking, it made me work harder to find my inner voice as he called it. Even though professors are also integral to university life, there are numerically more male professors than female professors.

Additionally, male professors receive the rank of full professorship at higher rates than females. Another layer of complexity is that of female professors. Female professors of Color numerical rates are lower than their White female counterparts. Moreover, the cultural taxation that faculty of Color carry creates stress and what Smith (2011) has coined as racial battle fatigue.

The reality of being a woman in leadership is an arduous task. How *Cross-Cultural Examination of Women in Higher Education and the Workplace* successfully interweaves the stories of women in higher education is an incredibly delicate balancing act of addressing educational inequities and finding ways to dismantle barriers. Moreover, the authors hail from various countries worldwide; however, the crux of the book remains the same. The general perspective of the existing female marginalization and how women must overcome these barriers are discussed in detail. Readers - men and women alike - will be able to relate to the stories and experiences

Foreword

that are explained within these pages. The authors have made the content relatable because educators from all levels - albeit PK-12 or higher education - can relate to the misconceptions that occur when a woman is in a leadership position (whether in the classroom or administration). I can personally relate to this situation since I have taught and been an administrator at every grade, from PK-6 to 7–12, to higher education and beyond. One overarching theme is prevalent: a woman must prove herself initially and constantly; in addition, she must work harder to go less far.

Although the authors in this book are women and men, they are all writing about the marginalization of women who work in higher education and the workplace. Herein these pages, the authors describe the hardships that women experience in the workplace. These hardships are those of marginalization, glass ceilings, cultural taxation, lack of access to "a seat at the table," misogyny, stereotypical behavior from colleagues, sexual harassment, and other forms of unethical and unprofessional behavior that goes "unnoticed" and overlooked within the workplace setting.

By crossing cultural boundaries and sharing various perspectives of higher education and the workforce, the readers will understand that perspective matters. Additionally, cultural relativity impacts how one sees the world. Ultimately, it is up to society to embrace the notion that our world is changing. The demographics of our nation are becoming more culturally diverse. Women are a staple within our society and workforce, and it is time to begin to come to terms with our assumptions and misconceptions that have created hurdles along the way.

It is time for society to reflect on what has worked and has not worked. *A Cross-Cultural Examination of Women in Higher Education and the Workplace* is a great place to do just that. The stories within the pages of this book provide the space to have honest, open conversations about the changing landscape in higher education and the workplace. In addition, the experiences that are shared in this book are an excellent springboard for discussing how to create a safe space for students, faculty, and staff to create a socially just and equitable workplace environment. In order to move forward, society must study the past. Dr. Reem A. Abu-Lughod's edited book is a perfect springboard for critical conversations. It is this author's hope that one day, this world will be a place where women, especially women of Color in higher education, will be added to every list of nostalgic remembrances alongside our favorite college football team and fight song.

Patricia Lane
California State University, Fresno

Preface

Many countries around the world have introduced initiatives aimed at promoting the advancement of women roles in their respective societies. These initiatives encompass various aspects such as women's right to vote, political participation, and access to education and employment opportunities. This book addresses these movements, shedding light on the policy implications and resources that have played a crucial role in propelling women forward on different fronts. A key focus of this book is on strategies that have been proposed or put into practice to address ethical dilemmas and gender-related challenges.

This topic crosses over many sub-disciplines within the social and behavioral sciences, particularly those that align with my academic teachings and research publications. These include social stratification, women's studies, race & ethnic studies, public policy, ethics, and more.

Furthermore, the book covers literature that offers insights on how to bolster the presence of women in higher education and the workforce across diverse societies. It emphasizes the importance of fostering communication and embracing a cross-cultural perspective across various disciplines.

While the 21st century has seen a significant increase in the number of women entering the workforce and achieving higher levels of education, their numbers remain disproportionate compared to their male counterparts. As such, this book examines the marginalization of women in higher education and the workplace, exploring the various factors that have contributed to this disparity. These factors include cultural norms, socio-economic factors, race and ethnic biases, and societal perceptions of women's roles. Through a cross-cultural lens, this book compares the experiences of women in different societies, examining the policies and practices that have either supported or hindered women's advancement in education and the workforce. By shedding light on these issues, the book aims to provide a deeper understanding of the challenges women face in achieving equality and empowerment in these domains.

This book will be invaluable to:

- Educators in higher education across disciplines
- Researchers engaged in women's studies

- Government agencies focusing on the advancement of women
- Agencies across various sectors led by women

We hope this collection provides valuable insights and fosters a deeper understanding of the challenges and opportunities for women in higher education and the workplace globally.

ORGANIZATION OF THE BOOK

Chapter 1: One Stride at a Time: Women Breaking Through the Glass Ceiling in the MENA Region

Reem Ali Abu-Lughod

Gender disparities are a prevalent issue that impedes the progress of women in higher education and the workforce on a global scale. This chapter specifically examines the Middle East and North Africa (MENA) region, shedding light on women's roles in higher education and employment, which play a crucial role in advancing women's positions in various fields and professions. It explores the influence of traditional and patriarchal societies in the MENA region, which often subconsciously steer women towards domestic roles as homemakers and caregivers. Despite these challenges, the chapter underscores significant strides made in promoting women in higher education and the workforce within the MENA region, while also advocating for enhanced regional cooperation to further these initiatives.

Chapter 2: Post-Pandemic Agents and Culture Vultures Women in Higher Education

Catherine Hayes

This chapter addresses the persistent marginalization of women in the workforce, with a specific focus on higher education, exacerbated by the COVID-19 pandemic. Despite the challenges brought on by the pandemic, it has also provided women with opportunities to showcase their skills and surpass their male counterparts in traditionally male-dominated roles. The chapter explores the existential crisis that Higher Education Institutions (HEIs) have faced post-2020, using this as a framework to explore broader issues surrounding governance and policy implementation. It examines the representation of women in various leadership roles and delves into discussions surrounding the agency of women in these positions. It further emphasizes the importance of strategic and inclusive policymaking in higher education to ensure the advancement and empowerment of women in leadership roles.

Chapter 3: Profess*Her: The Revelatory Power of the Black Female Professor

Catherine Saunders

The rise in Black women entering academia as professors in the twentieth and twenty-first centuries has been marked by notable professional and personal challenges. This chapter moves beyond traditional narratives to explore the unique experiences of Black female professors, through the concept of "Profess*Her." This term symbolizes their transformative ability to uncover systemic issues and push for essential reforms within academic settings. By shedding light on their struggles and triumphs, the chapter advocates for a reassessment of diversity and inclusion initiatives to foster genuine liberation and equity for Black female professors.

Chapter 4: Black Women Professors' Healing Theories and Practices for Well-Being in Teacher Education

Rosalynne Duff

Black women professors have cultivated distinctive theories and practices for promoting well-being, often through memoirs and social movements. This chapter explores these healing practices within the context of teacher education, a field currently grappling with a crisis marked by excessive demands, limited autonomy, and inadequate compensation. Through an analysis of the memoirs of six Black women professors, this chapter seeks to elevate their healing theories and practices from the periphery to the forefront of knowledge disseminations. It advocates for recognizing these practices as indispensable elements of activism, scholarship, and pedagogy, fostering well-being and holistic education in teacher training programs.

Chapter 5: A Social-Ecological Model for Racially Diverse Women in Higher Education: Organizational Support and Affirmative Action

Lolita Kincade

Systemic and structural inequities present significant obstacles for women of color in higher education. This chapter introduces a Social-Ecological Model of Support (SEM) as a framework for developing effective interventions within social environments. The focus is on organizational practices and policies that promote diversity opportunities for racially diverse women in higher education roles. Additionally, the chapter examines the impact of race and gender-based affirmative action, highlighting the overrepresentation of White women and the need for more inclusive affirmative action initiatives. Recommendations are provided to address gendered racism and intersectional discrimination, with the goal of enhancing the recruitment, retention, and advancement of racially diverse women in higher education.

Chapter 6: Women in the Academy: Challenges, Barriers, Promising Practices and Policies

Sandy Watson

This chapter examines the status of women in higher education, focusing on the obstacles and barriers they encounter. It explores the prevalent challenges in recruitment, retention, and career advancement policies, while also showcasing various strategies aimed at overcoming these hurdles. These strategies encompass a range of interventions, including structural supports such as childcare facilities and lactation centers, pipeline initiatives like equity advisors and ombudspersons, program such as peer networking and mentoring, policies like tenure clock extensions, and climate initiatives that address unconscious bias and promote bystander interventions. The chapter emphasizes the critical need for institutional transformation to create a more supportive and inclusive environment that fosters the progress and success of women in higher education.

Chapter 7: Advocating for Quota System as a Model for Women Participation in Political Affairs in Southern Africa: The Case of Zimbabwe

Menard Musendekwa

Despite the implementation of various gender-based policies and initiatives, the progress of women's participation in political affairs in Zimbabwe has been slow. This chapter suggests advocating for the full implementation of a Quota System (QS) to boost women's political involvement. It offers a historical perspective on advocacy efforts for women's political engagement in Zimbabwe and examines the potential benefits and challenges of adopting a QS model in the Southern African region. The chapter posits that a QS has the potential to greatly improve women's representation and impact in political decision-making processes.

Chapter 8: Hispanic Women Professors in Higher Education in the US

Antonio Juan Rubio, Jimmy Hernandez

The Hispanic population is the largest minority group in the United States; however, Hispanic women remain underrepresented in higher education as both tenured and non-tenured professors. This chapter examines the factors contributing to the limited presence of Hispanic female professors and showcases specific cases that exemplify the obstacles they encounter. It sheds light on the overall lack of awareness surrounding this issue and emphasizes the need for heightened initiatives to advocate for and elevate Hispanic women in academic positions. The chapter underscores the significance of representation and diversity in higher education to accurately mirror the demographic realities.

Chapter 9: The Western Gaze and African Feminism: Twin Peaks in the Global Higher Education Workforce

Catherine Hayes

This chapter provides a critical analysis of the historical and traditional Western approaches to African feminist epistemology, which have been influenced by colonialism. It advocates for the importance of acknowledging and validating African feminist perspectives within their own cultural and contextual frameworks. The chapter aims to move away from the superficial Western interpretations towards genuine portrayals of African women's lived realities. Through this shift, it strives to promote a more inclusive and accurate understanding of African feminism within the global higher education sector.

Chapter 10: Examining Women Leaders' Role in Broadening Participation in STEM at HBCUs

Kimarie Engerman, Angelicque Tucker Blackmon, Camille McKayle, Elizabeth Jaeger

This chapter examines the pivotal role of women academic leaders in enhancing participation in Science, Technology, Engineering, and Mathematics (STEM) disciplines at Historically Black Colleges and Universities (HBCUs). HBCUs are instrumental in cultivating a diverse STEM workforce, with women leaders renowned for their innovative leadership styles and approaches. Through the utilization of Interpretative Phenomenological Analysis (IPA), the chapter explores leadership attributes of women at HBCUs and their impact on STEM achievements. The results highlight the substantial impact of women leaders in advancing student, faculty, and institutional success within STEM fields.

Chapter 11: Micro-Enterprises, Performance Factors and the Role of Gender

Chelo Durante, Michel Plaisent, Cataldo Zuccaro, Jean-Pierre Gueyie, Prosper Bernard

Preface

Micro-enterprises, frequently established and operated by women, play a vital role in the informal economy of developing countries. This chapter examines key performance indicators of these micro-enterprises, such as access to micro-financing, networking, innovation, and overcoming challenging business environments. It sheds light on the specific obstacles encountered by women entrepreneurs, stemming from stereotypes and cultural norms. Drawing from a cross-sectional study involving 200 entrepreneurs, the chapter evaluates different hypotheses regarding success factors and offers valuable insights into the distinct challenges and prospects for women entrepreneurs in developing countries.

Chapter 12: Inclusive Practices in Higher Education and Workplaces: Strategies for Empowering Women

Mustafa Kayyali

This chapter explores the ever-changing landscape of inclusive practices in higher education and workplaces, with a specific focus on strategies to empower women. It covers the historical context of gender inequality, contemporary issues, cross-cultural perspectives, success stories, and best practices. The chapter emphasizes the importance of intersectionality and mental health support in fostering inclusive environments. Through the celebration and analysis of these inclusive practices, the chapter aims to offer a thorough understanding of the path towards gender equality and the empowerment of women in diverse cultural contexts.

IN CONCLUSION

In compiling *A Cross-Cultural Examination of Women in Higher Education and the Workplace*, we have worked diligently to illuminate the multifaceted challenges and triumphs experienced by women across different cultural and societal landscapes. Each chapter provides a unique perspective that helps us gain a deeper understanding of the intricate dynamics of gender, culture, socio-economic influences, and institutional policies that impact women in academia and the professional world.

Our esteemed contributors have offered a wealth of valuable insights, ranging from the remarkable progress of women in the MENA region to the pioneering leadership of Black women professors in the United States. We have examined the persistent obstacles faced by women globally, including the underrepresentation of Hispanic women in academia and the systemic inequities encountered by racially diverse women in higher education. Nevertheless, we have also celebrated the resilience and empowerment of women who, in spite of these challenges, are spearheading transformative initiatives in their respective fields and communities.

The diverse perspectives showcased in this volume underscore the critical importance of fostering cross-cultural dialogue and collaboration. They emphasize the need for implementing comprehensive strategies that address both the visible and invisible barriers hindering women's progress. These strategies encompass policy reforms, organizational support systems, and inclusive practices that not only empower women but also enhance the institutions and societies in which they operate.

In my role as editor, I am hopeful that this book will serve as a catalyst for further research and action. I envision a future where gender equality is not merely an aspiration but a tangible reality in higher education and the workplace. I extend an invitation to educators, policymakers, researchers, and leaders from all sectors to engage with the insights and recommendations presented here, and to join me in fostering environments where women can thrive and make meaningful contributions.

In conclusion, while significant strides have been made, the journey toward gender equity remains ongoing. It demands sustained dedication, unwavering commitment, and a readiness to challenge and transform existing frameworks. We are confident that the perspectives and strategies deliberated in this book will inspire and guide those committed to advancing women's roles in higher education and the workforce, paving the way for a more equitable and inclusive future for all.

Introduction

Historically, women were faced with barriers in pursuing higher education and employment, limiting their opportunities for success and advancement. However, in recent years, there has been a significant shift in promoting gender equality in these two domains, all while recognizing the need and value for diversity and inclusion. This is a multifaceted subject that stems across various cultures, societies, and time eras. In *A Cross-Cultural Examination of Women in Higher Education and the Workplace*, authors aim to shed light on very important issues that encompass a wide range of topics focusing on women's advancements, exploring their struggles and achievements in reaching success in higher education and work.

Each chapter in the book is unique in that it provides the reader with an understanding of policies that have either promoted or inhibited the advancement of women across various levels in society. Additionally, authors have included information on current changes that are driving a movement toward gender equality in higher education and work. For example, in their contributions, authors focus on the importance of having professors in higher education that come from diverse racial and ethnic groups. Those contributions not only focus on the desperate need for diversity in higher education, but also the enriching experiences students gain from that.

Additionally, diversity in higher education is emphasized as it provides representation for minority students who, over the years, have not seen themselves represented in positions of authority within academe. This representation in higher education serves as a move toward breaking stereotypes and biases by embracing diversity and enhancing more inclusive practices and curricula. This, as it has been proposed, fosters cultural and global awareness that challenges academic institutions to think critically and develop competence among faculty of diverse racial and ethnic backgrounds, as well as promote a subculture of viewpoints across curricula.

In addition to women in higher education, authors' contributions have also presented on the importance of women in the workforce. In their writings, authors have highlighted ways women have been able to break barriers and stereotypes that have long hindered their advancement. Furthermore, authors focus on the shift in the workforce, promoting more female inclusion and changing workplace dynamics by examining policies that allow women to break through the metaphorical glass ceiling. However, authors are also cautious to point out that while there have been advancements in policies promoting equity in the workforce, women continue to face struggles in the persisting wage gaps between men and women and the disparities in promoting a more diverse and inclusive workplace.

Another important point authors bring to the discussion is the limited female representation in leadership positions and their underrepresentation in top executive roles. The metaphorical glass ceiling barrier, as it is pointed out, continues to create obstacles for women seeking promotions and advancements at their places of employment, that only systematic changes in organizational cultures and policies and practices promoting gender diversity and inclusion can eventually overcome. Nevertheless, women from cross-cultural and global perspectives are making strides in breaking through the glass ceiling and challenging stereotypes. Some of the noted strategies are seen through promoting women-led initiatives, exploring resources and training focused on professional development, advancement, and mentoring, and pursuing higher education.

Globally and cross-culturally, it is crucial to address unconscious biases through policy changes and legislative efforts that can not only help in breaking barriers for women to advance in their careers, but also address the urgent need for equal opportunity and inclusivity in the workforce. Education and awareness, as the chapters present, are essential in combatting stereotypes, providing training programs on gender sensitivity and inclusivity that would promote diversity at different levels.

Contributions to this book are also diverse in topics associated with ethnic minority women's experiences in teaching and teacher education. One important aspect that is pointed out is the well-being among minority professors; an understated aspect that is significant when examining barriers in higher education that may impact the overall emotional and mental health of ethnic minorities. Through an interdisciplinary approach, authors present theories focusing on the importance of practices imbedded in curricula that can contribute to an integrative approach of healing through education, social dynamics, and spirituality.

As such, navigating through stereotypes in the workplace and ensuring that they have access to resources for personal health, marginalized groups can have better academic success and job satisfaction, positively contributing to their overall health. This outcome is a moral imperative and perceived to have a reciprocal reaction, in which both the educator and student benefit in generating an inclusive culture that is supportive and thriving in any learning environment.

Moreover, focusing on a social ecological model when addressing the need for diversity in higher education and the support and promotion of women of color has also been addressed through the historical context of affirmative action. This

Introduction

contribution further emphasizes the need to strengthen gender-based affirmative action initiatives in a way that would aid higher education institutions in improving diversity and promoting research focused on programs that support a positive organizational structure that is critical in addressing gender and racial parity at different levels of the academic institution.

While contributions to this book are primarily focused on the gender aspect of inclusion in higher education and the workplace, they are also cross-cultural in that they focus on different regions across the world. For example, as authors point out the challenging racial and ethnic dynamics in the U.S., others introduce trends in Africa and the Middle East. Specifically, in a study of Zimbabwe, the author examines the importance of addressing policies that would include more women representation in politics and decision making, and presents the challenges globally, bringing to the discussion China, Russia, Brazil, India, and South America. Furthermore, the author addresses the importance of the quota system in ensuring that women are represented in local and parliamentary councils, a process that is predicted to overcome gender biases and work to limit systematic barriers that exclude women from political participation.

Interestingly, the book contributions undoubtedly show that, despite progress being made, evidence suggests that women, *globally*, are still challenged by policies that somewhat limit their opportunities for advancement and their power to break through the metaphorical glass ceiling. Gender inequities are present, and women aspiring for a work-life balance while fighting to progress in their leadership roles, continue. However, the progress made, at a more global perspective, also give hope that (albeit slow), the role of women in higher education and the workforce have substantially contributed to the economic productivity of their respective societies.

Chapter 1
One Stride at a Time:
Women Breaking Through the Glass Ceiling in the MENA Region

Reem Ali Abu-Lughod
Royal University for Women, Bahrain & School of Social Sciences and Education, California State University, Bakersfield, USA

ABSTRACT

Gender inequalities are a worldwide phenomenon hindering women's progress in higher education and the workforce. To fully grasp the current manifestations of this problem, it is crucial to examine the reasons behind it and shed light on the changes in policies that have moved toward overcoming it. This chapter focuses on women in the Middle East and North Africa (MENA) region; it specifically explores the roles of women in pursuing higher education and employment, as the two are intertwined in the complexity of advancing women in different disciplines and professions. The chapter also highlights how traditional and patriarchal societies in the MENA region place an unconscious bias on women, placing an expectation on them to be homemakers and caretakers for their families. Finally, the chapter presents how, despite more work to be done, the MENA region has advanced in promoting more women in higher education and the workforce but that a call for more collaboration in the region is needed.

Gender inequalities are a worldwide phenomenon, hindering women's progress in higher education and the workforce. To fully grasp the current manifestations of this problem, it is crucial to examine the reasons behind it and shed light on the changes in policies that have moved toward overcoming it. This chapter focuses

DOI: 10.4018/979-8-3693-0102-9.ch001

on women in the Middle East and North Africa (MENA) region; it specifically explores the roles of women in pursuing higher education and employment, as the two are intertwined in the complexity of advancing women in different disciplines and professions. The chapter also highlights how traditional and patriarchal societies in the MENA region place an unconscious bias on women, placing an expectation on them to be homemakers and caretakers for their families. Finally, the chapter presents how, despite more work to be done, the MENA region has advanced in promoting more women in higher education and the workforce but that a call for more collaboration in the region is needed.

A woman caring for her children; a woman striving to excel in the private sector; a woman partnering with her neighbors to make their street safer; a woman running for office to improve her country – they all have something to offer, and the more our societies empower women, the more we receive in return. ~ Queen Rania of Jordan

WOMEN IN EDUCATION

Education in the Arab World has seen a significant increase in recent decades (Campante & Chor 2012; UNESCO, 2015; UNESCO, 2020), particularly with the implementation of policies directed toward schooling and the advantage of oil revenues that have contributed to the expansion of the educational system (Daun & Arjmand, 2002. Interestingly, in 2019, more girls were enrolled in schools, making significant progress toward gender parity in enrollment (UNESCO, 2020). According to the Global Gender Gap report (2020), 15 Arab countries scored above 0.81 in 2020, with the highest possible score being 1 in the educational attainment.

Moreover, the advancement in education also suggests that there are human capital gains that *can* contribute to better labor markets (Daun & Arjmand 2002). However, the MENA region has also been impacted by a series of events that have obstructed a positive correlation between education and employment (World Bank, 2012). For example, during the Arab Spring in 2010, it was clear that young people in the MENA region were desperate for better opportunities in pursing education and finding employment, even more so for women, emphasizing the importance of their roles in education and employment (Nazier & Ramadan, 2018). It was also a movement that addressed the need for empowering people with skills to overcome economic hardships and engage in social developments within the region. This movement, and others in the region, have raised awareness to empower young people with the skills necessary to tap into policies that emphasize a positive correlation between higher educational attainment and employment (Campante & Chor 2012; Putnam 1995,). Similarly, political conflicts in Yemen and Syria have left over 2 million children out of school (UNICEF, 2019), a phenomenon that will undoubtedly challenge the advancements of rising education in the region.

Despite the political turmoil, traditional societal and cultural norms limiting female education and career opportunities in the MENA region (Price, 2016), countries in the Gulf Cooperation Council (GCC) have witnessed progress in the labor force participation rate of females (ages 15+) in 2022; Bahrain at 44%, Kuwait at 48%, The United Arab Emirates (UAE) at 55%, and Qatar leading the way at 60% (ILO, 2023). These number are important particularly that the MENA region cannot be viewed as a monolithic entity, given the region's heterogeneity in subcultures, nationalities, religions, and socio-economic factors (Mojab, 2022).

Historically, women have been marginalized in higher education, facing discrimination and limited opportunities for intellectual growth. Higher education has historically been male dominated, with limited opportunities available for women. According to Moghadam (2003, 2005), society held the belief that women's place was primarily in domestic roles, hindering their ability to pursue higher education. Despite these obstacles, women fought for their right to education, leading to increased enrollment and access to higher education for women. The late 19th and early 20th centuries marked a turning point for women in higher education. With the emergence of women's rights movements and the gradual dismantling of gender barriers, women have demonstrated nation-building and social mobility in their respective societies (Mojab, 2022).

Today, women constitute a substantial percentage of university students, particularly in the MENA region (Mojab, 2022), bridging the gender gap and establishing a foundation for their career aspirations (Roudi-Fahimi & Moghadam, 2003). This phenomenon has been positively impacted by legislative reforms, that include equal access to higher education, and scholarships that reflect state policies aimed at endorsing women's participation as a catalyst in building human capital, termed as Arab state feminism (Hatem, 1995). As a result, more women are pursuing higher education in the MENA region and have access to a broader range of disciplines, including Science, Technology Engineering, and Mathematics (STEM), which have been traditionally male dominated (Liben & Coyle, 2014).

As such, these efforts have been instrumental in breaking down gender stereotypes and barriers by fostering female engagement in these fields (McKinnon, 2022). For example, more women in the MENA region are pursuing STEM fields, such as Dr. Heba Alzaben, a Jordanian scientist who was selected to receive the 2021 L'Oreal-UNESCO for Women in Science Levant Young Talents Program, following Dr. Lina Dahabiyeh in 2020 and Dr. Nouf Mahmoud in 2019. Similarly, Her Excellency Sarah Al-Amiri, Chair of the United Arab Emirates (UAE) Space Agency and Minister of State for Advanced Technology, led the successful operation of the Hope Probe to Mars; making the UAE the fifth nation (and first Arab country) to successfully orbit a satellite around the red planet (Shaheen, 2020). However, it is important to note that despite an increasing number of women in STEM, their labor force lags below 40% in the STEM workforce (UNESCO Institute for Statistics, 2024).

As evidenced, women in higher education have in fact made significant strides, with more women enrolling in and completing advanced degrees than ever before (Mojab, 2022). Consequently, many women in the MENA region have overcome historical barriers and gender biases, meeting the challenges of growing societies in an era of globalization (Baki 2004; Mills 2003). This progress paved the way for future generations of women to pursue advanced degrees and contribute to academia, all while breaking barriers (Saucerman & Vasquez, 2014) and excelling in their chosen fields.

By contrast, Athey et al. (2000) and Burbridge (1994) observe that while progress has undoubtedly been made, women in higher education continue to face challenges such as gender bias, lack of mentorship opportunities, and the elusive glass ceiling. Further, despite women achieving parity in undergraduate degrees, the representation of women in higher-level positions such as professorships and administration remains unequal (Jackson & O'Callaghan, 2009). This inequality creates a scarcity of female role models (Casad et al., 2018) and undermines the voices and contributions of women in academia.

One significant step towards gender equity in higher education has been the implementation of initiatives and programs aimed at supporting women's advancement (AIWF, 2024). Many universities have established women's centers, mentoring programs, and scholarships specifically designed to address the unique challenges faced by women. These initiatives promote gender parity, advocate for equal opportunities, and provide support throughout the academic journey. Increasing female representation in higher education therefore brings numerous benefits. Women's perspectives and experiences contribute to a more comprehensive understanding and analysis of various subjects. Diverse voices spark creativity, innovation, and critical thinking within academic institutions. Moreover, increasing female representation inspires future generations of women, offering young girls tangible role models (Casad et al., 2018) to look up to. This representation, in turn, promotes social equality by challenging societal norms and stereotypes.

To continue advancing gender inclusivity in higher education, universities must take proactive steps, such as reviewing admission policies, fostering research on gender equality, and creating more opportunities for female leadership. Institutions should prioritize diversity and inclusion in hiring practices and provide mentorship and support networks for female faculty and students. Additionally, addressing the gender pay gap in academia is crucial to attracting and retaining talented women scholars.

From a theoretical perspective, human capital (World Bank, 2005) argues that education plays a role in reducing poverty levels and promoting economic growth, at the national and household levels. Moreover, education is considered one of the key protections against authoritarian governments and a condition for achieving democracy (Akkari, 2004). Education is also a component that drives feminists' goals of achieving equal citizenship in their respective society. Undoubtedly, access to education and educational equality go hand in hand with women's rights globally. However, access to education is also equally important to the role of women in voicing their views and participating in active citizenship. Hence, women are eager to be part of decision-making processes, refusing passivity that may be expected of them.

Denying women access to education or limiting opportunities for educational advancement further contributes to gender segregation and reaffirms the ideological perspective that stereotypes their role in society. This adversely impacts the socialization process in which women are expected to lead traditional roles (Hasso, 2010; Olmsted, 2005) limiting their prospects to becoming active members of the workforce.

Policies promoting more women in education in the MENA region have been implemented to address gender disparities in educational opportunities. These policies aim to increase access to education for girls and women, combat cultural and social barriers, and promote gender equality (Dandan & Marques, 2017). Some specific initiatives include providing scholarships and financial support for female students, establishing girls' schools and colleges, promoting female representation in educational institutions and leadership roles, and raising awareness about the importance of girls' education. These efforts seek to empower women, enhance their skills and knowledge, and contribute to their social and economic advancement (Nazier & Ramadan, 2018).

As such, women's participation in education in the MENA region has increased significantly over the years. Governments and organizations in the region have made efforts to improve access to education and promote gender equality. Many countries in the Middle East have implemented laws and policies to ensure equal education opportunities for both men and women. As a result, more girls and women are enrolling in schools, colleges, and universities. However, challenges such as societal norms, traditional gender roles, and gender-based discrimination still exist and can hinder women's education in some areas. Women's higher education and employment in various sectors and across many countries in the MENA region have seen significant support and improvement when examining gender-related indices (Deniz & Dogruel, 2008). In addition to governmental support, engaged civil societies and feminists advocating for women's rights have also promoted women's empowerment.

For instance, one of the most important aspects in achieving more female engagement in higher education and the workplace is literacy rates, which are significantly high in the MENA region, with exceptions of a few countries, including Yemen and Morocco, not exceeding 70% (UNESCO, 2015). Literacy rates among women (ages 15-24) in the Arab world was at 80% in 2020, an increase from 74.5% in 2000 (Gapminder, 2024). Male literacy rate in the same age group is approximately at 80% but decreasing since 2000 (Gapminder, 2024). Given these statistics, it is important to note that, undoubtedly, one of the setbacks to learning in the MENA region was the COVID-19 pandemic. For example, limited access to technology, school learning resources, overall school closures, lack of economic viability and others have created a subculture of learning poverty (Kobakhidze, 2020; The World Bank, 2020).

Education and access to learning environments can only empower women's socialization and in turn increase the likelihood of their creativity in various sectors across the workforce, overcoming their personal and societal struggles. Overall, there has been progress in advancing women's education in the Middle East and Arab world, but further work is needed to achieve full gender equality in the education sector.

WOMEN AT WORK

Gender inequality continues to be a pressing issue in modern society, particularly in the realm of work and employment (Ryan, 2022), where women worldwide only constitute 37% of leadership roles (World Economic Forum, 2022). The roots of gender inequality can be traced back to historical norms and perceptions that have perpetuated discriminatory practices (Koenig et al., 2011; Schein, 1973). Women were conventionally confined to domestic roles, while men were deemed the primary breadwinners, a phenomenon often referred to as "patriarchal bargain" (Moghadam 2003, 2005; Sharabi 1988). These deeply ingrained societal expectations of what women and men *are* like (Ellemers, 2018) and what they *should* be like (Heilman, 2012), have created and sustained a gendered division of labor, with profound repercussions for today's workplace dynamics.

While progress is made toward having more women included in executive positions worldwide, their representation remains significantly lower than their male counterparts. For example, while the 1970s and 1980s illustrate the progress of women accessing position of power and authority, the 1990s showed a more delayed progress (Stainback & Tomaskovic-Devey, 2012). Furthermore, 14.6 percent of executive officers were women, a decrease from 15.7 percent in 2002 (Catalyst, 2005, 2014). Attempts have been made to understand the dynamics of the gender dichotomy observed in the workforce, but the causes are rooted in various aspects of societies in the global context (Padavic, Ely, & Reid, 2019).

Historically, women have faced disadvantages in trying to reach their career success, particularly given the stereotypical belief that women lack qualities to succeed (Leslie et al., 2017; Heilman, 2012; Ibarra et al., 2010;) and that they're more likely to be dependent upon men taking on more traditional roles in familial caretaking (Foroutan, 2009). This perspective of self-reliant women who are financially dependent on men is particularly pervasive in the MENA region (Negm, 2017), compared with women's progress in Western countries. However, over the past two decades, laws and policies targeted toward gender equality in the Middle East and North Africa (MENA) region have been witnessed (CAWTAR 2007). Particularly important are laws that have focused on promoting more female representation in higher education and the workplace (Moghadam, 2005).

Gender stereotypes and discriminatory practices persist in various workplaces (Cundiff & Vescio, 2016), hindering women's opportunities and contributions. Preconceived notions regarding women's competency, commitment, and ability to lead often limit their professional growth and increase gender inequalities (Koenig et al., 2011; Schein, 1973). Overcoming these deeply entrenched biases requires raising awareness, creating inclusive environments, and promoting diverse leadership. As the evidence suggest (Fox, 2016; Metcalfe, 2007) women in the MENA region have made progress in playing an active and very important role in the region's workforce and development. Particularly so, is the phenomenon of a younger generation of women with skills (Liben & Coyle, 2014) and educational attainment who are expressing greater interest in unconventional fields such as technology, entrepreneurship, public policy, and others. The openness and equitable opportunity available to women, in advancing both their education and work, is recognized by the UN Women as a human rights issue, setting the stage for sustainable cities to accomplish the 2030 vision, including gender equality at different levels (UN Women, 2016). This is one way the 21st Century has marked a new dimension in making progress toward gender equality as part of the global humanitarian agenda (Joshi at al., 2015).

Despite women's overall low economic participation, women leaders in high profile positions are steadily changing this trend (Business Today, 2016). The emergence of working women in the MENA region contributes to numerous socioeconomic benefits (Nazier and Ramadan, 2018), by tapping into an underutilized female workforce, as such, the region gains the potential to expand its labor force (Roudi-Fahimi & Moghadam, 2006), increase productivity, and foster economic growth. Additionally, women's economic empowerment leads to upward mobility, poverty reduction, improved health and education outcomes, and enhanced gender equality in society (Alzuabi, 2016; Ferrant, 2010; Burgess, 2007)

As this chapter presents, women in the MENA region are in fact pursing higher education, which does not explain why women's unemployment rate is high in the region (Rutledge et al., 2011). For example, despite high literacy rates for women in the region, they are still unutilized (Al Masah Capital Limited, 2015). In 2021, Jordan had a literacy rate for 98.1% among females 15 years of age and higher, followed by the United Arab Emirates (UAE), at 97.6% in 2022, and Kuwait (2020) with a 95.4%. Saudi Arabia (2020), had a 96% literacy rate, followed by 93.6% in Lebanon (2019). For Tunisia (2022), Algeria (2018) and Egypt (2022), the literacy percentages for the same population were 77.9%, 75.3%, and 69% respectively (Gapminder, 2024).

One factor that cannot be denied in possibly contributing to unemployment of women in the region, is the sociocultural values embedded in Middle Eastern and Arab cultures (Medichie & Gallant, 2012; Dechant & Al Lamky, 2005), providing a limitation on how far women can advance in their professional careers, confirming the gender stereotypes of what women *can* and *should* do (Gallant & Pounder, 2008; Tlaiss, 2015). Women's work is viewed as less important, since their primary responsibility is assumed to be the household. Related to this, employers believe that male employees tend to be more committed to their jobs and are cheaper to employ compared to women who would prioritize their families, leave their jobs for their children, or incur maternity and childcare costs (ILO, 2017; Al Khatib, 2020).

Therefore, despite efforts set in place to make the workplace a more gender-inclusive environment, women in the MENA region may still face challenges of the family-work balance. Research has shown that women are often faced with trying to overcome the conflict between their family obligations and their long working hours which, in many instances, may hinder their professional advancement (Padavic, Ely, & Reid, 2020). As such, a male-dominated and patriarchal society as the one present in the MENA region, can inevitably create boundaries for women's place of work (e.g. domestic work), while continuing the cycle of promoting men to be the breadwinners (Tlaiss, 2015; Moghadam, 2005; Sharabi, 1988).

In addition, due to the expectation that raising children is perceived almost exclusively as a woman's job, the work-life balance becomes an even more challenging commitment for women to attain (Ghoson, 2015), particularly given the societal and organizational challenges (Tlaiss, 2014). While achieving a work-life balance is a challenge for both women and men, societal expectations and stereotypes regarding caregiving responsibilities predominantly fall on women, resulting in added burdens that can impede their career progression. Addressing these imbalances in caregiving expectations is crucial to achieving gender equality in the workplace.

The stagnation in women's advancements has been explained in a work-family research context, in which a stagnation to women's gains have been explained in women's family obligations conflicting with their professional jobs' long hours (Ely et al., 2014; Ramarajan et al., 2012) with proposed solutions to providing policies offering flexible work arrangements to mitigate these challenges (Perlow & Kelly, 2014; Galinsky et al., 2010;). While such policies are proposed to help reduce gender inequality in the workplace, it is a double-edged sword in a way that flexibility may backfire by hindering women's possibilities of advancing their careers.

Despite the work-family explanation being viewed as simplistic (Cha, 2013; Damaske, 2011; Stone, 2007) it is undoubtedly embedded in culture; more specifically in the MENA region. It is argued that women, in many instances, fail to reach the top because they "find other parts of life more fulfilling" (Belkin, 2003) and they prioritize family over work (Ely et al., 2014).

Gender inequality in work and employment is further manifested is further manifested in the limited opportunities for women to reach hierarchical positions and secure promotions. This is particularly seen in the glass-ceiling phenomenon, which typically affects women at the lower managerial level (Said et al., 2022), consequently contributing to the lowest number of female CEOs in the MENA region (13%), compared with a 21% rate in other developing countries (International Labour Organization, 2016). The glass ceiling and gender biases often hinder women's career advancement prospects, limiting their access to senior roles and executive positions (Ryan, 2022). This underrepresentation of women in leadership exacerbates gender inequality, perpetuating existing discriminatory patterns. For instance, as of 2022, the labor force participation rate for the female population (ages 15 and over) in the MENA region showed varying statistics. At the top of the spectrum were mainly countries in the Gulf Cooperation Council (GCC); Qatar (60%), the UAE (55%), Kuwait (48%), and Bahrain (44%) and a much lower labor force participation rate were Algeria (16%), Egypt (15%), Jordan (15%), and the West Bank (19%) (World Bank 2021).

Despite the increased numbers of female employment in the region, there is undoubtedly a call for more women participation in the workforce (Nazier & Ramadan, 2018; Ross, 2008). This is particularly important as worsening regional events, including political unrest, economic struggles and social climates may only contribute to a risk of regression. These instabilities may also contribute to societal conflict, giving rise to more imbalanced influence from patriarchal governments reinforcing structural inequities. The battle for legal, civil, social, and educational equality is therefore a central element of woman's rights, not only regionally, but also globally.

Some efforts to overcome the obstacles witnessed in bridging the workplace gender gap, are embedded in initiatives such as gender quota systems (Tlais, 2014; Rutledge et al., 2011) and other proactive measures to combat workplace gender biases are being implemented to ensure women's access to employment opportunities. As an illustration, in 2020 in Bahrain, women comprised 19% of all participants in the Legislative Authority; 15% were elected in the parliament, 23% appointed in the Shura Council, and 23% in the Municipal Council. Similarly, the United Arab Emirates' initiative to a reserve 50% of their gender quota seat for their national assembly puts them among the top three countries in the world in terms of female parliamentary representation (the other two are Rwanda and Cuba) (IPU 2022). The changes show, that despite cultural barriers and stereotypes of what women can and cannot do, gender quotas have been instrumental in impacting legislative reform and increasing women's presence in MENA politics (Wellborne and Buttorff 2022). Compared with their Western counterparts, Arab countries (in the past two decades) have increased at twice the rate (Tripp, 2012). To further illustrate, in 2020, Egypt (27.7%), Tunisia (26.3%), Djibouti (26.2%), and Iraq (28.9%) surpassed the U.S. Congress (23.3%) in their female representation in 2018, following the 2018 midterm elections (IPU, 2019).

While challenges persist, it is important to emphasize that the MENA region has witnessed notable advancements in gender equality in higher education and the workforce. The considerable progress made in empowering women in the MENA region should serve as a source of inspiration for continued efforts towards gender parity. More to the point, sustained support, coupled with comprehensive policy reforms, continued advocacy, and inclusive initiatives, will be instrumental in ensuring a brighter future wherein women thrive intellectually and professionally in the MENA region (World Bank, 2001; 2012).

While the literature shows significant diversity in the MENA region, women continue to face a variety of social, cultural, and legal challenges that may affect their lives and opportunities. Some common issues include limited access to education, restrictive gender norms, and unequal opportunities in the workforce. As such, in recent years, there has been an increasing recognition of the importance of women's empowerment and gender equality in the MENA region. Efforts have been made to address these challenges, such as implementing legal reforms, promoting women's education, and encouraging women's participation in politics and leadership roles. However, progress is uneven across countries, and significant work is still needed to ensure equal rights and opportunities for women throughout the region.

Government initiatives in the MENA region directed toward implementing policies that promote female labor force participation are an indication that governments in the region recognize and support women's economic empowerment (Nazier, 2019). Over the years, these initiatives have encompassed legislative reforms, such as equal pay provisions and maternity leave entitlements, as well as programs to enhance women's access to education and vocational training. As such, governmental support is instrumental in facilitating the transition towards a more inclusive and empowered workforce. For example, launched in 2021 by the Container Control Programme (CCP), "Customs, Cargo and Women: A Talk for Her," works to address the gender gaps in the MENA region. Through networking sessions, facilitations, and other inter-regional study visits, the initiative is also directed at changing mindsets and structures in the workplace. In September 2022, the CCP MENA team brought together decision-makers across government structures in Iraq, Jordan, Lebanon, Morocco and Tunisia to discuss recruitment, retention, and promotion processes.

Similarly, the Women's Economic Empowerment Platform (WEEP) in Kuwait is another opportunity directed at fostering gender equality for women's empowerment in the workplace and community as a whole; all while contributing to economic growth and sustainability in the Gulf, Arab States and beyond. It is also part of the Agenda 2030 and the achievement of Sustainable Development Goal 5 (SDG 5: achieve gender equality and empower all women and girls) (Nazier & Ramadan, 2018) and Kuwait's national development priorities on growth and social protection (UN WOMEN, 2016)

As for Egypt, women-focused economic policies are critical, where women make up 73.1 percent of nursing staff in the private sector and 91.1 percent of nursing staff for the Ministry of Health, 42.4 percent of doctors, and 56.8 percent of employment in service sector. In addition, 18.1 percent of Egyptian women are heads of households. Several of the measures Egypt implemented to support women include exceptional leave for mothers, an expansion in conditional cash transfers, increased monthly income for rural women, allowances for medical staff and 500 cash allowances for irregular workers, 40 percent of whom are women, and special programs for women with disabilities (from Wilson center, 2021).

The strategies that have been implemented to promote more employment opportunities for women in the MENA region are crucial for achieving gender equality and economic development in the region. For example, providing quality education and skill training for women, including vocational training and entrepreneurship courses, can empower them with the necessary qualifications and knowledge to enter the workforce. Additionally, advocating for equal pay, and promoting maternity rights can help in assisting women with a work-life balance without comprising their professional advancement. Overall, this reflects a comprehensive approach that addresses systemic challenges, promoting education, skill development, as well as addressing ways to engage women in the private sector, business ownership, and other aspects of developing family-friendly policies and gender inclusive environments that are conducive to providing opportunities for women in the region.

Private sector engagement is also crucial for the advancement of working women in the MENA region. By promoting gender inclusivity through the adoption of gender-sensitive policies, companies can contribute to breaking down barriers (Saucerman & Vasquez, 2014) and fostering an enabling environment for female employees. Increasing women's leadership skills (Atir, 2022) and representation in decision-making positions is equally vital, as it drives gender equality within organizations and aids in dismantling glass ceilings.

CONCLUSION

The MENA region has historically featured cultural and social norms that restrict women's involvement in the public sphere. However, the global progressive stance towards gender equality, coupled with a pressing need for socioeconomic development, has paved the way for a shift in attitudes (Cassola, 2014). This emerging trend has resulted in the integration of increasing numbers of women into various industries, promoting gender empowerment and overall societal progress. The growing participation of women in the MENA labor market represents significant progress towards gender equality and socioeconomic development. While challenges persist, initiatives from governments, combined with private sector engagement and a shift in societal perceptions, provide substantial opportunities for working women in the region.

Despite promising developments, working women in the MENA region face various challenges. For example, cultural perceptions, prevailing gender-based discrimination, and deep-rooted gender stereotypes (Ellemers, 2018; Eagly et al., 2000;) continue to hinder their progress. Moreover, social expectations surrounding traditional gender roles, limited access to education and professional development opportunities, and inadequate childcare facilities pose significant barriers to women's full integration into the labor market.

It is critically important that by addressing deeply ingrained societal perceptions and cultural norms is essential for unlocking the full potential of working women in the MENA region (World Bank, 2020). A shift in societal attitudes towards gender roles and labor market inclusion is needed to create an environment that encourages and supports women's professional aspirations. Engaging in dialogue, raising awareness, and challenging norms are integral steps towards empowering women and achieving sustainable progress.

In all, collaboration among MENA countries is crucial in fostering women's economic empowerment. Next, sharing best practices, experiences, and lessons learned can help overcome common challenges and pool resources, facilitating more efficient interventions. Last, but not least, regional economic integration strategies should also prioritize gender mainstreaming, ensuring that the benefits of economic development are equally distributed among all members of society.

REFERENCES

Akkari, A. (2004). Education in the Middle East and North Africa: The Current Situation and Future Challenges. *International Education Journal*.

Al Khatib, M. (2020). Facilitating female employment in Jordan: Key Issues and Trends. *UNESCO*. Retrieved August 14, 2020, from https://unevoc.unesco.org/yem/Female+unemployment+in+Jordan+YEM+Blog&context

Belkin, L. (2003). The opt-out revolution. *New York Times Magazine*, 26, 42–47.

Burgess, P. (2007). *Women Empowered: Inspiring Change in the Emerging World*. Rizzoli.

Campante, F. R., & Chor, D. (2012). Why was the Arab World Poised for Revolution? Schooling, Economic Opportunities, and the Arab Spring. *The Journal of Economic Perspectives*, 26(2), 167–188. doi:10.1257/jep.26.2.167

Cassola, A., Raub, A., Foley, D., & Heymann, J. (2014). Where do Women Stand? New Evidence on the Presence and Absence of Gender Equality in the World's Constitutions. *Politics & Gender*, 10(2), 200–235. doi:10.1017/S1743923X1400004X

Catalyst. (2005). *Catalyst census of women corporate officers and top earners of the Fortune 500*. www.catalyst.org/system/files/2005_Census_Fortune_500_Women_Corporate_Officers.pdf

Catalyst. (2014). *Statistical overview of women in the workplace*. http://www.catalyst.org/ knowledge/statistical-overview-women-workplace

Center of Arab Women for Training and Research (CAWTAR). (2007). https://cawtar.org/en/nged-network

Cha, Y. (2013). Overwork and the persistence of gender segregation in occupations. *Gender & Society*, 27(2), 158–184. doi:10.1177/0891243212470510

Damaske, S. (2011). *For the Family? How Class and Gender Shape Women's Work*. Oxford University Press.

Dandan, M. M., & Marques, A. P. (2017). Education, Employment and Gender Gap in Mena Region. *Asian Economic and Financial Review*, 7(6), 573–588. doi:10.18488/journal.aefr.2017.76.573.588

Daun, H., & Arjmand, R. (2002). Arab Countries: Oil Boom, Religious Revival and Non Reform. In H. Daun (Ed.), *Educational Restructuring in the Context of Globalization and National Policy*. Routledge.

Deniz, Z., & Dogruel, A. (2008). Disaggregated Education Data And Growth: Some Facts From Turkey And Mena Countries. Topics. In *Middle Eastern & North African Economies*. Proceedings Of The Middle East Economic Association.

Ely, R. J., Stone, P., & Ammerman, C. (2014). Rethink what you know about high-achieving women. *Harvard Business Review*, *92*, 101–109.

Ferrant, G. (2010). *A New Way to Measure Gender Inequalities in Developing Countries: The Gender Inequalities Index. CES working Report*. The University of Paris, the Sorbonne.

Galinsky, E., Saka, K., Eby, S., Bond, J. T., & Wigton, T. (2010). Employer-provided workplace flexibility. In K. Christensen & B. Schneider (Eds.), Workplace Flexibility: Realigning 20th-century Jobs for a 21st-century Workforce. Ithaca, NY: Cornell University Press.

Gapminder. (2024). www.gapminder.org/data/

Global Gender Gap Report. (2020). World Economic Forum. https://www3.weforum.org/docs/WEF_GGGR_2020.pdf

Hatem, M. (1995). Political Liberalization, Gender and the State. Political Liberalization and Democratization in the Arab World, 187–205.

Information and Research Center – King Hussein Foundation (IRCKHF). (2019). *Gender Discrimination in Jordan*. Retrieved August 14, 2020, from http://irckhf.org/en/project/gender-discrimination/jordan

International Labour Office (ILO). (2017). *Jordan: Young women's employment and empowerment in the rural economy*. Retrieved August 14, 2020, from https://www.ilo.org/wcmsp5/groups/public/---ed_emp/documents/publication/wcms_622766.pdf

International Labour Organization. (n.d.). *ILO Modelled Estimates and Projections database*. ILOSTAT. Accessed September 05, 2023. Ilostat.ilo.org/data.

Jaramillo, A., Ruby, A., Henard, F., & Zaafrane, H. (2011). *Internationalization of Higher Education in MENA: Policy Issues Associated with Skills Formation and Mobility*. World Bank.

Kobakhidze, N. (2020). *Pandemic Changes Global Dynamics in Education*. Academic Press.

Koenig, A., Eagly, A., Mitchell, A., & Ristikari, T. (2011). *Are Leader Stereotypes Masculine? A meta-analysis of three research paradigms. National Library of Medicine. National* Center for Biotechnology Information.

Liben, L. S., & Coyle, E. F. (2014). Developmental interventions to address the STEM gender gap: Exploring intended and unintended consequences. In L. S. Liben & R. S. Bigler (Eds.), Advances in child development and behavior, Vol. 47. The role of gender in educational contexts and outcomes (pp. 77–115). Elsevier Academic Press. doi:10.1016/bs.acdb.2014.06.001

Modern Diplomacy. (n.d.). Retrieved from https://moderndiplomacy.eu/2023/05/04/the-covid-19-pandemicchanges-global-dynamics-in-education/

Moghadam, V. M. (2005). Women's Economic Participation in the Middle East: What Difference Had the Neoliberal Policy Turn Made? *Journal of Middle East Women's Studies*, *1*(1), 110–146. doi:10.2979/MEW.2005.1.1.110

Mojab, S. (2022). *Women and Education in the Middle East and North Africa*. Oxford Research Encyclopedias. doi:10.1093/acrefore/9780190264093.013.1544

Nazier, H. (2019). *Women's Economic Empowerment: An Overview for the MENA Region. Strategic Sectors.* Economy and Territory.

Nazier, H., & Ramadan, R. (2018). What empowers Egyptian women: Resources versus social constraints? *Review of Economics and Political Science*, *3*(3/4), 153–175. doi:10.1108/REPS-10-2018-015

Padavic, I., Ely, R., & Reid, E. (2020). Explaining the Persistence of Gender Inequality: The Work-family Narrative as a Social Defense against the 24/7 Work Culture. *Administrative Science Quarterly*, *65*(1), 61–111. doi:10.1177/0001839219832310

Perlow, L., & Kelly, E. L. (2014). Toward a model of work redesign for better work and better life. *Work and Occupations*, *41*(1), 111–134. doi:10.1177/0730888413516473

Putnam, R. (1995a). Bowling Alone: America's Declining Social Capital. *Journal of Democracy*, *6*(1), 65–78. doi:10.1353/jod.1995.0002

Ramarajan, L., McGinn, K., & Kolb, D. (2012). *An outside–inside evolution in gender and professional work*. Harvard Business School Working Paper, 13–051.

Roudi-Fahimi, F., & Moghadam, V. (2003). *Empowering Women, Developing Society: Female Education in the Middle East and North Africa. From*. Population Reference Bureau.

Roudi-Fahimi, F., & Moghadam, V. (2006). Empowering Women, Developing Society: Female Education. In *The Middle East And North Africa. Women's Studies* International.

Ryan, M. (2022). Addressing Workplace Gender Inequality: Using the Evidence to Avoid Common Pitfalls. *British Journal of Social Psychology*. PMID:36415906

Shaheen, K. (2020). First Mars Mission from UAE Aims to Inspire a New Generation of Space Scientists. *National Geographic*. https://www.nationalgeographic.com/science/article/uae-mars-mission-hope-aims-inspire-new-generation-space-scientists

Stainback, K., & Tomaskovic-Devey, D. (2012). *Documenting Desegregation: Racial and Gender Segregation in Private Sector Employment since the Civil Rights Act*. Russell Sage Foundation.

Stone, P. (2007). *Opting Out? Why Women Really Quit Careers and Head Home*. University of California Press. doi:10.1525/9780520941793

UNESCO. (n.d.). *Education for All: Regional Synthesis Report of the 2015 National Reviews in the Arab States Region*. https://www.unesco.org/new/fileadmin/MULTIMEDIA/FIELD/Doha/pdf/UNESCOEFAReviewArabStatesENG.pdf

United National Children's Fund (UNICEF). (2019a). *Syria Crisis Fast Facts*. Available at: https://www.unicef.org/mena/reports/syria-crisis-fast-facts

United Nations Children's Fund (UNICEF). (2019b). *To keep children in education, UNICEF starts incentives for school-based staff in Yemen*. Available at: https://www.unicef.org/press-releases/keep-children-education-unicef-starts-incentives-school-based-staff-yemen

United Nations Organization for Education, Science and Culture (UNESCO). (2020). *UIS Institute for Statistics*. Available at: http://data.uis.unesco.org/#

Weeks, K. (2011). *The Problem with Work: Feminism, Marxism, Antiwork Politics, and Postwork Imaginaries*. Duke University Press.

Wilson Center. (2021). *Education in the Arab World: A Legacy of Coming Up Short. Part of the Viewpoints Series*. Author.

World Bank. (2001). *Engendering Development: Through Gender Equality in Rights, Resources, and Voice*. Author.

World Bank. (2005). *Introduction to poverty analysis*. http://siteresources.worldbank.org/PGLP/Resources/PovertyManual.pdf

World Bank. (2012). *Capabilities, Opportunities and Participation: Gender Equality and* Development in the Middle East and North Africa Region, A companion to the World Development Report. http://siteresources.worldbank.org/INTMENA/Resources/World_Development_Report_2012_Gender_Equality _ Development_Overview_MENA.pdf

World Bank. (2020). *COVID-19 Could Lead to Permanent Loss in Learning and Trillions of Dollars in Lost Earnings.* Retrieved from https://www.worldbank.org/en/news/press-release/2020/06/18/covid-19-could-lead-to-permanent-loss-in-learning-and-trillions-of-dollars-in-lost-earnings

World Bank. (2021). *Labor Force Participation Rate, female (% of female population ages 15+) (modeled ILO estimate)-Middle East & North Africa.* Author.

World Economic Forum. (2020). *The Global Gender Gap Report.* Available at: http://www3.weforum.org/docs/WEF_GGGR_2020.pdf

Chapter 2
Post-Pandemic Agents and Culture Vultures:
Women in Higher Education

Catherine Hayes
University of Sunderland, UK

ABSTRACT

The marginalization of women across the 21st century workforces remains a fundamental issue for address in terms of global economies where factors contributing to inequality and inequity pervade. This chapter illuminates the agency of women in the context of higher education institutions where the COVID-19 pandemic provided an opportunity for them to undertake skills and outperform their male counterparts, in situations which up until that point history had maintained as the preserve of men. The existential crisis facing higher education institutions (HEIs) as a direct consequence of 2020 has served as a lens through which other facets of ambiguity and contingency also influence meta-thinking concerning their strategic governance and operationalization of policies in practice. Just how representative these women leaders were of those working across diverse leadership contexts and settings is also something that remains open to scrutiny, and this chapter explores debates of the agency of women in leadership roles.

"Equality is leaving the door open for anyone who has the means to approach it; equity is ensuring there is a pathway to that door for those who need it." (Caroline Belden, 2021)

DOI: 10.4018/979-8-3693-0102-9.ch002

The impact of the COVID-19 pandemic has ensured not only that humanity has dealt with a sudden and harsh reminder of its own position relative to the risks man lives with on an everyday basis, but also the opportunities to initiate and manage change that these bring, specifically for women in business (Peters et al, 2020). The existential crisis facing Higher Education Institutions (HEIs) as a direct consequence of 2020 has served as a lens through which other facets of ambiguity and contingency also influence meta-thinking concerning their strategic governance and operationalisation of policies in practice (Pellegrini et al, 2020). Facing ethical dilemmas, institutional leaders also must grapple with compounding intraneous and extraneous variables which exacerbate the current crisis situations HEIs now face (Rapanta et al, 2020). For the purposes of this chapter the term gender can be operationally defined as pertaining to the social and cultural construction of the terms male and female. Within the context of this chapter, it is acknowledged that work alluded to applies particularly to Europe, the UK and USA rather than for potential global application. The author's own positionality as a British woman can be attributed to this lens of perspective, when considering the experience of women in the workplace. It is acknowledged that this chapter has provided only a brief insight into global perspectives, which is reflective of the author's stance as a British academic. This is certainly something which can be further explored on both a practical and theoretical level.

Whereas the majority of HEIs across the globe work within specific methodological and management methodologies, the capacity for flexible adaptation, creativity, and innovation in crisis, arguably manifests more commonly amongst women leaders than their male counterparts (El-Besomey, 2020). The gender balance and diversity that women bring to executive leadership positions during times of crisis provides a correspondingly more diversified epistemic standpoint through which crises can be considered (Aldrich and Lotito, 2020). These often subtle but diverse differences in knowledge positionality serve to be more transformative than transactional and as such are often more contextually and situationally relevant to immediately pressing issues, offering a wider lens through which to present, frame and articulate considered solutions (Martinez-Leon et al, 2020). Crises impact upon the theoretical underpinnings of the institutional rationales, designs, and operations of these contexts – within HEI and in parallel fields of praxis, where women have been witnessed at executive leadership levels, coping better and more appropriately than their male peers, almost as if facing a hypothetical wartime battle (Benziman, 2020; Maas et al, 2020).

The malalignment of the theoretical framework of HEI relative to the disciplinary perspectives of education has long been annotated as an issue for address (Barnett, 1990), however this was framed at a particularly politically volatile time as a means of highlighting larger ethical issues of concern, rather than crisis as an independent concept (Jandrić et al, 2020). The most recent challenge, presented by COVID-19, is to ensure that pedagogic practice across HEIs can adapt to new teaching and assessment methodologies, whilst at the same time ensuring an optimal quality and student experience for those joining academic programmes of study at HEIs (Rapanta et al, 2020) These experiences will potentially form the foundational bedrock which will ultimately underpin their future careers, lives and capacity for wider civic societal contributions.

Media reports that women in leadership roles have greatly outperformed men in the strategic management of the implications of COVID-19 globally, have become an everyday source of interest and intrigue. The positive lauding of female prime ministers, presidents and politicians has also been counterbalanced by accounts from women with more standard positions on career trajectories, for whom home working, home schooling and the attempted continuance of everyday norms amidst a global pandemic are, by their very nature, far more routine and mundane prospects (Whitty-Collins, 2020). On an even more negative and resonant note, the media have reported on the increased incidence and prevalence rates of domestic violence crimes committed against women, which further detail the challenges that some women (and their children) in 21st Century society also face (Wenham, Smith and Morgan, 2020).

The scope and parameters of this chapter do not permit a consideration of all issues that all women face, rather this chapter provides an insight into the agentic roles of women leaders in global crises, which have ensured their credibility and dependability in times of greatest challenge to the context of Higher Education (HE) leadership across the world. A collective insight into the roles of women leaders within the COVID-19 pandemic has featured widely in the international press, where multi-agency perspectives on their actions and reactions have been largely positive (Trent, 2020). Belying this media frenzy, however, lies a far deeper debate in just how representative these women leaders are of those working within diverse HE leadership contexts and settings and indeed how far transferable their situational skills of leadership actually are (Henley and Roy, 2020).

The individual positionality of all women is equally important to those who operate as strategic heads of state and whose lives are largely characterised by the privilege of hierarchical positions and the status accompanying them (Bright, Acosta and Parker, 2020; Inman, 2020)). This chapter aims to explore the fundamental impact of how gendered leadership in Higher Education Institutions can shape culture, context, and the civic progression of women's roles across professional contexts and differing contexts of situational specificity reflected within Higher Education (Tshivhase, 2020).

In its entirety, this chapter also serves to deconstruct the characteristic and agentic qualities of women leaders amidst global crises, which are also reflected in the traits of women managing in more recognisable and relatable leadership roles in the context of Higher Education leadership (Thomas, 2020). The core acknowledgements that on a global level the impact of crises inevitably leads to a disproportionate impact on women, a lack of prioritisation of global impetus to address levels of gender inequality and the embedded role of gender equity in relation to human progression and development on a macro level is apparent (Power, 2020; WHO, 2020). This global perspective illuminates the inequalities that women educators face and the impact that this has on the broader scope of professional development through educational impact (Barba and Iraizoz, 2020). Whilst situational specificity is significant in terms of the context of HE leadership, the universality of human experience underpinning them remains the connecting thread, which enables the deconstruction of meaning making in applied educational leadership experiences.

PROACTIVE APPROACHES IN CRISIS MANAGEMENT

Crisis management of any variety necessitates a proactive response, rooted in complex ambiguity, which is non-conventional and is underpinned by active application of cognition, metacognition, and epistemic cognition to practice. In terms of temporal issues, response times can necessitate an immediacy of thinking and correspondingly rapid response, all of which may have potentially long-term consequences, necessitating leaders to be both accountable and responsible for their actions. Parallel to this lies Mezirow's (2009) Perspective Transformation Theory, posited by Mezirow, in relation to transformative learning as,

"... the epistemology of how adults learn to reason for themselves - advance and assess reasons for making a judgement - rather than act on the assimilated beliefs, values, feelings and judgements of others..."

In terms of overall cognitive processing in the contexts of crisis, how gender is of direct relevance is rooted in the increased capacity women have, relative to men, to think flexibly, adaptably and with compassion (Villiers, 2019). This is not to denigrate the gender attributable skill sets of male employees across HEIs but to acknowledge that how people problem solves and react can often have its basis in concepts which are adjuncts to, rather than facets of gender. Whereas men are geared towards objective problem solving in binary 'black and white' fashions as opposed to the capacity to think in shades of grey, which women more clearly demonstrate, what is clear, is that situation and context are the pivotal deciding variables in terms of the need for immediacy of action (Cahdriyana, et al, 2019). These problematic frames of reference, described by Mezirow in the context of education, serve to explain how humans monitor their problem-solving capacities, once engaged in contexts and settings of complex ambiguity, where contingency planning comes to the fore (Mezirow, 2009).

UNEXPECTED, COMPLEX, AND DISRUPTIVE AMBIGUITY

Within the context of complex and disruptive ambiguity in crisis, the capacity for both critical reflection and critical reflexivity are paramount. Self-awareness features highly as one of the core aspects of being able to undertake either optimally and effective action, since how responsive behaviours may be viewed by others, and the interrelationship of this with the alternative perspective of others can be indicators of potential success in crisis management. Illuminating this awareness enables a further conceptual consideration of the gender delineation occurring naturally because of the agentic qualities and attributes of women in the context of crisis management. What is pivotal in these incidences is the capacity for and subsequent integration of tacit knowledge to practice, which stems from not only an extant evidence base but also experiential learning and wisdom, rather than any certainty or concretisation of new knowledge (Dewey, 1933). It is this which is transformational rather than transactional in terms of application and use in leadership praxis and aligns directly with the traditional gender traits of women and men in executive leadership positions, respectively. Through the advancement of the body of work in cognitive psychology at the turn of the 21st century, and the understanding of epistemic assumptions, models such as 'the reflective judgement model' posited by King and Kitchener (2004) (see Table 1 overleaf) lend themselves to adapted application in relation to gender delineation. Whilst all of these are evidence based on the extant literature, the issues of situational specificity and context are pivotal in any consideration of complex ambiguity in crisis, not least because of the relative certainty of knowledge within them.

CONTEMPLATING WHETHER REFLEXIVITY CAN BE INFLUENCED BY GENDER

Axiologically identifiably fixed and typically white male, middle-aged, middle-class mindsets have shaped the society within which corporate leadership operates, with global Higher Education Institutions being no exception. The perspectives these fixed mindsets are rooted in, stems not only from professional bias, but the constraints of cultures which seek to categorise, label and define men and women in relation to biology rather than their capacity to function as leaders, where gender

Table 1. A gender delineation adaptation of the King and Kitchener (2004) reflective judgement model

Thinking Stage	Potential Impact on Gender Based Agentic Qualities
Stage 1 Pre-reflective	Knowledge is absolute and concrete, no reason to ask why, I believe only what I have seen and thus know it to be true-single category belief system – exposure to diversity of thinking.
Stage 2 Pre-reflective	Knowledge is absolutely certain but not readily available to everyone, the right person in authority needs to be sought– some people hold right beliefs and some people hold wrong beliefs - similar to Perry's dualism observed or taught by an authority figure.
Stage 3 Pre-reflective	Knowledge is assumed to be absolutely certain or temporarily uncertain and believe that absolute truth will be manifest in concrete data sometime in the future. Implicitly they maintain that ultimately all problems have solutions.
Stage 4 Quasi-reflective	Knowledge is no longer certain, there is always a layer of ambiguity, limitations of the knower are acknowledged and without certainty knowledge cannot be validated. Well-structured problems such as arithmetic can be described completely, and ill-structured problems are afforded legitimacy at this stage.
Stage 5 Quasi-reflective	Knowledge is contextual and subjective, interpretations are different, so knowledge is different.
Stage 6 Reflective	Knowing is uncertain and knowledge must be understood in relation to the context from which it was derived. Knowledge is constructed through evaluation, comparing knowledge and opinions across contexts, an initial basis for forming judgement/solutions to ill-structured problems.
Stage 7 Reflective	Knowing is uncertain and subject to interpretation and epistemically justifiable claims can be made about the best solution to the problem. Knowledge as an outcome and a process of evaluation. Re-evaluation, new methods of inquiry, or new perspectives become available over time.

is and ought to be regarded as matterless. What is evident is that the characteristic agentic qualities of both genders differ but what is equally clear is that these have been socially constructed over the course of lifetimes and it is a change in the fixed mindset of modern society that is gradually enabling recognition and acknowledgement of this. Sadly, whilst the COVID-19 pandemic may increase access to educational opportunities and potentially widen participation, the economic effects will have a greater negative impact, restricting even basic access to educational opportunity. In May 2020 the World Bank estimated that 60 million people at risk of being pushed into extreme poverty worldwide as a result of Covid; erasing all progress made to alleviate poverty over the past 3 years. This will likely adversely impact upon women.

Tversky & Kahneman (1974) provided some of the first insights into how judgements under uncertainty, which primarily rely on three heuristics are made. The first, is the probability or likelihood of something, the second is the plausibility of it occurring at all and finally the capacity to develop dual process thinking. Considering all three in the context of the COVID-19 pandemic, has necessitated an instinctual and emotional response, which fits into Tversky and Kahneman's definitive System 1 thinking, whereas System 2 tends to engage logic and systematic thinking. The agentic qualities of women and men, although attributable to societal construction correspond with these Systems of duality. What enables coping in crisis situations, is not actually an innate capacity to cope, but the recognition and address of complex ambiguity. Where the agentic qualities of women are an advantage here, is that they have a tendency for relationality and transformation as opposed to the functionalism and transactional approaches traditionally adopted by men.

BRIEF SUMMARY OF EVIDENCE FROM THE EXTANT LITERATURE

Using Bronfenbrenner's Ecological Systems as a theoretical lens through which to view globally published literature to date is useful. It provides a means of relating to macro, meso and micro levels of infrastructure which directly impact upon the policy level, institutional level, and individual levels in which gender continues to influence and matter.

MACRO (POLICY LEVEL)

Gender-Based Admonishment of Women has had a global impact on the capacity for women to mobilise their active contribution to the workplace and frame an identity within it. Within and between culturally diverse geographical regions across the world, this has had a significant impact on the potential of women to also begin to address the ongoing existence of physical and emotional violence against them. Globally, in tandem with this there are huge grass roots implementation gaps in policy, which would empower women to establish their own professional identities and career trajectories. Having policy commitment could potentially revolutionise these cultures and provide a mechanism of making gendered differences everyone's moral responsibility. Because of traditionalist approaches to gendered leadership there has also been a prioritisation of men in leadership roles, particularly across Asia and Africa, with the exception of female dominated professions such as nursing and childcare. Sociocultural perspective lenses frame backgrounds and serve as significant constraints to women who wish to follow an academic career trajectory across these continents. The appropriateness of women's work was often positioned within gendered roles of care and nurture, which is reflective of this workforce today. To increase women's representation, this ought to be addressed. Alongside this the intersectionality of structural inequalities within social class, caste, religion, ethnic origin and language remain key issues.

MESO (INSTITUTIONAL LEVEL IMPLEMENTATION)

Across strategic studies of the gendered workplace the core enablers for women have been identified as approaches to internationalisation, courses of study and learning in leadership which have been tailored and designed specifically for women's only strategic development planning. Often, organisational culture is rooted to an endemic patriarchal culture, which is reflective of wider societal and communal expectation. This can lead to issues of gender discrimination and incorporate both conscious and unconscious bias and even violence in some international Higher Education Institutions.

MICRO (LEVEL OF INDIVIDUAL IMPACT)

At an individual level, across multiple global societies and communities, women still experience active gender discrimination in the context of work-based practice. This two-tier system of regard has led to an increasing subculture of women who feel unworthy of promotion and an aspirational sense of value and consequently rarely apply for leadership roles or positions. This has the negative impact of further consolidating male dominated workplaces. Whilst family circumstances can practically constrain the level of input women can have in the Higher Education workplace due to the cultural expectation that women will be primary caregivers for their children, it remains pivotal that if women are to succeed in the workplace that they have a degree of support in their endeavours so that career progression can even be contemplated.

GENDERED LEADERSHIP IN HIGHER EDUCATION

Despite HEI's making formal recognition of barriers to women reaching senior management positions across their organisational hierarchies, their executives have done relatively little to address issues of structure and agency in relation to antiquated practices that perpetuate these identified inequities (O'Connor, 2020). The situational and contextual backdrops which influence these inequities globally are, of course, largely defined, as outlined previously, by subcultures and contexts at macro, micro and meso levels – the ecological perspectives of where change has been lost in translation in an effort to quite often tokenistically address gender inequity in the workplace are often clearly tangible (Grimson and Grimson, 2019). However authentic approaches to tackling the provision of opportunities for women are rooted too, in wider societal actions and agencies which women respond to prior to and in the early development of establishing a professional identity. The perpetuation of an underrepresentation of women in senior management positions within the labour market generally, and the higher education senior leadership market specifically, is an issue for address. The commonality of issues surrounding women in HEI leadership positions within and between diverse countries, is widely reported as something which transcends cultural barriers and contextual specificities. What unites the relative framing and positioning of these roles is the inflexibility of organisational infrastructures to accommodate diversity beyond feminist tokenism, which contributes directly to a lack of accessibility to leadership roles for women. This is a historical legacy characterised predominantly by dated approaches to the integration of women into the labour market at executive leadership levels (O'Connor, 2019). Remuneration levels are all too often aligned with this inequity and what is evident is that whereas globally most institutions are making moves to close the gender pay gap, they are doing relatively little to change the infrastructure and support for potential women leaders, which impacts on the degree of opportunity afforded to them during their career trajectories (Heymann et al, 2019; Taylor et al, 2017). These career trajectories, by virtue of biological function, are still inevitably interrupted by maternity leave and caring responsibilities to a larger extent than the traditional careers of their male counterparts. However it has to be acknowledged that a far greater percentage of males now do share caring responsibilities and do take equal amounts of paternity leave, so to some extent the redress has been balanced. Equality and diversity initiatives at national levels in the UK, now ensure that many organisations are designated the status of equal opportunities employers, which have seen the rise of initiatives such as the Athena Swann mark emblazoned across HEI provider websites, reflecting their articulated capacity to advocate and support equal opportunities in the workplace. Whether this impacts authentically on these wider issues of structures and agency is something only longer-term evaluation will reveal.

Whilst equality proofing quality initiatives serve well in the identification of the impact of policies which have unintentionally negative impacts on women in practice, one key challenge is being able to identify and filter out the factors underpinning them. In the context of wider professional practice measures these can potentially serve to identify unintended policy impacts but serve neither to identify mechanisms to monitor or reverse the ongoing masculinisation of HEI provision.

THE COMMODIFICATION OF HIGHER EDUCATION AND WOMENS' LEADERSHIP

The implications of neoliberal, managerial HEI ought also to be recognized within this context as contributing to the discriminatory impact within which women work. It is not the purpose of this chapter to examine this in detail, but its relevance remains irrefutable. Neoliberalism has had an extraordinary impact on the structure and agency of HEIs, with the commodification of education necessitating a new wave of managerialism which has been equally entrenched with misogyny as an integral part of the realms of traditional academia (Meyers, 2013). Characterised by a culture of often toxic masculinity, the tangible and lasting impact, which actively disadvantages women leaders, is well reported in the existing published evidence base surrounding this issue (Canaan and Shumar, 2008). On a global level, this impact varies in relation to the extent of the emergence of managerialism in HEIs, where female academic presence is predominant in humanities and those disciplines perceived as 'soft' in comparison to their overtly male led empirical science disciplines. The interrelationship with poor opportunities for external research funding across these female dominated academic disciplines has provided a now historically visible delineation between the genders, with the motivational climate for progression being negatively affected since there is little to no opportunity for the development and integration of creativity and imagination (Bagilhole, 2019).

This has not only had an impact at a disciplinary level for women, it also directly impacts on their future likelihood of being able to gain full professorships, a pathway which is often necessary to gain an academic senior management position in reputable and credible HEIs. Since the relative number of women operating at professorial level is significantly different across countries, and particularly in countries such as Ireland, which has the least proportion of women employed at either professorial or associate professorial levels, then it is also still evident that these women have least opportunity for promotion to executive roles in HEIs (Bailes and Guthery, 2020). As an adjunct to these statistics, is the fact that women also are far more likely to shoulder additional responsibilities in relation to caring for children, elderly relatives. This, alongside having to continually make a stand against the gender stereotyping which characterises 21st Century HEI workplaces paints a picture, which to some women leaders can be perceived as overwhelming and not worth the additional effort needed to challenge them. By continually instilling and reinforcing this culture into the contexts and settings of where women work in academia, these women often also begin to recognise that the gate keeping which prevents their progression in organisations, also ensures that their perception of a career trajectory at professorial level and consequently in executive management is fundamentally illusory to them (ibid, 2008).

To move beyond the tokenism that characterises male hegemony in HEIs globally, a key issue for address is the minimal representation of women within senior management positions. The challenges faced by women who do venture into these positions often serves to further highlight the extent of male domination at senior management level that exists within these HEIs. This tokenism has also ensured that women are not in positions where they can actively challenge either toxic masculinity or the supplementary structure and agency that prevail in today's HEI workplaces and which continue to resonate in the context of HEI women leadership (Wheaton and Kezar, 2019).

DRIVERS OF GENDER EQUITY AND EQUALITY IN HIGHER EDUCATION

The longevity of male dominance in particular disciplinary subjects such as mathematics, science and engineering has done little to positively enhance the quality and duration of HEI women leaders' career trajectories. An evidence-based insight into this reveals a clear deficit of female professors across these disciplines, which bears witness to the corresponding longevity and history of education locally, nationally, and globally. One of the first steps to deconstructing this inequality is, as the STEM initiative in the UK has focused upon, to encourage equity and new awareness of careers available in traditionally male dominated professions via the consideration of the concept of 'signature pedagogies' (Shulman, 2005; Fitzgerald, 2020). Where gendered organisational culture and processes are evident in favour with male employees, it is apparent from the literature that, conformity is also more widely valued than attributes of creativity, and, as a by-product, innovation. This has been both historically and contemporaneously apparent in the body of literature available but amidst crisis with the advent of the COVID-19 pandemic, has never been more relevant. In HEIs which have demonstrably lower levels of women at senior executive levels across their organisations, this brings into question the purist epistemic assumptions which are clearly non diverse and non-aspirational in terms of equality, diversity and therefore creativity. The exponential reach afforded by a clear capacity for a diverse workforce, not merely constructed of ideological representation, but one of operationalised knowledge and skill, is immeasurable and has been clearly evidenced by the progression of parallel fields of practice. As an active consequence of these dilemmas which have pervaded organisations for the best part of half a century, issues of gatekeeping, the impact of gendered cultures and infrastructures policies and initiatives are at last beginning to feature mechanisms of moving forward positively but they also indicate the extreme way to go that organisation must correct these systemic imbalances. What is clear is that if central policy does not change to reflect these needs, the governments, which also reflect an imbalance in the representation of women in executive roles, will persist in influencing the macro levels of society at which meso and micro levels are then by default poised to remain indefinitely.

DISPELLING TRADITION AND THE PERPETUATION OF STEREOTYPICAL THINKING

Research has been conducted which conclusively identifies that senior managers of HEI organisations believe or hold assumptions that women, from a signature pedagogy perspective, are far more likely to work in the context of disciplines such as the social sciences, arts and humanities - those often termed 'soft subjects' or those which are responsible in health and medical care in the remit of 'caring' such as nursing (Dilnot, 2018; Henderson et al, 2018). They also perceived those empirical sciences due to the cultural necessity of maintaining the status quo of daily operations would potentially be interrupted by career breaks and the accommodation of caring responsibilities. In contrast to this perspective though, remains the fact that women's choice of study during school and university years also demonstrates that relatively few young women wish to study subjects such as science, technology, engineering and mathematics and as the current initiatives in UK educational settings indicate, this has become an identified area for redress in terms of changing the misconceptions that girls have about academic study in the post-compulsory sector (Lannelli and Duta, 2018). At a macro level, the labour market dictates the value of subject disciplines by leaders of global societies, where the representation of women leadership is also comparatively low. Reflective of this, is the fact that a corresponding hierarchy of subjects and disciplines exist, which is positively reinforced by the masculine perspectives driving their need. Because of this, fewer women follow maths, technology and sciences in preferences to the arts, humanities and social sciences. Aligned with the capacity for maximal earning capacity in the labour market are the opportunities to work in disciplines of these empirical studies, hence widening the gap between men and women in the potential to gain highly paid roles. Again, the redress of this balance would serve to close the gender income gap which characterises global economies. Research also highlights that those disciplines with which women more readily engage, also contribute widely to the development of the skill sets which men are known to lack. Gender segregation in the early stages of student learning at school can be regarded as a key cause of the gender gap, both economically and in terms of leadership opportunity that women experience throughout their academic careers. Where these are of greatest concern is in relation to the concepts of citizenship, which HEIs often claim to incorporate as an integral part of their organisational strength across global communities. Within this context, diversity and equality are two issues upon which capacity for citizenship and capacity for active civic reach, can hinge.

The active delineation of leadership from management is important. It was perhaps best operationally defined for the context of HEIs by Gardner (1995), when he defined it, accounting for both task and relationship dimensionality, as 'The ability to influence, either directly or indirectly, the behaviour, thoughts, and actions of a significant number of individuals'.

Since temporality, situation and context are inherently dynamic and altered at any given point, it can be stated that there is no such thing as definably perfect leadership. It is optimal leadership and not management which is the greatest determinant of organisational success. This was a key mechanism for solving both public and private sector challenges, often many of which are politically underpinned in the context of HEI settings.

In times of societal crisis, the words of Fitzgerald (2003) resonate harshly in the culture and climate of today's HEI organisations, when the assertion 'Conceptualisations of leadership without full account of both gender and ethnicity are futile'. Recent impacting factors on how we consider all leaders, not merely based on their gender, add an extra dimension to how best crisis ought to be managed and how long held assumptions and pre-suppositions can be actively challenged in practice.

Critical to this is the capacity for self-reflection and the desire to implement critical reflexivity at the heart of crisis environments. Mezirow's now seminal work on transformative learning can be seen as the keystone that enables all people to be seen as more than simply a collection of qualifications and experience, towards knowing people who know themselves. This is arguably one of the few mechanisms of being able to claim true and authentic approaches to the leadership and management of self, alongside organisations and institutions whose infrastructures serve to permeate wider society as an integral part of their civic contribution to society.

THE CONSIDERATION OF DEFICIT MODELS

Within longstanding published literature it is well established that the skills that leading in the context of HEIs entails are not actually gendered at all (Burke and Crozier, 2014). More recently it has been recognised that these skills are centred around the capacity and capability for endurance in relation to hard work, strategic vision, evidence of reputational impact in research, the courage to manage in the context of taking measured risk and the resilience and integrity to operationalise what is necessary for success (Meletiadou, 2022). From an axiological standpoint, it is more often the case that the value placed upon what women leaders do, stems from the value of the disciplinary perspectives from which they emerge, rather than any overt judgement surrounding gender (Jamali et al, 2022). Within the context of male senior management there are far more likely to be male academics from traditionally masculine subjects such as science and engineering, whereas, due to the historical legacies and patterns of humanities and caring professions, women are far less likely to have worked with and alongside them (Bauer and Taylor, 2022).

New public governance of organisations has meant that a strategic revamp of most of the organisational structuring has taken place across HEIs globally, however whilst these have shifted things predominantly towards a consumer led market perspective, the impact on the gendered leadership in HEIs has arguably been only vaguely considered. Therefore, these axiological standpoints are often little more than tokenism in relation to the practical application of values based strategic vision to practice. Arguably the best starting point for axiological underpinnings to be addressed, lies at the heart of organisational structures and cultures, which enable the authentic agency of women to flourish and to be genuinely valued (Tiwary and Gupta, 2022). Since core values lie at the credibility of every HEI across the globe, these remain ongoing areas for address and further research.

Women leaders are far more likely to express a capacity for collective and relationship behavioural approaches in practice, than male leaders, who are more likely to adopt purely transactional leadership strategies and operationalise these in practice. Because of this approach, women are often deemed to be less effective since their capacity to deal with complex ambiguity often entails detailed critical thinking as opposed to the binary decision making associated with transactional approaches (O'Connor et al, 2022). This is wholly dependent on the situational specificity of organisational contexts, which ultimately provides a platform for leadership execution and the ethos evident within it, in relation to differing leadership styles and approaches (Ruben, Mahon and Shapiro, 2022).

ORGANISATIONAL INFRASTRUCTURES AND IMPACT ON GENDERED AGENCY

The formal administration structures of HEIs have altered little in a century. Still featuring a pyramidal structure where women notoriously occupy the bottom rung of the organisational hierarchy, remains a typical profile for the majority of global HEIs. In European and American HEIs, initiatives aimed specifically at addressing gender equity in education, are thriving, which aim to provide transformational leadership opportunities and development for women. These provide bespoke training, education, and progression pathways for those who wish to further their academic career trajectories but are limited in availability and opportunity to access them is often lacking in equity of opportunity. The central issue of capacity for women leaders in HEIs is not actually the number of women in HEIs across the globe but rather the positions they occupy, which tend to be traditionally clustered at the bottom of the organisational hierarchy with minimal degrees of representation at higher levels, As a consequence, women rarely progress to the level of Dean, but do occupy their subordinate positions as Associate Deans, Directors or Pro Vice Chancellors, rather than linchpin positions at the top. This is a source of blocking women's access to powerful positions and thus exerting a vision for the next generation of female leaders. Perhaps the greatest danger in this dynamic is the sheer invisibility of organisational and gender-based bias, which serves to block female progression. As a key aspect of social justice and equity in action, as both process and goal this is a fundamental area for address across the globe where untapped potential and the provision of opportunity warrant redress (McNair, Bensimon, and Malcom-Piqueux, 2020; Okoli et al, 2020).

Men are far more likely to attribute the underrepresentation or lack of women in executive level positions to the breaks they necessarily take in relation to family caring responsibilities, career interruptions due to pregnancy and their comparative and relative lack of research impact in HEI praxis. In contrast women's perceptions of the same experience are littered with reports of actively overt and covertly demonstrated workplace discrimination, fuelled by the basis of their gender. Unlike the successes of Merkel and Thatcher in a political setting, where transformative learning is valued, the opposite has been found to be largely true in the context of HEI settings, where the higher women climb within the organisational hierarchy, the more they assume the character traits represented by male leaders, where they become deliberately and overly transactional (Allen and Flood, 2018). As a direct consequence of this, they progressively develop the same perspectives, that recruitment on the basis of gender is something that ought to be tokenistic rather than something actually addressed in HEI professional practice. These deficit models are potentially damaging, but even more so where this is often unintentionally reinforced by members of their own gender because of the cultural normalisation of gender stereotyping (Teelken and Deem, 2013). Göransson, et al (2008) stated that gendered organisational cultures are in turn linked to gendered knowledge, which means the naturally occurring agentic qualities with which women are wired to lead, are often masked by the bureaucracy and culture of organisations, rather than anything else. Therefore, the hegemonic and often toxic masculinity which drives organisations pervades into the wider cultural climate and becomes entrenched and difficult to address. At the heart of addressing these issues is the nature of recruitment and the nature of actively retaining women through to the point where they have visibly recognisable opportunities to apply for promotion or at least seek a career trajectory reflective of their capacity and capability. This is apparent across many professional disciplines out with the context of Higher Education (Hayes and Graham 2020; Bellini et al, 2019). The nature of women's participation is also an issue, since they need the basis of equity and inclusivity to participate on an equal footing with their male counterparts. Those pragmatic issues which serve as barriers to this, are often found in the institutional operational policies within which all staff are required to work, regardless of academic or professional discipline (Cardel et al, 2020).

ACTIVE PARTICIPATION VERSUS VISIBILITY OF GENDER IDENTITY IN EDUCATION

The agentic qualities that women do bring to the context of executive leadership within the context of HEIs are based around their capacity for creativity and as a direct consequence the bridge to innovation that this secures (Lipton, 2015). They are also widely reported as enhancing capacity for effective communication and an authentic approach to dealing with both the professional and personal needs of others.

Perhaps dwelling overly on long held debates of both the metaphorical glass ceiling and glass escalator ought to be diminished by the consideration of women, who whilst largely atypical of female representativeness across HEIs, provide important lessons surrounding the agentic qualities which have underpinned their success (Arriaga, Stanley and Lindsey, 2020).

Presenting these women as exemplars, however runs two distinct risks which have important implications for professional practice (Jameson, 2019). Firstly, the situations and contexts within which all women operate as leaders are largely unique and therefore the opportunity to emulate success is limited and secondly, women who are unable to transfer approaches into the context of their own workplace have an increased potential to perceive they will fail. In relation to the concept of failure, there are far wider independent variables and contextual issues at play, which correspondingly align with the far wider cultural challenges of organisational norms (Benslimane and Moustaghfir, 2020). One of the most insightful set of perspectives are those presented by Syed (2019) whose perspectives on the need for accuracy rather than creativity in the progressive development of change on major world issues such as feminism. His debate that during COVID-19 some leaders have demonstrated a clear capacity to pivot between leadership styles via the integration of both diverse views and binary decision-making processes. Reconciling the perceived tension that arises when seeking to increase diversity within established meritocracies remains a pivotal debate in any consideration of women and their opportunities to use innate agency within crisis. Doubtless this will prevail, although the pandemic has provided a forum for the illumination of not just exceptional women from the higher echelons of society but all those coping in more everyday settings of the home, the office and beyond.

CONCLUSION

This chapter has explored the fundamental impact of how gendered leadership in Higher Education Institutions can shape culture, context, and the civic progression of women's roles across professional contexts. It is possible to see from this work that the global political implications of gendered workplace discrimination remain a key challenge, particularly across Asia in countries such as Afghanistan, Pakistan, India, Sri Lanka and Bangladesh. If monitored at all records and statistics of women in Higher Education Institutions are rarely recorded, other than in relation to student numbers. Specific focus in Western culture has led to an emphasis on the development of capacity within the disciplines of Science and Technology, with gender becoming almost a tokenistic addition to key considerations of curriculum quality rather than equal opportunities for women, which can be offered through, for example Universal Design for Learning, which ensures equity of opportunity as well as equality. The sociocultural power which men provide across the globe, means from an international perspective women are still very much regarded as domestic commodities, who ought never to have authority over men.

The chapter has also provided a theoretical insight into how the gender balance and diversity that women bring to leadership positions can strategically influence recovery from crisis, such as the global pandemic. It has been possible to consider how traditional signature pedagogies and disciplinary perspectives can often serve to stereotype and create assumptions about the need for leadership styles which are traditionalist, outmoded and lacking in creativity. The agentic roles occupied by women, as outlined in the chapter enable the illumination of workplace issues such as emotional labour and mental health to highlight core issues in the professional context of Higher Education Institutes. The proactivity that global responses to crisis necessitate have ensured that the universality of human experience, is now an integral part of not only the dynamic management of crisis but also recovery from it. Gender delineation and theoretical consideration of how crisis impacts on the agentic qualities of leadership in crisis has been a fundamental part of considering how best to address progressive thinking in the context of future progression in educational leadership in this chapter, within which capacity for critical reflexivity is essential. It is here that the relational capacity of women and their ability to undertake processes of metacognition which not only impact on functional responses but the potential impact of them, can be considered. Creativity and innovation that stems from unlocked diversity of thought will be sorely needed to address both the educational delivery challenges presented by the COVID-19 and adaptations necessary to deal with its long-lasting economic impact. The ongoing challenge for women, is to engage these as opportunities to be grappled with, as opposed to avoiding them for any perceived lack of confidence, knowledge and skill which has arisen from the projection of wrong assumption and traditionally male dominated organisational cultures and climates.

REFERENCES

Aldrich, A. S., & Lotito, N. J. (2020). Pandemic Performance: Women Leaders in the Covid-19 Crisis. *Politics & Gender*, *16*(4), 1–9. doi:10.1017/S1743923X20000549

Allen, T. G., & Flood, C. T. (2018). The Experiences of Women in Higher Education: Who Knew There Wasn't a Sisterhood? *Leadership and Research in Education*, *4*, 10–27.

Arriaga, T. T., Stanley, S. L., & Lindsey, D. B. (2020). *Leading While Female: A Culturally Proficient Response for Gender Equity*. Corwin.

Bagilhole, B. (2019). Against the odds: Women academics' research opportunities. In *Gender, teaching and research in higher education* (pp. 46–56). Routledge. doi:10.4324/9781315254548-5

Bailes, L. P., & Guthery, S. (2020). Held Down and Held Back: Systematically Delayed Principal Promotions by Race and Gender. *AERA Open*, *6*(2), 2332858420929298. doi:10.1177/2332858420929298

Barba, I., & Iraizoz, B. (2020). Effect of the Great Crisis on Sectoral Female Employment in Europe: A Structural Decomposition Analysis. *Economies*, *8*(3), 64. doi:10.3390/economies8030064

Barnett, R. (1990). *The idea of higher education*. McGraw-Hill Education.

Bauer, N. M., & Taylor, T. (2022). Selling them short? Differences in news coverage of female and male candidate qualifications. *Political Research Quarterly*.

Bellini, M. I., Graham, Y., Hayes, C., Zakeri, R., Parks, R., & Papalois, V. (2019). A woman's place is in theatre: Women's perceptions and experiences of working in surgery from the Association of Surgeons of Great Britain and Ireland women in surgery working group. *BMJ Open*, *9*(1), e024349. doi:10.1136/bmjopen-2018-024349 PMID:30617103

Benslimane, M., & Moustaghfir, K. (2020). Career development practices and gender equity in higher education. *International Journal of Management Education*, *14*(2), 183–211.

Benziman, Y. (2020). "Winning" the "battle" and "beating" the COVID-19 "enemy": Leaders' use of war frames to define the pandemic. *Peace and Conflict*, *26*(3), 247–256. doi:10.1037/pac0000494

Bright, A., Acosta, S., & Parker, B. (2020). Humility Matters: Interrogating Our Positionality, Power, and Privilege Through Collaboration. In Handbook of Research on Diversity and Social Justice in Higher Education (pp. 19-40). IGI Global.

Burke, P. J., & Crozier, G. (2014). Higher education pedagogies: Gendered formations, mis/recognition and emotion. *Journal of Research in Gender Studies*, *4*(2), 52.

Cahdriyana, R. A., Richardo, R., Fahmi, S., & Setyawan, F. (2019, March). Pseudo-thinking process in solving logic problem. *Journal of Physics: Conference Series*, *1188*(1), 012090. doi:10.1088/1742-6596/1188/1/012090

Canaan, J. E., & Shumar, W. (Eds.). (2008). *Structure and agency in the neoliberal university* (Vol. 15). Routledge. doi:10.4324/9780203927687

Cardel, M. I., Dhurandhar, E., Yarar-Fisher, C., Foster, M., Hidalgo, B., McClure, L. A., ... Willig, A. L. (2020). Turning chutes into ladders for women faculty: A review and roadmap for equity in academia. *Journal of Women's Health*, *29*(5), 721–733. doi:10.1089/jwh.2019.8027 PMID:32043918

Dewey, J. (1933). *How We Think A Restatement of the Relation of Reflective Thinking to the Educative Process*. Heath & Co Publishers.

Dilnot, C. (2018). The relationship between A-level subject choice and league table score of university attended: The 'facilitating', the 'less suitable', and the counter-intuitive. *Oxford Review of Education*, *44*(1), 118–137. doi:10.1080/03054985.2018.1409976

El-Besomey, D. A. M. (2020). The Contemporary Vision of Universal Strategic Planning for Facing (COVID-19) Crisis in the Field of Higher Education Via Virtual Learning-Training. *European Journal of Education*, *3*(2), 151–164. doi:10.26417/869dvb85y

Fitzgerald, T. (2020). Mapping the terrain of leadership: Gender and leadership in higher education. *Irish Educational Studies*, *39*(2), 1–12. doi:10.1080/03323315.2020.1729222

Gardner, H. (1995). *Leading Minds*. Harper Collins.

Göransson, K. E., Ehnfors, M., Fonteyn, M. E., & Ehrenberg, A. (2008). Thinking strategies used by Registered Nurses during emergency department triage. *Journal of Advanced Nursing*, *61*(2), 163–172. doi:10.1111/j.1365-2648.2007.04473.x PMID:18186908

Grimson, J., & Grimson, W. (2019). Eliminating gender inequality in engineering, industry, and academia. In *The Engineering-Business Nexus* (pp. 315–339). Springer. doi:10.1007/978-3-319-99636-3_15

Hayes, C., & Graham, Y. N. (2020). Prophylaxis in Action:# MeToo for Women of Medical and Surgical Disciplines. In Gender Equity in the Medical Profession (pp. 270-279). IGI Global.

Henderson, M., Sullivan, A., Anders, J., & Moulton, V. (2018). Social class, gender and ethnic differences in subjects taken at age 14. *Curriculum Journal*, *29*(3), 298–318. doi:10.1080/09585176.2017.1406810

Henley, J., & Roy, E. A. (2020). Are female leaders more successful at managing the coronavirus crisis. *Guardian*. https://www.theguardian.com/world/2020/apr/25/why-do-female-leadersseem-to-be-more-successful-at-managing-the-coronavirus-crisis

Heymann, J., Levy, J. K., Bose, B., Ríos-Salas, V., Mekonen, Y., Swaminathan, H., ... Darmstadt, G. L. (2019). Improving health with programmatic, legal, and policy approaches to reduce gender inequality and change restrictive gender norms. *Lancet*, *393*(10190), 2522–2534. doi:10.1016/S0140-6736(19)30656-7 PMID:31155271

Inman, A. G. (2020). Culture and Positionality: Academy and Mentorship. *Women & Therapy*, *43*(1-2), 112–124. doi:10.1080/02703149.2019.1684678

Jamali, A., Bhutto, A., Khaskhely, M., & Sethar, W. (2022). Impact of leadership styles on faculty performance: Moderating role of organizational culture in higher education. *Management Science Letters*, *12*(1), 1–20. doi:10.5267/j.msl.2021.8.005

Jameson, J. (Ed.). (2019). *International perspectives on leadership in higher education: Critical thinking for global challenges*. Routledge. doi:10.4324/9781315122410

Jandrić, P., Hayes, D., Truelove, I., Levinson, P., Mayo, P., Ryberg, T., ... & Jackson, L. (2020). Teaching in the Age of Covid-19. *Postdigital Science and Education*, 1-162.

King, P. M., & Kitchener, K. S. (2004). Reflective judgment: Theory and research on the development of epistemic assumptions through adulthood. *Educational Psychologist*, *39*(1), 5–18. doi:10.1207/s15326985ep3901_2

Lannelli, C., & Duta, A. (2018). Inequalities in school leavers' labour market outcomes: Do school subject choices matter? *Oxford Review of Education*, *44*(1), 56–74. doi:10.1080/03054985.2018.1409970

Lipton, B. (2015). A New" ERA" of Women and Leadership: The Gendered Impact of Quality Assurance in Australian Higher Education. *Australian Universities Review*, *57*(2), 60–70.

Maas, B., Grogan, K. E., Chirango, Y., Harris, N., Liévano-Latorre, L. F., McGuire, K. L., ... Primack, R. B. (2020). Academic leaders must support inclusive scientific communities during COVID-19. *Nature Ecology & Evolution*, *4*(8), 1–2. doi:10.1038/s41559-020-1233-3 PMID:32493950

McNair, T. B., Bensimon, E. M., & Malcom-Piqueux, L. (2020). *From equity talk to equity walk: Expanding practitioner knowledge for racial justice in higher education.* John Wiley & Sons. doi:10.1002/9781119428725

Meletiadou, E. (2022). The lived experiences of female educational leaders in higher education in the UK: Academic resilience and gender. In *Handbook of Research on Practices for Advancing Diversity and Inclusion in Higher Education* (pp. 1–19). IGI Global. doi:10.4018/978-1-7998-9628-9.ch001

Meyers, M. (2013). The war on academic women: Reflections on post-feminism in the neoliberal academy. *The Journal of Communication Inquiry*, *37*(4), 274–283. doi:10.1177/0196859913505619

Mezirow, J. (2009). Transformative learning theory. In J. Mezirow & E. W. Taylor (Eds.), *Transformative Learning in Practise: Insights from Community, 39 Workplace, and Higher Education* (pp. 18–32). Jossey Bass.

Milovanović, A., Kostić, M., Zorić, A., Đorđević, A., Pešić, M., Bugarski, J., Todorović, D., Sokolović, N., & Josifovski, A. (2020). Transferring COVID-19 Challenges into Learning Potentials: Online Workshops in Architectural Education. *Sustainability (Basel)*, *12*(17), 7024. doi:10.3390/su12177024

O'Connor, P. (2019). Gender imbalance in senior positions in higher education: What is the problem? What can be done? *Policy Reviews in Higher Education*, *3*(1), 28–50. doi:10.1080/23322969.2018.1552084

O'Connor, P. (2020). Creating gendered change in Irish higher education: Is managerial leadership up to the task? *Irish Educational Studies*, *39*(2), 139–155. doi:10.1080/03323315.2019.1697951

O'Connor, P. J., Jimmieson, N. L., Bergin, A. J., Wiewiora, A., & McColl, L. (2022). Leader tolerance of ambiguity: Implications for follower performance outcomes in high and low ambiguous work situations. *The Journal of Applied Behavioral Science, 58*(1), 65–96. doi:10.1177/00218863211053676

Okoli, G. N., Moore, T. A., Thomas, S. L., & Allen, T. T. (2020). Minority Women in Educational Leadership. *Handbook on Promoting Social Justice in Education*, 1711-1727.

Pellegrini, M., Uskov, V., & Casalino, N. (2020). Reimagining and Re-Designing the Post-COVID-19 Higher Education Organizations to Address New Challenges and Responses for Safe and Effective Teaching Activities. Law and Economics Yearly Review Journal, 9(part 1), 219-248.

Peters, M. A., Rizvi, F., McCulloch, G., Gibbs, P., Gorur, R., Hong, M., ... Quay, J. (2020). Reimagining the new pedagogical possibilities for universities post-Covid-19: An EPAT Collective Project. *Educational Philosophy and Theory*, 1–44.

Power, K. (2020). The COVID-19 pandemic has increased the care burden of women and families. *Sustainability: Science. Practice and Policy, 16*(1), 67–73.

Rapanta, C., Botturi, L., Goodyear, P., Guàrdia, L., & Koole, M. (2020). Online university teaching during and after the Covid-19 crisis: Refocusing teacher presence and learning activity. *Postdigital Science and Education*, 1-23.

Ruben, B., Mahon, G., & Shapiro, K. (2022). Academic Leader Selection, Development, Evaluation, and Recognition: Four Critical Higher Education Challenges. In International Perspectives on Leadership in Higher Education (Vol. 15, pp. 115-138). Emerald Publishing Limited.

Shulman, L. S. (2005). Signature pedagogies in the professions. *Daedalus, 134*(3), 52–59. doi:10.1162/0011526054622015

Syed, M. (2019). Rebel Ideas: The power of diverse thinking. Hachette UK.

Taylor, L. L., Beck, M. I., Lahey, J. N., & Froyd, J. E. (2017). Reducing inequality in higher education: The link between faculty empowerment and climate and retention. *Innovative Higher Education, 42*(5-6), 391–405. doi:10.1007/s10755-017-9391-1

Teelken, C., & Deem, R. (2013). All are equal, but some are more equal than others: Managerialism and gender equality in higher education in comparative perspective. *Comparative Education, 49*(4), 520–535. doi:10.1080/03050068.2013.807642

Thomas, S. (2020). Women in Higher Education Administration Leadership and the Role of Institutional Support. In *Accessibility and Diversity in the 21st Century University* (pp. 234–249). IGI Global. doi:10.4018/978-1-7998-2783-2.ch012

Tiwary, A. R., & Gupta, T. (2022). Stereotypical Barriers Affecting Women Aspiring High-ranking Leadership Role in Higher Education. In *Role of Leaders in Managing Higher Education* (Vol. 48, pp. 99–116). Emerald Publishing Limited. doi:10.1108/S2055-364120220000048007

Trent, R. J. (2020). *Women's Perspectives on the Role of Organizational Culture in Their Career Advancement to Leadership Positions: A Generic Inquiry* (Doctoral dissertation, Capella University).

Tshivhase, M. (2020). Personhood: Implications for Moral Status and Uniqueness of Women. Handbook of African Philosophy of Difference, 347-360.

Tversky, A., & Kahneman, D. (1974). Judgment under uncertainty: Heuristics and biases. *Science, 185*(4157), 1124-1131.

Villiers, C. (2019). Boardroom Culture: An Argument for Compassionate Leadership. *European Business Law Review*, *30*(2), 253–278. doi:10.54648/EULR2019012

Wenham, C., Smith, J., & Morgan, R. (2020). COVID-19: The gendered impacts of the outbreak. *Lancet*, *395*(10227), 846–848. doi:10.1016/S0140-6736(20)30526-2 PMID:32151325

Wheaton, M. M., & Kezar, A. (2019). Interlocking systems of oppression: Women navigating higher education leadership. In *Challenges and opportunities for women in higher education leadership* (pp. 61–83). IGI Global. doi:10.4018/978-1-5225-7056-1.ch005

Whitty-Collins, G. (2020). *Why Men Win at Work:...and How to Make Inequality History*. Luath Press Ltd.

World Health Organization. (2020). COVID-19 and violence against women: what the health sector/system can do, 7 April 2020 (No. WHO/SRH/20.04). World Health Organization.

ADDITIONAL READING

Aldossari, M., Chaudhry, S., Tatli, A., & Seierstad, C. (2023). Catch-22: Token women trying to reconcile impossible contradictions between organisational and societal expectations. *Work, Employment and Society*, *37*(1), 39–57. doi:10.1177/09500170211035940

Ansar, A. (2023). Bangladeshi women migrants amidst the COVID-19 pandemic: Revisiting globalization, dependency and gendered precarity in South–South labour migration. *Global Networks*, *23*(1), 31–44. doi:10.1111/glob.12368 PMID:35599743

Cronshaw, S., Stokes, P., & McCulloch, A. (2022). Online communities of practice and doctoral study: Working women with children resisting perpetual peripherality. *Journal of Further and Higher Education*, *46*(7), 959–971. doi:10.1080/0309877X.2021.2023734

Fine, C., & Sojo, V. (2019). Women's value: Beyond the business case for diversity and inclusion. *Lancet*, *393*(10171), 515–516. doi:10.1016/S0140-6736(19)30165-5 PMID:30739677

Mate, S. E., McDonald, M., & Do, T. (2019). The barriers and enablers to career and leadership development: An exploration of women's stories in two work cultures. *The International Journal of Organizational Analysis*, *27*(4), 857–874. doi:10.1108/IJOA-07-2018-1475

Merma-Molina, G., Urrea-Solano, M., Baena-Morales, S., & Gavilán-Martín, D. (2022). The satisfactions, contributions, and opportunities of women academics in the framework of sustainable leadership: A case study. *Sustainability (Basel)*, *14*(14), 8937. doi:10.3390/su14148937

Mousa, M., Boyle, J., Skouteris, H., Mullins, A. K., Currie, G., Riach, K., & Teede, H. J. (2021). Advancing women in healthcare leadership: A systematic review and meta-synthesis of multi-sector evidence on organisational interventions. *EClinicalMedicine*, *39*, 101084. doi:10.1016/j.eclinm.2021.101084 PMID:34430838

Pervin, N., Mokhtar, M., & Haque, N. Z. (2023). A Conceptual Study of Urban Spaces in Bangladesh: Exploring Patriarchy From a Feminist Perspective. In *Urban Poetics and Politics in Contemporary South Asia and the Middle East* (pp. 240–268). IGI Global. doi:10.4018/978-1-6684-6650-6.ch012

Sougou, N. M., Ndiaye, O., Nabil, F., Folayan, M. O., Sarr, S. C., Mbaye, E. M., & Martínez-Pérez, G. Z. (2022). Barriers of West African women scientists in their research and academic careers: A qualitative research. *PLoS One*, *17*(3), e0265413. doi:10.1371/journal.pone.0265413 PMID:35353842

Wilkinson, J., & Male, T. (2023). Perceptions of women senior leaders in the UK Higher Education during the COVID-19 pandemic. *Educational Management Administration & Leadership*. doi:10.1177/17411432221150079

KEY TERMS AND DEFINITIONS

Crisis: A time of intense difficulty or danger, when the immediacy of decision making, and strategic leadership is paramount.

Critical Reflection: A process of identifying, questioning, and assessing our deeply held assumptions.

Critical Reflexivity: The capacity to see one's own perspective and assumptions and understand how one's perspective, assumptions and identity are socially constructed through critical reflection.

Emotional Labour: The management of emotional response in order to present the outward image of control and reassurance in order to continue interaction with other people in a certain way while doing a job in stressful circumstances.

Inequality: Inequality in this chapter refers to the phenomenon of unequal and/or unjust distribution of resources and opportunities among members of a given society, in this instance female leaders.

Neoliberalism: Neoliberalism is a political philosophical term used to signify the political reappearance of 19th-century ideas associated with free-market capitalism, and in this chapter refers to the commodification of global Higher Education provision.

Positionality: Refers to the social and political context that creates your identity in terms of race, class, gender, sexuality, and ability status.

Signature Pedagogy: Refers to the forms or styles of teaching and instruction that are common to specific disciplines, areas of study, or professions and as such can unintentionally define and constrain them.

Chapter 3

Profess*Her:
The Revelatory Power of the Black Female Professor

Catherine Saunders
https://orcid.org/0000-0003-2547-4491
Howard University, USA

ABSTRACT

*The twentieth and twenty-first century has conveyed a notable increase in the number of Black women joining the professoriate. While triumphant, Black female presence has yielded significant professional and personal hardships for the Black woman. These hardships, often undervalued or dismissed by the institution, silences stories of mistreatment to maintain the illusion of diversity and inclusion. My chapter makes a notable departure from scholarly dialogue on the Black female professor that conceptualizes her trajectory through the looking glass of what Patricia Hill Collins called controlling images in Black Feminist Thought (2000). Instead, my project highlights the unique position of the Black female professor in the academy through a concept I call Profess*Her. The term references the unique, revelatory power of the Black female professor that exposes what is and what must change in order to stride toward true freedom as actualized and encouraged by the academic institution.*

DOI: 10.4018/979-8-3693-0102-9.ch003

Copyright © 2024, IGI Global. Copying or distributing in print or electronic forms without written permission of IGI Global is prohibited.

AN EARLY ENCOUNTER: MY INTRODUCTION TO THE PROFESSORIATE

I often think back to an early encounter in my teaching career. This encounter occurred by way of classroom observation where the Department Chair advised me to *teach* my students rather than "do the work for them." The observation report stated that while circling the room to engage with students doing groupwork I told a struggling student that I would do the work for them. My refutation to this untrue assessment proved brief and fueled a confident proclamation that she only wrote what she "heard me say." This memory—a testament to an oppressive effort to maintain power by any means necessary—demonstrates the truth as inconvenient to anyone whose power remains vested in a mythic, national narrative. This experience would assume countless forms throughout my time in the institution, each more sinister than the last to ensure that I knew my presence was not only unwelcome, but unqualified and unworthy—the point often arriving at the expense of my colleague's personal dignity and outside the bounds of respectability. In recalling this moment and others like it, I want to be sure not to afford adversity central placement. Instead, I appoint the unique positionality that my presence produces as a gateway to my interiority; notably, I appoint this position as a lane past the perils of my superficial presence and as an entry point into the power that lies beneath. Thus, while unpleasant, these experiences illuminate that the Black female professor harbors a lesson that becomes unteachable simply because so many refuse the invitation to unlearn (and subsequently unravel) what belies her presence as a conflict and not a conduit.

BACKGROUND

The university is, of course, a microcosm of the world at large, academia reflecting American prejudice (Kuradusenge-McLeod 2021). Also like the larger national culture, the academy often states that it prioritizes and values diversity and inclusion despite exhibiting behavior to the contrary (Kuradusenge-McLeod 2021). In their essay "'Scholaring' While Black: Discourses on Race, Gender, and the Tenure Track," Eva Michelle Wheeler and Sydney Freeman Jr note that "despite the modern American cultural sensitivity to racial issues (especially as reflected by the notion of political correctedness) empirical data show the Black faculty are still underrepresented in academia (Wheeler and Freeman 2018, 58) This assertion is perhaps best supported by the glaring dearth of Black presence in the twenty-first century academy. In 2018, the Black woman comprised only 4% of Assistant Professors, her presence slightly larger than the 3% of Black male Assistant Professors (Wheeler and Freeman, 2018). These numbers showed an unremarkable increase in Black female presence from a decade earlier where Black professors comprised only 3% of tenured faculty (Wheeler and Freeman, 2018). Recent scholarship on the subject notes that Black women make up slightly more that 2% of tenured faculty and less than 2% of full professors (Gayles 2022). The dwindling of an already modest population reflects the heavy weight of racial fatigue on Black female professors despite overt attempts to diversify the academy (Gayles 2022). According to a 2016 Washington Post article, these numbers reflect the desires of the institution. Specifically, the article argues that the predominately white institution lacks diversity as a reflection of faculty and administrative values (Wheeler and Freeman, 2018). The statement proves a bold proclamation of institutional choice that becomes more jarring (and true) in juxtaposition to the statistical representation (and decrease) of Black presence in an academy that remains predominately white. What is true for the Black female academic, however, is not necessarily true for all people of color. A 2017 survey reveals that Asian professors were the most represented minority of full-time professors (Department of Education 2017). Conversely, Black professors were the largest minority group of part-time faculty (Department of Education 2017). These statistics suggest an institutional preference for a transient Black presence and a predilection for certain minority groups over others. Moreover, the statistics on Black presence in the academy posit institutional commitment to diversity and inclusion as conditional if not cognitively dissonant. It does, however, remain imperative to acknowledge that the non-white presence remains essential to the larger white presence. What I mean here is that Black presence in the academy maintains the cultural hierarchies that permeate the larger culture—a hierarchy that only works if the non-white presence comprises the minority.

Despite their small statistical presence, the Black female professor has certainly warranted increased visibility. This increased visibility of Black female presence in the professoriate comes alongside a rising Black female presence in several other industries (like reality television) that socially reproduce the caricatures that ornament her past. In her essay "Black female faculty, Resilient Grit and Determined Grace of 'Just Because everything is different doesn't mean anything has changed,'" Rachel Alicia Griffin argues that despite some changes, "the world has yet to conquer the systemically orchestrated misrecognition of Black femininity as deviant, bereft, and anti-intellectual" (Griffin 2016, 366). Popular depictions of Black women often prove saturated in portrayals that posit these adjectives as true, but this systemically orchestrated misrecognition is perhaps most pronounced in the trajectory of the Black female professor.[1]

IN AND OUT: THE BLACK FEMALE PRESENCE IN ACADEMIA

In his essay "'Admirable or Ridiculous?': The Burdens of Black Women Scholars and Dialogue in the Work of Solidarity," Darrius D'wayne Hills notes that the Black female professor remains "pressed to shoulder a matrix of raced and gendered expectations and perceptions that negatively impact their personal and professional quality of life" (Hills 2019, 5). Much of the scholarly dialogue on the Black female professor views these raced and gendered expectations as reflecting the racist controlling images that ornament a not-so-distant past. The most frequent parity between the Black female professor and these controlling images is between the Black female professor and the mammy. In "You is kind, You is smart, You is important: The Black Female Professor as 'The Help,'" Lauren K. Alleyne aligns Black female professor expectation with the mammy arguing that "we're meant to care for our students in a way that is beyond the contract of the classroom" (Alleyne 2021, 176). Lori Walkington makes a similar argument in her essay "How Far Have We Really Come? Black Women Faculty and Graduate Students' Experiences in Higher Education." Here, she contends that the Black female professor remains expected to embody a contemporary mammy figure who showers their white male counterparts with reverence and allows and comforts questions of her competence (Walkington 2017, 53).

The Black female professor, therefore, shoulders the burden of excessive caregiving in her place of work. So, although seemingly graduated from the domestic work of her foremothers, the Black female professor illustrates expectations of self-less service as attached to the Black woman. But what makes the mammy's role so detrimental to Black professorship is the implications of its resurfacing. Particularly, the Black female professor as mammy is not just about physical servitude, but about the service Black women are expected to play in the larger national narrative. To this contention Alleyne notes that the children who suckled the Black woman's breasts "eventually assumed hierarchical position above her—history activated when Black women assume the position of professor of white students" (Alleyne 2021). Alleyne's image poignantly highlights the Black female professor's service role as instrumental in reproducing the forces that oppress her.

As a result, the Black female professor comes to occupy an 'outsider-within' status where she must "contend with the socially constructed, negative images of Black womanhood that deem all Black women—regardless of their education, status, or position—as inferior, subservient, hostile, domineering, hypersexual or overly masculine" (Jones, Wilder, Lampkin 2013, 327). This outsider-within status speaks specifically to Black female presence at predominately white institution and Black female proximity to a "hidden curriculum" that is "deeply embedded within the institutional structure and processes of many graduate programs" (Jones, Wilder,

Lampkin 2013, 327). Alleyne argues that she combats this hidden curriculum by challenging white students to give up their power perceiving her position in the academy as "to (re) construct and maintain my personhood so that I can encourage, support, and be of service to my students as we do the work of deconstructing the structures that would deny us all on our full humanity" (Alleyne 2021). Jones, Wilder, and Lampkin, like Walkington, combat this hidden curriculum with mentorship and advisement for Black female doctoral students prior to their formal entry into the professoriate. These suggestions highlight the power of the intra-cultural ecosystem to mitigate institutional mistreatment and mirror the talk some Black families have with their children pertaining to the systemic injustice that awaits them. My argument strives to contemplate the Black female professor's ability to expose the interiority of the academic institution, an exposition that bears notable promise to add nuance to the world around her. However, while I build on twentieth and twenty-first century discourse on the Black female professor, my argument makes a notable departure from the scholarly dialogue on the topic.

CONCEPTUAL FRAMEWORK

Much of the discourse on the Black female professor meditates on parallels between her mistreatment and what Patricia Hill Collins called controlling images to reference the caricatures that historically encapsulate Black female identity (Collins 2000). While these parallels rightfully depict the cyclical encounter with the Black woman in America, this frequent and persistent reference conveys an unsettling image of Black women through a racialized lens. This result is a form of invisibility gifted to those relegated to the social peripheries that demand a means to contemplate Blackness and Being beyond oppressive lenses that bind Black people and Black culture to racist ideations. So, while I do not discount the institutional wrath as yielding significant damage to the Black female professor, I argue that to conceptualize the Black female as an institutional victim plays into myths of Black inferiority. Instead, I make a firm distinction between the Black female professor and what I am calling the Profess*Her, the latter conveying the Black woman as occupying a unique pedagogical position that exposes what is and what must change to incite genuine cultural ascension.

My chapter builds on Jones, Wilder, and Lampkin's contention that the Black female subject occupies a unique position in the academy. My reliance on the unique experience of the Black female professor also corresponds to the work of Moya Bailey, namely her term misogynoir which speaks to the specificity of Black female oppression (Bailey 2018). Profess*Her appoints the Black female trajectory in the academy as a bridge to understanding her systemic mistreatment beyond victimhood and toward embracing her underdiscussed power. My methodology echoes the expansive perspective that the late Toni Morrison conveys in her novel *Song of Solomon*. Morrison conveys this perspective through her character Pilate who sees Blackness as a rainbow. It is the ability to see multiplicity in the singularity of oppression and systemic violence that harbors the revelatory power of the Black Profess*Her. The term builds on Trans*, a term that Christina Sharpe introduces in her text *In the Wake: On Being and Blackness* to reference the multiple transformations engendered from the transatlantic slave trade. Essential to conceptualizing Sharpe's term is the plural use of Trans*, a plurality and layering that I mirror in my use of the term "Profess." Profess is an obvious reference to the professoriate but it also encompasses its additional definitions which include a "vowel," declaration," and "affirmations," actions that correspond to Black female bondage and liberation. The "Her" component deviates from feminist discourse and instead references gender and its proximity to social mimetic ordering as contributing to Black female mistreatment in the professoriate. Therefore, the *Her* illustrates that which must also change to ameliorate the institutional peril as displaced onto the Black female professor.

My project proceeds with three objectives. First, I look at how the Black female Profess*Her acts as a revelatory agent and exposes both the ways of the world that inform the anxieties of the institution. The revelatory power of the Black female Profess*Her appoints her experience as both a window and mirror, her trajectory a lens into the present and the future. I contend that the Profess*Her exposes the present state of being, revealing the social cement that binds the bricks of the academy, and conveys the mimetic ordering as held in place by her experience as "outsider within." I pair these matrices with themes in Black female professor trajectory: expendability, institutional betrayal, and likeability to highlight how they reflect her powerful position and the larger potential for change. I place these themes in two counter stories that pick the scars of institutional wounds to bleed a truth told poignantly through stories that speak into the silence often demanded of the Profess*Her. This silence proves the result of the isolation that many Black scholars face in the academy and the high cost of advocacy and camaraderie (Allison 2008). Furthermore, while the history that precedes Black female entry into the academy may make her entry into the institution appear tantamount to entering a burning house, Profess*Her challenges readers to view the Black female professor as flames bearing the destructive power to forge a new path forward.

Profess*Her

THE BLACK WOMAN, "LIKEABILITY," AND INSTITUTIONAL BETRAYAL

The first counter story reflects an experience that frequents the trajectory of many Black female professors: petitions, or student effort to engender their institutional departure. The Black female professor in this narrative is a young woman who recently graduated and relocated to her hometown to do what she started across the country: teach. After a brief encounter with her students that consisted of listing her credentials, reviewing the syllabus, and facilitating a diagnostic, she prepares to return home. Before she would arrive at the train station, she received a call from the chair of her department, an elderly man of the majority who refused to let her grade student exams as if she did not mirror the academic credentials of her white male supervisor. He informed her that there was a petition started to have her fired after allegations that she was "talking down to the students." The accusations were, of course, particularly concerning given that she had barely spoken at all and the introduction to the course was not unlike any introduction that she had throughout her college career, minus the diagnostic exam. The resulting procedure was an in-class hearing where students articulated complaints ranging from "there was just the *I* and no *we*" to a complaint about the way she looked at someone. The hearing featured no commentary on pedagogy, course content, or instructor ability to teach; instead, the white male chair encouraged several superficial complaints. Upon his exit he seemed pleased with both himself and the students and sought no feedback or response from the Black female instructor. When word got to the provost about what happened, she rushed the Black female professor's narrative along, preferring to hear the story from a woman of the majority despite being a Black woman herself.

The counter story depicts a layered portrayal of institutional betrayal that highlights the systemic treatment of Black female presence in the professoriate as undervalued and subject to the racist terrorism of the institution. The counter story conveys a miscarriage of institutional authority in a humiliation ritual designed to remind the Black female professor of her outside status despite her positionality inside the ivory tower. Her status as "outside" makes the Black female professor subject to expendability for superficial reasons. The collection of signatures to eject an instructor after one brief encounter as supported by the institution rather than encouraging disgruntled students to drop the course or simply test the waters of a new course, illuminates the Black female professor as expendable—a gesture echoed by the faculty response. The faculty response to the student petition depicts a fusion of ideas on the student-faculty level. Because student prejudicial complaints matched the ingrained prejudice of the institution, it is the Black female professor, not the racist ideology, that must be eliminated. This shared and internalized belief also mirrors the passive and uncaring response of the Black female provost who also viewed the young Black female professor's racist experience as a scorched wall that needed to be painted over and not a fire that needed to be put out.

Despite sharing an experience with the Black female professor, the provost views the concerns as a burden, as she understands her position as watering a tree built over the unmarked graves of her ancestors, not to uproot it and implement a nuanced foundation. Her lack of support, like the white male chair, functions under the veil of impartiality, but details the cement that holds the academy together and as anchored in Black female exclusion. This Black female exclusion, however, conceptualized under the gaze of the Profess*Her, details Black female exclusion as a force in the academy's role in cultivating whiteness for its white male heirs to ascend to their racial thrones (Wilder 2013). The academy proved instrumental in cementing gender as a face of social order that also proved a repository for racism and other social evils. Thus, the Black female Profess*Her treatment, as evidenced in the counter-narrative, conveys the original structure of the academy as held in place by Black female treatment in the academy—her mistreatment an institutional effort to maintain the founding principles of the country as upheld and institutionally reproduced by the academy.

The Black female provost's behavior, in addition to playing into the ruse of impartiality, also panders to the politics of likeability displaced onto the Black female professor. In his twentieth century essay "Stranger in the Village," James Baldwin remarked on the politics of likeability during his visit to a predominately white European village. He contended that a "great part of the American Negro's education (long before he goes to school) that he must make people 'like' him," noting that "no one, after all, can be liked whose human weight and complexity cannot be, or has not been admitted" (Baldwin 1955, 165). The politics of likability detail the institutional as anchored in the belief of Black female expendability—her likability more significant that her professional accomplishments, her intentions for the course, or her pedagogical style. My early years in the academy featured countless claims from Department Chairs and advisors who saw fit to inform me if a student "did not like me," an elementary sentiment institutionalized as a vehicle to displace racist beliefs as the fault of the oppressed, because the unstated sentiment posits likeability as what follows competence. Likeability, therefore, functions as a sign of competence that implies that "they would like you if you were any good." This likeability is perhaps most pronounced in student evaluations where "serious" professors are labels "stuck up," "boring," or "unlikeable" because they fail to entertain their students and socially reproduce ideas of Black inferiority and white superiority. In "Free to Be Me? Black Professors, White Institutions," Donnatrice C. Allison notes that Black faculty tends to experience more institutional issues if they "fail to conform to stereotypical views" (Allison 2008, 642). Thus, the politics of likeability for the Black female professor remain rooted in racial expectation.

Profess*Her

The politics of likeability encapsulates the superficial regard that her professional presence demands. Likeability, of course, aligns with early ideations of Black minstrelsy remanifested in contemporary Black roles that convey animated (if not exaggerated) depictions of Black people as seen in reality television and the sexually suggestive images that ornament popular culture and social media. These images, like the Black female professor's institutional response to the Black female professor, depict degradation as the cost for Black female likeability. In their essay "Killing My Spirit, Renewing My Soul: Black Female Professors' Critical Reflections on Spirit Killings While Teaching," Jemimah L. Young, and Dorothy E. Hines call this systemic behavior "spirit-breaking," a behavior they align with the systemic murder of Black women vindicated by her presumed criminality. The Black female Profess*Her's trajectory details that though alignment with systemic murder seems far-fetched—the pervasive effort to destroy the psyche and dwindle the spirit of Black people, proves profoundly connected. The "unliked" Black female Profess*Her is deemed criminal for divorcing her allegiance to entertainment and for her exposition. However, to conceptualize the Black female professor as Profess*Her reveals that it is not the Black female Profess*Her that is "unliked" but her exposure of the ways of the world as fiction, evoking emotions that history said dissipated and embodying a power that they said they did not have.

To contemplate the power of the Profess*Her, it is imperative that the counter story graduate the Black female professor from the reigns of victimhood. As Audre Lorde remarked upon contemplating the transition from silence to articulation in her essay "The Transformation of Silence into Language and Action:" "I am not only a casualty, but I am also a warrior" (Lorde 1983, 41). The counter story depicts the Black female professor's experience as a casualty of a larger system and a symptom of a larger plague but does not purport her as victim. To perceive the Black female professor as a victim assumes the subjugated stance that informs her institutional mistreatment and overlooks the power vested in her vantage point. The Black female professor as victim perpetuates the collective plague that she exposes as individualistic, positing an understanding of the Black experience as one of singular, devastating circumstance. Thus, to perceive the Black female professor's trajectory as that would purely harm the Black woman, details the academy as plagued with circularity. This linearity demonstrates the black female professor as the necessary force to make a circular narrative linear. As Profess*Her the Black female professor affirms the larger state of the world and reveals institutional diversity initiatives as vehemently espoused to traditional ideations veiled by nuanced phrasing. The Profess*Her posits the Black female hire as reflecting no real place for her in a space that would not exist if it were not for exclusion and whose presence presents the thread to unravel the institutional plague. The Black female Profess*Her emerges as the ultimate figure of Black studies whose trajectory yields a roadmap for what must be present to yield more than pseudo diversity and inclusion. Diversity is not about looking different yet working together to institutionally foment a hidden agenda, and inclusion is not about what (or who) looks good on paper and sounds good but remains designed to fit an unsettling mold. The Profess*Her presents a point of departure from workshops that posit racism as equally experienced and perpetuated by any and all and suggests that its heighted persistence in her presence references the need for more interior work.

LUST IN EXPOSITORY FORM: HYPERSEXUALITY AND BLACK FEMALE PRESENCE IN THE ACADEMY

The second counter story presents what seems to counter the "likeability" dynamic with a Black female professor who is liked too much by a student. A Black female professor receives a sexually suggestive essay from a male student where he articulates his desire in expository form. She takes the essay to the white female dean who destroys the evidence and reassigns the student to another class only after his indignation (incited by what he perceived as rejection) spills over in a (verbally) violent explosion. After this reassignment the white female Dean states that the student is doing "exceptionally well" in their new placement.

The (literal) disregard for the Black female professor's concerns depicts an inability to perceive the Black woman as warranting any kind of sexual integrity. Therefore, rather than document the incident in case of escalation, the Black female professor's concerns remain silenced in the Dean's effort to maintain her own conjugal sanctity. The Dean's response conveys an inability, or willingness, to see the student's actions as violating Black female respectability in the reluctance to acknowledge its existence. Central to conceptualizing the Black female professor as Profess*Her is to contemplate the Dean's role in creating and maintaining gender exclusivity. Though the academy traditionally excluded women of the majority, this exclusion proved a pillar in establishing her social stature as woman despite her overt absence. This exclusion proves integral to distinguishing the Black woman from women of the majority and other woman of color. Yes, the traditional academy excluded all women, but their physical omission proved integral to consummate their conceptual role and social visibility. Of course, the opposite is true for the Black woman.

Moreover, while it is tempting to perceive this scenario as reflecting the jezebel controlling image, as a Profess*Her, the dynamic appears far more sinister. Sexuality is, of course, a means of control—thus, to sexually pursue the Black female professor is an attempt to accost her position and power, depicting her "likeable" attributes as a vehicle for her institutional denigration. The Profess*Her, therefore, emerges a figure of sexuality studies, her sexuality a continual systemic weapon that in its oppressive force delineates a form of invisibility.

BLACK FEMALE TRAJECTORY IN THE ACADEMY: A REVEALING ACT

To examine the extent of the Profess*Her's discourse, it is perhaps imperative to examine the structural conflict faced by women of color in the academy. Scholarly discourse on the non-white presence in the academy details the university as wielding institutional violence in variant. While the Black woman is often perceived as a "mammy," the Latina woman is often viewed as preoccupied with the ingredients of domestic life, and the Asian woman is often regarded as passive (Pittman 2010). Research also depicts the woman of color as sharing similar issues with respect and threatening encounters with white male students (Pittman 2010). In their essay, "Narratives from Latina Professors in Higher Education," Catherine Medina and Gaye Luna note that Latina presence in the professoriate is a direct result of the 1960s civil rights movement, notably the 1964 civil rights act. Like the Black female professor, the Latina has also maintained a very low presence in the academy, this dearth reflective of secondary schooling where Latina women were often burdened with low standards of their potential which discouraged many from pursuing higher education (Medina and Luna, 2000). Perhaps the most poignant component of their essay is the assertion that "academe is a model based on commonalities—not a community built around the concept of diversity" (Medina, Luna 2000). These commonalities prove glaring in discussions of non-white presence in the academy that often lump the peripheral groups into a single category connoting a shared, singular experience. Similarly, while the woman of color does not share the systemic power of her white counterparts, the university does present a shared role in their social function.

The Black female professor reveals a crossover, or becoming white process, to which the Black woman can never materialize due to the structural axis of the western world. In *Ebony and Ivy*, Craig Wilder notes that the academy originally yielded a becoming white process, a process that still manifests centuries after its conception. I want to be clear here that I do not mean to suggest that the woman of color becomes white pe se; I do, however, wish to note that the woman of color maintains a proximity to American identity, and the corresponding upward mobility, that the Black woman does not. My contentions are perhaps best illustrated by the "model minority" trope that maintains proximity to women of color and the continental African. While the model minority trope is inherently racist, it also observes notable privileges in the assistance it affords the cultural hierarchy which places blackness at its proverbial bottom.

Another revelatory component of the Profess*Her is that she reveals the systemic power of the white male as socially produced in color. Much of the scholarship pits Black against white—over looking the adversity that plagues the academy as re-presented in color. The revelation illuminates the perils of stagnancy and reveals the lingering stench of racism as finding a new home in prejudice. For clarity, I do not discount that the root of the institutional wrath that Black women face reflect an over prioritization of whiteness—it does—but that the manifestation of this power demonstrates that the epidemic has (and continued to) spread. This revelation takes me back to a resonant moment during my research on this topic. In her essay "Race and Gender Oppression in the Classroom: The Experiences of Women Faculty of Color with White Male Students," Chanelle Pittman includes testimony from a Black female professor who says that despite being faculty, she felt detached from the authority that typically accompanied the position. The professor details this detachment with unfortunate encounters with white male students who self-appoint themselves to authorial positions in her class under the premise that "as a white male, he's automatically my peer" (Pittman 2010, 189). The professor's testimony reveals a tendency for students of the majority to assume the position of colleague to a Black female professor despite her years of work to even qualify for this position. The Profess*Her reveals that while rooted in whiteness, this is occurrence manifests in many colors that assume their knowledge as commensurate to that of the Black female professor. This experience takes me back to the Black female student who brought in a high school worksheet to aid me with my pedagogy and the evaluations commentary I once received that mention that the student "didn't learn anything" as if there was simply nothing to learn from a Black female professor.

Taken together, the provided examples refute the claims made in the 2016 Washington Post article that examines what they regard as a lack of diversity in the academy. Rather, the revelatory power of the Profess*Her reveals that diversity is ever-present in the academy as the wrath of its center has spread with the virality of a plague. This spreading depicts the effect of unchecked bias and admonishes the consequences that await should the present state of affairs proceed without intervention.

THE NUDGE OF NUANCE: THE PROFESS*HER AND INSTITUTIONAL RESOLUTION

In contemplating the Profess*Her and the solutions her experience inspires, research on Black female presence in the professoriate reveals the Black woman as more likely to take on heavier teaching loads than her white male counterparts (Pittman 2010). This imbalance reveals the Black woman as a pillar in the institutional structure maintained by her degradation and over extension just like her foremothers. Several articles also note that the Black woman is often required to teach contentious subjects to students unsettled by its discourse (White 2007). Thus, it is imperative that dialogue concerning solutions for race and gender-based conflict in the academy do not suggest that Black women bear the brunt of teaching racial literacy. I do think that Black women must occupy primary roles in structuring cultural enlightenment. These roles, however, must be rooted in the understanding and acceptance that it is not the Black woman's job to reconcile institutional issues with her existence. To echo the feedback of my former colleague, it is essential that the Black female professor does not "do the work" for students of her experience. Moreover, it is equally as important to acknowledge that race and prejudice are not that which can be trained away.

My suggestions and insight arrive in the post-pandemic era informed by the global moment of reflection and resistance fomented by George Floyd's murder. The post-Floyd America has resulted in global commitment to diversifying previously white spaces and a string of nuanced diversity trainings. While surfacely advancing the evils that killed him, it is imperative to acknowledge the grace that systemic efforts afford offending parties despite appearing to prioritize marginalized communities. Derek Chauvin's feckless act of murder was neither the result of bad training nor is he a rotten apple. Chauvin, just like his institutional counterparts, prove products of a rotten tree that mist be gradually uprooted by tackling the tangled forest of mythos that pollutes the minds of the masses. Perhaps most importantly, Chauvin, like the countless others who came before him, illuminate the poison that spreads when racial prejudice continues to convey the low value of Black life.

It is also important to note that the institutional experience that frames the Black female professor does not just yield professional adversity but personal health issues. In her essay "Disrupting institutional erasure: Organizational exit, remembrance, value, and the need to matter," Katherine Grace Hendrix suggests that the health issues that come to ail the Black woman after years in the academy must be considered as consequences of their systemic adversity (Hendrix 2021). The detriment of the Black female trajectory, of course, does not just yield consequences for her; the extent of her treatment is that which proves the power to plague any and everyone in its path.

Strides toward a solution make it so that the Black female professor be hired for the richness of her palette not to re-present the racist mythos of an institution constructed for her exclusion or to right the wrongs of racism at the cost of isolation or elimination. It is imperative that the discomfort amongst students be anticipated, encouraged, but not seen as reflective of Black female incompetency—but of a starting point that the institution plans to challenge and re-construct by graduation. To do this it remains imperative that diversity be seen not as de-centering whiteness, as such a perspective still prioritizes the national center; instead, diversity must come to mean prioritizing the liberation and centralizing of peripheral cultures beyond the realms of sports and entertainment.

HEIRS TO A NEW KIND OF THRONE: CONCLUDING THOUGHTS

The ivory tower maintains a prominent role in what Sylvia Wynter called the "over-representation of Man," a phrase that reflects a Eurocentric perception of humanity. I implement Wynter's work to highlight ideations of humanity as a pillar of racial discourse. While I do not consider discussion of Black humanity a worthwhile (or debatable) pursuit, I do, however note that de-humanization of peripheral culture maintains prominent placement in contemporary conceptualizations of humanity. In addition to departing from scholarship that discusses the need to systemically "humanize" Black female identity, I also want to be clear that my intentions are not to suggest that the Black woman be perceived or welcome with open arms; I do not believe that this realistic or necessary. What I do hope to have conveyed is an understanding of how maladaptive institutional processes details the Black female Profess*Her as a barometer for the institution— that provides cause to question how far any institution can move from the dimensions of its origins.

A figure of Black Studies, Sexuality, and Gender—the Profess*her proves emblematic of nation in her institutional placement in the academy. As Profess*Her, the Black female trajectory proves one of destruction—she who destroys the ways of the western world and with every petition, sexual proposition, and prejudiced evaluation—depicts cracks in the institutional structure filled by initiatives, new hires, and manifestos that reproduce institutional behavior under the veil of change. The issue of change, when discussed in proximity to the benefactors of institutional terror often inspire comments that reflect an unwillingness to villainize those in overt positions of power. Despite the predictability of this sentiment, it provides a useful means to conceptualize the Profess*Her. Particularly, if one wishes not to villainize those who inherit from the generations that precede them it is perhaps dutiful to confront the inheritance. The academy embodies this cultural inheritance, which has, in large part, showered its spoils diversely. Because this inheritance has come to include those who aid in multiplying its means and uplifting its heirs, perhaps the Profess*Hers greatest feat is revealing issues of inheritance and lighting a spark that suggests that one should not strive to be heirs to such a hegemonic throne.

REFERENCES

Alleyne, L. K. (2021) "You Is Kind, You Is Smart, You Is Important: The] Black Female Professor as 'the Help.'" Teaching Black: The Craft of Teaching on Black Life and Literature, edited by Ana-Maurine Lara and Drea Brown, University of Pittsburgh Press, pp. 172–77. JSTOR, https://doi.org/. Accessed 17 Jan. 2024. doi:10.2307/j.ctv22tnmhk.23

Allison, D. C. (2008). Free to Be Me? Black Professors, White Institutions. *Journal of Black Studies*, *38*(4), 641–662. https://doi-org.proxyhu.wrlc.org/10.1177/0021934706289175. doi:10.1177/0021934706289175

Artz, B., & Welsch, D. M. (2014) "The Effect of Peer and Professor Gender on College Student Performance." *Southern Economic Journal*, vol. 80, no. 3, pp. 816 38. *JSTOR*, https://www.jstor.org/stable/23809653. Accessed 17 Jan. 2024.

Bailey, M.Moya Bailey & Trudy. (2018). On misogynoir: Citation, erasure, and plagiarism. *Feminist Media Studies*, *18*(4), 762–768. doi:10.1080/14680777.2018.1447395

Baldwin, J. (1955). "Stranger in the Village." Notes of a Native Son. Beacon.

Collins, P. H. (2000). *Black Feminist Thought: Knowledge, Consciousness, and the Politics of Empowerment*. Routledge.

Gayles, J. G. (2022). Does Anyone See Us? Disposability of Black Women Faculty in the Academy. *Diverse*. https://www.diverseeducation.com/opinion/article/15295726/doesanyone-see-us-disposability-of-black-women-faculty-in-the-academy

Griffin, R. A. (2016). Black female faculty, resilient grit, and determined grace or "Just because everything is different doesn't mean anything has changed". *The Journal of Negro Education*, *85*(3), 365–379.

Hendrix, K. G. (2021). Disrupting institutional erasure: Organizational exit, remembrance, value, and the need to matter. *Gender, Work and Organization*, *28*(4), 1323–1336. https://doi-org.proxyhu.wrlc.org/10.1111/gwao.12609. doi:10.1111/gwao.12609

Hills, D. D. W. (2019). "Admirable or Ridiculous?": The Burdens of Black Women Scholars and Dialogue in the Work of Solidarity. *Journal of Feminist Studies in Religion*, *35*(2), 5–21.

Jones, T. B.,….. (2013). "*Employing a Black Feminist Approach to Doctoral Advising: Preparing Black Women for the Professoriate.*" The Journal of Negro Education, vol. 82, no. 3, pp. 326-38. *JSTOR*, . Accessed 3 Feb. 2024.

Kuradusenge-McLeod, C. (2021). Multiple Identities and Scholarship: Black Scholars' Struggles for Acceptance and Recognition in the United States of America. *International Studies Review*, *23*(2), 346–369. https://doi-org.proxyhu.wrlc.org/10.1093/isr/viaa098. doi:10.1093/isr/viaa098

Lorde, A. (2007). *"The Transformation of Silence into Language and Action." Sister Outsider*. Crossing.

Medina, C., & Luna, G. (2000). Narratives from Latina Professors in Higher Education. *Anthropology & Education Quarterly, 31*(1), 47 66. https://www.jstor.org/stable/3196270

Morrison, Toni. (1977). Song of Solomon. Vintage. Oxford Languages. (2013). 7th ed.). Oxford English Dictionary.

Pittman, C. T. (2010). Race and Gender Oppression in the Classroom: The Experiences of Women Faculty of Color with White Male Students. *Teaching Sociology*, *38*(3), 183–196. https://www.jstor.org/stable/27896528. doi:10.1177/0092055X10370120

Sharpe, C. (2016). *In the Wake: On Being and Blackness*. Duke.

Spillers, H. J. (1987). Mama's Baby, Papa's Maybe: An American Grammar Book. *Diacritics*, *17*(2), 65–81. doi:10.2307/464747

Stanley, C. A. (2006). Coloring the Academic Landscape: Faculty of Color Breaking the Silence in Predominantly White Colleges and Universities. *American Educational Research Journal*, *43*(4), 701–736. https://www.jstor.org/stable/4121775. doi:10.3102/00028312043004701

U.S. Department of Education. (2017). Integrated Postsecondary Education. *Data Systems*.

Walkington, L. (2017). How Far Have We Really Come? Black Women Faculty and Graduate Students' Experiences in Higher Education. *Humboldt Journal of Social Relations*, *39*(39), 51–65. https://www.jstor.org/stable/90007871. doi:10.55671/0160-4341.1022

Wheeler, E. M., & Freeman, S. Jr. (2018). "Scholaring" While Black: Discourses on Race, Gender, and the Tenure Track. *Journal of the Professoriate*, *9*(2), 57–86.

White, D. G. (2007). "Matter out of Place": Ar'n't I a Woman? Black Female Scholars and the Academy. *Journal of African American History*, *92*(1), 5–12. https://www.jstor.org/stable/20064150. doi:10.1086/JAAHv92n1p5

Wilder, C. S. (2013). *Ebony and Ivy: Race, Slavery, and the Troubled History of America's Universities*. Bloomsbury.

Wynter, S. (1989). Beyond the Word of Man: Glissant and the New Discourse of the Antilles. *World Literature Today*, *63*(4), 637–648. doi:10.2307/40145557

Young, J. L., & Hines, D. E. (2018). Killing my spirit, renewing my soul: Black female professors' critical reflections on spirit killings while teaching. *Women, Gender, and Families of Color*, *6*(1), 18–25.

ENDNOTE

[1] Though my essay meditates on the Black female professor's trajectory, I do note a shared experience (in part), with her Black male counterpart.

Chapter 4
Black Women Professors' ART for Well-Being in Teacher Education

Rosalynne Elisabeth Duff
Georgia State University, USA

ABSTRACT

Within the academy, Black Women professors have cultivated theories and practices for well-being, utilizing memoirs for theorization and social movements. However, their theories and practices should be more valued within the literature on holistic or healing pedagogies or teacher education (Muhammad et al., 2020). Teacher education is in a crisis with reports of high demands and stress levels with low autonomy and pay (Doan et al., 2023). This is an exploratory study of six Black Women professors' healing theories and practices produced through the genre of memoirs. Therefore, this chapter aims to inform professors, teacher educators, and educational leaders about Black Women's healing practices as creative expressions of their activism, research, and teaching (ART) (Tyson, 2001) and ways of well-being. In this way, it aims to move Black Women's healing theories and ways of knowing from the margins to the center of knowledge production in the context of teacher education.

INTRODUCTION

Within the academy, Black Women have cultivated theories and practices for well-being, utilizing memoirs as a vehicle for theorization and social movements. However, Black Women's theories and practices are valued less within the literature on holistic or healing pedagogies and teacher education (Muhammad et al., 2020).

DOI: 10.4018/979-8-3693-0102-9.ch004

Copyright © 2024, IGI Global. Copying or distributing in print or electronic forms without written permission of IGI Global is prohibited.

Historically, Black Women's theories and practices, such as culturally relevant teaching (Ladson-Billings, 2021), intersectionality (Collins & Bilge, 2016), and abolitionist teaching (Love, 2019), have innovated teacher education. Yet, Black Women receive less recognition and respect from their colleagues for their work in colleges and universities. In this chapter, I explore how Black Women professors who desire to be well, liberated, and culturally authentic maintain well-being in the academy with its history of hurt and harm toward Black Women (Perlow, Wheeler, Bethea, & Scott, 2018; Winters, 2020; Walker, 2020; Njoku & Marshall, 2024). Therefore, this chapter aims to inform professors, teacher educators, and educational leaders about Black Women's healing practices as creative expressions of their activism, research, and teaching (ART) (Tyson, 2001) and ways of well-being as a call to action to center Black Women's educational theories in the teacher education curriculum. In this way, I also aim to move Black Women's healing theories and ways of knowing from the margins to the center of knowledge production in the context of teacher education.

According to a report on teacher well-being conducted by Rand Corporation, teachers recorded their intentions to stay or leave the profession based on different factors contributing to their well-being (Doan et al., 2023). Some key findings from the Rand teacher well-being report found that female teachers discussed feelings of burnout and were less likely to mention emotions related to resilience. Black teachers reported experiencing stress due to low salaries associated with teaching. Black teachers were found more likely to intend to leave the profession due to the impact of stress on their professional lives due to the culture and environment of schools in the U.S. context (Doan et al., 2023). Limiting curriculum that impacts the historical, political, and social conversation in K-12 and higher education in the classroom also affects the well-being of educators. "Despite very public efforts to promote "diversity" teacher education remains largely white supremacist in orientation, often "othering" People of Color in these programs and pushing them to the margins within the curriculum" (Player & Irizarry, 2022, p.592). In turn, teachers' well-being impacts students' whole (mind, body, and spirit) (Fu-Kiau & Lukondo-Wamba, 1988). Therefore, it is imperative to consider the impact of societal norms that shape our school cultures and negatively affect the well-being of Black Women professors as they navigate systems of oppression in higher education spaces.

This exploratory study draws upon data and findings from two studies utilizing Black Women's memoirs as mentors. I center the experiences of Black Women professors utilizing three excerpts from *Sisters of the Academy: Emergent Black Women Scholars in Higher Education* (Green & Mabokela, 2001) and three books: *Homecoming: Overcome Fear and Trauma to Reclaim Your Whole Authentic Self* (Bryant-Davis, 2022), *Holding Space: A Storytelling Approach to Trampling Diversity and Inclusion* (Cairo, 2021), and *Black Women's Yoga History: Memoirs of Inner*

Peace (Evans, 2021). The study's first phase centers on the voices of three Black Women professors who demonstrate ART (activism, research, and teaching) to resist oppression in the academy. The second phase builds upon the first by applying a holistic healing lens to Black Women's ART in the academy by examining three Black Women professors who published full texts about a particular healing practice cultivated outside the context of teacher education. Therefore, what follows is an analysis of six Black Women's experiences of creating from a position of leadership in higher education despite the "hegemonic normative whiteness" in order "to teach in a manner that is relevant, critical and humanizing while also socially and individually transformative" (Brown, 2014, p.326; Mattheis, 2022, p.570). The following sections of this chapter focus on how Black Women professors enact ART to create new knowledge in holistic and healing ways. Simultaneously, this study is my practice of synthesizing Black Women's theories within the literature on teacher education, professional development, and social well-being. Therefore, I demonstrate activism by centering marginalized voices of Black Women in my research as a pedagogy of practice, teaching through the well-being practices of Black Women.

THE WELL-BEING OF BLACK WOMEN PROFESSORS

Black Women professors' are the subject of this study because they have contributed a body of knowledge on holistic healing and well-being interdisciplinarily (Bryant-Davis, 2022; Cairo, 2021; Evans, 2021b). The role of a professor is to teach curriculum, mentor colleagues and students, and manage tasks of meeting deadlines on a day-to-day basis. One way Black Women professors have documented their well-being experiences in the workplace is through a strategy of memoir theorization. In Porcher and Austin's (2021) article, two Black Women professors of practice (PoPs) discuss racial inequity's mental and emotional impact, causing them to endure more labor and less compensation and recognition than their peers in teacher preparation. Porcher and Austin (2021) recognize their experiences are not unique but connected to a long legacy of inequity toward Black Women in society:

"*In Their Eyes Were Watching God,* Zora Neale Hurston (1937) states that "Black women are the mules of the world." Black women carry the load that white men, white women, and Black men refuse to carry; they do the work that no one wants to do, without praise or thanks" (p.117).

Despite existing on the lowest rank of the social caste system, Black Women students and professors continue to produce healing theories and practices for the academy without equity and justice or the professional recognition of their intellectual abilities, positioning them to stand up for their rights (Dixson, 2003; Evans-Winters & Twyman Hoff, 2011; Player & Irizarry, 2022). Marginalization of Black Women's ideas happens in the form of erasure in scholarship. For example, reviewing the book *Teaching with a Social, Emotional, and Cultural Lens: A Framework for Teachers and Teacher Educators* (Markowitz & Bouffard, 2020), the authors discussed Culturally Responsive Teaching without any mention of Geneva Gay (Gay, 2000) or Gloria Ladson-Billings' work on Culturally Relevant Teaching (Ladson-Billings, 1995). Gay and Ladson-Billings are the two Black Women at the forefront of conceptualizing these frameworks in teacher education. As researchers, framework developers, and scholars, how do we conduct ethical research using Black Women's theories without citing Black Women (Citeasista, n.d.)?

The short answer is that we cannot, and we should always give credit where credit is due to the Black Women whose ideas are foundational to our work in teacher education. Doing this creates a sense of righteousness for Black Women and restores historical harm in higher education.

Acuff's (2018) article "Confronting Racial Battle Fatigue and Comforting My Blackness as an Educator" discusses her personal and professional experiences with marginalization's impact on the emotions and psychology of Black educators, which she theorizes as racial battle fatigue. Racial battle fatigue (RBF) is defined as "exhaustion and stress associated with racial microaggressions [that cause] African Americans to experience various forms of mental, emotional, and physical strain" (Smith et al., 2006; Acuff, 2018, p.175). To counteract the narrative of Black Women as mules, going unrecognized for their work, and the emotional, mental, and physical stress put upon Black Women in the academy, Black Women professors have mitigated their marginalization to stay well by producing ART (activism, research, and teaching) through healing practices to benefit their students and the academy.

BLACK WOMEN'S ART IN THE ACADEMY: ACTIVISM, RESEARCH AND TEACHING

Black Women's activism, research, and teaching (ART) innovated educational theory (Muhammad et al., 2020; Tyson, 2001). The creativity of Black Women's educational theories was absent in my teacher preparation experience, and reflecting on that fact feels detrimental to my well-being as a Black Woman. The experience left me questioning the value of my intelligence and my place in the academy. Studying the work of educational leaders such as bell hooks (1994), Cynthia Dillard (2000), and Stephanie Y. Evans (2007) was one way I mitigated the marginalization of Black Women in my teacher preparation program. Building upon the educational theories of these Black Women scholars, I focused my intelligence on resisting and dismantling the systems of oppression at the root of education in America by studying the well-being experiences of Black Women in higher education (Wallace et al., 2020), which developed into the critical reflection of Black Women's memoirs as mentors as a pathway toward healing and professional development of teacher educators and Black Women professors.

THE POWER OF BLACK WOMEN'S MEMOIRS

The power of Black Women's memoirs as mentors for holistic healing and well-being is captured through the work of Dr. Stephanie Y. Evans, author of *Black Women's Yoga History: Memoirs of Inner Peace* (2021). Before writing the book, she collected the titles of over five hundred Black Women's life writings, divided them into themes such as mental health, food, yoga, and meditation, and organized them on her website, africanamemoirs.net (Evans, 2013).

The stories Black Women share from personal testimonies provide a road map for understanding how to live well under adverse circumstances. "I investigate the inner peace practices that Elder black women have used to try to bring their lives into balance, especially after being subjected to personal, cultural, or structural violence" (Evans, 2021b, p. 6). The power of Black Women's memoirs is the wisdom transferred through life stories for others to learn ways to be well and act as mentors for the next generation (Evans, 2021a). Evan's research into the well-being practices of Black Women through memoirs is a catalyst to conceptualizing holistic healing and well-being in teacher preparation curriculum. Her work lays the foundation for this exploratory study examining the experience of Black Women professors. It provides insight into the value of Black Women's perspectives on how to be well in the context of higher education for others interested in workplace wellness.

THEORETICAL FRAMEWORK

My theoretical perspective on Black Women professors encompasses three concepts: critical consciousness (Friere, 1968; hooks, 1994), critical contemplative pedagogy (Kaufman, 2017), and womanist theory (Maparyan, 2012). To properly understand the onto-epistemology of Black Women professors, I engaged with intersectionality (Hill Collins & Bilge, 2016), four levels of social location: micro, mezzo, macro, and global (Kirk & Okazowa-Rey, 2010), and the two frameworks from *Flat-Footed Truths*, the "beautiful, healing, and ugly truths" and "self, reclamation, resistance, and transformation" (Bell-Scott & Johnson-Bailey, 1999). The work of Black Women like Audrey Lorde, Dr. Maya Angelou, and bell hooks, among other phenomenal Black Women memoirists, also influence this inquiry. Throughout this study, I utilized the contemplative practices of journaling, meditating, prayer, and nature walks combined with reading Black Women's memoirs to think more deeply about the well-being practices of Black

Woman professors in the U.S. context of the academy. Combining the three perspectives into one, I conducted this study from the stance of a critical contemplative womanist. Shelley P. Harrell's (2018) work also captures this stance in her conceptualization of soulfulness, a framework for understanding the meditative practices of African Americans. The soulfulness and spirituality of Black Women, intertwined within their culture and gender, is also represented through Maparyan's (2012) conceptualization of womanism. Therefore, I applied a critical contemplative womanist framework to this two-part exploratory study of the experiences of Black Women professors.

SISTERS OF THE ACADEMY

Reflecting on my initial inquiry about the well-being of Black Women in the academy, I set out to create a composite of what Black Women endure mentally, emotionally, and spiritually as educational leaders. I chose the book *Sisters of the Academy* because it "does not dwell on these negative portrayals of women of African descent but rather highlights and celebrates their contributions and successes in academic environments that are not always supportive." (Green & Mabokela, 2001 p.vx). It traces the trajectory of Black Women in higher education and addresses "historical, social, cultural, political, and academic issues that affect Black Women in the academy" (Bell-Scott & Johnson-Bailey, 1998). I chose to explore *Sisters of the Academy* because the editors include essays balanced between acknowledging the oppression felt by Black Women and celebrating their ways of knowing and being in the world.

The book is an anthology of thirteen essays in different genres of writing. To begin my analysis, I created a rubric to determine which essays were written in the memoir genre. Next, I examined the table of contents and identified six memoirs. Then, I analyzed the six memoirs by reading the author's biographies and each chapter to compare and contrast the narratives. Almost immediately, three memoirs emerged, along with Tyson's (2001) ART framework of activism, research, and teaching. The three memoirs of Dr. Lisa Williams, Dr. Cynthia Tyson, and Dr. Thandeka Joyce F. Kirk act as mentor texts for the first phase of this memoir study. In terms of each author's social location, at the time of publication, Williams was a professor of Women's Studies at the University of Massachusetts, Amherst; Tyson was a Language, Literature, and Culture Assistant Professor at Ohio State University; and Kirk was an Associate Professor at the University of Wisconsin-Milwaukee in Africology. All three professors wrote within the context of a historically white institution (HWI).

Each memoir from *Sisters of the Academy* is connected to a Black Women's Memoirs framework for the literature on "beautiful, healing, and ugly" truths of their experiences (Bell-Scott & Johnson-Bailey, 1998). For example, Maya Angelou's (2014) *Letters to My Daughter* demonstrates beautiful truths, Ida Keelings' (2018) *Can't Nothing Hold Me Down* expresses healing truths, and Tarana Burke's *Unbound* (2021) reveals ugly truths about Black Women's experiences in society. As I analyze the work of Williams (2001), Tyson (2001), and Kirk (2001), I connect each one to Bell-Scott & Johnson-Bailey's (1998) "beautiful, healing, and ugly" truths framework in the context of teaching and higher education. Williams (2001) writes about beautiful truths, Tyson (2001) reflects healing truths, and Kirk reveals the ugly realities of being a Black Woman professor. Together, the life writings of Williams (2001), Tyson (2001), and Kirk (2001) created a dynamic profile of a Black Women professor. To add complexity and depth to my analysis, I also applied Bell-Scott & Johnson-Bailey's (1998) framework of "self, reclamation, resistance, and transformation" to the findings and conclusion of the analysis for all three memoirs.

Dr. Lisa D. Williams: Telling One's Own Life (Self)

I moved what waz my unconscious knowledge of being in a colored woman's body into my known everydayness -Ntozake Shange as cited by Bell-Scott & Johnson-Bailey, 1998

In her memoir essay, "Coming to Terms with Being a Young, Black Female Academic in U.S. Higher Education," Dr. Lisa D. Williams (2001) tells her life in the way Ntozake Shange calls "everydayness" as she advocates for herself, Women of Color, and blazes the trails of equity and justice for young scholars coming into the academy. Her memoir centered on her own experience as a "doctoral student, faculty member, and researcher" at a predominantly white institution (PWI) (Williams, 2001, p.93). Her research is framed through an intersectional lens of race, gender, and positionality in the academy. She shares, "There needs to be a deeper understanding and analysis of Black Women in the academy and not a simplified one that masks the multiple layers of their different identities" (Williams, 2001, p.93). Her reflection is an essential reminder of the self-work required to maintain well-being in the academy. Black Women must continue to recover their intersectional identities through self-study. The academy must acknowledge Black Women's cultural, political, historical, and academic contributions to education at all levels. Significant contributions Williams (2001) discusses in her essay include the complexity of intersectional identity and the interrelated connection between race and gender because, for Black Women, the two concepts are never separated. An intersectional lens uplifts the complexity of Black Women's perspectives, allowing for more than one experience to exist simultaneously. Williams (2001) ends the essay by saying:

There is a continuing need to tease out the dynamics that contribute to the multifaceted experiences of young Black women and to place much-needed attention on the role they play as researchers, faculty, and students. Finally, we must continue to create a critical space in which to transform and challenge misconceptions about young Black women in higher education (p.101).

Through her teaching, she shifts the conversation toward whose knowledge gets centered in the academy, the value of mentorship, the role of voice, and connecting to other Black Women in the academy. She shared, "I wasn't just teaching the subject, I became the subject-a young, Black female who was shifting the experiences of Black Women from the margins to the center" (Williams, 2001, p.97). Moving from the margins to the center exemplifies her activism within her teaching. Williams (2001) also points out the importance of challenging misconceptions about Black Women because doing so contributes to everyone's well-being and growth in the academy. She challenged these misconceptions about having Black Women as guest speakers during her Black Women and Activism course. By doing so, she also learned through Black Women's memoirs as mentors in her professional development and charting a path forward to center Black Women's onto-epistemologies in research and teaching. Anything less than centering Black Women's theories in education contributes to the devaluation and dehumanization process through the status quo of a narrow view of research, teaching, and learning in higher education. Her memoir confirmed the importance of self-study in teacher education as a means for valuing the perspectives of teachers and students to contribute to everyone's holistic health and well-being.

Dr. Cynthia A. Tyson: Claiming Lives Lost (Reclamation)

And where the words of women are crying to be heard, we must each of us recognize our responsibility to seek those words out, to read them and share them and examine them in their pertinence to our lives -Audre Lorde, 1997

The life writing of Dr. Cynthia A. Tyson's (2001) essay "From the Classroom to Higher Education" is her personal and professional journey of navigating systems of oppression while persevering to create meaningful ART (activism, research, and teaching). Her memoir is similar to Williams's but differs in how the information is presented. Williams (2001) writes her memoir as an essay, while Tyson's writing provides the methodology and framework for understanding Black Women's ART, which is also reflected in William's (2001) memoir. Tyson also writes through the lens of intersectional identity. However, she self-identifies through her ARTist roles.

"There is the possibility that after reading my story, one more sister will understand the struggles and triumphs, and the sacrifices and rewards that allow commitments to teaching, research, and activism to find a place in the academy" (Tyson, 2001, p. 139). Tyson's memoir provides in-depth insight into teacher as an activist, researcher as an activist, and the importance of mentoring Black Women (and men) in the academy. Her essay creatively demonstrates her reclaiming of Black Women's worth in the academy through ART.

Tyson's memoir is connected to the critical contemplative womanist framework by centering the work of other Black Women activists in education, such as Angela Davis (1989). Both contribute a critical lens to inequities in education, contemplative spirituality, and awareness of the interconnection between the experiences of Black Women at a soul level, and both share a womanist perspective by uplifting and appreciating the experiences of Black Women. Tyson's work helps to transform education by encouraging Black Women to reclaim themselves as teacher-activists and researcher-activists to decolonize education at all levels.

Tyson's (2001) memoir is a mentor for claiming and reclaiming lives otherwise lost by centering Black Women's voices in activism, research, and teaching to reclaim researcher-activist, continuing the legacy of liberation, and sharing knowledge and wisdom with the next generation of students and scholars. Teacher educators and professional learning facilitators can reclaim the role of teacher-activist by creating a curriculum based on the culture of students (teachers), encouraging educators to work for equity and justice, to bring healing into education, starting with personal and professional identity work leading to systemic changes through teaching and learning.

Dr. Thandeka Joyce F. Kirk: Telling Lives As Resistance (Resistance)

We can learn to work and speak when we are afraid in the same way we have learned to work and speak when we are tired. For we have been socialized to respect fear more than our own needs for language and definition, and while we wait in silence for that final luxury of fearlessness, the weight of that silence will choke us -Audre Lorde as cited by Bell-Scott & Johnson-Bailey, 1998

Dr. Thandeka Joyce F. Kirk's life writing reflects resistance to national and global systems of oppression. Williams (2001) writes her memoir like an essay, Tyson (2001) produces a methodology, and Kirk (2001) writes her chapter, "Not an Honorary White: Conducting Research During the Days of Apartheid," in a journalistic style to convey her teacher and researcher experiences in the academy. She shares, "This chapter is concerned primarily with my experience as an African American female graduate student doing field research in South Africa for the first time from October 1981 to January 1983" (Kirk, 2001, p. 183). Unlike the others, Kirk (2001) chronicles a research journey but, similar to Williams (2001) and Tyson (2001), approaches the work from the perspective of an activist. Kirk's activism is unique as she is navigating the apartheid system in solidarity with South Africans; therefore, she renounces her American privilege to have accommodations similar to the South African whites.

She reflects on her experience:

Thinking back over my sixteen months of fieldwork in South Africa during the days of apartheid, I wondered how to explain my everyday life, which included events that had less to do with research in archives or the library and much more to do with being Black and living under apartheid (Kirk, 2001, p. 184).

Because of her international experience as a researcher, her perspective includes an intersectional lens of race, color, and language. More than anyone else, she names white supremacy and defines it in the context of South African apartheid. Her identity, the self, is centered in her reflective writing style while reclaiming her power by renouncing the more human treatment she received from whites once she displayed an American accent. She transforms by resisting the "honorary white" treatment and undergoing a renaming ceremony. She continues to resist by continuing to visit South Africa. Her teaching is less subtle than Tyson's (2001) and Williams (2001). Still, it is evident in how she chronicles her experience as an African American graduate researcher experiencing South African apartheid. Kirk's work makes a broader connection to discourse on equity, justice, and decolonizing the academy by making the personal, professional, and professional political. "Doing field research during the days of apartheid meant it was difficult, if not impossible, for me not to become involved in the politics of the country" (Kirk, 2001, p.202). In this way, she centered her experience as a Black Women professor writing through memoirs about race, gender, and cultural politics in her research and teaching in the academy. In my analysis of all three memoirs using the ART framework, Kirk is the only one who does not explicitly mention teaching. However, her teaching is also implied through her work as a tenured professor. Therefore, each professor demonstrated a commitment to activism, research, and teaching that could be considered a healing practice in higher education.

BLACK WOMEN'S MEMOIRS: SAVING OUR LIVES (TRANSFORMATION)

The combined life writings of Williams, Tyson, and Kirk in *Sisters in the Academy* (Green & Mabokela, 2001) illustrate a transformative profile of Black Women in the academy at all stages of their career. Williams (2001) describes her life by highlighting her transition from a doctoral student to becoming a professor focusing on the self. Tyson (2001) reclaims the lost ART of Black Women in the academy by highlighting her transition from a classroom teacher to a professor as an activist. Kirk (2001) resists white privilege, practices, and policies of apartheid, highlighting her growth from taking doctoral courses to conducting fieldwork in South Africa from the perspective of an African American. In this way, the life writings of Williams (2001), Tyson (2001), and Kirk (2001) act as mentors for Black Women's well-being in the academy.

Each memoir separately provides wisdom, but when combined, they paint a solid portrait of the experiences of Black Women professors who know themselves, reclaim their roles as teacher-activists and researcher-activists, and resist systems of oppression in the academy by any means necessary.

Lastly, emerging from the data gathered from the text is Tyson's (2001) framework of ART (activism, research, and teaching) in the academy, which reminds me of CaShawn Thompson's popular #BlackGirlMagic (For Harriet, 2020). Because the ART of Black Women transpires in an environment of racism, white supremacy, and systemic oppression, it is devalued or undervalued but mythicized as something no one else can do. Black women in the academy are sometimes considered mythical characters who somehow shoulder tasks that others are unable or unwilling to undertake. Yet, through the life writings of Williams (2001), Tyson (2001), and Kirk (2001), it is imperative to note that Black Women's activism, research, and teaching are to the benefit of the next generation of scholars because the memoirs unashamedly share the beautiful, healing, and ugly truths Black women professors' experiences.

The ART of Black Women professors is revolutionary and a "freedom dream" toward liberatory education (Kelley, 2002; Coles & Stanley, 2021). My freedom dream for liberation is a new world of teacher education that centers holistic healing and well-being in the learning process. I think centering the healing theories and practices of Black Women in the curriculum of teacher educators could impact teacher education with a ripple effect into the ethers of education for generations to come. I am reminded of the brilliance of Septima Clark, whose activism, research, and teaching were foundational to the Civil Rights movement through literacy and civic education (Charron, 2012). The acknowledgment and intentional use of Black Women's knowledge of the social systems-level change, social and emotional development, and their fifty-year legacy of activism, research, and teaching in the academy positions them as the experts on healing and well-being.

BLACK WOMEN'S HEALING PRACTICES OF
HOMECOMING, HOLDING SPACE, AND INNER PEACE

Discovering the ART of Black Women professors is foundational in understanding how Black Women maintain their well-being in the academy to produce publications on healing theories and practices. Based on Black Women's memoirs, well-being is maintained through healing practices such as storytelling or writing narratives about Black Women's ways of being well and healing education. The catalyst for healing practices is the oppression Black Women encounter in the workplace (in multiple areas of their lives) and the erasure of their intellectual genius theory and research (Muhammad et al., 2021). However, this phenomenon is not new or rare (Chance, 2021, p50). Therefore, as I consciously build a case to center the voices of Black Women in the teacher preparation curriculum and demonstrating a strong connection between theory and practice, I transition into examining how three Black Women offer unique, culturally centering, and historically- rooted healing practices from different fields of education to contemplate how Black Women professors demonstrate well-being in higher education to begin to conceptualize holistic healing and well-being in teacher education.

Each author in the following sections is an expert in their field of study. The second phase of this study aims to move toward conceptualizing well-being through the healing theories and practices of Black Women who are making a concerted effort to contribute new knowledge through ART (activism, research, and teaching). What follows is not a review of each text but a multidimensional, interconnected, interdisciplinary, and intersectional analysis. It expands beyond education to bring the knowledge of experts in psychology, sociology (African American and Women and Gender studies), and anthropology to conceptualize well-being and wellness as it pertains to education broadly and teacher preparation specifically. The three texts are samples, and further research can be conducted using a more extensive data set.

Dr. Thema Davis Bryant's Practice of Homecoming (Psychology)

Dr. Thema Davis-Bryant (2022) is the President-elect of the American Psychological Association and the author of *Homecoming: Overcome Fear and Trauma to Reclaim Your Whole, Authentic Self.* She is a psychologist and a Christian minister. Her book offers anecdotal evidence of healing emotional wounds and trauma through her healing theory and practice of homecoming. Homecoming is not a physical space but a return to an inner space of self-acceptance. She refers to it as an emotional and spiritual space of belonging, appreciation, and love" (Bryant-Davis, 2022, p.4). A space where one can be authentic and traverse the problematic work of inner healing to find inner peace. The most prolific memoirist, Dr. Maya Angelou, also wrote about returning to the inner space of a home that requires you to face what may make you uncomfortable. "A part of our homecoming is healing the wounds that have caused us to disconnect so we can awaken to our emotional consciousness" (Bryant-Davis, 2022, p.17).

Liberation is a theme in Homecoming. Her work aligns with my conceptualization of well-being and wellness through a liberation psychology framework and a socio-political context. This framework "outlines how people understand, resist, and overcome oppression to achieve psychological well-being" (Prilleltensky, 2003). Bryant-Davis (2022) and Prilleltensky (2003) believe in the interconnected dimensions of psychology and the political self, where people can access an aspect of their well-being. "He further asserts that the liberation of oppressed people has both psychological and political impact, such that the liberation for the individual is interconnected with the liberation of larger groups and communities" (Wyatt & Ampadu, 2021, p.215). In facilitating professional development for preservice and experienced educators, I use liberatory practices to describe many ways to engage in self-care. For Black Women educators who face oppression in the workplace, having a self-care practice grounded in liberation from oppression is vital to their ability to thrive in the profession.

Blackness and culture are other themes emerging from the practice of homecoming.

"Once therapists understand the barriers facing the most marginalized from practicing wellness, in this case, Black Women and others marginalized by gender, they are more prepared to assist these clients in achieving their wellness goals"(Gamby et al., 2021, p.233). Dr. Bryant-Davis identifies herself as a Black Woman and writes about how she conceptualizes her identity in her work. "African psychology and other indigenous psychologies resist the false dichotomy between the sacred and secular. Not only do we pray with our mouths, but we also pray with our actions" (Bryant-Davis, 2022, p.137). She is not only preaching and teaching about Blackness and culture; she is acting out (practicing) her beliefs in her work. Her healing practice is rooted in the culture and identity of her clients. Lastly, she understands the importance of dismantling racism and white supremacy in the healing process of BIPOC as opposed to assisting systems of oppression by learning " to strive to be twice as good, to work twice as hard, and to prove to others that they are worthy of respect, humanity, and a livable wage" (Bryant-Davis, 2022, p.35). This notion also connects to the liberation psychology mentioned in the prior paragraph. To get free, we have to change our habits of mind. Bryant-Davis says we must relearn to slow down and "reject the pressure of self-erasure and perpetual busyness" (Bryant-Davis, 2022, p.35) to heal and come home to ourselves genuinely.

As a minister, Dr. Bryant-Davis does not shy away from incorporating the spirit in her work. She mentioned Dr. Shelly P. Harrell's soulfulness, an African American approach to contemplative practices. In another text by Dr. Harrell, she connects the spiritual dimension of well-being, often neglected in the conceptualization of well-being, contributing to the process of dehumanization that takes place and threatens "the vitality of one's spirit and faith" (Akbar, 1991; Harrell, 2000, p.48). In coming home to ourselves and healing in education, we must bring all the dimensions of well-being into educational spaces. "When you have to leave parts of yourself out of the equation, it delays our journey home. I hope you can cultivate spaces where you can be your full self, including your spiritual self, whatever that looks like for you" (Bryant-Davis, 2022,p.140). Dr. Bryant-Davis's theory and practice of homecoming are how she expresses her ART.

Dr. Aminata Cairo's Healing Practice of Holding Space (Anthropology)

Dr. Aminata Cairo (2021) is a Suriname anthropologist, artist, activist, and educator who lives and works in the Netherlands. Her memoir, *Holding Space: A Storytelling Approach to Trampling the Diversity and Inclusion,* similar to Dr. Bryant-Davis, uses anecdotal stories to teach a complex healing practice, holding space. Holding space is a fairly new term I encounter in professional learning and contemplative educational spaces. There is much ambiguity around what it means to hold space, and Dr. Cairo did not provide a concrete definition. The closest definition I could find was a quote about the importance of acknowledging our humanity (Cairo, 2022, p.302). At the same time, as a facilitator trained in meditation and yogic practices, I know what it feels like to hold space and have space held for me. Halifax (2012) and Pyles (2020) think that professionals who are in the service of clients sometimes lack the compassion necessary to avoid "moral injury" (Pyles, 2020, p.179). When we can hold space and acknowledge our humanity collectively, in our workplaces or our homes, we are doing the "love work" (Cairo, 2022) that brings us home to ourselves (Bryant-Davis, 2022).

A theme emerging from Cairo's work is working on yourself (inner work), which she terms "love work." However, this work of changing conditioned habits of mind is not for navel grazing. It is to practice within yourself how to best be in community with others and use your gifts for others through holding space. In the love work, we become in tune with ourselves."It requires us to ignore no longer the signals that alert us when things go off-kilter in our space (Cairo, 2021, p. 303). We must spend time coming home to ourselves, being honest, and taking the necessary actions to change. Once we have done our "love work," we can meet our community's needs. Love work " requires that we take the collective as a starting point, rather than the individual, and through understanding our connectedness, persevere to regard all people in their humanness and all of nature as our extended selves"(Cairo, 2021, p.

303). It is also imperative to hold space using the arts, for example like dance and singing to begin the embodiment process of the love work. She enjoys "...singing, dancing, or theater activities,...to have fun and to lower inhibitions, but also to build on that muscle of embodied knowledge..." (Cairo, 2021, p. 250). Learning or (re)learning to love ourselves requires us to do what Dr. Bryant-Davis says: slow down. Cairo takes it a step further and says, do nothing.

The second theme emerging from Cairo's work on the healing practice of holding space is the art of doing nothing. On any given day, there are more than enough demands for our time and attention, not to mention when we get entangled in arguments with loved ones, miss a deadline at work, or forget an appointment, we become overwhelmed and stressed. "These stressors can have a strong impact on well-being" (Chakraborty & Mahanta, 2019, p. 19). Cairo agrees with the literature on well-being. She acknowledges that we live in a world obsessed with the production of "doing" rather than "being," and it affects our "health and well-being" (Cairo, 2021, p. 292). She offers the contemplative practices of "grounding, breathing, and appreciation" as starting points for holding space for ourselves and others (Cairo, 2021, p. 292)."Neutral might be seen as boring, but it grants us a space of being rather than doing, where multiple parties are allowed to be without judgment" (Cairo, 2021, p. 267). Black Women need healing spaces, sister circles, and time to relax because Black Women teachers have historically led the charge for educational equity (Dixson, 2003; Lee & Thomas, 2022, p.1).

Black Women teachers leading movements for educational equity require action and change. Another theme of Cairo's work is transformation, a process, and an outcome. Holding spaces for yourself and others is an act of transformation involving a particular disposition and a set of skills, which are applied over time and then become embodied habits. Transformation is a practice embedded in the practice of holding space. "Transforming is the power to (change) the energy in the room by using all the key ingredients of awareness, care, courage, humility, trust, listening, seeing, speaking, silence, neutrality, embodiment, and surrendering to do so" (Cairo, 2021, p. 274). The literature on well-being for social workers links healing justice, holistic care, and transformation as a self-care practice (Pyles, 2020). The need for transformation stems from the disharmony caused by stress, burnout, and the impact of the oppressive systems we interact with daily. The goal is for individual and collective transformation through vulnerability. "Ultimately, the transforming agent is to transform the space so that some type of crack can be caused to create a potential growth opportunity" (Cairo, 2021, p. 274). In her book, Cairo devotes an entire chapter to the crack and the transformation. Dr. Cairo's theory and practice of holding space is how she expresses her ART.

Dr. Stephanie Y. Evans' Healing Practice of Inner Peace (Sociology)

Dr. Stephanie Y. Evans (2021) is a professor of African American studies and Women and Gender studies at Georgia State University. Her book, *Black Women's Yoga History: Memoirs of Inner Peace,* is foundational to this study on wellness and well-being (Evans, 2021). Her course in Black Women's memoirs influenced this and my previous study on *Sisters in the Academy* (Green & Mabokela, 2001). Her work is interconnected, intersectional, and interdisciplinary. The study of yoga is multi-dimensional. "Yoga, a holistic health practice that encompasses meditation, is a topic of research in several academic disciplines, including psychology, religious studies, education, sociology, political economy, human development, kinesiology, public health, and several areas of medicine" (Evans, 2021, p. 8). Yoga is a self-care practice referred to in the literature on wellness and well-being as it is a billion-dollar industry.

However, Evans' approach to yoga sheds light on her personal and professional journey grounded in Africana studies, a culturally centered lens, and an intersectional framework on Black Women's stories.

The first theme emerging from the text is self-care. The practice of inner peace is synonymous with self-care in Evans' work. She clearly states that yoga is an umbrella term that includes meditation, music, and movement (dancing). Her writing is in alignment with the literature on wellness and well-being because the research argues that yoga can "create mental, spiritual, and physical balance, counteract the stress impact of racism and sexism, and improve quality of life by relieving a range of illnesses and health conditions" (Evans, 2021, p. 8). The impact of racism is echoed in the work of Wyatt and Ampadu (2021) and other texts in the literature review that situation wellness and well-being are a cultural and historical framework for BIPOC and the LGBTQIA+ communities that encounter oppression and discrimination daily (p. 218). "Societal barriers to reconnecting with ourselves include poverty and discrimination, which can be sources of stress and trauma that cause us to shrink our stuff and prepare for the worst"(Bryant-Davis, 2022, p.33).

Evans (2021) notes that Black Women are well-versed in developing stress management and inner peace due to their struggle against the socialization system as advocates and activists (p. 4). Wyatt and Ampadu (2021) define wellness in terms of radical self-care that can resist the process of dehumanization. "Furthermore, self-care models that center on the health and wellness of Black people also become radical given that they are part of a society that threatens their well-being"(Wyatt & Ampadu, 2021, p.215). Therefore, Black Women's healing practices can revolutionize teacher education.

Blackness and culturally centered healing practices are other themes emerging in the literature and Evans' work. Wyatt and Ampadu (2021) acknowledge, along with other scholars, that Black folk's ways of being well or caring for themselves may look different than what is currently in the mainstream media. "For example, self-care behaviors for people of color may include engaging in an ancestral practice for spiritual self-care (Pérez, 2011) or engaging in healing circles (Richardson, 2018) with other members in their communities that also encounter oppression and discrimination (Hobart & Kneese, 2020; Wyatt & Ampadu, 2021, p.218).

Blackness and culturally centered self-care practices are echoed in Adeeke (2012), McQuillar (2010), and Gamby et al. (2021). Aspects of Blackness in self-care practice look like communal care, sister circles, and rootwork. Evans centers Black/African culture in her work while decentering whiteness in wellness and well-being practices that cause harm to marginalized communities.

The last theme is the dehumanization through violence that Black Women experience in society. Evans' memoir is intertwined with the memoirs of notable women in history. "Black women are disproportionately subject to personal, cultural, or structural violence..."(Evans, 2021, p. 3). Dr. Layli Maparyan, the author of *The Womanist Idea* (2012), identifies the impact of this type of violence as an imbalance. In 2008, Moya Baily conceptualized "misogynoir" to refer to "the uniquely co-constitutive racialized and sexist violence that befalls Black Women as a result of their simultaneous and interlocking oppression at the intersection of racial and gender marginalization" (Bailey, 2021, p. 1; Lee & Thomas, 2022, p.3). Misogynoir produces the imbalance that results in Black Women's need for Maparyan's model for defining self-care in three elements: "health, healing, and wellness" (Maparyan, 2012; Evans, 2021, p. 3). Black Women teachers are noted in the literature for their contribution to "practicing emancipatory pedagogy, they are tasked to do so while also navigating constant macro- and micro-level misogynoir" (Acosta, 2019; Acosta et al., 2018; Bailey, 2021; Dillard, 2022; Lee & Thomas, 2022, p.3). It is essential to consider in my study how Black women teachers and educators stay well in higher education. Simultaneously, I recognize Evan's work of conceptualizing Black Women's practice of inner peace addresses issues of multidimensional violence in ways that can heal education. Dr. Evans's theory and practice of inner peace are how she expresses her ART.

CALL TO ACTION: CENTER THE VOICES OF BLACK WOMEN IN THE ACADEMY

Black Women in the academy have historically contributed theories and practice in teacher preparation and to the academy more broadly (Dillard, 2006; Evans, 2007;

Muhammad et al., 2020). However, the playbook for educational change has erased and marginalized the names of Black Women educational leaders to the determinant of the field of education. (Dixson & Dingus, 2008; Muhammad, et. al, p. 420). Professional organizations, like the Association of Women in Higher Education (Association of Black Women in Higher Education, n.d.) and the Women's Higher Education Network (*WHEN Equality*, n.d.), are devoted to centering the voices of Black Women in higher education. "Inclusion of Black Women's theories and biographies will support the authentic integration of unique and largely untapped approaches for improving educational practices" (Muhammad et al., p. 421). Solutions to the most pressing dilemmas in teacher education can be revolutionized by studying Black Women's intellectual history and healing practices in the academy.

Love (2019) and Neal and Dunn (2020) think it is necessary to center intersectionality in Black Women's work to create the conditions for dialogue about how teachers and students can bring their authentic selves into the education process. "It is from a place of intersectionality, where humanity and wholeness are central, that all students can thrive and not simply survive" (Love, 2019; Neal & Dunn, 2020, p.60). Healing education requires an environment where teachers and students are seen, heard, and accepted; our humanity depends upon it. To broaden our lens to center well-being in teacher education, we must apply the intersectional lens to value gender and race and recognize that an intersectional lens is foundational to understanding the journey toward well-being and healing education through multiple lenses simultaneously (Goleman & Senge, 2015). For example, it is imperative to recognize systemic oppression and continue to move toward systems-level liberation to heal education, which requires a lens of intersectionality.

Patricia Hill Collins (2000) theorized intersectionality as "particular forms of intersecting oppressions, for example, intersections of race and gender, or sexuality and nation" (Lee, 2012, p. 468). It is through the lens of intersectionality that I recognize the complexities and interconnectedness of oppression and suffering within myself and, in turn, recognize it in the memoirs of Black Women. "Intersectional paradigms remind us that oppression cannot be reduced to one fundamental type and that oppressions work together to produce injustice (Hill Collins, 2000; Lee, 2012, p. 468). Therefore, the approach to healing education must be multidimensional and interconnected.

As a Black Woman, I identify with the historical, intellectual activism of Black Women in the academy. "Black Women educators have historically engaged in educational practice as social activism" (Muhammad et al., 2020, p. 425). According to the Center for Contemplative Mind in Society, activism is a contemplative practice (*The Tree of Contemplative Practices – the Center for Contemplative Mind in Society*, 2021). Black Women's pedagogical practices are easily associated with activism, but rarely is it translated into a contemplative pedagogy. Black Women's pedagogy is most often associated with critical pedagogy, but here and more in-depth in my dissertation, I reclaim Black Women's pedagogy as contemplative criticality. I also argue that Black Women's intellect, creativity, and pedagogy is a revolutionary art historically at the center of teacher preparation but is erased to uphold the system of racism and white supremacy in the context of U.S. education. Muhammad and colleagues agree with me:

There is a dearth of research on Black Women's historical contributions to education; however, we can point to historical markers that indicate the broad and varied ways that Black Women have contributed to transforming the landscape of educational practice and theory (2020, p. 425).

Through activism, research, and teaching, Black Women have a stake in higher education. The ART inspired me in the article "The Black Feminist Mixtape" (Wallace et al., 2020). It creatively addresses the "beautiful, healing, and ugly" truths of what Black Women endure in spaces of higher learning. "We dream of a day where our stories are centered without the work being on our backs. A day when our very being and existence as Black Women are celebrated within and beyond the academy" (Wallace et al., 2020, p.1). I, too, dream of a day when the ART of Black Women's healing practices is relegated to its proper place in academia.

BLACK WOMEN'S HEALING ART IN TEACHER EDUCATION

The memoirs of Black Women professors have produced healing theories and practices to benefit well-being curricula for teacher education. For example, Tricia Hersey's work on rest has revolutionized teacher education. Author of *Rest Is Resistance: A Manifesto,* Hersey (2022) deconstructs the interlocking system of oppression as "grind culture"(Hersey, 2022). The U.S. schooling system is the headquarters of "grind culture," hegemony, and alienation, reproducing racism and white supremacy (Hersey, 2022). American physician Dr. Camara Jones, in a TEDx Emory talk, described the system of oppression in the allegory of the gardener and two flower boxes. As Jones explains, in the system of racism and white supremacy, one flower box receives nutrients in the soil while the other box does not receive the nutrients (TEDx Talks, 2014). The gardener is reminiscent of teachers in the classroom where particular students receive the care and concern needed to grow while Black and Brown students experience marginalization in the curriculum. Our schools are not sites of freedom but violence and spirit murder (Williams, 1987; Love, 2019). Therefore, it is necessary to move toward well-being, transformation, and humanizing pedagogy while uplifting the marginalized theories of Black Women in the academy and teacher education more specifically.

There are many harmful impacts of decentering Black Women's work in teacher education that impact the health and well-being of teachers and students. "Racism and white supremacy ideology are at the foundation of the American schooling system, which compromises the well-being of teachers and learners" (Ighodaro & Wiggan, 2010; Neal & Dunn, 2020). Throughout the study of the experiences of Black Women professors through examining their memoirs, I deconstructed and reconstructed knowledge toward a vision of healing education and different ways of knowing and being well in the world. "Therefore, we (re)member the freedom dreams of Black women abolitionist teachers and glean from their well of brilliance, wisdom, and joy to inform new generations of teachers and teacher educators to persist in the struggle for change and dream up an education that is equitable and just" (Neal & Dunn, 2020, p.60). To follow in the footsteps of Neal and Dunn, this study considered the connection between Black Women's well-being theories and practices through ART, which is currently innovating education, sociology, psychology, anthropology, spirituality, and history.

As I conclude this chapter, I reflect on the voices of Black Women centered in this study whose memoirs advanced my intellect and whose stories shape my worldview. Voice comes from an individual's experience and allows them to be in a community with others. "...the struggle for voice begins when a person attempts to communicate meaning to someone else" (Showunmi, 2021, p.7). This exploratory study positioned the voices of African American/Black women as experts in ways of well-being. Black Women are experts at integrating the personal and professional, the private and public, the physical and spiritual for purposes of centering the (ART) activism, research, and teaching through healing practices of homecoming (Bryant-Davis, 2022), holding space (Cairo, 2021) and the inner peace practice of yoga (Evans, 2021) grounded in the current literature on wellness, well-being, and intersectionality. The call to action is to continue to create ART in the Academy (teacher preparation) that centers marginalized voices, such as Black Women. Still, for someone else, it might be another demographic. Centering well-being in the academy is another call to action to dismantle the "grind culture" (Hersey, 2022) headquartered in higher education to deconstruct oppressive systems and calls for us to theorize and practice well-being for self, social, and systems change.

REFERENCES

Acosta, M. M. (2019). The paradox of pedagogical excellence among exemplary black women educators. *Journal of Teacher Education*, *70*(1), 26–38. doi:10.1177/0022487118808512

Acosta, M. M., Foster, M., & Houchen, D. F. (2018). "Why seek the living among the dead?" african american pedagogical excellence: Exemplar practice for teacher education. *Journal of Teacher Education, 69*(4), 341–353. doi:10.1177/0022487118761881

Acuff, J. (2018). Confronting racial battle fatigue and comforting my blackness as an educator. *Multicultural Perspectives, 20*(3), 174–181. https://doi.org/ Adeeke, A. (2012). Seed of Osun. https://www.seedofosun.com doi:10.1080/15210960.20 18.1467767

Akbar, N. (1998). *Know thy self.* Mind Productions & Associates.

Arie, India – strength, courage & wisdom. (2001). Genius.com. https://genius.com/Indiaarie-strength-courage-and-wisdom-lyrics Association of Black Women in Higher Education. (n.d.). *ABWHE.* ABWHE. Retrieved April 24, 2022, from https://abwhe.org/

Bailey, M. (2021). *Misogynoir transformed: Black womens digital resistance.* New York University Press.

Bell-Scott, P., & Johnson-Bailey, J. (1999). *Flat-footed truths: telling Black women's lives.* Henry Holt.

Brown, K. D. (2014). Teaching in color: A critical race theory in education analysis of the literature on preservice teachers of color and teacher education in the US. *Race, Ethnicity and Education, 17*(3), 326–345. doi:10.1080/13613324.2013.832921

Bryant-Davis, T. (2022). *Homecoming: Overcome fear and trauma to reclaim your whole, authentic self.* Tarcherperigee.

BUILD series. (2019, October 3). *Amanda seales has honest advice for young black women entering the workforce.* Www.youtube.com. https://youtu.be/umNsNBy9JJY

Burke, T. (2021). *Unbound my story of liberation and the birth of the me too movement.* Flatiron Books.

Cairo, A. (2021). *Holding space: A storytelling approach to trampling diversity and inclusion.* Aminata Cairo Consultancy.

Chakraborty, A., & Mahanta, M. (2019). Employee well-being – are organizations addressing it the correct way? *IRA-International Journal of Management & Social Sciences (ISSN 2455-2267), 14*(2), 17. https://doi.org/ 3 doi:10.21013/jmss.v14.n2sp.p

Chance, N. L. (2021). Resilient leadership: A phenomenological exploration into how black women in higher education leadership navigate cultural adversity. *Journal of Humanistic Psychology*, *62*(1), 44–78. doi:10.1177/00221678211003000

Charron, K. M. (2012). *Freedom's teacher: The life of septima clark*. Univ of North Carolina Press.

Citeasista. (n.d.). *#CiteASista: Today & Everyday*. #CiteASista: Today & Everyday. Retrieved May 26, 2023, from https://citeasista.com/

Coles, J., & Stanley, D. (2021). Black liberation in teacher education: (Re)Envisioning educator preparation to defend black life and possibility. *Northwest Journal of Teacher Education*, *16*(2). Advance online publication. doi:10.15760/nwjte.2021.16.2.6

Crenshaw, K. (1991). Mapping the margins: Intersectionality, identity politics, and violence against women of color. In R. Kennedy & K. Bartlett (Eds.), *Critical Race theory: Readings in Law and Gender* (pp. 116–162). Routledge.

Davis, A. Y. (1989). Black women in the academy: Defending our name 1894-1994. In J. James (Ed.), *The Angela Y. Davis reader* (pp. 222–231). Blackwell.

Dillard, C. B. (2000). The substance of things hoped for, the evidence of things not seen: Examining an endarkened feminist epistemology in educational research and leadership. *International Journal of Qualitative Studies in Education : QSE*, *13*(6), 661–681. doi:10.1080/09518390050211565

Dixon, A. D. (2003). "Let's do this!" Black women teachers' politics and pedagogy. *Urban Education*, *38*(2), 217–235. doi:10.1177/0042085902250482

Doan, S., Steiner, E., Pandey, R., & Woo, A. (2023). *Teacher Well-Being and Intentions to Leave Findings from the 2023 State of the American Teacher Survey*. Rand Cooperation. https://www.rand.org/pubs/research_reports/RRA1108-8.html

Evans, S. Y. (2007). *Black women in the ivory tower, 1850-1954: An intellectual history*. University Press of Florida.

Evans, S. Y. (2013). *Africana Memoirs*. Sesheta. http://www.africanamemoirs.net/

Evans, S. Y. (2021). "Letters to Our Daughters: Black Women's Memoirs as Epistles of Human Rights, Healing, and Inner Peace." In The Black Intellectual Tradition: African American Thought in the Twentieth Century (pp. 100–125). University of Illinois. doi:10.5622/illinois/9780252043857.003.0006

Evans, S. Y. (2021). *Black women's yoga history: Memoirs of inner peace*. Suny Press. doi:10.1515/9781438483658

Evans-Winters, V. E., & Twyman Hoff, P. (2011). The aesthetics of white racism in pre-service teacher education: A critical race theory perspective. *Race, Ethnicity and Education, 14*(4), 461–479. doi:10.1080/13613324.2010.548376

For Harriet. (2020, April 11). *How the Creator of #BlackGirlMagic Got Erased from the Movement She Started.* Www.youtube.com. https://youtu.be/y2Ko-mgo1DU

Forman, R. (1998). If you lose your pen. In *Flat-Footed Truths.* Henry Holt and Company. Freire, P. (1968). *Pedagogy of the oppressed.* Bloomsbury Academic. https://envs.ucsc.edu/internships/internship-readings/freire-pedagogy-of-the-oppressed.pd f Fu-Kiau, K. B., & Lukondo-Wamba, A. M. (1988). *Kindezi: the Kôngo art of babysitting.* Imprint Editions.

Gamby, K., Burns, D., & Forristal, K. (2021). Wellness decolonized: The history of wellness and recommendations for the counseling field. *Journal of Mental Health Counseling, 43*(3), 228–245. doi:10.17744/mehc.43.3.05

Gay, G. (2000). *Culturally responsive teaching: Theory, research, and practice* (1st ed.). Teachers College Press.

Goleman, D., & Senge, P. M. (2015). *The triple focus: A new approach to education.* More than Sound.

Green, A. L., & Mabokela, R. O. (2001). *Sisters of the academy: emergent Black women scholars in higher education.* Stylus Pub.

Halifax, J. (2018). *Standing at the edge: Finding freedom where fear and courage meet.* Flatiron Books.

Harrell, S. P. (2018). Soulfulness as an orientation to contemplative practice: Culture, liberation, and mindfulness awareness. *The Journal of Contemplative Inquiry, 5*(1), 9–32.

Hersey, T. (2022). Rest is resistance: A manifesto. Little Brown Spark. Hill Collins, P. (1990). Black feminist thought. Routledge.

Hill Collins, P. (2000). Gender, black feminism, and black political economy. *The Annals of the American Academy of Political and Social Science, 568*(1), 41–53. doi:10.1177/000271620056800105

Hill Collins, P., & Bilge, S. (2016). *Intersectionality.* Polity Press.

Hobart, H. I. J. K., & Kneese, T. (2020). Radical care survival strategies for uncertain times. *Social Text, 38*(1), 1–16. doi:10.1215/01642472-7971067

Hooks, B. (1996). Teaching to transgress: Education as the practice of freedom. *Journal of Leisure Research, 28*(4), 316.

Hooks, B. (1997). Homeplace: A site of resistance. In Undoing place? A geographical reader (pp. 33-38). Routledge.

Hooks, B. (1997). from Bone Black: Memories of girlhood. *Critical Quarterly, 39*(3), 80–83.

Ighodaro, E., & Wiggan, G. (2010). *Curriculum violence*. Nova Novinka.

Jones, B., & Williams, J. (2020, July 30). *OPINION: When institutions fail black women in academia*. The Hechinger Report. https://hechingerreport.org/opinion-when-institutions-fail-black-women-in-academia/

Kaufman, P. (2017). Critical Contemplative Pedagogy. *Radical Pedagogy, 14*(1).

Keeling, I., & Anita Doreen Diggs. (2018). *Can't nothing bring me down: chasing myself in the race against time*. Zondervan.

Kelley, R. D. G. (2002a). Beyond the "real" world, or why black radicals need to wake up and start dreaming. *Souls, 4*(2), 51–64. doi:10.1080/10999940290105228

Kelley, R. D. G. (2002b). Freedom dreams: The black radical imagination. Beacon Press, [20]08.

Kirk, G., & Okazowa-Rey, M. (2010). Identities and social location. In M. Adams, C. (Rosie) Castaneda, W. J. Blumenfeld, & X. Zuniga (Eds.), Readings for Diversity and Social Justice. Routledge.

Kirk, T. J. F. (2001). Not an honorary white: Conducting research during the days of apartheid. In A. L. Green & R. O. Mabokela (Eds.), *Sisters of the Academy* (pp. 183–204). Sterling Publishing.

Ladson-Billings, G. (1995). But that's just good teaching! The case for culturally relevant pedagogy. *Theory into Practice, 34*(3), 159–165. doi:10.1080/00405849509543675

Lee, K. (2012). Rethinking with patricia hill collins: A note toward intersectionality as interlocutory interstitiality. *The Journal of Speculative Philosophy, 26*(2), 466–473. doi:10.5325/jspecphil.26.2.0466

Lee, S. J., & Thomas, S. (2022). Protect black women teachers: Influencing sustainability through mental health literacy. *Urban Education*. Advance online publication. doi:10.1177/00420859221086524

Lorde, A. (1997). *The collected poems of Audre Lorde*. W.W. Norton & Company.

Love, B. (2019). *We want to do more than survive: Abolitionist teaching and the pursuit of educational freedom.* Beacon.

Maparyan, L. (2012). *The womanist idea.* Routledge. doi:10.4324/9780203135938

Markowitz, N. L., & Bouffard, S. M. (2020). *Teaching with a social, emotional, and cultural lens: a framework for educators and teacher educators.* Harvard Education Press.

Mattheis, A., Corado, J., & Gutierrez, A. III. (2022). Intersectionally developing community and solidarity through queer studies in education. In C. D. Gist & T. J. Bristol (Eds.), *Handbook of Research on Teachers of Color and Indigenous Teachers.* American Educational Research Association. doi:10.2307/j.ctv2xqngb9.47

McQuillar, T. L. (2010). *Rootwork: Using the folk magick of Black America for love, money, and success.* Simon & Schuster.

Muhammad, G. E., Dunmeyer, A., Starks, F. D., & Sealey-Ruiz, Y. (2020). Historical voices for contemporary times: Learning from Black women educational theorists to redesign teaching and teacher education. *Theory into Practice, 59*(4), 419–428. doi:10.1080/00405841.2020.1773185

Neal, A. M., & Dunn, D. (2020). Our ancestors' wildest dreams (re)membering the freedom dreams of black women abolitionist teachers. *Journal of Curriculum Theorizing, 35*(4).

Njoku, N., & Marshall, D. (2024, January 15). *Ring the alarm: A call to action for black women to address wellness in the academy.* Diverse: Issues in Higher Education. https://www.diverseeducation.com/opinion/article/15661985/ring-the-alarm-a-call-to-action-for-black-women-to-address-wellness-in-the-academy

Pérez, E. (2011). Spiritist mediumship as historical mediation: African American pasts, black ancestral presence, and afro-cuban religions. *Journal of Religion in Africa. Religion en Afrique, 41*(4), 330–365. doi:10.1163/157006611X604760

Perlow, O. N., Wheeler, D. I., Bethea, S. L., & Scott, B. M. (2018). *Black women's liberatory pedagogies: Resistance, transformation, and healing within and beyond the academy.* Palgrave Macmillan Imprint Published by Springer Nature. doi:10.1007/978-3-319-65789-9

Player, G. D., & Irizarry, J. G. (2022). Dismantling the "wall of whiteness": How teacher education simultaneously pursues diversity and reinscribes whiteness. In C. D. Gist & T. J. Bristol (Eds.), *Handbook of Research on Teachers of Color and Indigenous Teachers*. American Educational Research Association. doi:10.2307/j.ctv2xqngb9.48

Porcher, K., & Austin, T. (2021). "Black Women are the Mules of the World": Black Women Professors of Practice in Teacher Education Programs. *Journal of African American Women and Girls in Education*, *1*(3), 109–129. doi:10.21423/jaawge-v1i3a54

Prilleltensky, I. (2003). Understanding, resisting, and overcoming oppression: Toward psychopolitical validity. *American Journal of Community Psychology*, *31*(1-2), 195–201. doi:10.1023/A:1023043108210 PMID:12741700

Pyles, L. (2020). Healing justice, transformative justice, and holistic self-care for social workers. *Social Work*, *65*(2), 178–187. Advance online publication. doi:10.1093/sw/swaa013 PMID:32236450

Richardson, J. L. (2018). Healing circles as black feminist pedagogical interventions. In *Black women's liberatory pedagogies* (pp. 281–294). Palgrave Macmillan. doi:10.1007/978-3-319-65789-9_16

Showunmi, V. (2021). A journey of difference: The voices of women leaders. *Frontiers in Education*, *6*, 548870. Advance online publication. doi:10.3389/feduc.2021.548870

Smith, W. A., Yosso, T. J., & Solorzano, D. G. (2006). Challenging racial battle fatigue on historically white campuses: A critical race examination of race-related stress. In Faculty of color: Teaching in Predominately White Colleges and Universities (pp. 299–327). Jossey Bass.

Smith, W. A., Yosso, T. J., & Solórzano, D. G. (2007). Racial Primes and Black Misandry on Historically White Campuses: Toward Critical Race Accountability in Educational Administration. *Educational Administration Quarterly*, *43*(5), 559–585. doi:10.1177/0013161X07307793

The Tree of Contemplative Practices – The Center for Contemplative Mind in Society. (2021). The Center for Contemplative Mind and Society. https://www.contemplativemind.org/practices/tree

Tyson, C. (2001). From the classroom to the field: Teacher, researcher, activist. In A. L. Green & R. O. Mabokela (Eds.), *Sisters of the Academy* (pp. 139–149). Sterling Publishing.

Walker, R. (2020). *The unapologetic guide to black mental health*. New Harbinger Publications.

Wallace, E. R., Adams, J. D., Fullwood, C. C., Horhn, E.-B., & Loritts, C. (2020). The black feminist mixtape: A collective black feminist autoethnography of black women's existence in the academy. *Journal of Critical Scholarship on Higher Education and Student Affairs*, 5(3).

WHEN Equality. (n.d.). Www.whenequality.org. Retrieved April 24, 2022, from https://www.whenequality.org/

Williams, L. D. (2001). Coming to terms with being a young black female academic in u.s. higher education. In A. L. Green & R. O. Mabokela (Eds.), *Sisters of the Academy* (pp. 93–102). Sterling Publishing.

Winters, M.-F. (2020). *Black fatigue: how racism erodes the mind, body, and spirit*. Berrett-Koehler Publishers, Inc.

Wyatt, J. P., & Ampadu, G. G. (2021). Reclaiming self-care: Self-care as a social justice tool for black wellness. *Community Mental Health Journal*, 58(2), 213–221. Advance online publication. doi:10.1007/s10597-021-00884-9 PMID:34478022

Chapter 5
A Social–Ecological Model for Racially Diverse Women in Higher Education:
Organizational Support and Affirmative Action

Lolita L. Kincade
https://orcid.org/0009-0007-5070-4806
SUNY Plattsburgh, USA

ABSTRACT

Systemic and structural inequities have created barriers to the success of women of color in higher education. In the U.S., racially diverse women are underrepresented among faculty and senior leaders, and they experience complex challenges because of their intersectional identities. This chapter builds on a Social-Ecological Model of Support (SEM), designed to guide the development of effective interventions through social environments. There is a focus on the organizational level, which promotes practices and policies that advance diversity and opportunity for racially diverse women in higher education roles. An examination of race and gender-based affirmative action and its effects, to include increased representation of White women as higher education faculty and senior leaders is provided. Also outlined are recommendations to strengthen affirmative action programs in ways that promote diversity, mitigating issues of gendered racism and intersectional discrimination, which compromise recruitment, retention, and advancement of racially diverse women in higher education settings.

DOI: 10.4018/979-8-3693-0102-9.ch005

INTRODUCTION

Women of color in the United States are disproportionately underrepresented in the higher education academy (Chance, 2021; Gause, 2021; Taylor, 2020). Systemic and structural inequities create barriers to attracting, advancing, and keeping members of this population as faculty and leaders. They experience significant obstacles in the hiring and promotion process, in large part due to their intersectional identities (Chance, 2022; Griffin, 2019). Given the complex challenges associated with the intersectional experience, Kincade (2023) postulates a Social-Ecological Model (SEM) of support for women of color in higher education. This model centers the unique experiences of women of color academicians and leaders, relative to their counterparts. It provides guidance for developing successful interventions through social environments, provided racial and gender-based stressors commonly highlighted as aspects of the lived experiences of racially diverse women employed in higher education settings (Al-Faham, Davis & Ernst, 2019; Colon-Alverio & Flowers, 2022; Love, Templeton, Ault, & Johnson, 2021). Further, the model highlights actions and practices that support the success and professional advancement of these women. The researcher asserts that the SEM model is useful in identifying points of leverage and intervention at individual, interpersonal, organizational, community and societal levels. The application of the model to women of color in the academy is organized into five nested, hierarchical levels:

1. The individual level consists of specific characteristics that combat race-based stress, including self-care practices and healthy work-life balance.
2. The interpersonal level promotes increased understanding of institutional culture and climate, as well as relationships and social networks among people of shared identities to foster a supportive and collegial workplace.
3. The organizational level considers practices that can be adopted by higher education institutions, including upholding protections for professionals victimized by discrimination and workplace bullying, providing professional development opportunities, and engaging in equity practices.
4. Community structures offer relationships with professionals across universities and opportunities to engage with organizations and networks geared specifically toward women of color.
5. Equal opportunity for women of color to advance in public sectors is important, as it relates to society and public policy (Kincade, 2023). See *Table 1*.

Table 1. A Social-Ecological Model (SEM) of support for women of color in higher education

Level [1] Individual	Level [2] Interpersonal	Level [3] Organizational	Level [4] Community	Level [5] Society & Public Policy
1a. **Practice self-care** ■ Mindfulness ■ Meditation ■ Managing the amount of time devoted to work 1b. **Address internalized oppression** ■ Relevant mental health services, including therapy with a focus on Race-Based Traumatic Stress	2a. **Increase knowledge & understanding of culture and climate of predominantly White institutions** 2b. **Build social support networks** ■ Shared gender, racial/ethnic/ immigrant and class-based identities ■ Friendships with other faculty/ research colleagues of color ■ Safe and private venting spaces to discuss similarities in experiences 2c. **Demonstrated support in the workplace by women of color** 2d. **Peer Mentoring** ■ Other women of color in higher education leadership/ administration	3a. **Greater representation of women of color** 3b. **Address wage inequity issues** 3c. **Uphold protections for those facing discrimination, bullying & verbal abuse** 3d. **Professional development training addressing:** ■ Cultural humility ■ Unconscious bias ■ Collegiality ■ Intersectional experiences	4a. **Peer mentoring and support groups across universities** ■ Virtually or on social media ■ Face-to-face gatherings by region 4b. **Empowerment seminars aimed at racially diverse women** 4c. **Formal and professional organizations geared toward women of color employed in higher education**	5a. **Proactive plan of action to ensure equal opportunity in employment & university programs and activities** 5b. **Support for women of color in politics** 5c. **Acknowledge and address racial capitalism** ■ White allies to relinquish power and reallocate resources to minority populations.

This chapter has a focus on level three, the organizational level, which promotes standards, procedures, and policies that advance diversity and opportunity for racially diverse women in higher education roles. Since university affirmative action policies are expected to support full workplace opportunities for racially diverse women, the author provides an examination of race and gender-based affirmative action. A fundamental commitment to eradicating racism and inequality in higher education leadership requires careful development, implementation, and monitoring of policies and plans designed to meet the needs and standards of the academic community. Corrective policies may also be necessary to overcome effects of any barriers that perpetuate discrimination or disadvantage for women of color faculty and leaders.

The goal of this chapter is to establish the importance of the SEM Model of support for women of color in higher education as a frame of reference to inform diversity, equity, and inclusion efforts, with a particular emphasis on the organizational level. Moreover, readers will gain an increased understanding of the history of affirmative action in the United States, including the intended goals, and narratives of fierce opposition. Also explored are the effects of affirmative action among White women, to include their increased representation as higher education faculty and senior leaders, relative to the perpetual underrepresentation of women of color. The author synthesizes common misconceptions about the nature of affirmative action programs, and highlights ways to analyze and professionally address inconsistencies or concerns with these plans in the interest of women of color in the academy.

This analysis of race and gender-based affirmative action is an important endeavor, as it reinforces efforts to achieve structural and systemic transformation across colleges and universities. Implementation of best practices to recruit, retain, and support women of color leaders in higher education remains essential to institutional advancement, strategic visioning, and to the development of critical strategic priorities.

A SOCIAL-ECOLOGICAL FRAMEWORK

Kincade (2023) explains that the environmental context of colleges and universities impacts women of color in unique ways, since these institutions are embedded in larger social and economic structures. Further, historian Rubio (2009) asserts that affirmative action, based on the common law principle of equity, is also broadly experienced and exists in a multifaceted social dynamic. This notion is adeptly aligned with the Social-Ecological framework, which assists us in understanding social systems and interactions between individuals and environments. A social-ecological approach is helpful to understand the complexity of these experiences and can inform long-term solutions to the nuanced issues affecting racially diverse women in their varying higher education roles. Transformative interventions at interactive and reinforcing levels (e.g., individual, interpersonal, organizational, community, society, and public policy) can support the demographic of interest in reaching their full personal and professional potential as higher education faculty and administrators. Particularly, at the organizational level recruitment and retention of women of color in higher education positions is the critical goal. Recommendations to increase representation, to support parity in pay, and to uphold protections for those experiencing discrimination, bullying or verbal abuse, for example, are also aligned with well-intended affirmative action and equal opportunity plans. Yet, women of color are not only underrepresented in leadership and full-time faculty positions across the United States, but they are also under-retained (Chambers, 2023; Colby and Fowler, 2020). Therefore, a critical assessment is essential to ensure that standards and procedures are nondiscriminatory both in principle and in practice. We begin with a review of the history and implications of affirmative action in American society.

AFFIRMATIVE ACTION HISTORY AND LEGITIMATE PURPOSE

A comprehensive understanding of affirmative action requires deconstruction of American racism. American racism is deeply rooted in the myth of white Anglo-Saxon racial superiority, where early colonists believed that they personified racial purity, physical prowess, beauty, independence, and prided themselves on their ability to create democratic institutions (Hudon, 1999). Hudson (1999) explains that over time being white became synonymous with being "American," and radical views of race, separatism, and superiority became the creed of American democracy. Racism and inequality became institutionalized, shaping government, American rights, and citizenship. A body of laws were designed by and for affluent white males (the "majority") to protect their property and privilege, while excluding or limiting rights for persons of color, women, and the poor. Enslaved Black Americans, for example, were considered property, while free persons of color were subjects, not citizens. White women and members of poor white groups were regarded as citizens with limited rights. Similar restrictions were imposed on who could become a citizen. Citizenship was limited to free white persons, while persons of color throughout the world were excluded from eligibility to become citizens of the United States.

Once established, these barriers endured for centuries, and the political, social, and economic ramifications persisted even after the laws changed. Particularly for women of color, the legacy of slavery, legal segregation, unequal treatment, and pervasive discrimination in education, employment, and other sectors compromised full empowerment and participation in mainstream American life. As a corrective measure, affirmative action programs were established, and were an important step in dismantling the legal structure of racial segregation and inequality in the United States (Hudson, 1999).

The earliest affirmative action measure in America included an executive order mandating that government contractors "take affirmative action" in all aspects of hiring and employing minorities. The order was later amended to include women, with the understanding that they also experienced discrimination and barriers to equal opportunity, like people of color. As such, the objective of race and gender-conscious affirmative action policies were to provide opportunities for these groups to advance in American society. This is significant, since minority groups and women were commonly underrepresented and excluded from high-status, well-paying jobs, while their White male counterparts benefited from preferential treatment in employment (Garrison-Wade & Lewis, 2004; Rai & Critzer, 2000).

The seminal work of researchers such as Benokraitis and Feagin (1978) explains that affirmative action requires removal of all barriers, however informal or subtle, that would prevent access by minorities and women to their rightful places in employment and educational institutions of the United States. In lieu of this, attempts to create institutions, workplaces, and a society in which individuals or groups are not stigmatized or excluded from opportunities based on race, ethnicity or gender is the moral and ethical foundation of affirmative action plans (Rosenfeld, 1991; Soni, 1999).

The United States is but one of many countries and continents that have some form of affirmative action to support members of these groups. Some policies predate those in the US, while the notion of affirmative action is a more recent development in other countries (Jenkins & Moses, 2014). Even beyond American borders, however, there have been shifts from race toward other categories of disadvantage (Gururaj, Somers, Fry, Watson, Cicero, Morosini, & Zamora, 2021; Jenkins & Moses, 2014). Particularly as it relates to higher education, the inclusion of women has been a prevalent form of affirmative action globally (Jenkins & Moses, 2014).

Gururaj and colleagues (2021) offer a comparative review of the historical and legal evolution of affirmative action, reservations, quotas, and positive discrimination in Brazil, India, South Africa, and the United States. It was noted that the effects of these policies vary according to culture and context, but generally they are established to acknowledge differential treatment of individuals with diverse identities and historically discriminated groups, so they can participate in society. Thus, equity and access are widely promoted.

Gisselquist, Schotte and Kim (2023) built a global dataset of affirmative action policies, consisting of standardized data from 53 countries (spread across all five world regions). They examined the design and modalities of affirmative action policies, their adoption, implementation, impact, and common controversies. They also conducted a systematic review of literature to determine whether the policies were effective. Of the 194 studies reviewed, 63% concluded that policies and programs improved outcomes for targeted populations and helped groups to attain access to better education and employment. The researchers underscored potential benefits of affirmative action–correcting historical injustices, supporting marginalized groups, and promoting equality in sectors of education and employment–as well as potential pitfalls, especially as it relates to perceptions of fairness and societal conflict. They emphasized that public debate over the appropriateness of affirmative action is heated across diverse contexts, regardless of what empirical research shows about policy and program success around the world.

Opposition to Affirmative Action

It can be argued that historically there has been a critical need for government leaders to disrupt patterns of structural and systemic inequality, and to take purposeful and aggressive action in eradicating discrimination. Only, such change has been met with criticism and fierce opposition, particularly in the United States. However well-intended some opponents of affirmative action suggest that it is reverse discrimination, and harmful to the White population, particularly White males. It has been framed as a system of handouts, quotas, and racial preferences, undeservedly benefitting people of color. This narrative seems to reflect what historian Rubio (2009) refers to as an *ideology of whiteness*, wherein Black disadvantage is thought to exist through a combination of personal failure and some past discrimination, that is no longer relevant and should not interfere with White positions that are presumably earned. Thus, opposition to affirmative action among this group is fueled by a desire to protect privileges, though the existence of said privileges and the drive to maintain them are frequently denied (Rubio, 2009, p. 173-175).

The notion of reverse discrimination in employment is assumed to occur when women and minorities are hired over presumably "better qualified" White males (Soni, 1999). It is not uncommon, for example, for women of color who are employed in academia or higher education leadership to be categorized as "affirmative action hires." They are constantly challenged to prove that their success is not an effect of opportunity hiring, or tokenism, since frequently they are a member of an extreme minority group (Chance, 2020; Chance, 2022).

Pincus (2003) explains that the concerns of reverse discrimination expressed by White men are inconsistent with most of the available data on education and economic well-being collected by the federal government. Historical patterns and findings suggest that White males are the advantaged group in terms of education, income, and employment. More recent labor force statistics by race and ethnicity also reflects this trend (U.S. Bureau of Labor Statistics, 2023).

Further, White women have gained more from affirmative action as women than they have lost as members of the White race. In fact, one of the greatest beneficiaries of affirmative action, and especially in higher education, is White women (Hall, 2017; Rai & Critzer, 2000; Niemann & Maruyama, 2005). This can be seen when we analyze Integrated Postsecondary Education Data. According to recent statistics by the US Department of Education (2020) women of color are least represented among faculty, and in higher academic ranks. Underrepresented minorities make up only 12.9 percent of full-time faculty members in the country, despite making up nearly 33 percent of the US population. Underrepresentation and opportunity gaps are particularly pronounced among Hispanic or Latino and Black or African American women.

This demonstrates how affirmative action has been an equalizer for White women in education and in the workforce. In fact, some scholars suggest that from its inception the inclusion of women in affirmative action policies centered race and class-privileged women. Crenshaw (1989), for example, explains how dominant conceptions of subordination condition us to think about discrimination that affects women using a single-axis framework, wherein the intersectional experiences of Black women and other women of color are excluded and essentially erased from antiracist and antisexist policy discourse. In essence, women of color have been less served by affirmative action policies and practices because they are seen for their race before their gender.

Despite the various ways that White women have benefited from affirmative action, literature on racial attitudes regarding group-based policies suggests that they are arguably among the most ambivalent groups (Cho, 2002; Hall, 2017; Hunt & Smith, 2022). Researcher Hall (2017) explored this dissonance in a study on White fragility and affirmative action. It was hypothesized that higher levels of fragility would yield lower levels of support for affirmative action policies. White fragility" is defined as:

A state in which even a minimum amount of racial stress becomes intolerable, triggering a range of defensive moves. These moves include the outward display of emotions such as anger, fear, and guilt, and behaviors such as argumentation, silence, and leaving the stress-inducing situation. These behaviors, in turn, function to reinstate White racial equilibrium (DiAngelo, 2011, p.54).

Findings suggested that White women have a greater propensity to oppose affirmative action in higher education due to "White fragility" (Hall, 2017). This fragility exists because White women believe that affirmative action has led them to lose something of value (e.g., employment, promotions, or other opportunities) to less qualified minorities (Hall, 2017). Hall's (2017) research also recognizes that affirmative action is commonly presumed to be a pro-Black policy. Therefore, White women's opposition to affirmative action is also a substitute for their position on race relations. Despite racial attitudes and perceived threats, White women are disproportionately *more* likely to benefit from affirmative action policies compared to their counterparts, demonstrated by their significant gains in educational and workforce achievement, including full-time professional and administrative jobs.

THE EFFECTS OF AFFIRMATIVE ACTION AMONG WHITE WOMEN: THREATS TO DIVERSITY

In modern society, workplace diversity continues to be of importance. Given the disproportionality previously described and the effects of affirmative action, White women continue to expand their representation in senior levels of leadership in higher education more often and at twice the rate of women of color (Melidona, Cassell, Chessman, & Cecil, 2023).

There exists an apparent lack of diversity in senior-level positions within higher education organizations, and women of color are among the most underrepresented groups. Data from the American College President Study reported by Melidona and colleagues (2023) of the American Council on Education (ACE) suggests that fewer women than men are employed as university presidents across colleges and universities. Compared with men, women account for about 33% of senior leaders. However, nearly 70% of women presidents are white. In contrast, 14% of women presidents in the study identified as Black or African American, while 8% identified as Hispanic or Latina. Sample sizes of other races were so small (e.g., Asian American, and American Indian) that conclusions could not be summarized about these women presidents. Moreover, since faculty bodies tend to serve as a pipeline to leadership positions, the data is an indicator of the underrepresentation of women of color in academia overall.

A recent report on racial and ethnic equality in US higher education further indicates that faculty members from underrepresented populations are less likely to be represented and ascend the ranks than their White counterparts, due to changing structures in academia and perpetual patterns of inequality in society (Ellsworth, Harding, Law, & Pinder, 2022). Further, the McKinsey analysis found that 88% of (not-for-profit) colleges and universities have full-time faculties that are less diverse than the US population, and that number rises to 99% for institutions defined as R1 (Ellsworth et al., 2022). Predictions indicate that at current rates, it would take more than 1,000 years to diversify full-time faculty ranks to match the total population, and R1 institutions would never reach parity (Ellsworth et al., 2022). Despite national and federal investments, and stated commitments to diversity, equity, and inclusion, there are several barriers to advances in senior level leadership among racially diverse women.

A partial explanation of this disparity is the cultural adversity commonly experienced by women of color in their professoriate and higher education roles. There is a growing body of literature that documents the lived experiences of racially diverse women. They experience adverse challenges of intersectionality to include the interplay of racism, sexism, and ageism, as well as tokenism and social stereotypes (Chance, 2022; Hill et al., 2016). They have limited role models in higher education, and struggle to find belongingness due to exclusion and isolation (Chance, 2022; Geyton, Johnson & Ross, 2022). Further, gendered racial microaggressions can lead to traumatic stress symptoms, including depression and psychological distress (Moody and Lewis, 2019; Williams & Lewis, 2019). The intense hardship experienced by these higher education leaders has a significantly negative impact on their overall mental health and well-being. Therefore, racially diverse women may not be retained in these roles.

Following years of service and tenure at the rank of Professor, "Jade," a highly credentialed and qualified professional became the first Black woman to lead her academic department as a mid-level manager. She felt prepared, willing, and able to lead, but soon found herself sitting at the intersection of discrimination and gender and race-based biases in her new role. She regularly endured scrutiny, experienced microaggressions, and subtle workplace bullying. Her colleagues questioned her judgement and abilities, and she did not feel as though she were fully supported by senior-level administration. Jade described the compounding effects of these factors on her physical and mental health, resulting in burnout. The work itself and the conditions became undesirable, and the emotional costs too high. After about three years Jade resigned from her leadership position, and her role in academia overall. She made the decision to relocate her family, and transition into private practice. The unique pressures and challenges experienced by Jade and countless other women of color in this sector has a profound impact on the pipeline for recruitment, retention, and ultimately representation of diverse women in these roles.

Dominance among White women higher education leaders is also reinforced by hiring practices that are counter to efforts to equalize opportunities for other women. Take for example leadership appointments that are made at the executive level, with no faculty input, without the assembly or involvement of a hiring committee, or a national search. This is especially detrimental in cases where the employee population is not representative of the available or qualified population for the role. This issue was raised by a professional colleague employed at a Predominantly White Institution (PWI) in the southern region of the United States, where a senior leader commonly "created" roles, or appointed members of their personal network to assume available leadership positions. An observable pattern was recognized, where only professionals who reflected the identity of the senior leader were considered for promotion. As such, appointees were almost exclusively White women.

Such practices eliminate opportunities for placement goals to be established, which are designed to encourage committees and hiring officials to monitor their pool demographics at each stage of the hiring process. Moreover, this work should be done in collaboration with affirmative action staff, who play an important role in ensuring that search processes are inclusive. Ideally, when applicant pools are not representative, outreach or other recruitment actions are taken to promote and enhance diversity. Therefore, in hiring senior leaders, recruitment beyond usual networks is essential. Approaches like those described, however, undermine affirmative action and equal opportunity goals, further limiting opportunities for women of color to advance in the academy.

It is important to consider the prevalence of racial discrimination that exists in the United States overall, which continues to impact the experiences of women of color in the academy and in their daily lives. Some researchers have sought to measure everyday experiences of unfair treatment due to race or other status-based characteristics (Boutwell et al., 2017; Lee et al., 2019). Using data from the Pew Research Center's Racial Attitudes in America Survey, Lee, and colleagues (2019) explored the prevalence of discrimination experiences among various racial groups, including White, Black, Hispanic, and Asian respondents (N = 3,716). Study results indicated that all racial minority groups (e.g., Black, Hispanic, and Asian) reported facing more racial discrimination in comparison to Whites (63%), with Blacks reporting the most among all the groups analyzed. Incidences of discrimination are likely even higher than what is reported, however. Only cases of discrimination can be difficult to prove, and victims may be ambivalent to confront related challenges. Generally, however, racial discrimination continues to be part of the landscape of American society, as well as a prevalent feature in the lives of the demographic of interest.

Given this prevailing notion we can draw inferences about robust discrepancies or discrimination that occurs in the hiring of higher education leaders, even with existing affirmative action programs and policies. Researchers Quillian, Pager, Hexel and Midtbøen (2017) performed a meta-analysis to investigate changes over time in the level of hiring discrimination against African Americans and Latinos in US labor markets. They examined every available field experiment of hiring discrimination between 1989 and 2015, using callback rates of 55,842 applications submitted for 26,326 positions. They further analyzed the relationship of discrimination ratios to years in which the data were gathered to provide an estimate of the trend in discrimination. On average, White applicants received 36% more callbacks than African Americans who were equally qualified, representing a substantial degree of direct discrimination. In contrast, White applicants received on average 24% more callbacks than Latinos. According to these results, as it relates to hiring decisions, Black or African American candidates remain substantially disadvantaged relative to equally qualified whites, and there has been little indication of progress over time. The researchers observed no change in the level of hiring discrimination against African Americans for nearly 30 years. As such, the researchers caution against prevailing assumptions about waning stereotypes, implicit bias, and prejudice. In fact, they explain that hiring discrimination persists at a distressingly uniform rate, and for African Americans especially there is little evidence to suggest that it is disappearing, or even gradually diminishing.

STRENGTHENING AFFIRMATIVE ACTION PROGRAMS

Since the structures and systems established to create differential outcomes still exist, maintaining affirmative action as a legal framework is necessary, and serves as a mechanism to help enforce ideals of equity and inclusion in higher education leadership. Diverse leadership is fundamental to institutional success and critical to transforming academic structures, policies, and practices. Affirmative action can support workforce diversity, and ongoing critical assessment of affirmative action programs helps to ensure that standards and procedures to promote diversity are nondiscriminatory both in principle and in practice.

With consideration for the organizational level of the Social Ecological framework and given what we have come to understand about barriers to equal participation in leadership among women of color, colleges and universities can take critical steps to operationalize affirmative action goals with clear and directive implementation plans. Varying recommendations are outlined here to assist in strengthening affirmative action programs for all protected groups, but with a particular focus on women of color. These outlined strategies serve to guide higher education institutions and leaders in developing new affirmative action plans, or in analyzing and addressing inconsistencies or concerns with existing plans. The outlined strategies are also expected to help mitigate issues previously described, including: (1) Gendered racism and intersectional discrimination (2) Practices that compromise equal employment opportunities and (3) Hiring discrimination.

Strategic Visioning

As part of their commitment to affirmative action, colleges and universities must promote relevant priorities and values in their institutional strategic plans. One of the fundamental purposes of strategic visioning in higher education is to encourage and assist institutions to address opportunities and develop solutions to problems or threats that have the potential to impede institutional success (Hunt, 1997; Williams, 2021). One of the major criticisms of strategic planning among some scholars is that such plans are more general, figurative, and short-term, as opposed to practical plans for action (Haan, 2014; Williams, 2021). Further, it has been noted that top-down approaches may be used, where senior leaders design plans, in some cases, only to appease external stakeholders, government funders, alumni, parents and/or the public (Chance, 2010; Williams, 2021). Strategic planning can also be elaborate and complex, depending on the unique characteristics of institutions. This can lead to confusion, frustration, ineffective planning, and results. As such, higher education institutions are encouraged to move toward the use of simplified strategy models with more transparency and visible outcomes (Jalal and Murray, 2019).

Williams (2021) proposes an action research framework to facilitate more simplified and effective strategic planning initiatives in higher education. The B-VAR Model emphasizes brainstorming, visioning, action, and results, and is expected to mitigate many of the common issues that surface in the design and development of strategic planning initiatives. According to this model, the brainstorming stage includes the formation of ideas resulting from consultation, as well as formal and informal research efforts. Institutional leaders and stakeholders are encouraged to participate in both structured and unstructured focus groups to dialogue about the direction of the institution, and to document ideas about potential ways to accomplish that mission and vision.

Targeted meetings with the executive leadership team are organized during the visioning stage, where reflection and assessment are a priority. The senior leadership team reflects more carefully on information gleaned from brainstorming, including feedback received from consultation. They reflect on the projected direction of the institution, and analyze internal and external environments, using primary and secondary data. During this stage, analytical tools such as Strengths Weaknesses Opportunities and Threats (SWOT) Analysis can be beneficial in examining strengths, weaknesses, opportunities, and threats. Visioning should result in a one-page draft document outlining the vision, mission and strategic goals as agreed upon by the planning team (Williams, 2021).

The action stage requires participation and involvement from the entire institution, and the formation of teams to review output from the visioning and brainstorming stages. These teams are tasked with developing new proposals and identifying new directions based on their own research and evaluation of internal and external systems or environments impacting the institution. This stage also involves retreats, consultations, and actions from key operational and strategic members of the institution. Collaboration should happen both at the higher corporate governance level and within smaller campus units, including faculties, schools, departments, and centers (Williams, 2021).

Finally, a small strategy development team works collectively to process all the information gathered during the earlier stages. The results stage entails detailed discussions on concepts, meanings, measurement, accuracy of data, and related factors. Team members also come to a consensus on the most comprehensive and concise approach to present the data, ensuring clarity on the finalized strategies and strategic outcomes. This stage should result in the completion of the strategic plan document to be used as the basis for communication with all internal and external stakeholders. The team should also gain approval of the plan from the various committees previously described. Following any necessary iterations of the document, the plan should be implemented accordingly. Initiation of the plan should be organized in collaboration with the marketing and communications departments, as well as the core strategic planning team (Williams, 2021).

A multi-campus international university comprised of nearly 50,000 students, with higher education partnerships throughout North America, Latin America, Asia, Africa, and Europe, emphasized elements of the B-Var Model in the design and implementation of a revised strategic plan. The Vice Chancellor led brainstorming sessions, which included meetings with heads of governments, alumni, private sector groupings, multilateral organizations, leadership partners at other Higher Education Institutions, and community stakeholders. The University's Office of Planning carried out research to increase understanding of internal and external environments of the institution and higher education sector. This research was followed by focused retreats with senior executives, which resulted in a brief summary of the institution's vision, mission, core values, broad strategic goals, alignment, and responsiveness. Finally, with engagement from the entire campus community (e.g., departments, centers, institutes), the visioning document was critiqued and modified to better address and reflect unique institutional needs, taking into account important initiatives and targets. Following retreats, focus groups, interviews, and research, activities were carried out in the university's Office of Planning in order to derive a draft document of the plan. The draft was presented to various governance bodies for feedback, adjustments, and final approval by the University Council. After final approval, the Offices of Marketing and Planning rolled out a campaign, to formally launch the strategic plan (Williams, 2021). The university's Central Planning Office in collaboration with a steering committee, helped to monitor and evaluate quantitative outcomes, as well as overall progress and achievement of strategic goals. Following successful execution of the B-Var Model, the institution was on target to meet most of its goals and objectives between 2017-2022. Some achievements included the opening of an additional campus, and several other satellite locations across the world, resulting in increased industry engagement, international partnerships, educational access, and global research opportunities for students (Williams, 2021).

This example demonstrates the potential impact and effectiveness of the B-Var Model. As it relates to the phenomena of interest, the model can be useful in addressing affirmative action goals and actions designed to promote and hire diverse university faculty and leaders, and particularly women of color. Research to include workforce analysis, an assessment of the utilization and underutilization of protected groups, placement goals, as well as labor market availability data can be useful. Recruitment practices that reduce the potential for bias in selection, retention, and the impact of the institutional climate on these groups are also important considerations for senior leaders and teams evaluating research on internal and external environments, wherein the higher education institution is operating. Such factors should be accounted for in the strategic planning process, and solutions should be derived. The benefits of the action research framework proposed is that the management process can be easily monitored. Further, the model also allows for innovation and adaptability in reaching the desired outcomes.

During the process of strategic brainstorming, visioning, results, and action, it will also be important to clarify common myths and misconceptions about affirmative action, to protect fairness and equality. Examination of empirical evidence to counter narratives of preferential treatment and unfair advantage, and to demonstrate the value and benefits of race and gender conscious policies and frameworks can support such efforts. The university community should be educated about the intended goals. Also, consultation and collaboration with human resources and affirmative action staff will be essential.

Development of Core Teams

While various stakeholders and constituencies have an important role in the strategic visioning process, the assembly of a Core Team or steering committee with a clearly defined purpose and focus on strengthening affirmative action programs can be beneficial. Core Teams should be represented by an affirmative action officer or designee, faculty, staff, and volunteers, with a demonstrated commitment to positive and transformative leadership. Members will serve as decision makers, reviewers, and advisors. They should engage in data-driven analysis to ensure that affirmative action plans are effective and adeptly aligned with the vision, mission, and values of the institution's strategic plan. This might be done in collaboration with an Office of Institutional Effectiveness (or a similar office), that is typically charged with providing campus leadership and others with data and analyses to support planning, decision-making, and assessment. For example, it may be important to review employment activity data, including the number of racially diverse applicants for available positions, hiring rates, and promotions. The Core Team's review of job postings and proof of targeted recruitment efforts can also be helpful. This information can be used to track progress toward placement goals and/or to establish hiring benchmarks.

The work of the Core Team should also inform the development and implementation of equity-minded practices and policies, in the interest of achieving a more inclusive and diverse work (and academic environment) across the college or university. Their commitment should include ensuring equal opportunities for women of color and working to buffer unique barriers that have the potential to impede success among members of this group.

An extension of the university's Core Team might also include an affirmative action advisory council, made up of community members or other professionals with relevant expertise, who work collaboratively with the Core Team toward the identified goals and objectives. The advisory council is tasked with reviewing written reports, activities, and recommendations of the Core Team. Members of the advisory council are also empowered to provide resources and education to the Core Team. While diverse representation on the council is imperative overall, the inclusion of members who represent the special interests of women of color is particularly important, given the specific charge outlined in this chapter.

Training and Development

Members of the Core Team should engage in ongoing professional development and training that is rooted in inclusive excellence. Equity advocacy trainings, competency workshops, intergroup dialogue spaces, community "listen-ins" and "teach-ins" provide opportunities to build skills and knowledge in the interest of strengthening affirmative action programs and plans.

Generally, equity advocates gain useful information and skills that allow them to better understand local, national, and global issues and trends impacting the workforce. They identify behaviors and judgments that might have a disparate racial effect in hiring (Cahn, Gona, Naidoo & Truong, 2022). As advocates and members of a Core Team, they act as consultants and advisors to university search committees, who play a pivotal role in sourcing, recruiting, assessing, and recommending the most qualified and diverse candidates for employment. Equity advocates may also serve as voting members of search committees (for units or divisions they are not a member of), since they are uniquely trained to advocate for principles and practices related to diversity, equity, and inclusion (DEI) throughout the search. Advocates are encouraged to utilize an equity lens to think critically about the ways that structural and systemic issues impact vulnerable populations (Columbia University, 2016; Davey, Johnson, Webb & White, 2021; Nosek & Smyth, 2007; Sue, 2010). These may include racism, sexism, gender-based identity, discrimination, or other concerns. Further, the equity lens aims to disrupt biases and misuse of power that often manifests during hiring processes. Therefore, equity advocates must engage in ongoing training that addresses unconscious bias, labor market discrimination, understanding microaggressions, and techniques for interviewing diverse candidates. Follow-up with affirmative action officers and/or professionals who coordinate DEI efforts on university campuses is important to ensure quality improvement, and to evaluate and assess the effectiveness of affirmative action programs and practices.

It will be beneficial for other training opportunities to emphasize dimensions of the Association of American Colleges and Universities' (2015) inclusive excellence model. This model provides a comprehensive framework for infusing diversity into an institution's recruiting and hiring processes, training, and administrative structures and practices. Researchers Milem, Chang, and Antonion (2005) highlight the significance of institutional expectations and commitment, which reflects diversity in the mission and goals, at the highest levels of campus leadership, and ongoing funding and support for diversity programs and initiatives. This more systematic and multidimensional approach to assessing affirmative action policies and procedures, for example, will help to maximize institutional diversity efforts.

The development of critical consciousness about racial, ethnic, and cultural diversity should also be a major component of education and training for Core Team members. Critical consciousness is the ability to recognize, analyze, and act against oppressive political, economic, and social forces shaping society (Seider, El-Amin & Kelly, 2020). Some content areas might include anti-oppression, identity and socialization, bias (conscious and implicit), and racial frames. With a heightened critical consciousness, Core Team members will be able to better assess how policies may inadvertently impede advancement for women of color, which should in turn inform updates or changes to affirmative action plans.

Intergroup dialogue (IGD) is an example of a brave space, which fosters the development of critical consciousness, relationships, and capacities for promoting social justice (Frantell, Miles, & Ruwe, 2019). IGD is a small group intervention that allows people to connect across differences. In this context, the goal for Core Team members should be to develop their understanding of the social identities of women of color, social inequalities, and conflicts. Similarly, participation in flagship events such as community "listen-ins" allow members to engage in dialogue and receive guidance from subject-matter experts on equity-related issues, while "teach-ins" may focus on engagement, participatory discussions, and academic scholarship that supports access and opportunities for the population of interest.

Recruitment and Outreach

In an earlier section of this chapter, we learned from the B-VAR model about the importance of organizing affirmative action plans in partnership with university marketing and communications departments. Core Team members, who may also be hiring committee members and equity advocates, are encouraged to work in collaboration with these departments, to identify and implement best practices for recruitment and outreach to qualified, underrepresented groups (e.g., women of color faculty and leaders). This is essential, since marketing and communications professionals are trained in proven inclusive recruitment strategies that support the creation of a more diverse workforce. To target women of color specifically, outreach and partnerships are necessary with entities that represent women of color and/or sponsored events uniquely designed for them (e.g. networking or career events, community groups, professional organizations, etc.) Crafting hiring announcements and job postings that also appeal to women of color is critical to building an inclusive recruitment strategy.

Marketing and communications teams can also be instrumental in helping to promote and encourage academic scholarship among members of the campus community, that has the potential to inform affirmative action policy and practice.

External Searches

When filling new leadership positions in higher education administration, sometimes universities need a culture fit, and in other cases the goal may be to achieve a culture change. While there are undoubtedly some benefits associated with promoting or hiring senior higher education leaders from within, there may also be limitations to *only* hiring internal candidates, and especially at PWIs. Some concerns include the limited applicant pool, as well as the creation of an entrenched or inflexible work culture. In contrast, external candidates may offer fresh perspectives, new skills, and innovative ideas to help to advance the mission and strategic vision of the university. Otherwise, routinization, stagnation or ineffective systems can become the status quo. The potential for new ideologies and practices can strongly support institutional advancement. Also, there is the possibility that the internal candidate(s) may not be best suited for the position. Perhaps, they are hardworking and have sustained a long career at the university, but they've also had inadequate training or preparation for the role. An inclusive recruitment strategy then includes both internal and external recruitment when filling available positions. Qualified, racially diverse internal candidates should not be overlooked. Further, national searches provide equal opportunity for qualified external applicants, a standard important to proactively recruiting women of color to senior leadership positions in higher education.

Periodic Reviews

Regular updates to affirmative action plans, and ongoing efforts to strengthen policies should be initiated by the college or university's Core Team. Researching and studying initiatives being implemented across other institutions is an important practice. Campus leadership can learn from and avoid risks or pitfalls that have the potential to impede success. They can also assess affirmative action needs, identify best practices, and opportunities to improve programs and plans.

Periodic review of affirmative action programs should also include assessment of funding, resources, and support. This assessment will allow the Core Team to set priorities and develop strategies for the best ways to implement plans. It also helps to identify gaps that may require buy-in or additional support from campus leadership or other important stakeholders.

Analysis of the data and research that results from brainstorming and visioning sessions led by members of the Core Team is not only important to implementation of affirmative action programs and plans, but also helps to inform program evaluation. Core members should consider and reconsider measures of effectiveness and the program's overall objectives. Assessment can be most effective when the evaluation process is continuous.

Following successful recruitment and appointment of racially diverse faculty and leaders there should also be a periodic review of the effectiveness of efforts to create an environment where protected groups can thrive. Reports regarding work culture and/or complaints of discrimination are a critical area for review in the affirmative action program. Any concerns should be effectively addressed through appropriate planning systems and procedures, like those outlined in this chapter.

Accountability and Responsibility

To maintain the integrity and intended purpose of affirmative action programs, follow through on actions for protected groups is crucial. Campus leaders, members of Core Teams and other constituents must take positive steps to end discrimination, to prevent its recurrence, and to create new opportunities for women of color, who have been previously denied. The United States Equal Opportunity Commission sought to guide the public and address employer use of affirmative action plans, stating that:

An affirmative action plan must be designed to achieve the purposes of Title VII [of the Civil Rights Act of 1964]; i.e., to break down old patterns of segregation and hierarchy and to overcome the effects of past or present practices, policies, or other barriers to equal employment opportunity. It must be a concerted, reasoned program rather than one or more isolated events (Equal Employment Opportunity Commission, 1981, vol. 28, sec. 1608).

To accomplish this, it is critical for those who are leading affirmative action efforts to prioritize and advocate for structural change; to uphold campus values, and exercise power with good intent. Rhetoric of diversity, equity, and inclusion must lead to actionable policies and measurable outcomes. Leaders have a responsibility to both avoid and speak against strategies of institutional resistance to change and transformation. Understanding, leading and enacting change, however, can be a challenge. Practicing campus leaders, higher education practitioners, scholars, faculty, and staff can be impactful in mitigating these issues.

Kezar (2018) offers research-based principles for those who desire to be agents of change in their own institutions. The researcher proposes a framework that aids in identifying the type of change needed, the context of change, leadership, and theoretical approaches that may be scientific, evolutionary, political, social, cultural, or institutional. The main theories emphasize the importance of using data and benchmarks, consultation, planning, negotiating, mapping different interests, and drawing upon resources to affect change. Other key strategies may include understanding and appealing to values, creating coalitions, developing a collective vision, and mobilizing people and resources.

Further, having been met with challenges in leading change efforts in higher education, the author has found some success in other fundamental practices such as working to build trusting relationships, demonstrating how proposed changes align with relevant goals and objectives, involving faculty, staff and stakeholders in the process of change, being willing to learn from open discussions, adapt to feedback, and maintain clear and consistent communication throughout the change process.

CONCLUSION

This chapter addressed the need for a Social Ecological Model in identifying points of intervention to support the promotion and success of women of color in the academy. At the organizational level, colleges and universities are well positioned to develop, implement, and promote programs and policies that provide equal and equitable opportunities. The strategies outlined in this chapter can serve as a guide for institutional leaders and others who are engaged in the work of establishing a culture and practices that support a diverse higher education workforce. By correcting or strengthening gender-based affirmative action initiatives, we improve efforts to mitigate issues of gendered racism and intersectional discrimination that compromise recruitment, retention, and advancement of racially diverse women in higher education settings. There is great value in fostering more diverse and equitable practices, structures, and societal institutions (Kincade, 2023) in the interest of this population.

Women of color are invaluable assets to university institutions, systems, and structures. Their agency and commitment to positively impacting their campus community and the society at large supports the development and implementation of successful initiatives, programs, goal-driven and research-based strategies. Their strong connections to and engagement with diversity, equity, and inclusion sparks innovation, and drive positive organizational change across institutions. Moreover, institutions stand to benefit financially from implementing and improving diversity initiatives. Students benefit from the unique perspectives of women of color, their mentorship, and leadership. They help to center the diverse experiences of marginalized and underserved students, creating opportunities to improve student outcomes and student success. These are but a few examples of the ways that women of color directly influence and support the advancement of colleges and universities. Hence, efforts to promote gender diversity is an important priority at all levels of higher education organizations, but actionable plans, to include effective recruitment and retention of racially diverse women are especially critical to achieving gender and racial parity at all levels of leadership. It cannot be ignored, however, how such efforts are being undermined, regulated, and restricted at state levels.

While programs and plans to ensure equal opportunity in the workforce remain lawful for employers, pre-existing, and new bans on race-conscious affirmative action in college admissions, cutbacks, and legal attacks on Diversity, Equity, and Inclusion (DEI) initiatives pose critical concerns. Anti-DEI movements are a major threat to the goals outlined in this chapter to support progress and equitable opportunities among racially diverse women. Thus, continued development of anti-racism educational innovations, legislative and legal advocacy, and communicating best practices for the types of activities and programs that can legally occur in states with bans (Orr et al., 2023) is imperative moving forward, as more restrictions and limitations are being imposed. Lange and Lee (2024) suggest a proactive defense that centers on what advocates and educators are fighting *against*, as well as what we're fighting *for* across higher education institutions.

REFERENCES

Al-Faham, H., Davis, A. M., & Ernst, R. (2019). Intersectionality: From theory to practice. *Annual Review of Law and Social Science, 15*(1), 247–265. doi:10.1146/annurev-lawsocsci-101518-042942

Association of American Colleges and Universities. (2015). *Committing to equity and inclusive excellence: A campus guide for self-study and planning.* ERIC Clearinghouse.

Benokraitis, N. V., & Feagin, J. R. (1978). *Affirmative Action and Equal Opportunity: Action.* Inaction and Reaction.

Boutwell, B. B., Nedelec, J. L., Winegard, B., Shackelford, T., Beaver, K. M., Vaughn, M., Barnes, J. C., & Wright, J. P. (2017). The prevalence of discrimination across racial groups in contemporary America: Results from a nationally representative sample of adults. *PLoS One, 12*(8), e0183356. doi:10.1371/journal.pone.0183356 PMID:28837680

Cahn, P. S., Gona, C. M., Naidoo, K., & Truong, K. A. (2022). Disrupting bias without trainings: The effect of equity advocates on faculty search committees. *Innovative Higher Education, 47*(2), 253–272. doi:10.1007/s10755-021-09575-5 PMID:34456457

Chambers, C. (2023). *African American Women Leaders in Higher Education: An Examination of Job Satisfaction* (Doctoral dissertation, St. John's University (New York)).

Chance, N. L. (2020). *"Nevertheless, She Persisted": Exploring the Influence of Adversity on Black Women in Higher Education Senior Leadership* (Doctoral dissertation, Indiana Institute of Technology).

Chance, N. L. (2021). A phenomenological inquiry into the influence of crucible experiences on the leadership development of Black women in higher education senior leadership. *Educational Management Administration & Leadership, 49*(4), 601–623. doi:10.1177/17411432211019417

Chance, N. L. (2022). Resilient leadership: A phenomenological exploration into how black women in higher education leadership navigate cultural adversity. *Journal of Humanistic Psychology, 62*(1), 44–78. doi:10.1177/00221678211003000

Chance, S. (2010). Strategic by design: Iterative approaches to educational planning. *Planning for Higher Education, 38*(2), 40–54.

Cho, S. (2002). Understanding white women's ambivalence towards affirmative action: Theorizing political accountability in coalitions. *UMKC Law Review, 71*, 399.

Colby, G., & Fowler, C. (2020). *Data snapshot: IPEDS data on full-time women faculty and faculty of color.* American Association of University Professors.

Colon-Alverio, I. D., & Flowers, T. D. (2022). The Racial Battle Fatigue of Black Graduate Women in the Academy. In Black Women Navigating Historically White Higher Education Institutions and the Journey Toward Liberation (pp. 69-87). IGI Global. doi:10.4018/978-1-6684-4626-3.ch004

Columbia University. (2016). Guide to best practices in faculty search and hiring.

Crenshaw, K. (1989). Demarginalizing the intersection of race and sex: A black feminist critique of antidiscrimination doctrine, feminist theory and antiracist politics. University of Chicago Legal Forum, Volume 1989, Article 8.

Davey, T. L., Johnson, K. F., Webb, L., & White, E. (2021). Recruitment inclusive champions: Supporting university diversity and inclusion goals. *Journal of Faculty Development*, *35*(2), 50–57.

DiAngelo, R. (2011). White fragility. *The International Journal of Critical Pedagogy*, *3*(3), 54–70.

Ellsworth, D., Harding, E., Law, J., & Pinder, D. (2022). *Racial and ethnic equity in US higher education*. McKinsey and Company.

Equal Employment Opportunity Commission. (1981). Affirmative action appropriate under title vii of the civil rights act of 1964, as amended. Code of Federal Regulations, vol. 29, sec. 1608. Retrieved from CM-607 Affirmative Action | U.S. Equal Employment Opportunity Commission (eeoc.gov).

Frantell, K. A., Miles, J. R., & Ruwe, A. M. (2019). Intergroup dialogue: A review of recent empirical research and its implications for research and practice. *Small Group Research*, *50*(5), 654–695. doi:10.1177/1046496419835923

Garrison-Wade, D. F., & Lewis, C. W. (2004). Affirmative action: History and analysis. *Journal of College Admission*, *184*, 23–26.

Gause, S. A. (2021). White privilege, Black resilience: Women of color leading the academy. *Leadership*, *17*(1), 74–80. doi:10.1177/1742715020977370

Geyton, T., Johnson, N., & Ross, K. (2022). 'I'm good': Examining the internalization of the strong Black woman archetype. *Journal of Human Behavior in the Social Environment*, *32*(1), 1–16. doi:10.1080/10911359.2020.1844838

Gisselquist, R. M., Schotte, S., & Kim, M. J. (2023). *Affirmative action around the world: insights from a new dataset* (No. 2023/59). WIDER Working Paper.

Griffin, K. A. (2019). Institutional barriers, strategies, and benefits to increasing the representation of women and men of color in the professoriate: Looking beyond the pipeline. Higher Education: Handbook of Theory and Research: Volume 35, 1-73.

Gururaj, S., Somers, P., Fry, J., Watson, D., Cicero, F., Morosini, M., & Zamora, J. (2021). Affirmative action policy: Inclusion, exclusion, and the global public good. *Policy Futures in Education*, *19*(1), 63–83. doi:10.1177/1478210320940139

Haan, H. H. (2014). Where is the gap between internationalisation strategic planning and its implementation? A study of 16 Dutch universities' internationalisation plans. *Tertiary Education and Management*, *20*(2), 135–150. doi:10.1080/13583883.2014.896407

Hall, P. D. (2016). White fragility and affirmative action. *The Journal of Race & Policy*, *12*(2), 7.

Hill, C., Miller, K., Benson, K., & Handley, G. (2016). *Barriers and bias: The status of women in leadership*. American Association of University Women. https://www.aauw.org/resources/research/barrier-bias/

Hudson, J. B. (1999). Affirmative action and American racism in historical perspective. *The Journal of Negro History*, *84*(3), 260–274. doi:10.2307/2649005

Hunt, C. M., Oosting, K. W., Stevens, R., Loudon, D., & Migliore, R. H. (1997). *Strategic Planning for Higher Education*. Haworth Press.

Hunt, M. O., & Smith, R. A. (2022). White Americans' Opposition to Affirmative Action, Revisited: New Racism, Principled Objections, or Both? *Social Currents*, *9*(2), 107–117. doi:10.1177/23294965211024679

Jalal, A., & Murray, A. (2019). Strategic planning for higher education: A novel model for strategic planning process for higher education. *Journal of Higher Education Service Science and Management*, *2*(2), 1–10.

Jenkins, L. D., & Moses, M. S. (2014). *Affirmative Action Matters*. Routledge. doi:10.4324/9781315795744

Kezar, A. (2018). *How colleges change: Understanding, leading, and enacting change*. Routledge. doi:10.4324/9781315121178

Kincade, L. L. (2023). At the Crossroads: A Social-Ecological Model of Support for Women of Color in Higher Education Leadership. In Stabilizing and Empowering Women in Higher Education: Realigning, Recentering, and Rebuilding (pp. 87-105). IGI Global. DOI: doi:10.4018/978-1-6684-8597-2.ch006

Lange, A. C., & Lee, J. A. (2024). Centering our Humanity: Responding to Anti-DEI Efforts Across Higher Education. *Journal of College Student Development*, *65*(1), 113–116. doi:10.1353/csd.2024.a919356

Lee, R. T., Perez, A. D., Boykin, C. M., & Mendoza-Denton, R. (2019). On the prevalence of racial discrimination in the United States. *PLoS One*, *14*(1), e0210698. doi:10.1371/journal.pone.0210698 PMID:30629706

Love, B. H., Templeton, E., Ault, S., & Johnson, O. (2021). Bruised, not broken: Scholarly personal narratives of Black women in the academy. *International Journal of Qualitative Studies in Education : QSE*, 1–23.

MelidonaD.CassellA.ChessmanH.CecilB. G. (2023). The American College President: 2023 Edition. *Available at* SSRN 4689236.

Milem, J. F., Chang, M. J., & Antonio, A. L. (2005). *Making diversity work on campus: A research-based perspective*. Association American Colleges and Universities.

Moody, A. T., & Lewis, J. A. (2019). Gendered racial microaggressions and traumatic stress symptoms among Black women. *Psychology of Women Quarterly*, *43*(2), 201–214. doi:10.1177/0361684319828288

Niemann, Y. F., & Maruyama, G. (2005). Inequities in higher education: Issues and promising practices in a world ambivalent about affirmative action. *The Journal of Social Issues*, *61*(3), 407–426. doi:10.1111/j.1540-4560.2005.00414.x

Nosek, B. A., & Smyth, F. L. (2007). A multitrait-multimethod validation of the Implicit Association Test: Implicit and explicit attitudes are related but distinct constructs. *Experimental Psychology*, *54*(1), 14–29. doi:10.1027/1618-3169.54.1.14 PMID:17341011

Orr, C. J., Raphael, J. L., Klein, M., Corley, A. M., Tatem, A., Li, S. T. T., Pitt, M. B., Gustafson, S., & Lopez, M. A. (2023). Moving toward diversity, equity, and inclusion: Barriers, consequences, and solutions. *Academic Pediatrics*, *23*(8), 1524–1525. doi:10.1016/j.acap.2023.07.019 PMID:37543084

Pincus, F. L. (2003). *Reverse discrimination: Dismantling the myth*. Lynne Rienner Publishers. doi:10.1515/9781626374874

Quillian, L., Pager, D., Hexel, O., & Midtbøen, A. H. (2017). Meta-analysis of field experiments shows no change in racial discrimination in hiring over time. *Proceedings of the National Academy of Sciences of the United States of America*, *114*(41), 10870–10875. doi:10.1073/pnas.1706255114 PMID:28900012

Rai, K. B., & Critzer, J. W. (2000). *Affirmative action and the university: Race, ethnicity, and gender in higher education employment*. U of Nebraska Press.

Rosenfeld, M. (1991). *Affirmative action and justice: a philosophical and constitutional inquiry*. Yale University Press. doi:10.12987/9780300159547

Rubio, P. F. (2009). *A history of affirmative action, 1619-2000*. Univ. Press of Mississippi.

Seider, S., El-Amin, A., & Kelly, L. L. (2020). The development of critical consciousness. The Oxford handbook of moral development: An interdisciplinary perspective, 203-221.

Soni, V. (1999). Morality vs. mandate: Affirmative action in employment. *Public Personnel Management, 28*(4), 577–594. doi:10.1177/009102609902800407

Sue, D. W. (2010). *Microaggressions in everyday life: Race, gender, and sexual orientation*. John Wiley & Sons.

Taylor, M., Turk, J. M., Chessman, H. M., & Espinosa, L. L. (2020). Race and ethnicity in higher education: 2020 supplement. American Council on Education (ACE).

US Bureau of Labor Statistics. (2023). Labor force characteristics by race and ethnicity, 2023. *BLS Report no. 1100*.

U.S. Department of Education, National Center for Education Statistics, IPEDS, 2020, HR Survey component (provisional data).

Williams, D. A. (2021). Strategic planning in higher education: A simplified B-VAR model. *International Journal of Educational Management, 35*(6), 1205–1220. doi:10.1108/IJEM-08-2020-0382

Williams, M. G., & Lewis, J. A. (2019). Gendered racial microaggressions and depressive symptoms among Black women: A moderated mediation model. *Psychology of Women Quarterly, 43*(3), 368–380. doi:10.1177/0361684319832511

Chapter 6
Women in the Academy:
Challenges, Barriers, Promising Practices, and Policies

Sandy White Watson
https://orcid.org/0000-0002-8885-6203
University of Louisiana at Monroe, USA

ABSTRACT

In this chapter, the author examines the state of women in higher education, including a discussion of roadblocks and deterrents. The author reveals deterrents/roadblocks in common recruitment practices, retainment requirements, and advancement policies. She then focuses on initiatives designed to mitigate those deterrents that act to transform institutions, starting with research and evaluation, identifying and forming pipeline initiatives designed to encourage women to apply for positions in higher education. These initiatives are classified as structures (such as childcare facilities, lactation centers, family resource centers, etc.), pipeline initiatives (equity advisors, ombudspersons/offices, etc.), programs/initiatives (peer networking, mentoring, etc.), policies (tenure clock extensions, etc.), and climate initiatives (addressing unconscious bias, bystander interventions, etc.).

INTRODUCTION

According to the National Center for Education Statistics (2019) the percentage of university/college female faculty decreases across ranks: 54% of all assistant professors are female, 47% of associate professors are female, and only 33% of full professors are female. In 2013, 48% of all tenure-track positions were occupied

DOI: 10.4018/979-8-3693-0102-9.ch006

Copyright © 2024, IGI Global. Copying or distributing in print or electronic forms without written permission of IGI Global is prohibited.

by women, but only 37.5% of tenured positions were held by females (IPEDS, 2013). Further, fewer women than men hold leadership positions in academia, including chairs, deans, provosts, and presidents (Bartel, 2018), while only 30% of college presidencies are held by women, and of those, only 5% are held by female minorities (American Council on Education, 2017). One false narrative for this disparity is the notion that men dominate in these positions because there are not enough qualified females to fill them. This is simply not true because the number of women in doctoral programs has outnumbered men since 2006 (National Center for Education Statistics, 2019). Moreover, many women in academia possess the skills, abilities, and aspirations necessary for these positions, but systemic barriers embedded within the culture and organization of higher education act to impede their access to such positions (Fitzgerald, 2008). This phenomenon clearly reflects a leaking pipeline for women in academia (Ysseldyk et al., 2019). There are multiple reasons for this gender inequity among higher education faculty that can be grouped into three categories: recruitment, retainment, and advancement. In this chapter, the author will provide a literature review synthesis of challenges, barriers, promising practices, and policies regarding women in the academy.

Recruitment

When an individual begins an academic job search and locates a position that matches their expertise, they often search the website of the institution posting the advertisement for information about the university in general, its policies related to hiring, tenure and promotion, benefits, information related to the department housing the position, courses in relevant programs, etc. The information present or not present on the websites can influence whether or not a potential candidate moves forward with a formal application for the position. In addition, how position descriptions are worded can impact whether or not women choose to apply for them. Women who might be qualified for a position may opt out of applying for various reasons related to the position description or information found (or not) on the website. Common reasons women choose to pass on applying for positions include: (1) position descriptions with masculine wordings that allude to competitiveness, independence, strength, etc. (Gaucher et al., 2011; Lester, 2008); (2) the lack of readily locatable website information related to equitable structures and policies unique to women in university settings such as tenure clock extensions for childbirth or adoption reasons and family-friendly policies (Lundine et al., 2018); (3) mistakenly thinking they must meet 100% of the advertised qualifications to apply for the position– interestingly, males will apply for a position if they believe they meet only 60% of the posted qualifications (Mohr, 2014); and (4) inequities in compensation between male and female hires (wage gaps) (DesRoches & Zinner, 2010).

From the university perspective, the search committee screen applicants' materials and makes initial and subsequent interview and hiring decisions that often favor makes over females.

These include (1) the preference for hiring a male over a female in general (Savigny, 2014) due to unconscious gender biases; (2) choosing a male applicant over a female to avoid a female's potential maternity leave absence (Ledford, 2017); (3) selecting a male over a female because the criteria utilized by search committees to rate applicant attributes are masculinized (Gorman, 2005); (4) declining to hire a female due to the potential for absences related to child care [a married female applicant with young children is 35% less likely to be hired for a faculty position than a married male applicant with young children and are 33% less likely to be hired than a single female who has no children (Goulden et al., 2011)]; and (5) the preference for a male applicant because of the presence of unconscious bias among search committee members that manifests in negative female stereotypes and attitudes (Foley & Williamson, 2018).

One of the first steps university search committees can take to ensure the diversity of position applicants, is to ensure their own diversity by confirming that all groups are represented across search committee members (AFT Higher Education, 2011). In no particular order, universities should: encourage more female applicants to apply for academic positions, and ensure that position descriptions and advertisements utilize gender neutral language (Gaucher et al., 2011). To be certain the language used is gender neutral, several apps and websites are available to scan wording (textio.com; gender-decoder.katnatfield.com). Search committees should also limit the number of required qualifications for positions advertised to the most necessary of attributes, check to be certain family friendly benefits are clearly stated and easily locatable and even better, should include these policies in their position advertisements. Finally, they should include a commitment statement for encouraging female applicants such as a statement communicating a desire to increase female faculty in STEM by 40% (recruit.academicpositions.com).

In addition to these recommendations, universities could also establish search committees that purposely promote equity and diversity practices, such as the Strength through Equity and Diversity (STEAD) faculty search committee at the University of California, Davis. This specific committee seeks to identify and hire diverse applicants and ensures they do so by (1) regularly examining their recruitment practices to identify and eliminate biases, (2) including targeted diversity statements along with position advertisements, (3) emphasizing the importance of service, teaching, and advising skills of applicants, not just primarily targeting research accomplishments (Casad et al., 2020). And, finally, colleges should consider utilizing female tenure and tenure-track faculty to identify and develop best practices for recruiting and retaining women faculty, a practice in place at California State

Polytechnic University in Pomona for warranting the recruitment of female STEM faculty (Casad et al., 2020).

Retainment

When women attain faculty positions, they are more apt to eventually abandon them than men holding the same positions with the same qualifications. There are multiple reasons women leave higher education including: (1) The unappealing nature of academia (the need for constant searches for research funding sources, its solitary nature, the competitiveness and aggressiveness among colleagues (especially in STEM areas), being forewarned that their gender will work against them, family sacrifices that may occur, etc. (Rice, 2012); (2) The imposter syndrome (feelings of incompetence and unworthiness and believing that any successes one experiences are due to luck rather than personal qualities, a phenomenon that women experience more than men) (Clarence & Imes, 1978); (3) Hostile, sexist work environments; (4) Difficulties balancing academic demands and family obligations; (5) Inequitable workloads with women receiving heavier workloads than males in service (Kachchaf et al., 2015), advising, teaching (Carrigan et al., 2011) and student mentoring (Lester, 2008), all undervalued components of professors' work (Baker, 2020; Carrigan et al., 2011), to the detriment of research, a criteria that is heavily considered in tenure and promotion decisions (Baker & Manning, 2021); (6) Consistently negative teaching evaluations that are gender biased against females and that contribute to imposter syndrome feelings (Madera et al., 2009); (7) Difficulty obtaining grant funding due to funders' perceptions that women applicants are less competent than male applicants (Magua et al., 2017); and (8) The belief that White male faculty hold all the power in academia (AFT Higher Education, 2011).

Advancement

The literature is rife with studies that prove female faculty are promoted less frequently than male faculty (Coleman, 2010; Fitzgerald, 2014; O'Connor, 2011). There are multiple reasons why women are not promoted as often as their male counterparts: (1) The presence of a "glass ceiling," a barrier created by race and/or gender that stops women from moving forward in their careers (Bruckmuller et al., 2014); (2) Sporadic or intermittent publication rates due to maternity leave, childbirth, childcare (Resmini, 2016); (3) Few available supports for women that are deemed critical for promotion (Pyke, 2013); (4) Bias in letters of support and recommendation for promotion specifically directed at females (Madera et al., 2018); (5) Inability to meet travel obligations for conferences and other events due to family obligations (Hardy et al., 2016); (6) Unclear and arduous promotion and tenure requirements that have varying interpretations (Francis & Stulz, 2020); (7) Barriers presented by competitive colleagues, often other women (Francis & Stulz, 2020); (8) Feeling undervalued, underacknowledged, and unrecognized discourages women from seeking tenure and promotion (Francis & Stulz, 2020); (9) Perceiving certain other faculty (rock-stars) as more valued by leadership in terms of awards and promotion, supports and opportunities (Francis & Stulz, 2020); and (10) Experiencing academic bullying (Pyke, 2013).

Numerous studies have been conducted and widely disseminated pertaining to educational systems that create exclusion and marginalization and how to mitigate such practices, yet exclusive and marginalized practices continue to exist in higher education. In fact, many "modern neoliberal universities' efforts toward equity, diversity, and inclusion agendas often amount to no more than institutional rhetoric, or 'cosmetic diversity'" (Tamtik & Guenter, 2019, p. 42). Cosmetic diversity manifests itself in inconsequential changes and strategically-worded mission statements (Henry et al., 2016) with little to no action. However, many institutions have taken bold steps to mitigate practices and policies that exclude and marginalize. These actions often begin with recognizing the existence of such negative practices and policies through a purposeful examination of an institution's equity climate and then developing an action plan to address the problem.

Next, the author will discuss how universities might assess for gender equity, and identify pipeline initiatives (structures, positions, programs/initiatives, and policies) and climate strategies (strategies related to gender equity education and attitudinal changes) that can be utilized to create a more gender equitable organization.

Institutional Transformation

To begin the process of transforming the culture and climate of a university to become gender equitable, leaders must first evaluate its equity climate. This is often accomplished via gender equity surveys, focus groups and interviews. Once results are obtained, climate and pipeline initiatives are identified and put into place to address any inequities revealed during the evaluation process.

Research and Evaluation

In preparation for transformational change, it is recommended that institutions evaluate climate in terms of the following indicators: representation, equity, and inclusion. Bilmoria et al. (2008) studied transformational change at 19 universities that were awarded National Science Foundation ADVANCE funding and identified two categories of initiatives: climate and pipeline. Climate initiatives are those actions focused on changing the attitudes, awareness, and practices of male colleagues via education/training and development (committees, mentorship training, professional development, etc.). Responding actions are then directed toward creating more equitable, transparent, and collegial departments (departmental strategic planning with a focus on change), cross-departmental collaboration, seminars and workshops, leadership coaching; and organizational efforts toward improving diversity awareness and inclusion (conferences, relevant presentations by senior women, gender awareness education, etc.) (Bilmoria et al., 2008).

Pipline initiatives are aimed at growing the numbers of females entering the tenure track pipeline (mentoring programs, information sessions, research funding, etc.); improving the processes and structures related to critical career transitions (hiring, tenure, rank and leadership promotions) such as training to identify biases among search, tenure, and promotion committees and training for increasing transparency; better preparing pre-tenured and tenured females for navigating the pipeline (providing mentors, celebrating accomplishments of women, funded professorates, research funding, etc.) (Bilmoria et al., 2008).

Pipeline Initiatives

Pipeline initiatives can be divided into three categories: structures (childcare facilities, lactation centers, etc.), positions (equity advisors, ombudsmen, etc.), and policies (tenure clock extensions, dual-career hiring, part-time policies, family-friendly benefits, equity action plans, etc.). Structures generally refer to concrete initiatives such as locations and facilities, positions refer to roles taken by individuals, and policies represent formal courses of action. The author will first discuss structures, followed by positions, then programs/initiatives, and will end with policies.

Structures. There are multiple structures that have been deemed effective for widening the academic pipeline for women entering into, staying in, and advancing through academia. These include childcare facilities and lactation centers.

Childcare facilities. The American Association for University Professors (AAUP) has stressed the importance of access to quality childcare facilities for university professors and advocate for universities accepting some responsibility for providing such childcare services to their faculties (aaup.org – 2023). In particular, on-site childcare facilities can lead to more productive and satisfied faculty. In the event that on-site childcare is not feasible, the AAUP recommends attaining cooperative agreements with nearby organizations, resources and cost-sharing (aaup.org, 2023).

Lactation centers. To communicate the value of women as workers in the workforce, lactation spaces began to be developed in work settings in the early 2000s (Vilar-Compte et al., 2021). According to the Fair Labor Standards Act (FLSA), nursing mothers who are employees must be provided break time in a private setting for breastmilk expression for up to one year after the births of their babies

(Porter & Oliver, 2015). What lactation centers look like and provide and policies associated with them differ according to location. According to Vilar-Compte et al (2021) services might include providing breast-pumps, offering work-from-home options or reduced work hours, offering flexible scheduling, providing private or semi-private spaces for milk expression for breastfeeding or pumping, and enacting policies to support breast-feeding women in the workplace.

Family resource centers. Family resource centers located on university campuses are excellent sources of support for parents who are students or faculty. Services offered by such centers include legal affairs, nutrition, disability support, early intervention, childcare assistance, therapy, peer and emotional support, insurance guidance, and more.

Positions. Colleges and universities have created numerous positions for the purpose of advancing gender equity. Examples of such positions include equity advisors, ombudspersons, and ombuds offices.

Equity advisors. Some universities have established equity advisor (EA) positions whose primary focus is equitable recruitment. The person(s) holding the position is often senior faculty who has been identified for the position due to their commitment to equity and their interpersonal and collaborative skills. Ideally, each department has a dedicated EA. EAs are tasked with ensuring equity among hiring practices, facilitating pay equality, mentoring initiatives, monitoring climate, advancing women, securing relevant equity work-shops for faculty, and more. The previously mentioned ADVANCE program has funded such initiatives at the University of California, Irvine (UCI), who credits its increased percentage of women faculty hires with the creation of an Equity Advisor position. Specific examples of the work of EAs include: ensuring the use of "gender-neutral selection criteria" (Stepan-Norris & Kerrissey, 2016 p. 227); monitoring hiring processes to ensure females are equally considered (which could involve holding departments responsible for their hiring decisions); hiring an external person to oversee the hiring process for gender equity- from reviewing position descriptions to reviewing applicant lists to meeting regularly with deans and faculty; analyzing pay equality among faculty; developing mentoring and networking initiatives for junior faculty; and, promoting the achievements of female faculty (Stepan-Norris & Kerrissey, 2016).

Ombudspersons/office. Ombudspersons were first utilized in university/college settings in the United States in 1967 at Michigan State University during a period of political unrest as a means for students to voice safety concerns. Since then, the roles of ombudspersons have expanded to serve faculty, staff, administrators, and external populations with university connections, such as donors, parents, and alumni (Morson, 2016).

According to the International Ombuds Association (IOA), an ombudsperson or ombuds office collaborates with individuals and groups to "provide a safe space to talk about an issue or concern, explore options to help resolve conflicts, and bring systemic concerns to the attention of the organization for resolution" (ombudsassociation.org). There are a variety of different types of ombuds including organizational, classical, advocate, hybrid, executive, legislative, and media. In the case of the university setting, an ombudsperson confidentially receives complaints from faculty and staff related to bullying, discrimination, harassment, threats, and more and can also be involved in annual performance, evaluation feedback, tenure/promotion decisions, and departmental conflict (Rubin, 2023). The ombudsperson not only consults with individuals and groups, but facilitates informal conflict management, resolution of disputes, advocates for the fair treatment of faculty and fair process for the university as a whole. In short, ombudspersons provide a means for hearing the voices of the less powerful.

Diversity, education and inclusion (DEI) officers. Individuals in DEI positions often specialize in one area and work with a team of other individuals with related specialties. Collaboratively, they work to increase an organization's diversity, education and inclusion and improve the well-being of its employees. Specific tasks of DEI officers include removing bias from application processes, increase the representation of women and others who are under-represented, review organizational policies and websites for non-inclusive language and practices, and more (bestcolleges.com).

Programs/Initiatives. Many universities have implemented effective programs and initiatives designed to promote gender equity. These include peer networking, group scholarship programs, equity action plans, gender action plans, and mentoring, among others.

Peer networking. Peer networking is an intervention for interrupting gendered norms, promoting career advancement, and counteracting feelings of isolation that involve bringing together a group of faculty members (such as assistant professors) on a regular basis for conversations about tenure and promotion, time-management, work-life balance, etc. In the case of peer networking for women, the faculty group often becomes a long-term cohort that is led by a female role model in a leadership position or at a senior rank who also facilitates the group's activities and conversations and schedules regular meetings (O'Meara & Stromquist, 2015). Research has revealed the effectiveness of such groups for developing strong ties across members, for safety in discussions and sharing confidences, and for the sharing of relevant information (Kezar, 2014). According to Hart (2008), peer networking has proven to serve as a change agent because they are uniquely positioned to support women faculty navigating gendered university workspaces why also establishing new norms and ideas. Additionally, women involved in peer networking indicate that they feel a sense of belongingness, are better able to overcome challenges, and adopt new perspectives for attaining tenure and promotion (O'Meara & Stromquist, 2015).

Group scholarship. The author of this chapter is involved in with a collaborative group of faculty members who represent multiple universities and disciplines across five states. This group's primary purpose is co- or reciprocal- learning between mentors and mentees and the promotion of one another's scholarship by sharing in group publishing projects. This Faculty Academy has jointly produced multiple books, articles and conference presentations over the last 15 years. Hence, the importance of collegiality cannot be overstated. Not only do junior faculty benefit from the knowledge and experience of senior faculty in such arrangements, group collaborations that result in funded grants and published products have been instrumental in positive tenure and promotion decisions (Francis & Stulz, 2020).

Mentoring. In general, the positive benefits of mentoring for women's career advancement have long been widely acknowledged and demonstrated (Burke, 1984; Dreher & Ash, 1990; Young et al., 1982). Mentorship relationships involving women in academia are especially beneficial for ameliorating job stress and providing workplace support (Nelson & Quick, 1985), and for positively impacting job success and satisfaction (Riley & Wrench, 1985). When women mentor other women in academia, mentees have reported the criticality of the empathy their mentors expressed for their concerns and feelings (Dreher & Ash, 1990) and have indicated that the mentoring they receive from other women is more supportive and personal than mentoring received from males (Burke, 1984). Other benefits of academic mentoring relationships for women include research collaboration opportunities and self-esteem and confidence growth (Wright & Wright, 1987). One such mentoring program is called The Launch Program at the University of Michigan, which assigns senior mentors to first-year STEM faculty for their entire first year, a strategy so successful, that it is now being duplicated in the Social Sciences and Humanities (Casad et al., 2020).

Equity action plans. Some higher education institutions have experienced success with departmental equity action plans for ensuring equitable workload across professorial ranks (Culpepper et al., 2020). One such plan developed by Culpepper et al. (2021) identified six conditions that facilitate equitable workloads among faculty: (1) *transparency*- departments have readily-available faculty work activities information (O'Meara et al., 2021); (2) *clarity*-departments have identified faculty work activity benchmarks that are well understood (O'Meara et al., 2021); (3) *credit*- departments show appreciation for extensive faculty work via rewards and recognition (O'Meara et al., 2021); (4) *norms*- departments ensure workload fairness by establishing and reinforcing norms/systems (O'Meara et al., 2021); (5) *context*-departments realize the uniqueness of their faculty and differing demands of the various positions they hold and thus are flexible in assigning workloads (O'Meara et al., 2021); and, (6) *accountability*: departments make sure that all faculty meet workload obligations and are credited appropriately for that work (O'Meara et al., 2021).

Gender action plans. Several European institutions have had successes with the implementation of gender action plans. One such plan is the INTEGER project (Institutional Transformation for Effecting Gender Equality in Research), which addresses gender inequities specific to STEM at multiple institutional levels by following a six step procedure: (1) Obtaining support from top university leadership (president/provost); (2) Engaging key decision-makers (senior management and college officers) with external gender equity experts to identify unconscious gender biases; (3) Providing training for leaders for building capacity; (4) Providing unconscious bias seminars for all university levels; (5) Requiring unconscious bias awareness/training for search committees (Gvozdanovic & Bailey, 2020).

Policies. The last category of pipeline initiatives are policies. Such policies include tenure clock extension, dual-career hiring, parental leave, part-time employment guidelines, and family friendly benefits. The author will now discuss each of these policies.

Tenure clock extension. Tenure timeline extensions mainly occur due to child-related events such as childbirth or adoption and generally extend tenure by one year. Policies related to extending the tenure clock timeline vary across universities. For example, at Villanova University, faculty (male, female or both) who give birth get an automatic one-year extension preceding the tenure decision year. McEacharn et al. (2019) conducted an analysis of 189 colleges/universities by searching the website for each institution to examine tenure-extension policies. Of the 189 institutions examined, 7.4% provided automatic extensions, 10/9% provided automatic extensions upon request, 67.4% required formal request and approval, 6.3% had vague extension policies, and 8.0% had no policy. For example, at Virginia Polytechnic Institute, new parents receive a one-year extension, whether new parenthood is because of the birth of a child or if it is because of adoption of a child under five years of age. At Miami University, a new parent must formally request a one-year extension, but the parent must have primary responsibility for the care of a child. And at the University of Southern Mississippi, new parents can request an extension of tenure application until their 7th year with the university, or later (McEacharn, et al., 2019).

It is interesting to note that male faculty tend to benefit more than female faculty from child-related tenure clock extensions as they receive rank promotions more than female faculty who also receive such extensions (Juraqulova et al., 2019). On the other hand, female faculty receiving tenure extensions are less likely to benefit in the same way, at least in economics at research-intensive institutions (Antecol et al., 2018).

Dual-career hiring. The increasing presence of women in academia has influenced the emergence of dual-career hiring in university settings. Dual-career hiring occurs when both members of a couple are hired together. Schiebinger et al. (2008) found that approximately 36% of faculty state they were hired as part of a dual-career academic couple. The hiring of the secondary member of a dual-career couple can be for a full-time tenure-track position (least common), a shared position, an administrative role, or for a part-time adjunct/lecturer/visiting professor position (most common) (Blake, 2022).

Dual-career hiring has been especially beneficial for increasing gender equity in natural science fields. For example, 83% of women faculty members in the natural sciences are partnered with another scientist, while 54% of male faculty have scientist partners (Schiebinger et al., 2008). Another study revealed that half of women physicists are married to other physicists and 30% of female physicists are married to other scientists (McNeil & Sher, 1999). These statistics demonstrate the impact hiring dual-career couples has on women's representation in the sciences in university settings (Blake, 2022).

Universities who actively recruit dual-career couples often have policies that facilitate this process, thus are often able to expedite hire offers (Blake, 2022). As an example, at Oregon State University if a person recruited for a tenure-track position has a partner who is also eligible for a tenure track position, the provost can consider waiving the search for the second position and instead approve jointly funding the primary hire and partner (facultyaffairs.oregonstate.edu). At the University of Houston (UH), when one partner is hired for a tenure-track position, the university helps to facilitate the job search process for the other partner, whether at UH as faculty or staff, or in the local community (uh.edu).

Dual-career hiring practices are not as transparent as other hiring procedures according to Schiebinger et al (2008). For example, these practices are often of concern to other faculty, who may question the fairness of hiring a dual-career couple, thus it is critical that the process be open and related policies be easily attainable. To further mitigate concerns, universities should require thorough vetting of both members of a dual career couple before they are hired (Blake, 2022). Further, Blake (2022) recommends that administration and faculty engage in open dialogue about the implications of dual-career hiring. In addition, any dual career-hiring policies should be communicated to all applicants and be readily available on university websites (Higginbotham et al., 2011) and a designated administrator should be targeted for handling dual-career hires and facilitating cross-departmental communication regarding such hires (Blake, 2022).

Parental leave. Because of the fluid nature and blurred boundaries of professors' work, maternity leaves are controversial (Myerchin, 2014). Across most institution of higher education in the U.S., there are no consistent or formal policies related to parental leave for faculty (Wilson, 2003), thus, it is not unusual for female academics to struggle balancing meeting the needs of their young children while fulfilling faculty job expectations. To better balance this struggle, many mothers who are faculty members plan pregnancies and births around the academic year. Even when parental leave is granted, there is often much stress and anxiety surrounding the impact of leave on tenure and promotion due to a loss in productivity and visibility during that time. Also problematic is parental leave for fathers in academia as the idea of providing parental leave for new fathers in academia is gendered and steeped in social stigmas (Winter & Pauwels, 2006).

Part-time policies. Contingent faculty positions were first developed when universities did not allow women to hold professorships. These part-time female faculty were referred to as "the housewives of higher education" (Schell, 1997, p. 40). The conditions for and perceptions of part-time faculty have improved little since adjunct positions were established. Contingent faculty earn between 22 - 40% less than individuals holding tenure-track assistant professorships, receive no benefits, and have no or only minimal possibilities for career advancement. Part-time faculty have been characterized as members of academia's permanent underclass (Harris, 2019), migrant laborers of higher education (Drozdowski, 2022), the new working poor (Rhoades, 2013), and second-class university citizens (Mathieu-Frasier, 2021), earning an average of $2700 per course (Flaherty, 2020). Alarmingly, 31% of contingent university/college faculty are living at or below the federal poverty level (American Community Survey, 2023), 4 in 10 receive government assistance in order to cover basic household expenses, 45% have postponed receiving health care, and 65% have forgone dental care (American Federation of Teachers, 2023). Women make up 54% of part-time, non-tenure track faculty (AAUP, 2023).

The increased reliance on part-time faculty has led to much discussion regarding their rights, roles, status, privileges, and responsibilities. It is the position of the AAUP that any part-time faculty member who carries loads equivalent to those of full-time faculty should be entitled to the privileges and rights held by full-time faculty members. For improving the conditions and job security of adjunct faculty, the AAUP recommends the following policy proposals: (1) *Tenure for Part-Time Faculty.* Regular contingent faculty should be offered tenure and the rights it offers; (2) *Employment Security.* Regular contingent faculty who teach courses year after year should have some degree of job security; they should not be routine last-minute hires when new courses must be quickly established, and ought to be compensated for time already spent in course preparation when courses must be unexpectedly canceled. In addition, adjuncts should have access to grievance procedures, just as full-time faculty do; (3) *Institutional Governance.* Part-time faculty with longer employment with universities should have the right to participate in institutional governance, have voting rights, and should be included in decisions related to the courses they teach, such as goals, schedules, techniques, assessments, etc.; (4) *Fringe Benefits and Pay.* Part-time faculty should be provided equitable pay, with some receiving flat rates per course and others receiving prorated pay, with each option dependent upon individual merit and seniority (aaup.org, 2023). Despite all of these recommendations, few universities have instituted any of these policies regarding contingent faculty.

Reasons women attain adjunct positions include the inability to obtain a full-time position; the need to provide full-time childcare to young children, including those with disabilities or health conditions; the desire for more family time in general; and obligations related to caring for elderly family members. Furthermore, many women accept such positions because they hope that they will eventually become full-time positions (American Federation of Teachers, 2023).

However, some adjunct faculty have organized to form unions so as to gain voices and votes. For example, at New York University, the Adjunct Faculty Union advocates for benefits, better working conditions, and fairer wages and has been successful, negotiating a third contract with the university that allowed for increased wages and expanded health benefits (Smith, 2016). At Duquesne University, the United Steelworkers union negotiated minimum adjunct pay to be increased from $2500 to $3500 per course. At the University of Chicago in 2018, adjunct faculty negotiated their first union contract, which resulted in pay raises, increased job security, and family leave. Other unions have stepped up to advocate for the rights of part-time faculty, including the American Federation of Teachers, the National Education Association, the United Auto Workers, the Service Employees Education Association, the United Electrical Workers and more (Tolley, 2018).

Family-friendly benefits. Increasingly, colleges and universities are providing family-friendly resources and benefits for faculty members. Examples of family-friendly benefits include maternity/childbirth leave and parental leave for new parents, extended sick leave benefits, childcare centers, sick-child services, excluding time from tenure clock due to dependent care, counseling services, LGBT faculty alliance services, flexible spending accounts, reduced tuition for faculty, spouses and eligible children, and more. Resources include work/life resource centers that help faculty balance their personal and work lives, help locate child and elder care, provide educational programming, and connect faculty with students who babysit, do yardwork, tutor, pet sit, provide housekeeping and more.

Some universities provide funds for adoption assistance, vacation and holiday pay, modified duties for active service faculty, deferral of personnel reviews due to family issues, grief and loss resources, prescription drug discounts, smoking cessation programs. Infertility services and resources, prenatal classes, various support groups, dementia family support programs, and more.

Climate Initiatives. To change the equity climate so that it is more welcoming to women, universities should provide education for male colleagues to increase their gender equity awareness, and create initiatives that serve to improve the collegiality, egalitarianism, and transparency of departmental practices, and increase awareness of issues related to diversity and inclusion at the organizational level in general (Bilmoria et al., 2008). Examples of such initiatives include training in unconscious bias and bystander intervention, workshops for learning to identify and correct inequitable behaviors, dissemination of literature related to increasing gender equity awareness, conducting surveys to faculty perceptions of gender bias in hiring, tenure, and promotion practices, etc. Next, the author will share particular strategies that have proven successful to improve equity climate in academic settings.

Addressing unconscious bias. Unconscious or implicit bias occurs when "we make judgements or decisions on the basis of our prior experiences, or our own deep-seated thought patterns, assumptions or interpretations, and we are not aware we are doing it" (Royal Society, 2015, p. 2). It also arises from culture, and retrieval and processing of information taken from media and other external sources (Gvozdanovic & Bailey, 2020). The consequences of gender-related unconscious bias can be gender inequality, where the viewpoints and needs of differing genders are disregarded, overlooked, or not present (Gvozdanovic & Bailey, 2020). Unconscious bias among faculty search committee members has been shown to influence hiring decisions against women. This is especially true for women candidates seeking science positions (Miller et al., 2015).

Research has revealed that university leadership are uniquely positioned for addressing such unconscious bias, therefore strategies for mitigating and preventing such bias should be incorporated into leadership training (Gvozdianovic & Maes, 2018). Unconscious bias awareness training is a popular strategy often utilized as a way to help male faculty become aware of their own gender biases, although the efficacy of such an approach has been questioned because its effectiveness has not been determined (Emerson, 2017). However, when unconscious bias training is coupled with additional targeted strategies, a reduction in implicit bias has been documented (Devine et al., 2012). Another such strategy is the use of bias observers, individuals who monitor biased behaviors in recruitment structures, for example, and then recommend actions that mitigate them. Examples of biased behaviors among members of search committees might include devoting more time to a male applicant over a female applicant, asking different questions of female applicants than male applicants, discussing applicants informally, and more (Gvozdanovic & Maes, 2018).

Bystander interventions. Bystander intervention training for male faculty members is helpful for showing them how to recognize misconduct directed by men toward women and how to appropriately and safely intervene and support victims afterwards. Examples of such misconduct include sexual harassment and abuse, bullying, discrimination, and micro- and macro-aggressions (Casad et al., 2020). Examples of such programs include the "Empowering (Geo)Scientists to Transform

Workplace Climate" program at the University of Kansas and "The Green Dot" programs at the University of California, Berkeley and Harvard University.

Workshops on recognizing and correcting inequitable behaviors. According to a 2009 Catalyst report, men are often an untapped source of transformation for gender equity, and when they become aware of their own gender biases, they are much more likely to realize the criticality of gender equality (Prime et al., 2009). Hence, it is imperative that men in academia be provided opportunities to examine their own biases and learn more about gender bias and its impact on the careers and wellbeing of their female counterparts. A perfect place for this self-examination and further exploration is within a dedicated workshop on recognizing and correcting unconscious biases. When training is provided, it becomes a tool for powerful individual and collective transformational change.

Funding Institutional Transformation

In this final section, the author will identify current funding sources for supporting many of the transformational programs and initiatives discussed in this chapter. Of all the funding sources listed, the National Science Foundation's ADVANCE Institutional Transformation program seems to have funded more and more innovative and effective initiatives than all of the others, as greater than 160 higher education institutions and STEM non-profit groups across 47 of the 50 states have been awarded ADVANCE grants to support the advancement of females in STEM, totaling approximately $270 M.

National Science Foundation's ADVANCE Institutional Transformation Program. The National Science Foundation's ADVANCE (Organizational Change for Gender Equity in STEM Academic Professions) program was developed to advance a more diverse science and engineering workforce by supporting the implementation of equity strategies in higher education. These strategies are developed to mitigate systemic policy and practice inequities such as policies and/or procedures that fail to alleviate implicit bias when decisions concerning hiring, promotion and tenure occur resulting in women and other minorities receiving evaluations that are less favorable (nsf.gov). This program has funded multiple initiatives across U.S. universities, including several of the initiatives and programs mentioned in this chapter (University of Michigan's Launch Program, the University of Kansas's Empowering (Geo) Scientists to Transform Workplace Climate program). Other initiatives funded by ADVANCE include the previously mentioned pipeline initiatives that serve to increase the number of women entering STEM university positions; efforts to revise academic policies related to recruitment, tenure, promotion, and leadership to make them more equitable; and preparing women faculty to successfully navigate the pipeline process (Bilimoria et al., 2008); and climate initiatives focused on providing education and development for male colleagues to increase their awareness and improve their practices, creating initiatives that serve to improve the collegiality, egalitarianism, and transparency of departmental practices, and increasing awareness of issues related to diversity and inclusion at the organizational level (Bilmoria et al., 2008).

The ADVANCE program has been effective in representing women in the science and engineering tenure-track pipeline as many of the universities with ADVANCE programs reported increased numbers of women entering all three ranks – assistant, associate, and full professor as well as leadership positions (Bilmoria et al., 2008). For example, the University of California, Irvine obtained ADVANCE funding that allowed them to expand their existing efforts at recruiting women in STEM to all other disciplines. As a result, they were able to hire a greater percentage of female faculty as compared to before receiving the grant.

National Science Foundation's Early-Career Academic Pathways in the Mathematical and Physical Sciences program. The funds for this initiative are intended to be utilized for broadening participation of members of under-represented groups in the mathematical and physical sciences by jumpstarting the research agendas of early career faculty (nsf.org).

National Science Foundation's Directorate for Computer and Information Science and Engineering (CISE): Broadening Participation in Computing PILOT. This initiative supports actions to increase the participation of under-represented groups (including women) in computing fields (nsf.org).

National Science Foundation's Directorate for Engineering: Broadening Participation in Engineering (BPE). Like CISE, this project supports actions to increase the participation of under-represented groups (including women) in engineering fields (nsf.org).

American Philosophical Association's Diversity and Inclusiveness in Philosophy program. This initiative aims to support the participation of women and other minorities in philosophy (apaonline.org).

Institute for Citizens & Scholars: Mellon Emerging Faculty Leaders Award. This award is provided to individuals who have successfully completed their mid-tenure review and wish to work toward eliminating disparities in their respective fields (humanities and social sciences) related to culture, civil rights, education, equity and inclusion (citizensandscholars.org).

CONCLUSION

In this chapter, the author described the current status of women in academia, shared the reasons women don't enter, aren't promoted, or leave higher education altogether, discussed the evaluation of an institution's gender climate, and identified pipeline (structures, positions, programs/initiatives, and policies) and climate initiatives for transforming university workspaces into gender equitable environments, ending with an examination of funding sources for transforming universities into gender equitable environments. In summary, it is time that all administrations in higher education recognize that women's unique experiences, perspectives, and scholarly and curricular contributions offer students immeasurable benefits. Thus, we all need to work together to be certain women in academia are treated justly and do not experience gender inequities.

REFERENCES

American Association of University Professors. (2023). *Faculty child care.* https://www.aaup.org/report/faculty-child-care

American Community Survey (2023). *U.S. Census Bureau.* Census.gov

American Council on Education (2017). Minority presidents. *American Council on Education.* aceacps.org

American Federation of Teachers, Higher Education. (2011). Promoting gender diversity in the faculty: What higher education unions can do. *American Federation of Teachers. Higher Education.*

American Federation of Teachers (2020). *Report reveals grave plight of contingent college faculty.* aft.org

Antecol, H., Bedard, K., & Stearns, J. (2018). Equal but inequitable: Who benefits from gender-neutral tenure clock stopping policies? *The American Economic Review, 108*(9), 2420–2441. doi:10.1257/aer.20160613

Baker, V. L. (2020). *Charting your path to full.* Rutgers University Press. doi:10.36019/9781978805972

Baker, V. L., & Manning, C. (2021). A mid-career faculty agenda: A review of four decades of research and practice. Higher education: Handbook of theory and research, 36, 1-66. doi:10.1007/978-3-030-43030-6_10-1

Bartel, S. (2018). *Leadership barriers for women in higher education.* https://bized.aacsb.edu/articles/2018/12/leadership-barriers-for-women-in-higher-education.

Bartels, L. K., Weissinger, S. E., O'Brien, L. C., Ball, J. C., Cobb, D., Harris, J., Morgan, S. M., Love, E., Moody, S. B., & Feldman, M. L. (2021). Developing a system to support the advancement of women in higher education. *Journal of Faculty Development*, *35*(1), 34–42.

Bilmoria, D., Joy, S., & Liang, X. (2008). Breaking barriers and creating inclusiveness: Lessons of organizational transformation to advance women faculty in academic science and engineering. *Human Resource Management*, *47*(3), 423–441. doi:10.1002/hrm.20225

Blake, D. J. (2022). Gendered and racialized career sacrifices of women faculty accepting dual-c areer offers. *Journal of Women and Gender in Higher Education*, *15*(2), 113–133. doi:10.1080/26379112.2022.2067168

Bruckmuller, S., Ryan, M. K., Rink, F., & Haslam, S. A. (2014). Beyond the glass ceiling: The glass cliff and its lessons for organizational policy. *Social Issues and Policy Review*, *8*(1), 202–232. doi:10.1111/sipr.12006

Burke, R. J. (1984). Mentors in organizations. *Group & Organization Studies*, *9*(3), 195–207. doi:10.1177/105960118400900304

Carrigan, C., Quinn, K., & Riskin, E. A. (2011). The gendered division of labor among STEM faculty and the effects of critical mass. *Journal of Diversity in Higher Education*, *4*(3), 131–146. doi:10.1037/a0021831

Casad, B. J., Franks, J. E., Garasky, C. E., Kittleman, M. M., Roesler, A. C., Hall, D. Y., & Petzel, Z. W. (2020). Gender inequality in academia: Problems and solutions for women faculty in STEM. *Journal of Neuroscience Research*, *99*(1), 13–23. doi:10.1002/jnr.24631 PMID:33103281

Clance, P. R., & Imes, S. A. (1978). The imposter phenomenon in high achieving women: Dynamics and therapeutic intervention. *Psychotherapy (Chicago, Ill.)*, *15*(3), 241–247. doi:10.1037/h0086006

Coleman, M. (2010). Women-only (homophilous) networks supporting women leaders in education. *Journal of Educational Administration*, *48*(6), 769–781. doi:10.1108/09578231011079610

Culpepper, D., Kilmer, S., O'Meara, K., Misra, J. & Jaeger, A. J. (2020. The Terrapin time initiative: A workshop to enhance alignment between faculty work priorities and time- use. *Innovative Higher Education, 45,* 165-179. https://doi.org/ 09490-w

DesRoches, C. M. & Zinner, D. E., Rao, S. R., Lezzoni, L. I., & Campbell, E.G. (April 2010). Activities, productivity, and compensation of men and women in the life sciences. *Academic Medicine, 85*(4), 631-639. https://doi.org/ doi:10/1007/s10755-019-

Devine, P. G., Forscher, P. S., Austin, A. J., & Cox, W. T. L. (2012). Long-term reduction in implicit race bias: A prejudice habit-breaking intervention. *Journal of Experimental Social Psychology, 48*(6), 1267–1278. doi:10.1016/j.jesp.2012.06.003 PMID:23524616

Doucet, A. (2006). Estrogen-filled worlds: Fathers as primary caregivers and embodiment. *The Sociological Review, 54*(4), 696–716. doi:10.1111/j.1467-954X.2006.00667.x

Dreher, G. F., & Ash, R. A. (1990). A comparative study of mentoring among men and women in managerial, professional, and technical positions. *The Journal of Applied Psychology, 75*(5), 539–546. doi:10.1037/0021-9010.75.5.539

Drozdowski, M. J. (2022, February). The plight of adjunct faculty on America's campuses. *Best Colleges.* bestcolleges.com

Emerson, J. (2017). Don't give up on unconscious bias training – Make it better. *Harvard Business Review.* https://publicsector.sa.gov.au/modern-manager-series-making-better- decisions-unconscious-bias-at-work/

Fitzgerald, T. (2008). The continued politics of mistrust: Performance management and the erosion of professional work. *Journal of Educational Administration and History, 40*(2), 113–128. doi:10.1080/00220620802210871

Fitzgerald, T. (2014). *Women leaders in higher education: Shattering the myths.* Routledge.

Flaherty, C. (2020, April). Barely getting by: New report on adjuncts says many make less than $3500 per course and live in poverty. Inside Higher Ed. insidehighered.com

Foley, M., & Williamson, S. (2018). Managerial perspectives on implicit bias, affirmative action and merit. *Public Administration Review, 79*(1), 35–45. doi:10.1111/puar.12955

Francis, L., & Stulz, V. (2020). Barriers and facilitators for women academics seeking promotion. *Australian Universities Review, 62*(2), 47–60.

Gaucher, D., Friesen, J., & Kay, A. C. (2011). Evidence that gendered wording in job advertisements exists and sustains gender inequality. *Journal of Personality and Social Psychology*, *101*(1), 109–128. doi:10.1037/a0022530 PMID:21381851

Gorman, E. (2005). Gender stereotypes, same-gender preferences, and organizational variation in hiring women. *American Sociological Review*, *70*(4), 702–728. doi:10.1177/000312240507000408

Goulden, M., Mason, M. A., & Frasch, K. (2011). Keeping women in the science pipeline. *The Annals of the American Academy of Political and Social Science*, *638*(1), 141–162. Advance online publication. doi:10.1177/0002716211416925

Gvozdanovic, J., & Bailey, J. (2020). Unconscious bias in academia: A threat to meritocracy and what to do about it. In E. Drew & S. Canavan (Eds.), *The gender-sensitive university* (pp. 110–123). Routledge. doi:10.4324/9781003001348-9

Gvozdanovic, J., & Maes, K. (2018). Implicit bias in academia: A challenge to meritocratic principle and to women's careers—And what to do about it. League of European Research Universities (LERU). Leuven.

Hardy, A., McDonald, J., Guijt, R., Leane, E., Martin, A., James, A., Jones, M., Corban, M., & Green, B. (2016, June). Academic parenting: Work–family conflict and strategies across child age, disciplines and career level. *Studies in Higher Education*, *43*(4), 625–643. doi:10.1080/03075079.2016.1185777

Harris, A. (2019, April). The death of an adjunct. *Atlantic (Boston, Mass.)*.

Hart, J. (2008). Mobilization among women academics: The interplay between feminism and professionalization. *National Women's Studies Association (NWSA). Journal*, *20*(1), 184–208.

Henry, F., Dua, E., Kobayashi, A., James, C., Li, P., Ramos, H., & Smith, M. S. (2016). Race, rationalization and indigeneity in Canadian universities. *Race, Ethnicity and Education*, *20*(3), 300–314. doi:10.1080/13613324.2016.1260226

Higginbotham, A., Bellisari, A., Poston, M., Treichler, P., West, M., & Levy, A. (2011). Recommendations on partner accommodation and dual-career appointments (September 2010). *Academic Bulletin of the American Association of University Professors*, *97*(5), 81–87.

International Ombuds Association (2023). Ombursassociation.org/

IPEDS. (2013). Full-time instructional staff, by faculty and tenure status, academic rank, race/ethnicity, and gender (degree-granting institutions): Fall staff 2013 Survey. Washington, D.C.: National Center for Education Statistics, IPEDS (The Integrated Postsecondary Education Data System).

Juraqulova, Z. H., McCluskey, J. J., & Mittelhammer, R. C. (2019). Work-life policies and female faculty representation in US doctoral-granting economics departments. *Industrial Relations Journal*, *50*(2), 168–196. Advance online publication. doi:10.1111/irj.12246

Kachchaf, R., Ko, L., Hodari, A., & Ong, M. (2015). Career-life balance for women of color: Experiences in science and engineering academia. *Journal of Diversity in Higher Education*, *8*(3), 175–191. doi:10.1037/a0039068

Kezar, A. (2014). Higher education and social networks: A review of research. *The Journal of Higher Education*, *85*(1), 91–124. doi:10.1080/00221546.2014.11777320

Ledford, H. (2017). US postdocs face steep challenges when starting families. *Nature*. Advance online publication. doi:10.1038/nature.2017.22200

Lester, J. (2008). Performing gender in the workplace: Gender socialization, power, and identity among women faculty members. *Community College Review*, *35*(4), 227–305. doi:10.1177/0091552108314756

Lundine, J., Bourgeault, I. L., Clark, J., Heidari, S., & Balabanova, D. (2018, May 5). The gendered system of academic publishing. *Lancet*, *391*(10132), 1754–1756. doi:10.1016/S0140-6736(18)30950-4 PMID:29739551

Madera, J., Hebl, M., & Marn, R. (2009). Gender and letters of recommendation for academia: Agents and communal differences. *The Journal of Applied Psychology*, *94*(6), 1591–1599. doi:10.1037/a0016539 PMID:19916666

Madera, J. M., Hebl, M. R., Dial, H., Martin, R., & Valian, V. (2018). Raising doubt in letters of recommendation for academia: Gender differences and their impact. *Journal of Business and Psychology*, 1–17. doi:10.1007/s10869-018-9541-1

Magua, W., Zhu, X., Battacharya, A., Filut, A., Potvien, A., Leatherberry, R., ... Kaatz, A. (2017). Are female applicants disadvantaged in National Institutes of Health peer review? Combining algorithmic text mining and qualitative methods to detect evaluative differences in R01 reviewers' critiques. *Journal of Women's Health*, *26*(5), 560–570. doi:10.1089/jwh.2016.6021 PMID:28281870

Mathieu-Frasier, L. (2021). An outsider looking in: Advocating a sense of community for adjunct faculty. *Faculty Focus*. facultyfocus.com

McDermott, M., Gelb, D. J., Wilson, K., Pawloski, M., Burke, J. F., Shelgikar, A. V., & London, Z. N. (2018). Sex differences in academic rank and publication rate at top-ranked U.S. neurology programs. *JAMA Neurology, 75*(8), 956–961. doi:10.1001/jamaneurol.2018.0275 PMID:29610899

McEarcharn, M., Boswell, K., Chauhan, K., & Siereveld, S. O. (2019). Tenure clock policy transparency for biological clock (family friendly) events. *Administrative Issues Journal: Connecting Education, Practice, and Research, 9*(2), 28–41. doi:10.5929/9.2.4

McNeil, L., & Sher, M. (1999). The dual-career-couple problem. *Physics Today, 52*(7), 32–37. doi:10.1063/1.882719

Miller, D., Eagly, A., & Linn, M. (2015). Women's representation in science predicts national g ender-science stereotypes: Evidence from 66 nations. *Journal of Educational Psychology, 107*(3), 631–644. doi:10.1037/edu0000005

Mohr, T.S. (2014, August). Why women don't apply for jobs unless they're 100% qualified. *Harvard Business Review.* hbr.org

Morson, J. (2016). A delicate balance: The role of the ombuds in resolving campus conflict. *Advice and News.* https://www.higheredjobs.com/

Myerchin, A. D. (2014). Experiences of female faculty with maternity leave at four-year universities in an upper mid-west state. *Journal of the Communication. Speech & Theatre Association of North Dakota, 26*, 1–13.

National Center for Educational Statistics. (May 2019). Characteristics of post-secondary faculty. https://nces.ed.gov/programs/coe/indicator_csc.asp

Nelson, D. L., & Quick, J. C. (1985, April). Professional women: Are distress and disease inevitable? *Academy of Management Review, 10*(2), 206–218. doi:10.2307/257963 PMID:10300087

Nielson, M. (2016). Limits to meritocracy? Gender in academic recruitment and promotion policies. *Science & Public Policy, 43*(3), 386–399. doi:10.1093/scipol/scv052

O'Connor, P. (2011). Irish universities: Male dominated? Limits and possibilities for change? *Equality, Diversity and Inclusion, 31*(1), 83–96. doi:10.1108/02610151211199236

O'Meara, K., Culpepper, D., Misra, J., & Jaeger, A. (2021). Equity-minded faculty work-loads: What we can and should do now. ACE. https://www.acenet.edu/Documents/Equity- Minded-Faculty-Workloads.pdf

O'Meara, K. & Stromquist, N.P. (2015). Faculty peer networks: Role and relevance in advancing agency and gender equity. *Gender and Education, 27*(3)m 338-358. doi:10.1080/09540253.2015.1027668

Oates, M. (2023, March). How it works: Gender equity in higher education. *Academic Diversity Search.* academicdiversitysearch.com

Porter, J., & Oliver, R. (2015). Rethinking lactation space: Working mothers, working bodies, and the politics of inclusion. *Space and Culture, 19*(1), 80–93. doi:10.1177/1206331215596488

Prime, J., & Moss-Racusin, C. A. (2009). Engaging men in gender initiatives: What change agents need to know. *Catalyst : Feminism, Theory, Technoscience.*

Prime, J., Moss-Racusin, C. A., & Foust-Cummings, H. (2009). Engaging men in gender initiatives: Stacking the deck for success. *Catalyst : Feminism, Theory, Technoscience.*

Pyke, J. (2013). Women, choice and promotion or why women are still a minority in the professoriate. *Journal of Higher Education Policy and Management, 35*(4), 444–454. doi:10.1080/1360080X.2013.812179

Resmini, M. (2016). The "leaky pipeline.". *Chemistry (Weinheim an der Bergstrasse, Germany), 22*(11), 3533–3534. doi:10.1002/chem.201600292 PMID:26878818

Rhoades, G. (2013). Adjunct professors are the new working poor. *CNN.* cnn.com

Rice, C. (2012). Why women leave academia and why universities should be worried. *The Guardian.* theguardian.com

Riley, S., & Wrench, D. (1985). Mentoring among women lawyers. *Journal of Applied Social Psychology, 15*(4), 374–386. doi:10.1111/j.1559-1816.1985.tb00913.x

Royal Society. (2015) *Unconscious bias briefing (Prof Uta Frith).* https://royalsociety.org/~/media/policy/Publications/2015/unconscious-bias-briefing-2015.pdf

Rubin, L. (2023). Faculty ombudsperson: Mission statement. Texas Woman's University. twu.edu

Savigny, H. (2014). Women, know your limits: Cultural sexism in academia. *Gender and Education, 26*(7), 794–809. doi:10.1080/09540253.2014.970977

Schell, E. E. (1997). Gypsy academics and mother-teachers: Gender, contingent labor, and writing instruction. *Cross Currents.*

Schiebinger, L. L., Henderson, A. D., & Gilmarting, S. K. (2008). Dual-career academic couples: What universities need to know. Michelle R. Clayman Institute for Gender Research, Stanford University.

Smith, M. (2016). Adjunct faculty union advocates for rights. *New York University.* nyunews.com

Stepan-Norris, J., & Kerrissey, J. (2016). Enhancing gender equity in academia: Lessons from the ADVANCE program. *Sociological Perspectives, 59*(2), 225–245. doi:10.1177/0731121415582103

Tamtik, M., & Guenter, M. (2019). Policy analysis of equity, diversity and inclusion strategies in Canadian universities – How far have we come? *Canadian Journal of Higher Education, 49*(3), 41–56. doi:10.47678/cjhe.v49i3.188529

Tolley, K. (2018). Why we should care about the unionization of adjunct faculty in higher ed. *Johns Hopkins University Press.* press.jhu.edu

Vilar-Compte, M., Hernandez-Cordero, S., Ancira-Moreno, M., Burrola-Mendez, S., Ferre-Eguiluz, I., Omaña, I., & Pérez Navarro, C. (2021). Breastfeeding at the workplace: A systematic review of interventions to improve workplace environments to facilitate breastfeeding among working women. *International Journal for Equity in Health, 20*(1), 110. doi:10.1186/s12939-021-01432-3 PMID:33926471

Wilson, R. (2003). Baby, baby, baby. *The Chronicle of Higher Education, 49*(25), A10.

Winter, J., & Pauwels, A. (2006). Men staying at home looking after their children: Feminist linguistic reform and social change. *International Journal of Applied Linguistics, 16*(1), 16–36. doi:10.1111/j.1473-4192.2006.00104.x

Wright, C. A., & Wright, S. D. (1987). The role of mentors in the career development of young professionals. *Family Relations, 36*(2), 204–208. doi:10.2307/583955

Young, C. J., MacKenzie, D. L., & Sherif, C. W. (1982). In search of token women in academia: Some definitions and clarifications. *Psychology of Women Quarterly, 7*(2), 166–169.

Ysseldyk, R., Greenaway, K. H., Hassinger, E., Zutrauen, S., Lintz, J., Bhatia, M. P., Frye, M., Starkenburg, E., & Tai, V. (2019). A leak in the academic pipeline: Identity and health among postdoctoral women. *Frontiers in Psychology, 10*, 1297. Advance online publication. doi:10.3389/fpsyg.2019.01297 PMID:31231285

Chapter 7
Advocating for Quota System as a Model for Women's Participation in Political Affairs in Southern Africa:
The case of Zimbabwe

Menard Musendekwa
https://orcid.org/0000-0002-6644-8727
Reformed Church University, Zimbabwe

ABSTRACT

Despite the advent of gender-based policies and initiatives that have tended to dominate the participatory discourse both nationally and internationally, the literature on women and gender emphasises the slow pace of transition and development (Mapuva 2013). Severe decline of women participation in political affairs in Zimbabwe since 2008 may be indicators that women are continually drifting into the margins as far as politics is concerned. This research proposes that advocacy full implementation of Quota System (QS) may increase women participation in political affairs .The research is a historical reflection of advocacy towards women participation in political affairs in Zimbabwe as the case for Southern Africa.

DOI: 10.4018/979-8-3693-0102-9.ch007

INTRODUCTION

Research on women and gender emphasizes how slowly things are changing, even despite the implementation of gender-based laws and practices that tend to dominate the national and international participatory discourse (Mapuva, 2013).

According to Madeleine Albright, "success without democracy is improbable and democracy without women is impossible" (National Democratic Institute for International Affairs [NDI], 2010, p. 12). Democratic principles should, therefore, always provide equal opportunity between men and women to perpetuate democratic governance. States that profess to be proponents of democracy but fail to provide sufficient space for women lack integrity. The recognition that women's empowerment is a necessary condition for women's growth serves as the foundation for gender equality in society. The equality of men and women, women's rights to realize their full potential, and their right to self-determination and self-representation are the cornerstones of women's political empowerment (Fadia, 2014). According to Ajogbeje (2016), the limited representation of women in politics stems from the limited view on accommodating women in these domains, thereby questioning the integrity of democracy in those states that claim to be democratic.

The United Nations (UN) General Assembly passed 'The Convention on the Elimination of All Forms of Discrimination against Women (CEDAW)' in 1979. The bill is frequently referred to as a worldwide bill of rights for ending discrimination of any form against women and increasing their participation in political affairs. State commitments included the following: 1) incorporating the principle of equality between men and women into their legal systems; 2) establishing tribunals and other public institutions to ensure the effective protection of women against discrimination; and 3) ensuring the abolition of all acts of discrimination against women by individuals, groups, or businesses (Tufekci & Hashiru, 2019).

According to Tufekci and Hashiru (2019), emerging powers have also expressed concern over the empowerment of women. For example, in 2016, the BRICS nations—Brazil, Russia, India, China, and South Africa—organized the 8th BRICS summit in Goa, India, with the subject "Building Responsive, Inclusive, Collective Solution." In addition, they founded BRICS Feminist Watch. Preambles 32, 99, and 100 of the Johannesburg Declaration from the 10th BRICS Summit in July 2018 reaffirm the rising states' commitment to ensuring women's political engagement and empowerment in their member states. For example, Preamble 99 alludes to the way forward to further strengthening of BRICS exchanges in this regard, including of women parliamentarians. Such efforts by emerging powers indicate that women's participation in political affairs has been a global challenge. More than half of the world's population is female, but in many nations, women's involvement in the political and governing processes, where decisions about their lives are made, is minimal. Zimbabwe is also no exception to this global pattern.

THEORETICAL CONSIDERATIONS

The research applies The Structural Violence Approach (SVA). SVA is a methodology that focuses on how social factors such as poverty, peer pressure, gender inequality, and economic hardships, along with social structures like politics, religion, the economy, culture, and tradition, limit, harm, and shape people in society (Galtung, 1969). In a similar vein, Ho (2007) argues that structural violence demonstrates how systemic injustices routinely deny certain people access to fundamental necessities and human rights. The research focuses on gender imbalances in politics that have stimulated the development and application of policies that may address those imbalances.

Ho (2007) asserts that structural violence arises when certain classes, genders, nationalities, and other groups are presumed to have—and in fact do—more access to opportunities, resources, and goods than other classes, genders, nationalities, and other groups; this unfair advantage is ingrained in the social, political, and economic systems that control societies, states, and the global economy. Ho (2007) concurs that structural violence theorists characterize violence as the preventable discrepancy between one's capacity and actual satisfaction of one's basic needs.

Using Zimbabwe as a case study, structural violence served as a starting point for my evaluation of the quota system as a model for addressing women's participation in political affairs in Southern Africa. Gender inequality contributes to the fact that many women become victims of structural violence, as Farmer (1999) highlights. The study assesses how much political strategies like the quota system can aid in removing barriers to women's involvement in politics.

DEFINING QUOTA SYSTEM

The Quota System for Women can be defined as a method of ensuring proportional representation of women and men in Parliament. Initially, six female representatives were appointed from each of the ten provinces into the parliament, despite not being specifically voted for (Geisler, 1995). Appointing women for the sake of mere representation may not be sufficient. Such appointments may lack objectivity in a multi-party democratically elected government. Instead, each party should nominate their female candidates for election.

The Quota System in Southern Africa: A Catalyst for Women's Political Representation

The quota system has emerged as a pivotal mechanism aimed at enhancing women's political representation worldwide. Particularly in Southern Africa, where gender disparities in political leadership persist, the quota system has garnered attention as a potential solution to address these inequalities. This paper explores the implementation and effectiveness of the quota system in Southern Africa, drawing on case studies from the region.

In many Southern African countries, women remain significantly underrepresented in political decision-making processes, despite their substantial contributions to society. Factors such as patriarchal norms, socio-cultural barriers, and institutionalized sexism have historically hindered women's access to political power. The quota system, with its aim to reserve a certain percentage of political seats for women, seeks to counteract these barriers and promote gender equality in politics.

One example is Rwanda which is often hailed as a success story for gender parity in politics, Rwanda has made significant strides in women's representation through the quota system. Following the 1994 genocide, which left the country with a predominantly female population, Rwanda implemented a constitutional provision requiring at least 30% of parliamentary seats to be held by women. This quota was later increased to 50%, leading to Rwanda's ranking as the country with the highest proportion of women in parliament globally (Tripp, 2015).

Another important example to note is South Africa. Despite being a beacon of democracy in the region, South Africa still faces challenges in achieving gender parity in politics. The African National Congress (ANC), South Africa's ruling party, has implemented a voluntary party quota system, reserving 50% of its seats for women candidates. While this has increased women's representation within the ANC, women remain underrepresented in other political parties and governmental institutions (Hassim, 2019).

The last example given in this paper is Zimbabwe which is given more attention in this chapter. In Zimbabwe, efforts to increase women's political representation have been met with mixed results. The country's 2013 Constitution mandated a 30% quota for women in parliament, resulting in a notable increase in women's participation. However, challenges such as patriarchal attitudes, electoral violence, and limited access to resources continue to impede women's full political inclusion (Moyo, 2017).

Roots of Women's Participation in Political Affairs in Zimbabwe

Mbuya Nehanda's assertion that "our bones will rise" (*mapfupa edu achamuka*) symbolizes the spirit that animated the liberation struggle (Fontein, 2006:141). The desire to belong and contribute to future generations inspired acts of selflessness. For individuals whose wisdom transcends mortality and whose influence extends into eternity, death signifies not an end but a continuation. For those whose selfless sacrifices pave the way for the next generation, life extends beyond death, rendering the phrase "mafupa achamuka" apt.

Women in Zimbabwe were afforded an opportunity to challenge the colonial stereotype dictating their subservience to husbands, motherhood, and passive daughterhood during and after the liberation struggle. It is crucial to note that even women who did not directly engage in combat made invaluable contributions to the cause by providing logistical, material, and emotional support to the liberation fighters (Gudhlanga, 2013).

Seidman (1984) revealed that the influx of settlers brought with them British cultural norms steeped in inequality throughout the 19th century. Colonial administrators crafted regulations that portrayed women as dependent on their husbands and fathers. Colonial policymakers primarily viewed women as mothers, relegating them to the role of caregivers while men assumed the role of family providers, a stark departure from precolonial society where women served as both producers and reproducers.

The divergent treatment of boys and girls within colonial educational programs exemplifies how colonial administrators imposed their notions of women's societal roles on Zimbabwean society. Despite limited access to education for black individuals, girls were significantly less likely than boys to complete formal schooling (Seidman, 1984).

During the liberation struggle, various strategies were employed to encourage women and girls to participate actively. One such strategy emerged from the spiritual guidance of Mbuya Nehanda. Fontein (2006) notes that Nehanda played a central role in educating guerrilla youth, and her voluntary martyrdom by hanging in 1897 ignited the uprising. Her sacrificial act instilled a sense of commitment in new recruits, who viewed themselves as the resurrected bones she prophesied. Despite debates about the historical authenticity of ancient mythological figures, many women found inspiration in identifying with them, perpetuating their role in Zimbabwe's liberation history.

Zimbabwean youth who joined the liberation struggle were educated about colonial oppression and the heroic resistance of their ancestors. The symbolic hanging of statues depicting Mbuya Nehanda and Sekuru Kaguvi by colonial settlers served as a rallying cry for subsequent generations (Fontein, 2006). Despite their limited resources, these resistance fighters set an example through their selfless sacrifices for the future benefit of the entire nation. Their legacy serves as a reminder for present-day Zimbabweans to honor and continue the struggle initiated by their forebears.

Mwari shrines were also utilized to invoke nationalist myths, incorporating folklore associated with spirit mediums. These myths provided historical precedent, revived memories of past liberation battles, and mobilized the masses to support the quest for independence (Fontein, 2006). Thus, every individual, regardless of gender, is entitled to freedom.

Ultimately, the intellectual legacy of the liberation struggle was believed to determine the nation's leadership. Mbuya Nehanda was purported to have anointed Mugabe, validating his position as the unyielding leader (Musendekwa, 2011). Despite suggestions by Canaan Banana to incorporate national heroes' names into biblical narratives, Mugabe's eventual successor, Mnangagwa, continued to honor Mbuya Nehanda by erecting a statue in Harare.

As Nehanda is revered as revered ancestor spirit, the ruling party assumed the role of custodian of liberation narratives to validate their continuation of the struggle during the second Chimurenga. Mnangagwa's construction of the statue symbolizes his alignment with Nehanda's spirit, akin to Mugabe's connection. However, the failure to reinstate the second vice presidency, initially held by a female liberation fighter during Mugabe's tenure, marks a setback. Efforts to emphasize the quota system appear to have become problematic.

For many women, participation in the struggle for freedom signified a step toward national and personal liberation. By the end of the liberation struggle, thousands of women had enlisted in the military, constituting up to 25% of the 30,000 guerrillas who fought for ZANU-PF (Seidman, 1984).

Commander Teurai Ropa Nhongo, also known as "Spiller of Blood," gained widespread recognition across the country. According to Nhongo, assuming a command role allowed women to shed their inhibitions, and overcoming various challenges independently contributed to personal growth. In a departure from tradition, some women even led squads comprising both men and women (Seidman, 1984). Eventually, Nhongo was acknowledged by Mugabe and appointed as Vice-President.

Hamandishe (2018) emphasizes that Zimbabwe, as a signatory to numerous declarations promoting women's leadership, possesses a legal framework prioritizing gender equality and equity in politics. With the implementation of a quota system reserving 60 seats for women in proportion to the population under Zimbabwe's 2013 Constitution, the representation of women in parliament increased from 16% to 34%. This positive trend complements the constituency-based electoral system, which some view as highly competitive and unwelcoming to aspiring female lawmakers.

The quota system, set to expire in 2023 and not applicable to municipal government, lacks specific guidelines for integrating women. Thus, it appears that the political elite have yet to fully embrace gender equality and women's empowerment. However, if revised and made a permanent provision before the 2023 elections, proportional representation could be reinstated in the future.

Prior to the 2018 elections, only 33.2% of women were represented in Zimbabwe's National Assembly. The relationship between gender inequality and political engagement remains a critical consideration, particularly in light of upcoming harmonized elections. Despite constitutional mandates for gender parity and equal political opportunities, patriarchal attitudes persist, and political parties seem reluctant to adopt affirmative measures to promote gender equality.

According to Zikhali (2018), women in Zimbabwe, particularly within the ruling ZANU-PF party, are frequently visible at political rallies, events, and public spaces. Their active participation in singing and dancing distinguishes them, indicating their deep involvement in party politics and Zimbabwean politics as a whole. While such visible displays of support are often cited as evidence of women's political engagement since the liberation struggle, their representation in elite positions remains disproportionately low, constituting only 20% of the total upper and lower houses.

According to Zikhali (2018), women are now more represented on the African continent than they were before the Convention on the Elimination of All Forms of Discrimination Against Women (CEDAW). Because it promoted the 30% affirmative action of women in political and decision-making roles by the year 2005, CEDAW is a crucial step in the search for equality and equity in the political sphere. Sadly, most governments have failed to put the principles into practice after adopting them in rhetoric. This is true despite the fact that quota laws, permissive election systems like parliamentary representation, and egalitarian political cultures have all come together to contribute to significant changes on the continent.

Since the 2008 elections, when women's representation at the local level stood at 18%, there has been a decline in the number of women serving in local government in Zimbabwe. It dropped to 16% in 2013 and by an additional 2% in the election of 2018 to reach 14%. With the introduction of a Constitutional amendment in parliament, the fight for a quota for women in local government in Zimbabwe intensified by April 19, 2021. With 30% of seats reserved for women and divided according to Proportional Representation (PR), this aims to transfer the system in existence at the national level to the local level. The modifications, according to the Minister of Justice, Legal, and Parliamentary Affairs Ziyambi Ziyambi, would suggest a two-term maximum, as is the case with National Assembly proportional representation, and evaluate whether planned goals would have been accomplished. To put this policy orientation into reality, he declared, "we need legislation." President Emmerson Mnangagwa of Zimbabwe and his cabinet announced their full support and approval of a 30% women's quota at the local level in the country following the first-ever Women Councillors Indaba hosted by the Zimbabwe Local

Government Authority (ZiLGA), Women in Local Government Forum (WILGF), and Gender Links (GL) in December 2020. Since the adoption of a new constitution in 2013, Zimbabwe has had a legislated quota of 60 seats distributed among parties on a PR basis at the national level, in addition to the 210 seats open to women and men in the constituency or First Past the Post (FPTP) seats. Although Article 17 of the Constitution provides for equal representation of women and men in all areas of decision-making, local government is presently not included in the Constitutional quota. In the past ten years, GL is recognized with bringing gender issues to the attention of local governments all around the SADC region. At the Coalface: Gender and Local Government in Southern Africa, a groundbreaking study, served as the foundation for this work. The study inspired GL to collaborate with approximately 400 councils in ten nations that chose to establish themselves as Centres of Excellence for gender in local government activity. This was made possible by constant engagement with like-minded organizations and stakeholders through the use of different strategies, including UNWOMEN, the Ministry of Local Government and Public Works, the Ministry of Justice, the Zimbabwe Electoral Commission (ZEC), the Zimbabwe Local Government Association, the Women in Local Government Forum, civil society organizations, and the media. A similar effort by GL in Mauritius in 2012 resulted in a "gender-neutral" local government quota for women of at least one third of either sex running in local elections. In 2013, women's presence in local government in Mauritius increased by a factor of four, from 6% to 24%.

The tenets of democratic government and human rights, according to Hamandishe (2018), are predicated on the idea of equitable involvement by all citizens in any nation. For this reason, it's critical that women have fair representation and meaningful participation in all parts of governance.

ADVANTAGES AND DISADVANTAGES OF QUOTA SYSTEM

While the quota system has facilitated notable progress in women's political representation in Southern Africa, several challenges persist. Resistance from male-dominated political structures, tokenism, and a lack of enforcement mechanisms undermine the effectiveness of quota systems. Additionally, quotas alone cannot address deep-rooted gender inequalities and societal attitudes towards women in leadership roles.

However, the quota system also presents opportunities for transformative change. By providing women with access to political power, quotas can amplify their voices, priorities, and interests in decision-making processes. Moreover, quotas serve as a catalyst for broader societal shifts towards gender equality, challenging traditional notions of leadership and paving the way for more inclusive political systems.

Gaidzanwa (2006) highlights both the advantages and disadvantages of the quota system in political representation. One of the advantages of the quota system is its role in ensuring adequate representation of women in local and parliamentary councils (Gaidzanwa, 2006). By mandating a certain proportion of seats for women, the quota system addresses the historical underrepresentation of women in decision-making bodies. Moreover, this increased presence of women has facilitated heightened awareness of gender issues among legislators and policymakers. Additionally, the quota system has the potential to elevate the proportion of women in cabinet positions, thereby promoting gender diversity in leadership roles. Furthermore, by showcasing women as capable leaders, Members of Parliament (MPs) serve as role models, challenging misconceptions about women's competence in positions of authority and public accountability.

However, Gaidzanwa (2006) also delineates several disadvantages associated with the quota system. Firstly, the system perpetuates the misconception that women are inherently less competent than men, as it implies that women require special measures to compete with their male counterparts. Moreover, women legislators often lack the necessary networks, resources, and support systems to effectively fulfill their duties, undermining their effectiveness in office. Additionally, the quota system may inadvertently admit unqualified women into parliament, prioritizing numerical representation over qualifications. This quantitative emphasis may compromise the qualitative contributions of women in politics, potentially undermining the credibility of parliamentary proceedings. Furthermore, while the quota system addresses the numerical deficit of women in politics, it may not sufficiently dismantle the systemic barriers that impede women's (and men's) entry into political spheres.

Financial constraints pose a significant challenge for female politicians, as highlighted by Gaidzanwa (2006). Candidates, particularly in the Zimbabwean context, must finance their campaigns independently, including expenses for themselves and their campaign teams during primaries. Intense competition for seats exacerbates financial pressures, disproportionately affecting low-income individuals. Rising inflation rates further inflate campaign costs, particularly for essential items such as campaign materials. Consequently, financially privileged individuals, including young businessmen, increasingly dominate political candidacy, perpetuating inequities in political representation.

Moreover, Gaidzanwa (2006) underscores the additional financial burdens faced by candidates in rural constituencies, where infrastructure deficiencies compound logistical challenges. Candidates must navigate extensive travel distances and endure fatigue to attend campaign-related events, further straining their financial resources. Additionally, female candidates, balancing campaign responsibilities with household duties, incur additional financial costs and experience heightened vulnerability to burnout.

Furthermore, Gaidzanwa (2006) highlights the prevalence of gender-based hostility towards female candidates, particularly in traditional rural communities. Female candidates encounter verbal abuse and harassment from male colleagues and constituents, who often exploit private details to undermine their candidacy. Widowed, divorced, or single women face heightened scrutiny and stigmatization, further impeding their electoral prospects. Consequently, female candidates, especially those lacking established reputations, are vulnerable to exploitation by male counterparts seeking to secure electoral advantages.

In summary, while the quota system offers potential benefits in promoting gender parity in political representation, its implementation entails various challenges, including perpetuating gender stereotypes, exacerbating financial disparities, and exposing female candidates to gender-based hostility and exploitation.

Manifestoes for Women Participation

Rudo Gaidzanwa (2006) reported that the 2000 parliamentary elections witnessed the highest number of female candidates vying for office in Zimbabwe's history. One hundred forty-five women contested for 120 seats in the national assembly, representing five political parties. However, only 14 (or 25%) of the 55 candidates were elected. Compared to the outcome of the 1995 election, where women held 22% of the 150 parliamentary seats, this figure represents a mere 9.3% of the total. Women's groups expressed disappointment with this result, especially considering their efforts to mobilize support for female candidates and promote a women's agenda at a higher political level. However, it is essential to question the assumption that supporting female politicians is inherently desirable and that women must be educated about its importance (Gaidzanwa, 2006).

Ten women were nominated by Zimbabwe's newest opposition group, the MDC. However, it is crucial to note that many women dropped out of the race after the initial phase, underscoring the need for policies aimed at increasing the number of female candidates while ensuring their equal electoral opportunities (Gaidzanwa, 2006).

Given that women constitute the majority of voters (52%), it is anticipated that there would be a proportionately high number of female candidates. However, this expectation has not been met, leading to doubts about political parties' commitment to women's political empowerment (Zimbabwe Elections Observer Mission Report, undated).

Chinowaita (undated) argues that every society striving to rectify historical inequalities among its citizens requires a quota system to elevate women to the same level as men, who historically enjoyed unfair advantages over their female counterparts. The gender composition of party leaders and the procedures for selecting parliamentary candidates are cited as the primary factors hindering women's participation in politics in Zimbabwe. Men typically dominate these processes, limiting women's influence (Chinowaita, undated).

In the lead-up to the 2000 parliamentary elections, the ZANU-PF Women's League mandated that for every three positions held by men in the party, one must be filled by an elected female member. This decision was justified on the basis that societies aiming to address historical disparities must implement quota systems to ensure equal opportunities for women (Hungwe, 2000).

Prior to the 2000 election, Learnmore Jongwe, the MDC's secretary for information and publicity, asserted that women's prospects of holding elected office and prominent positions within their parties depended on party support and their own efforts. This highlights the importance of party programs and individual initiatives in determining women's success (Chinowaita, undated).

However, some male politicians have contested the notion of equal opportunities for women, arguing against preferences based on gender. Such remarks undermine the necessity of quota systems and emphasize the need for women to compete on merit alone (Chinowata, undated).

Gaidzanwa (2004) noted that the SADC Declaration on Gender and Development aimed to achieve at least 30% representation of women in positions of authority within political and decision-making organizations by 2005. Achieving this goal would require legislative and constitutional quotas, as well as electoral systems that ensure women's electoral success. The debate surrounding gender quotas, their benefits, and drawbacks has been ongoing, with increasing momentum since the adoption of the SADC Declaration on Gender and Development in 1997.

EVALUATIONS AND CONCLUSIONS

The nation needs more than just a framework for gender-sensitive legislation—it also needs the political will of people in positions of authority—to achieve meaningful representation of women in Parliament. According to the makeup of the candidates for the 2018 elections, political parties have mostly disregarded their pledge to gender parity. Despite developing sound ideas, Zimbabwean political parties have been unable to put them into action because they continue to let other 'political' factors dominate the selection of candidates. Only 27 of the 47 political parties with candidates for the National Assembly fielded at least one woman. Women make up 243 out of the 1 652 candidates running for the National Assembly, or around 15%, and 146 out of the 290 candidates running for the Senate. There were 40 candidates from political parties running for local authority positions, 12 of which were all men. Of the 6796 candidates, 17% are women and 83% are men.

In addition to a thorough legal framework, ensuring gender equality in Zimbabwe's political and electoral domains calls for the cooperation of important state and non-state actors. These include the Zimbabwe Electoral Commission (ZEC), the courts, government departments, gender-focused statutory commissions, the civil society, and Parliament. Some of these, particularly the civil society, have been important allies in the fight for equal political representation, peaceful elections, and institutional and legal protections that would ensure the full involvement of women.

The quota system remains a vital tool for promoting women's political representation in Southern Africa. While its implementation has yielded significant gains, ongoing efforts are needed to overcome challenges and ensure the meaningful participation of women in politics. By addressing structural barriers, fostering political will, and promoting gender-sensitive policies, Southern African countries can harness the potential of the quota system to advance gender equality and democratic governance.

REFERENCES

Ajogbeje, T. O. (2016). Women political participation and decision-making in Nigeria: The case of Edo State House of Assembly. *African Journal of Political Science and International Relations, 10*(9), 234–245.

Chinowaita, M. (undated). Does affirmative action benefit women? *Standard Online,* <www.samara.co.zw/standard>

Chinowaita, M. (undated). Organisation aims to politically empower women, Standard *Online,* <http:// www.samara.co.zw/standard/index>

Fadia, B. (2014). *Gender politics in global governance.* Routledge.

Farmer, P. (1999). *Pathologies of Power: Health, Human Rights, and the New War on the Poor.* University of California Press.

Fontein, J. (2006). *The Silence of Great Zimbabwe.* Weaver Press.

Galtung, J. (1969). Violence, peace, and peace research. *Journal of Peace Research, 6*(3), 167–191. doi:10.1177/002234336900600301

Geisler, G. (1995). Troubled sisterhood: women and politics in Southern Africa: case studies from Zambia, Zimbabwe and Botswana. *African Affairs, 94*(377), 545–578. doi:10.1093/oxfordjournals.afraf.a098873

Gudhlanga, E. (2013). Shutting them out: Opportunities and challenges of women's participation in Zimbabwean politics-a historical perspective. *Journal of Third World Studies*, *30*(1), 151–170.

Hamandishe, A. (2018). Rethinking women's political participation in Zimbabwe's elections. *Democracy (New York, N.Y.)*, *27*(4).

Hamandishe, T. (2018). Equitable participation in democratic governance: The role of women. *Journal of Democracy and Human Rights*, *15*(2), 78–89.

Hassim, S. (2019). Women's representation in South Africa's national and provincial legislatures: Lessons from the African National Congress' voluntary party quotas. *Women's Studies International Forum*, *73*, 130–137.

Ho, C. (2007). Understanding Structural Violence: A Social Structural Analysis. *Peace Review*, *19*(3), 331–337.

Ho, K. (2007). Structural violence as a human rights violation. *Essex Human Rights Review*, *4*(2), 1–17.

Hungwe, B. 2000. Women's League threatens to boycott congress, *Zimbabwe Independent,* 19 November 2000, <http://www.samara.co.zw/zimin/index>

Jephias, M. (2013). The feminist discourse and the development of a civic virtue in Zimbabwe: Case of Women of Zimbabwe Arise (WOZA). *Journal of African Studies and Development*, *5*(8), 261–270.

Mapuva, J. (2013). Women in politics: Zimbabwean perspective. In *Conference Paper of the Women's Global Leadership in Africa: Expanding the African Women's Voice and Visibility in Global Leadership*, Victoria Falls, Zimbabwe.

Moyo, S. (2017). Gender quotas, empowerment, and women's political participation in Zimbabwe. *Journal of African Elections*, *16*(1), 123–139.

Musendekwa, M. 2011. *Messianic expectations as prophetic responses to crises: a Zimbabwean perspective.* MTh Thesis, University of Stellenbosch, Stellenbosch.

Musendekwa, M. 2018. Messianic characterisation of Mugabe as rhetorical propaganda to legitimise his authority in crisis situations. *SHE* 44/3, 1-17. https://upjournals.co.za/index.php/SHE/ index.

National Democratic Institute for International Affairs. (2010). *Democracy and the Challenge of Change: A Guide to Increasing Women's Political Participation.* Washington: National Democratic Institute National Democratic Institute for International Affairs. (2010). *The role of women in political parties.* https://www.ndi.org/sites/default/files/The_Role_of_Women_in_Political_Parties.pdf

Seidman, G. W. (1984). Women in Zimbabwe: Postindependence Struggles. *Feminist Studies, 10*(3), 419–440. doi:10.2307/3178033

Tichagwa, W. 1998. in P Maramba (ed) Beyond inequalities: Women in Zimbabwe. Waldahl, R. 2004. Politics and persuasion: Media coverage of Zimbabwe's 2000 election. Avondale: Weaver Press.

Tripp, A. M. (2015). Rwanda: Women in post-genocide politics. In Women and Power in Postconflict Africa. Cambridge University Press.

Tufekci, O., & Hashiru, I. (2019). The Convention on the Elimination of All Forms of Discrimination against Women: A shift towards the empowerment of women in Africa. *Journal of Women's Empowerment, 3*(2), 98–115.

Tufekci, O., & Hashiru, M. (2019). Women Empowerment through Political Participation in Rising Powers: Comparison of Turkey and Nigeria. In M. İnce Yenilmez & O. B. Çelik (Eds.), *A Comparative Perspective of Women's Economic Empowerment* (pp. 219–233). Routledge. doi:10.4324/9780429053146-13

Zikhali, A. (2018). Women's representation in African politics: A review post-CEDAW. *Journal of African Politics, 20*(3), 45–56.

Chapter 8
Hispanic Women Professors in Higher Education in the US

Antonio Daniel Juan Rubio
https://orcid.org/0000-0003-3416-0021
Universidad de Granada, Spain

Jimmy Hernandez
Hispanic Association of Colleges and Universities, USA

ABSTRACT

Although the Hispanic population has become the largest minority group in the United States, this fact has not been reflected in their presence as tenured or non-tenured professors at the country's colleges and universities. And this is especially aggravated in the case of Hispanic females. The decreasing number of Hispanic female professors in Higher Education in the United States foretells this delicate situation. A major concern associated with the Hispanics' lack of involvement in higher education is the seeming lack of awareness among the general population that such a problem exists. Therefore, the objective of this chapter is to examine some specific outstanding and representative cases. Hispanic women professors continue to remain underrepresented in faculty and leadership position in the country.

INTRODUCTION

Although the Hispanic population has already become the largest minority group in the United States, this fact has not been reflected in their presence as tenured or non-tenured professors at the country's colleges and universities (Lacomba, 2022). This is especially aggravated in the case of Hispanic females (Mora, 2022). The

DOI: 10.4018/979-8-3693-0102-9.ch008

Copyright © 2024, IGI Global. Copying or distributing in print or electronic forms without written permission of IGI Global is prohibited.

decreasing number of Hispanic female professors in Higher Education in the United States foretells this delicate situation.

A major concern that is typically associated with the Hispanics' lack of involvement in higher education is the seeming lack of awareness among the general population that such a problem exists (Scherer & Mayol García, 2022). In general terms, Hispanic groups have yet to attain recognition of the existence of educational barriers for them on most US campuses (Krogstad et al., 2022).

Therefore, the objective of this chapter is to examine why there are so few Hispanic women in Higher Education in the United States as well as to research on some specific outstanding and representative cases. Despite the increase in their representation among college and university employees, Hispanic women professors continue to be underrepresented in faculty and leadership positions in the country.

Diana Natalicio (1939-2021) was an American academic administrator who served as the 10th president of the University of Texas at El Paso (UTEP) from 1988 to 2019. After growing up in St. Louis, Natalicio studied Spanish as an undergraduate, completed a master's degree in Portuguese, and earned a PhD in linguistics. She became an assistant professor at UTEP in 1971 and was named the university's first female president in 1988.

As a sign of her relevance, her 31-year tenure in the university's highest office stood as the sixth longest of any doctoral/research university president in history at the time of her retirement. It was also the longest term for a female president of a four-year public university at the time. Sadly, Diana Natalicio died in El Paso on September 24, 2021.

Before taking the helm as president, during her long and distinguished career at the university, Natalicio also served as vice president for academic affairs, dean of liberal arts, chair of the Department of Modern Languages, and professor of linguistics, among other academic appointments. The University of Texas System Board of Regents named her President Emerita in August 2019 in recognition of her outstanding career. According to Contreras et al. (2018), this clearly reflects the excellence of her resume and professional worth.

Her sustained commitment to providing all residents of the Paso del Norte region with access to excellent higher education opportunities helped make the UTEP a truly national success story. In addition, she was honored to have been the first woman, and therefore of Hispanic origin, to hold such a prominent position in higher education in the United States (Arciniega, 2012).

Natalicio served on numerous boards, including the Hispanic Scholarship Fund (HSF), the Rockefeller Foundation, Trinity Industries, Sandia Corporation, US-Mexico Foundation for Science (FUMEC), American Council on Education, National Action Council for Minorities in Engineering (NACME), and the Association of Public and Land-grant Universities (APLU). Besides, she was appointed by President

George H.W. Bush to membership on the Advisory Commission on Educational Excellence for Hispanic Americans and by President Bill Clinton to the National Science Board (NSB), where she served two six-year terms including three two-year terms as NSB vice-chair.

During Natalicio's tenure as president of the institution, UTEP's enrolment grew from 15,000 to nearly 24,000 students, reflecting the demographics of the Paso del Norte region, from which nearly 90% of them hail. More than 80% are Mexican American, and the other 5% travel to campus from Ciudad Juarez, Mexico (Nora & Crisp, 2019).

In addition, since 1988, UTEP's annual budget has steadily increased from $65 million to nearly $471 million, a seven-fold increase. UTEP is now regarded as a research and doctoral university that is nationally recognized for both the excellence and breadth of its academic and research programs. Accordingly, UTEP's annual research expenditures have grown from $6 million to more than $90 million per year, an eleven-fold increase, and doctoral programs from $1 million to $22 million during the same period (Corchado, 2019). And to accommodate steady growth in enrolment, academic, and research programs, the university has recently invested nearly $300 million in new and renovated expansion facilities in science, engineering, health sciences, and other infrastructure related to students' quality of life.

THEORETICAL FRAMEWORK

The Growing Role of Hispanic Faculty in Higher Education

Although the Hispanic population represent the largest and fastest growing minority population in the United States, the number of Hispanic students enrolled in higher education is only 15% of the total (Fry, 2012). If this percentage increases, an essential factor is to find a similar increase among Hispanic faculty and administrators at US universities.

The Hispanic Association of Colleges and Universities (HACU) is conducting tremendous work advocating for greater Hispanic access to higher education and for improving the quality and number of Hispanic faculty at institutions across the country. The association encompasses around 270 colleges and universities that enroll more than half of all Hispanics in higher education today (Krogstad, 2016).

According to Arciniega (2012), Hispanic students need to see real examples of Latinos in higher education to recognize their wide range of academic and professional possibilities. In addition, institutions need to have the expertise of Hispanic faculty as they understand the culture and background of the students and can ultimately help the university institution broaden its own understanding of its mission and approach.

It is true that, in the current era of US history, there is a tendency to see Hispanic faculty representatives as members of a minority rather than professors (Montemayor & Mendoza, 2004). Thus, it is to be expected from the Anglo-Saxon world that Hispanics are Spanish-speaking and well-versed in Hispanic culture and literature. This is why Hispanic university professors sometimes choose to specialize in Latin areas, and there is nothing perverse about that. The problem arises when there are unfounded assumptions that they will be experts on Hispanic issues, even if they are not their own chosen role because they are Hispanic (Nuñez et al., 2010).

Given the increasing scarcity of Hispanics as we move up the academic ladder, it is easy to deduce that Hispanics are more represented in adjunct faculty positions than in full professorships. Various studies have found that Hispanic professors benefit the nation's higher education by attracting students to the classroom (Aguirre & Martinez, 2006; Austin, 2012; Boice, 2010; Gandara & Contreras, 2009; Hubbard & Stage, 2009, among others). They also improved multilingualism on campus and conducted more and better research on racial communities.

One of the most compelling arguments for Latino faculty members is the direct impact of their teaching methods on student-learning outcomes. Researchers Urrieta and Chavez argue that most Latino faculty members conceive their classroom teaching as opportunities to "raise students' awareness and critical thinking skills even when met with some resistance" (Urrieta & Chavez, 2010, p. 15). Along with the retention of students of Latino origin, Hispanic university faculty also have a great impact on the scientific community due to their scholarships and are more relevant to the Latino community and individuals.

However, while much evidence points to the tangible and significant contributions made by Hispanic faculty to higher education, some research also highlights the challenging work environments they too often face. This research includes, among others, Castellanos and Jones (2003), Evans and Chun, (2007), Smith and Wolf-Wendel (2007), Gracia (2008), or Hubbard and Stage (2009). These challenges reflect the reality that these university faculty members endure when they are one of the few Hispanic members in their department or college.

Previous literature is overloaded with empirical evidence demonstrating that Latino faculty are more likely to have additional committee assignments than their White colleagues, as researcher Garza (1993) pointed out. These additional duties represent Hispanic teachers with a daunting daily reality that they are ultimately trying to ameliorate through the promotion process.

What we really mean is that many of these service commitments to the university community are undervalued when Hispanic members of the university are evaluated for promotion. This inherent tension between service obligations and promotion-related activities generally results in "physical and mental exhaustion and emotional drain for many Latino faculty", as Arrieta and Chavez asserted (Urrieta & Chavez, 2010, p. 576).

In a similar vein, other researchers argue that Hispanic professors often face barriers in their workplace that lack Hispanic cultural values such as "personalism, sympathy, familism, and allocentrism" (Delgado-Romero et al., 2000, p. 45). This challenging work climate is not universal but is more likely to occur when there are few Latino members in the workplace. Other researchers, such as Smith and Calasanti (2005), have argued that Hispanic professors may face isolation and alienation in the workplace.

In recent decades, researchers have examined how institutions of higher education often show a high degree of skepticism about Hispanic faculty members' academic work and that Latino scholarship is less relevant or less valued than others because it focuses solely on Latino issues. Among these researchers we can highlight Padilla and Chavez (1995), Ibarra (2003), De los Santos and De los Santos (2013), Harvey (2013) or Laden (2014).

Other researchers argue that knowledge production, as in academic journals, is a major problem and obstacle to the success of Hispanic faculty. In addition, some social science journals are less likely to publish research that focuses on racial or ethnic groups. However, despite these obstacles to research focused on Hispanic issues, many Hispanic scholars are deeply committed to advancing and expanding debates on Latino social issues (Urrieta & Chavez, 2010).

Hispanic Faculty in Higher Education in the United States: Contrastive Data

Prejudice is defined as any idea based on erroneous or emotional generalizations, whereas discrimination acts on these generalizations (Contreras et al., 2018). The level of acceptance that Hispanic faculty members perceive from the dominant majority group affects their comfort level in the work environment.

The underlying effect of discrimination, feeling unwelcome, despised, or simply not understood on American college campuses is reflected in a notable decrease in the retention rate of Hispanic faculty on college campuses, as demonstrated in an article published by several university professors (Gutierrez et al., 2012).

Alienation and discrimination are common among Latino faculty. White faculty remain dominant in many departments nowadays, and they also often hold the most powerful and influential positions: full professor, department chair, dean, etc. The low Latino representation, especially in these critical positions, is reminiscent of the systematic exclusion and discrimination that this segment of the university faculty suffers from the dominant majority, according to scholar Shorris (2015).

All these factors are logically reflected in the poor representation of Hispanic faculty in the US higher education system, especially in positions of administrative responsibility (president, dean, chancellor, etc.) or academic responsibility (department chair, full professor). This is especially alarming for Hispanic women (Lopez, 2013).

To elaborate on this chapter, we rely on the data compiled and contrasted by the US official government sources, especially the Department of Education and the National Center for Education Statistics Institute of Education Sciences, as well as the analysis of different scholars (Snyder & De Brey, 2016; Kena et al., 2016) and data provided by the HACU association. These statistics provide some illuminating data. For example, we can highlight that the percentage of full-time university faculty of Hispanic origin is barely 4% of the total, compared to 84% of the dominant Anglo-Saxon origin, according to data offered by Kena et al.

Some other representative data we can reflect on is that contained in the annual report published by the Department of Education. On this occasion, Snyder and De Brey offer detailed information on the presence of Hispanic faculty in the US university system. It especially stands out that of the almost 800,000 university professors in the US system, just over 33,000 are of Hispanic origin, representing a paltry 4.2% of the total number of professors, as can be seen in the following table:

This first table provides a general picture of the distribution of US professors in higher education according to their origin, in which Hispanics stand out for a fourth position in the rank despite being the largest minority group in the country. However, deepening a little further on Hispanic faculty members, we can appreciate that the total of 33,217 professors of Hispanic origin can also be classified according to their professional category, as we can see in Table 2:

Figure 1. Distribution of academic faculty
Kena et al. (2016, p. 223)

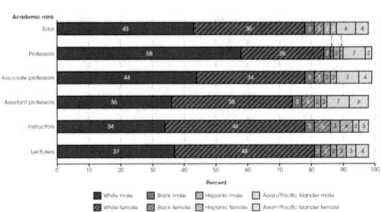

Table 1. Origin of US university faculty

Origin	Faculty	Percentage
White	575,491	72.7%
Asian/Pacific Islander	72,246	9.1%
Black	43,188	5.4%
Hispanic	33,217	4.2%
American Indian	3,538	0.4%
Others	63,711	8%
TOTAL	**791,391**	**100%**

Source: Snyder & De Grey (2015, p. 572)

Table 2. Origin of US university teaching staff by percentage

Rank	Faculty	Percentage
Professors	5,604	16.87%
Associate Professors	6,381	19.21%
Assistant Professors	7,130	21.46%
Instructors	6,340	19.08%
Lecturers	2,015	6.06%
Other faculty	5,747	17.30%
TOTAL	**33,217**	**100%**

Source: Snyder & De Grey (2015, p. 572)

As we can easily deduce from the content of the table above, the highest percentage of Hispanic teaching staff belongs to the category of assistant professors with 21.46% of the total, while the lowest percentage is in the category of full professors at 16.87%, which corroborates our previous findings. In between both sides of the scale, we come across the figures of associate professor (19.21%), instructor (19.08%), and other (17.30%)

However, we can still make another difference in terms of gender regarding the Hispanic faculty members. And the truth is that there is also a difference between the sexes within the same group of Hispanic teaching staff (Looney & Lusin, 2019). Among the 33,217 university professors of Hispanic origin, 17,198 were men, representing 51.77% of the total, while 16,019 were women (48.22%). This differentiation can be observed more graphically in Table 3:

Table 3. Distribution of US university faculty by gender

Rank	Male	Percentage	Female	Percentage
Professors	3,669	21.3%	1,935	12%
Associate Professors	3,533	20.5%	2,848	17.8%
Assistant Professors	3,624	22.6%	3,533	20.5%
Instructors	2,888	16.8%	3,452	21.5%
Lecturers	834	4.8%	1,181	7.4%
Other faculty	2,768	16.1%	2,979	18.6%
TOTAL	**17.198**	**51.77%**	**16.019**	**48.22%**

Source: Snyder & De Grey (2015, p. 572).

If we examine the information provided in this last table, we can affirm that, in principle, we could assume an almost technical parity between Hispanic male and female professors in overall numbers, which does not quite correspond to the reality of the numbers when we analyze the situation category by category (Orozco & Furszyfer, 2022).

This is particularly noticeable at the most influential or relevant positions. The difference between the two sexes is accentuated, for example, in the category of full professors, where Hispanic men represent 21.3% of the total (3,669 professors), compared to the 1,935 Hispanic women, with 12% of the total. In other words, there is almost a 10% difference between the two genders, which illustrates the extreme difficulties faced by female professors of Hispanic origin in US higher education.

The same occurs with the other two full-time categories: associate, and assistant professors. In the case of the former, associate professors, there were 3,533 males (20.5%) vs. 2,848 females (17.8%), almost a three-point difference. And in the case of the latter, assistant professors, we find 3,624 men (22.6%) against 3,506 women (20.4%), more than a two-point difference.

Curiously, in the case of non-permanent positions, such as instructors or lecturers mainly, we come across more women occupying those posts than their male counterparts. In the case of instructors, there were 3,452 Hispanic women (21.5%) versus 2,888 men (16.8%), a nearly five-point difference.

Hispanic Female Professors in Higher Education in the United States

In this section, after considering the overall data on Hispanic faculty in the US university system, we are going to focus on some relevant and particularly prominent

Hispanic female faculty members. Obviously, it is not possible to cover every individual case, so here, we present some significant examples.

Mildred Garcia (Chancellor, California State University, Fullerton)

Mildred Garcia was appointed the 11th chancellor of California State University (CSU), Fullerton in July 2023. Currently, Ms. Garcia serves as the president of the American Association of State Colleges and Universities (AASCU) and previously served as the president of CSU, Fullerton, and Dominguez Hills, where she was the first Hispanic president in the CSU system. She became the first-ever Latina appointed to lead the nation's largest and most diverse four-year university program.

Garcia is committed to multicultural partnerships and to the belief that these coalitions strengthen institutions and communities, as well as student self-development and opportunity. Her research in higher education focuses on the impacts of equity, diversity, and outreach on policy and practice. Garcia has been a participant and consultant in the policy work of the National Science Foundation, the American Educational Research Association, and the Middle States Commission on Higher Education (Takami, 2022). She served on President Obama's Commission on Educational Excellence for Hispanics. She has also served on the boards of directors of the Association of American Universities and the American Association of Hispanics in Higher Education.

Nilda Peragallo (Former Dean, School of Nursing and Health Studies, University of Miami)

Nilda P. Peragallo became the seventh Dean of the School of Nursing at the University of North Carolina in Chapel Hill in January 2017 and retired in January 2022. She was formerly a dean and professor at the University of the Miami School of Nursing and Health Studies. She is internationally recognized for her leadership in the areas of diverse health, cultural competency, and minority recruitment and retention in nursing. minorities in nursing.

A sought-after speaker, Peragallo has authored or co-authored many peer-reviewed publications and has been the principal investigator in numerous research grants (Martínez Riera et al., 2015). She was appointed by the U.S. Secretary of Health and Human Services to serve on the National Advisory Council of the National Center on Minority Health and Health Disparities. A Fellow of the American Academy of Nursing, Ms. Peragallo holds a joint appointment in the Department of Epidemiology and Public Health at the University of Miami Miller School of Medicine.

Teresa Leyva Ruiz (Former President, Glendale Community College)

Dr. Teresa Leyba Ruiz has served the students, faculty, staff, and community as an educator for over 30 years. She retired as President of Glendale Community College in the Maricopa County Community College District in January 2023, after 27 years of experience in higher education. Her administrative experience includes serving as a Vice President of Student Affairs, Associate Vice President for Academic & Student Affairs, and Dean of Academic Affairs.

Dr. Leyba Ruiz has been a math teacher at all levels of education in the last 16 years in the Community College District of Maricopa County. In January 2011, she accepted an interim assignment as an academic dean at Glendale Community College, where she participated in writing an academic strategic plan and developing a teaching and learning center.

Waded Cruzado (President, Montana State University)

Since January 2010, Dr. Waded Cruzado has served as the 12th President of Montana State University, and during that time, she has significantly reshaped the face and future of the state's first land-grant institution. An articulate and inspirational speaker on the role of the public university, President Cruzado is well known for her understanding of the Morrill Act, which created the land-grant university system nearly 160 years ago.

Prior to MSU, President Cruzado served as executive vice president and provost at New Mexico State University, a post she had held since September 1, 2007, and served as NMSU's interim president from 2008 to 2009. She also served as Dean of the College of Arts and Sciences at NMSU (2003–2007) and as Dean of the College of Arts and Sciences at Puerto Rico's land-grant university, the University of Puerto Rico at Mayaguez. She was a passionate champion of the land grant's tripartite mission of education, research, and public outreach.

Jane K. Fernandes (President, Antioch College)

Jane K. Fernandes is the first deaf woman to lead an American college. Born in Worcester, Massachusetts, Fernandes is a graduate of Trinity College in Connecticut and the University of Iowa. In Boston, she became the interim director of the American Sign Language Program at Northeastern University and then in Washington, DC, as the chair of the Department of Sign Communication at Gallaudet University. She was the Vice President of the Laurent Clerc National Center for Education of the Deaf in 1995 and was the Chancellor of the University from 2000 to 2006.

A native of Worcester, Dr. Fernandes has three decades of experience in higher education, including seven years as president of Guilford College in Greensboro, North Carolina, where she was also a tenured member of the faculty. She has provided senior leadership and held tenured faculty positions at other distinguished higher education institutions, including UNC Asheville, and Gallaudet University. (Myers, 2023). She has dedicated her career to making educational excellence accessible to all students by welcoming the fantastic range of human diversity to campus, including every voice in decision-making, and providing support, accommodations, and reparations to achieve equitable education through differences.

Joann La Perla-Morales (Former President, Middlesex County College)

Joann La Perla-Morales, former president of Middlesex County College, retired as president effective June 30, capping a 50-year career in higher education. Among many other achievements, Dr. La Perla-Morales oversaw creation of 55 new academic programs; led efforts for Middle States Self-Study and Reaccreditation; opened three new LEED-certified buildings; led the campus 10-year Master Plan effort that qualified for state bonding money for South Hall; successfully worked to establish strategic plans every three years with numerous accomplishments; wrote the grant to establish and maintain the Veterans Services Center; and responded to community needs by offering college facilities during Superstorm Sandy and the James Monroe school fire.

Prior to joining Middlesex, Dr. La Perla-Morales had been provost at New York College of Technology, dean of instruction at Nassau Community College, and held positions at Bloomfield College, Union County College, and Rockland Community College. She also served in the Peace Corps.

Dr. La Perla-Morales holds a doctorate and master's degree from Columbia University, and a bachelor's degree from the State University of New York, Oneonta. Dr. La Perla-Morales initiated new academic programs, restructured, and increased student services, and developed an honor program for high achieving students.

Renee D. Martinez (President Emeritus, Los Angeles City College)

Dr. Renee D. Martinez spent 12 years as Vice President of the Education and Economic Development Unit at East Los Angeles College. Within her duties at that institution, she oversaw the technology career and academic disciplines, and was involved in overall strategic planning. In her direction, the career technology program was first in the district, at the completion rate. Martinez has been a member of the executive committee for the past six years at Beverly Hospital at Montebello.

Reneé Martinez has worked in the field of community college education for over 42.5 years. Throughout her career, a top priority has been to serve as a role model for all students and staff members, demonstrating what can be attained by setting positive goals and working hard. She supports her staff members by encouraging them to be independent in their work environment, to further their education, and to provide good customer service to all needing their assistance and support.

Estela Mara Bensimon (Director, Center for Urban Education, USC Rossier School)

Estela Mara Bensimon is a professor of higher education at the USC Rossier School of Education and Director of the Center for Urban Education, which she founded in 1999. With a singular focus on increasing racial equity in higher education outcomes for students of color, she developed the Equity Scorecard, a process for using inquiry to drive changes in institutional practice and culture. Since its founding, CUE has worked with thousands of college professionals, from presidents to faculty to academic counsellors, helping them take steps in their daily work to reverse the impact of the historical and structural disadvantages that prevent many students of color from excelling in higher education (Polkinghmoe et al., 2013).

Dr. Bensimon has held the highest leadership positions in the Association for the Study of Higher Education (President, 2005-2006) and in the American Education Research Association, Division on Postsecondary Education (Vice-President, 1992-1994). She has served on the boards of the American Association for Higher Education and the Association of American Colleges and Universities. She was the Chair of AERA's Social Justice and Action Committee. In 2010, the University of Wisconsin system awarded Dr. Bensimon the 2010 Outstanding Women of Color in Education Award. In 2011, she was inducted as an AERA Fellow in recognition of excellence in research and received the ASHE's Council on Ethnic Participation Founders Service Award. She received the Association for the Study of Higher Education Research Achievement Award in 2013. She is a recipient of the USC Mellon Mentoring Award for faculty and Distinguished Service Award from the Association for the Study of Higher Education. In 2015, she received the American Association of Hispanics in Higher Education (AAHHE) Outstanding Latina Faculty Award for Research & Teaching. In 2017, she was elected to the National Academy of Education, and presented with the 2017 Social Justice in Education Award by the American Education Research Association.

Sylvia Hurtado (Former Director, Higher Education Research Institute, UCLA)

Sylvia Hurtado is a Professor of Education in the School of Education and Information Studies and directed the Higher Education Research Institute at UCLA for over a decade. She has written extensively on diverse students' college experiences, the campus racial climate, STEM pathways for underrepresented groups, and equity and diversity in higher education.

She was elected to the National Academy of Education in 2019; received the 2018 Social Justice in Education Award from the American Educational Research Association (AERA), and the 2015 Exemplary Research Achievement award from Division J. She was the past President of the Association for the Study of Higher Education (Newman et al., 2015). She now engages in collaborative work with UCLA's Center for Evaluation and Coordination, conducts research on the organizational impact of culturally aware mentor training for graduate program faculty in biomedical sciences, and directs a Howard Hughes Medical Institute project on how student-centered interventions at universities result in diversity and inclusion in science.

Rachel Moran (Distinguished Professor Emeritus of Law, University of California)

Rachel Moran is a Distinguished and Chancellor's Professor of Law at UCI Law. Before her appointment, she was Michael J. Connell Distinguished Professor of Law and Dean Emerita at UCLA Law. Before that, Prof. Moran was the Robert D. and Leslie-Kay Raven Professor of Law at UC Berkeley School of Law. She was also a founding faculty member in UCI Law from July 2008 to June 2010. Her expertise includes educational policymaking and law, Latino-related law and policy, race and law, legal education and the legal profession, and torts.

Throughout her career, Moran's work focused on the sources of inequality and opportunities. Her extensive and ongoing research on educational access and equity evaluates how public schools shape the lives of the nation's most vulnerable students, whether they are children of color, live in poverty, are undocumented, or speak a language other than English. Moran was selected to become the eighth dean of the UCLA School of Law, and the first Latina dean of one of America's top law schools.

Elsa Nuñez (Former President, Eastern Connecticut University)

Elsa M. Nuñez, the sixth president of Eastern Connecticut State University (2006 – 2013), retired in 2023. The first Latina to serve as a university president in New

England, Nuñez was credited with many significant accomplishments during her 18 years at the helm of Connecticut's designated public liberal arts university.

Dr. Nuñez's commitment to access faculty members is evidenced by data showing that Eastern has the highest percentage of minority faculty among all Connecticut colleges and universities. This and other factors have increased retention rates for underrepresented student populations and have also resulted in Eastern students making the largest gain in the six-year graduation rate of Latino students since 2004-10.

DIANA NATALICIO

Biographical Data

Diana Natalicio was born Diana Siedhoff to a working-class family in St. Louis in 1939 – "Natalicio" being her ex-husband's surname. Her father, Bill, owned a small retail business and her mother Jo was a homemaker. Neither of her parents attended college. Her father had finished two years of high school, while her mother had finished high school. Since they did not go to college, which was always a disappointment to both, they instilled values in her younger brother, Bill, and herself, that education was the most important thing in their personal formation.

She grew up in south St. Louis, in a lower-middle class neighborhood in the 1950s, the Eisenhower era, when people were optimistic and believed that a lot of good things could happen. She certainly had a stable childhood within the precariousness of the family. She went to a pretty good primary school, but high school was unsatisfactory. It was a secondary school that served the working population and did not set high aspirations for its students. The highest aspiration was for young people to work in various trades: electricians, plumbers, carpenters, or bricklayers. That is what the boys were predestined to do, and the girls were educated to marry and become housewives, like their mothers.

When she graduated, she went to work for a large manufacturing company in St. Louis as a secretary. She did shorthand, typed, and operated on a switchboard. For months, she learned new things but then gradually she realized that she didn't want to do that forever. So, she decided that she wanted to attend university. She talked to her parents about it and, as they were very enthusiastic and she had earned enough money, she was able to pay tuition.

She chose St. Louis University because it was the closest, and she could get there by bus and tram. She earned a B.A. in Spanish at St. Louis University, studied Portuguese in Brazil on a Fulbright scholarship, and earned her M.A. in Portuguese and her Ph.D. in linguistics at the University of Texas at Austin.

In 1971, Natalicio arrived at UTEP and was hired as an assistant professor. Despite being warned by friends that she would find El Paso a desert, she took an almost instant liking for the place. She enjoyed speaking Spanish and identifying with a working-class student body who struggled to balance school with work and family. Over the years, she taught linguistics, chaired the Department of Modern Languages, and served as the dean of the College of Liberal Arts and as the vice president for academic affairs.

Days after Diana Natalicio was named the first woman president of the University of Texas at El Paso in 1988, a local newspaper published an illustration of her as "the 48-year-old Wonder Woman". In many ways, the longest tenure at the head of a Texas public university among presidents still fits this description. Natalicio said: "I think the biggest difference between then and now is our confidence in ourselves as an institution. We were marginalizing ourselves, thinking that nobody was going to pay attention to us because we were here in the Chihuahuan Desert" (The Texas Tribune, 2013).

Natalicio served on numerous boards including The Holdsworth Center, the Hispanic Scholarship Fund (HSF), ACT, the Rockefeller Foundation, Trinity Industries, Sandia Corporation, the Mexican American Science Foundation (FUMEC), the National Action Council for Minorities in Engineering (NACME), and the Association of Public and Land-grant Universities (APLU).

In 2013, Natalicio also began a one-year term as the president of the American Council on Education, a national higher education research and advocacy group. She hoped that this role would allow her to highlight the work of large public institutions with underserved populations. Natalicio assumed her role during the 95th Annual Meeting of the American Council on Education (ACE) in Washington, DC.

She was appointed by President George H.W. Bush to the American Council on Education Advisory Commission and to the Advisory Commission on Educational Excellence for Hispanic Americans and by President Bill Clinton to the National Science Board, where she served two six-year terms, including three two-year terms as vice chair.

A good example of her personal imprint occurred in 2016 when the media reported a fainting spell she suffered on campus on her way to vote. For example, the "El Paso Herald Post" echoed her own statement upon leaving the hospital: "I am deeply grateful to UTEP Police Officer Bion Bell and the City of El Paso EMS personnel for their quick and skillful response to my emergency. I also greatly appreciated the expert recovery care I received from the dedicated health professionals at Providence Memorial Campus Hospital-nearly all of whom are UTEP graduates" (El Paso Herald Post, 2016).

The Presidency of Diana Natalicio at UTEP (1988 – 2019)

The leader of the UTEP for the past 28 years until last August, and the longest-serving president of a public research university in the United States, Diana Natalicio guided the UTEP's transformation into a national model for educating a 21st century student population. Recognizing the critical importance of pre-college preparation for student enrolment and success at UTEP, she has been a driving force in creating community partnerships to raise the educational aspirations and achievements of all young people in the Paso del Norte region.

Natalicio is a leading voice in national conversations on higher education, and a strong advocate for reaching past boundaries to develop strong international collaborations. When she was appointed president of UTEP in 1988, the first issue she wanted to address was the racial composition of the student body: "If you attract eighty-four percent of the students from El Paso County, you should look like the county" (Castellanos, 2003, p. 86). At that time, approximately half of the 14,000 students were Hispanic and after vigorous recruitment, approximately 66% of the 15,176 students were Hispanic, which does not include the 1,300 Mexicans, most of whom cross the border to attend classes every day. The UTEP is now the largest Hispanic-majority university in the country.

In Natalicio's opinion, talent is everywhere, it crosses gender and ethnic and geographic and socio-economic boundaries, and more than 80 percent of its students come from a particular region, so the university should probably look like the region. Not satisfied with that, her number one priority was to encourage more low-income and Hispanic young people to enroll at UTEP.

The second priority was to ensure that once that pathway was created, the education they would receive would be of high quality and allow them to graduate and compete with more influential peers of more prestigious means. As she thought about how to achieve that goal, she recognized that research activities on campus had to be increased to create a climate of high expectations. This would require recruiting more funding for faculty, which would require facilities and equipment, and more PhD programs, because the faculty she wanted to build would have to have PhD students form their research teams.

Natalicio was a strong believer in public universities with the mission of providing high-quality opportunities for people living in the region. Therefore, Natalicio hit the ground, lobbying for funds in Austin, Washington, D.C., and other centers of power. In UTEP's 84-year history, no one has ever shown such a concentrated effort, but the president succeeded as an old pro would have. The university budget, which was $64 million a decade ago, raised to $146 million. The UTEP used to offer one doctoral program and now has eight. And its profile is rising, both within the UT System and nationally.

Meanwhile, it used the school's traditional strengths in the sciences and engineering, UT-El Paso began as the Texas School of Mining and Metallurgy, to establish ties with the National Science Foundation. "I think we've overcome that fear of failure. We are now a much stronger institution because we have proven to ourselves that we can compete", said Natalicio, who was appointed to the foundation's board by Bill Clinton and served as its vice president (Castellanos, 2003, p. 95).

President Natalicio joined the UTEP in 1971 as a visiting assistant professor in the Department of Modern Languages. When she started, she recalled her own apprehensions as a first-generation college student: "I saw in many of my students' faces the same doubt I had felt, wondering, am I really university material?. Within weeks of joining the UTEP, I was sure that I had found a place where I could do for many other young people what St. Louis University had done for me, a place where I could pay it forward by creating opportunities for those following in my footsteps" (Ibarra, 2003, p. 35).

In 1987, the university initiated the Student Assistance Program, which allowed Mexican students to pay for in-state tuition. The university also partnered with the governor of Chihuahua, who offered scholarships for students from that state to obtain graduate or doctoral degrees at UTEP. Natalicio stressed the importance of this program in improving Mexican universities.

The UTEP currently enrolls more than 22,600 students, about 75% of whom are Mexican American, 12% of whom are Mexican, and half of whom commute daily from Ciudad Juárez. Natalicio said she wants to build an excellent university that reflects the diversity of the community: "I see it as our having assets that are very, very strong and unique, and we have an obligation to make those work for us and for the people we serve" (Ibarra, 2003, p. 93).

Former President Natalicio's sustained commitment to providing all Paso del Norte residents with access to exceptional higher education opportunities has made the UTEP a national success story. For three consecutive years, Washington Monthly magazine has recognized UTEP among the top 10 universities in the country and the number one university in the nation to improve the social mobility of its students.

Despite national plaudits, institutions such as the UTEP still face internal struggles. In the 2011 legislative session, the UTEP qualified to take advantage of the state's Competitive Knowledge Fund, an extra pot of money that only a small group of institutions can access. However, the university was denied access by the lawmakers.

Natalicio's term was also marked by questions about the UTEP's low graduation rates. Currently, 13% of UTEP undergraduates graduate in four years, down from 2.6% in 1999, according to the Texas Higher Education Coordinating Board. Natalicio attracted attention for openly rejecting the numbers and trying to forge a definition of success that she believed was better suited to the low-income, minority population of El Paso. In this regard, Natalicio pointed out that the total number of degrees awarded annually by the UTEP grew significantly. Last year, the total was more than 4,300, up from less than 2,200 years ago.

On the negative side of her presidency, since ascending to the top of the UTEP, she faced her own share of controversy. Her aggressive and hands-on management style clashed with some of her colleagues in the wrong way. For three years Natalicio was the focal point, though not the defendant, in a lawsuit that began when she rejected the candidacy of geology professor Kathleen Marsaglia even after the tenure committee had unanimously approved Marsaglia. Marsaglia said she was rejected because she had accused geology professor Nick Pingitore, a close friend of Natalicio's, of sexual harassment.

Worst of all, the university, which is known for its outstanding basketball program, was sanctioned for five years by the National Collegiate Athletic Association (NCAA), mainly for the use of ineligible players in various sports. Natalicio blamed poor record-keeping for the inclusion of ineligible players. She then replaced many of the athletic department staff members. She was also criticized for low graduation rates during her tenure (13% in 2016, compared to 2.6% in 1999), but in her defense Natalicio argued that graduation rates are not the most important measure of a university's success.

She was president of the UTEP for the past 28 years until her resignation in August, and the world of public higher education changed dramatically during that time. When she took on this role, the UTEP relied almost exclusively on its funding from the state appropriations formula and, to a lesser extent, tuition.

If this were a wealthy community, and if it served a predominantly high-income student population, tuition increases might have been a very easy solution. However, Natalicio intended to generate opportunities for people in this historically underserved region, knowing that they would have to be entrepreneurial to achieve educational access and quality. Tuition increases were simply not going to be the answer. Therefore, she began to work hard on developing other strategies that would generate revenue and allow students to grow and build quality, while continuing to ensure access and affordability for students of modest financial means.

Natalicio worked hard to diversify the university's asset portfolio. A major priority was to build research competitiveness by investing in infrastructure and faculty talents. She also had to attract several ancillary businesses, real estate, and many other assets, which helped make them a much stronger force for the future of this region.

The first big step was to start preparing the research injection and do everything possible to optimize the likelihood of obtaining external funding, not only from federal agencies, but also from corporate and foundation sources. This meant building an infrastructure on campus to support the faculty with talent and the potential to compete successfully. They needed to demonstrate to the faculty that, if they were entrepreneurial, they would support them. They also committed to reinvesting in their own capacity to generate more external funding. That meant building more facilities and creating more space for researchers to have room to perform their own work.

It learned early on to compete for large grants at the federal level because, if the inspection teams did not see the kind of physical facilities and equipment required to do the work, it was very doubtful that an upstart like the UTEP would be able to do the work. Therefore, they strategically invested and used the money they had, but limited, to acquire the necessary resources.

And the UTEP competed aggressively to match funds. Everyone on campus worked together to try to make this happen. They were firmly determined to become a research university, but, more importantly, they were also absolutely committed to not jeopardizing the quality and accessibility of the undergraduate experience for the economically constrained students they served and nurtured.

Thus, the commitment to developing a research agenda was closely tied to providing a higher-quality undergraduate experience and an even better deal for UTEP students who paid lower fees than their peers at most American public universities. They benefited from being surrounded by a research enterprise that made strategic infrastructure investments and created jobs on campus for them. There was a synergy between research and the quality of undergraduate education because everyone understood that it was a collaborative effort between those committed to accessible undergraduate education and high-quality teaching and learning, and those who were doing innovative research.

Honors and Awards

Diana Natalicio was the recipient of numerous honors and awards throughout her long career. In 2017, Natalicio was named one of the top 50 global leaders by Fortune magazine and being honored with the Hispanic Heritage Award in Science, Technology, Engineering, and Mathematics. The annual list honors pioneers in business, government, philanthropy, and the arts who build bridges to bring people together to solve problems and recognize reality while offering hope, according to the magazine.

The recipients were selected by Fortune magazine staff and a panel of experts from various fields. The ranking places Natalicio alongside prominent world leaders such as Pope Francis, Amazon founder Jeff Bezos, Canadian Prime Minister Justin Trudeau, singer-songwriter Shakira, and director Ava DuVernay.

In 2016, she was included in the TIME 100 list of the most influential people worldwide. Diana Natalicio's work at UTEP over the past 45 years has and has had everything to do with passion, determination, and a quest to make a difference in the lives of the residents of the Paso del Norte region. Her hard work and leadership are recognized on a global scale, making her worthy of such a distinguished citation. It is worth noting that in that year the magazine's nomination went to world figures such as US President Barack Obama, German Chancellor Angela Merkel, and French President Francois Hollande.

Thus, in statements made by TIME magazine when the decision was announced, Natalicio commented as follows: "I am humbled and deeply honored to have been named one of TIME magazine's 100 most influential people in the world. The work I have done would not have been possible without the creativity and courage of the UTEP faculty and staff, the high aspirations and hard work of our talented students, and the support of our alumni and friends, all of whom have enabled the UTEP to successfully combine academic and research excellence with genuine access and equity. The UTEP is the only doctoral/research university in the United States serving a predominantly Mexican-American student population, known for developing innovative strategies that level the playing field for students from historically underrepresented cultures and socioeconomic backgrounds. I am grateful to TIME for amplifying the UTEP story and our leadership role" (Time Magazine, 2016).

Paul L. Foster, Chairman of the University of Texas System Board of Trustees, said: "President Natalicio's impact on UTEP is immeasurable. She has spent more than four decades at this institution and has dedicated her life and her unparalleled talent and intellect to its success. She has led some of the nation's largest and most influential higher education organizations and committees, and her opinion has been sought by legislators and university leaders across the country and beyond. That she is one of the most influential people in the world will come as no surprise to her peers across the country, nor to her students and colleagues at the UTEP. We are delighted that TIME is recognizing her for her extraordinary achievements" (Time Magazine, 2016).

In 2015, the Carnegie Corporation of New York honored Natalicio with its prestigious Academic Leadership Award in recognition of her outstanding achievements in transforming UTEP into a national public research university. The same year she was named the El Paso Inc. person of the year. She said that she would donate her $1,000 award to UTEP's scholarship fund: "I don't think there is a better investment than talented young people. The return on investment is fantastic" (El Paso Inc., 2015). The selection of Natalicio was appropriate, and the editorial board felt that it was obvious to all that her focus on excellence over the past 15 years has gradually transformed the university into an increasingly research-oriented institution with national and global ambitions.

In 2011, the president of Mexico presented her with the "Mexican Order of the Aztec Eagle", the highest award given to foreigners who work to strengthen ties between the United States and Mexico. She was chosen by Mexican President Felipe Calderón for her efforts to maintain and foster a bilingual and bicultural environment at the university, while embracing the virtues and challenges of the El Paso-Juárez border region. Mexican Ambassador to the United States Arturo Sarukhan presented the award at the Mexican Cultural Institute: "Natalicio promotes policies of unity and inclusion and is a true source of inspiration at a time when voices that encourage fear and foster discrimination unfortunately seem to proliferate on this side of the border", said Sarukhan.

Natalicio said in an interview that she was very grateful to President Calderón and the Mexican government for recognizing the work that the UTEP had done to create opportunities in a truly binational environment. During her years as the president of UTEP, financial assistance programs increased, benefiting hundreds of Mexican students with financial needs.

In addition, the TIAA-CREF Institute, a research organization for universities, awarded Natalicio the Theodore M. Hesburgh Award for Excellence in Leadership, which is given to a university leader who embodies the spirit of the former president of the University of Notre Dame. As well as the Harold W. McGraw Award in Education in 1997, she was inducted into the Texas Women's Hall of Fame, received the Distinguished Alumna Award from the University of Texas at Austin, and was awarded honorary doctoral degrees from St. Louis University, North-eastern University, Victoria University (Melbourne, Australia), Georgetown University, Smith College, and the Autonomous University of Nuevo Leon.

Finally, when she resigned in August, another woman, Heather Wilson, was curiously elected to her post, and the UTEP Board of Regents named her "President Emeritus" of the institution in gratitude for her work over the past decades.

CONCLUSION

During the 2020-2021 academic year, the University of Texas at El Paso celebrated its centennial, and Diana Natalicio, the then president of the institution, marked her 28th anniversary of the university's most important job. That is a remarkably long period, but even more remarkable are the changes that the UTEP underwent during her administration. UTEP began as a mining school and annually graduates many engineers and scientists.

If the institution offered one doctoral program in 1988, it would now have twenty. In 1988, annual research expenditures amounted to approximately $5 million while last year the number was $84 million. And for the past few years, Washington Monthly magazine, using unconventional criteria, has named UTEP one of the top ten universities in the country.

While Diana Natalicio was very successful through her focus on access and excellence in increasing UTEP's enrolment by 50 percent and doubling the number of graduates, the unfinished task was to help create more high-skilled jobs in this region.

One of the challenges is that most must leave the area to secure meaningful and exciting work. That represents a huge brain drain when you consider the extensive investment that has been made in building the quality of undergraduate education and the competitiveness of research for them. So, one of her main priorities was to help make UTEP more of a catalyst for the economic development of skilled personnel.

In Natalicio's view, UTEP is there as a public university to provide educational opportunities for the residents of this region. That is the role of public universities and the reason why they are spread across the geography of a state as large as Texas: "If you lose sight of that fundamental mission, you've lost everything" (Comptroller Texas, 2017).

When she arrived at the UTEP, she thought she would stay for a year. However, after about two months of teaching, she was completely hooked: "I just loved the students. I thought they were great. And they were great because they were the kind of students who were here to work towards a better life. They weren't in class to have fun. They were just working-class people who wanted a better life. I have tremendous admiration for that" (Comptroller Texas, 2017).

The UTEP's impact on El Paso's economy has always been significant as a pathway for local students to enter businesses and professions. However, under Natalicio's leadership, the university was poised to make serious and sustained contributions to the nascent high-tech and entrepreneurial sectors of the growing regional economy. A legacy she hopes her successor will continue from now on.

REFERENCES

Aguirre, A. (2000). *Women and Minority Faculty in the Academic Workplace: Recruitment, Retention and Academic Culture*. ASHE-ERIC.

Aguirre, A., & Martinez, R. (2006). *Diversity leadership in higher education*. Jossey-Bass.

Arciniega, T. A. (2012). The Crucial Role of Hispanic-Serving Institutions in the Education of Latino/a Youth. *Journal of Latinos and Education, 11*(3), 150–156. doi:10.1080/15348431.2012.686348

Austin, A. E. (2012). Preparing the next generation of faculty: Graduate school as socialization to the academic career. *Journal of Higher Education (Columbus, Ohio), 73*(1), 94–122. doi:10.1353/jhe.2002.0001

Boice, B. (2010). *Advice for new faculty members*. Allyn Bacon.

Boyer, E. L. (1990). *Scholarship Reconsidered: Priorities of the Professoriate.* The Carnegie Foundation for the Advancement of Teaching.

Castellanos, J., Gloria, A. M., & Kamimura, M. (2003). The Latino Pathway to the PhD. *Stylus (Rio de Janeiro).*

Castellanos, J., & Jones, L. (2003). The Majority in the Minority: Expanding the Representation of Latino Faculty, Administrators and Students in Higher Education. *Stylus (Rio de Janeiro).*

Clark, R. L., & D'Ambrosio, M. B. (2015). *Recruitment, Retention and Retirement in Higher Education: Building and Managing the Faculty of the Future.* Edward Edgar.

Contreras, F. E., Malcom, L. E., & Bensimon, E. M. (2018). *Hispanic-Serving Institutions.* State University of New York Press.

De los Santos, A. G. Jr, & De los Santos, G. E. (2013). Hispanic-Serving Institutions in the 21st century: Overview, challenges, and opportunities. *Journal of Hispanic Higher Education, 2*(4), 377–391. doi:10.1177/1538192703256734

Delgado-Romero, E. A., Manlove, A. N., Manlove, J. D., & Hernandez, C. E. (2007). Controversial Issues in the Recruitment and Retention of Latino Faculty. *Journal of Hispanic Higher Education, 6*(1), 34–51. doi:10.1177/1538192706294903

Evans, A., & Chun, E. B. (2007). Are the Walls Really Down? Behavioral and Organizational Barriers to Faculty and Staff Diversity. *ASHE Higher Education Report, 33,* 1–139.

Fry, R. (2012). *Latinos in higher education: Many enroll, too few graduate.* Pew Hispanic Center.

Gandara, P., & Contreras, F. (2009). *The Latino education crisis.* Harvard University Press. doi:10.4159/9780674056367

Garza, H. (1993). *Second Class Academics: Chicana/Latino Faculty in US Universities.* Jossey-Bass.

Gracia, J. (2008). *Latinos in America: Philosophy and social identity.* Blackwell. doi:10.1002/9780470696484

Griffin, K. A., & Reddick, R. J. (2015). Surveillance and Sacrifice. *American Educational Research Journal, 48*(5), 1032–1057. doi:10.3102/0002831211405025

Gutierrez, M., Castañeda, C., & Katsinas, S. G. (2012). Latino Leadership in Community Colleges: Issues and Challenges. *Community College Journal of Research and Practice, 26*(4), 297–314. doi:10.1080/106689202753546457

Hamilton, R. (2013). After Quarter-Century on the Job, UTEP President is Still Making Waves. *The Texas Tribune*, 11th March.

Harvey, W. B. (2013). *Minorities in Higher Education: Annual Status Report.* American Council on Education.

Hubbard, S., & Stage, F. (2009). Attitudes, perceptions, and preferences of faculty at Hispanic serving institutions. *The Journal of Higher Education, 80*(3), 270–289. doi:10.1080/00221546.2009.11779013

Hurtado, S. (2001). *Linking Diversity and Educational Purpose: How Diversity Affects the Classroom Environment and Student Development.* Harvard Educational Publishing Group.

Ibarra, R. (2003). Latino Faculty and the Tenure Process in Cultural Content. *Stylus (Rio de Janeiro).*

Kena, G., Hussan, W., McFarland, J., De Brey, C., & Musu-Gillette, L. (2016). [National Center for Education Statistics.]. *The Condition of Education,* ●●●, 2016.

Krogstad, J. M. (2016). *5 Facts about Latinos and education.* Pew Research Center.

Krogtad, J., Passel, J. S., & Noe Bustamante, L. (2022). *Key facts about U.S. Latinos for national Hispanic Heritage month.* Pew Research Center.

LacombaC. (2022). Hispanic Map of the United States. *Observatorio Cervantes*, 1-126. https://doi.org/ doi:10.15457/OR084-02/2023EN

Laden, B. V. (2014). Hispanic Serving Institutions: What are they? Where are they? *Community College Journal of Research and Practice, 28*(3), 181–198. doi:10.1080/10668920490256381

Looney, D., & Lusin, N. (2019). *Enrollments in languages other than English in United States institutions of higher education.* Modern Language Association.

Lopez, M. H. (2013). *Three-Fourths of Hispanics say their community needs leader.* Pew Research Center.

Mactezuma, P., & Navarro, A. (2011). Internacionalización de la educación superior: Aprendizaje institucional en Baja California. *Revista de la Educación Superior, 40*(59), 47–66.

Martínez Riera, J. R., Ferrer, L., Cassiani, S. H., & Laverde, M. C. (2015). Envejecimiento: Retos y oportunidades para la investigación. *Revista Iberoamericana de Saúde e Envelhecimiento, 1*(1), 100–119. doi:10.24902/r.riase.2015.1(1).119

Montemayor, R., & Mendoza, H. (2004). *Right before our eyes: Latinos past, present and future*. Scholarly Publishing.

Mora, L. (2022). *Hispanic enrollment reaches new high at four-year colleges in the U.S. but affordability remains an obstacle*. Pew Research Center.

Myers, S. S. (2023). Building Bridges. In L. M. Pipe & J. T. Stephens (Eds.), *Ignite* (pp. 57–80). Vernon Press.

Newman, C. B., Tran, M. C., & Chang, M. (2015). Improving the rate of success for underrepresented racial minorities in STEM fails. *New Directions for Institutional Research*, *148*, 5–15. doi:10.1002/ir.357

Nora, A., & Crisp, G. (2019). *Hispanics and Higher Education: An Overview of Research, Theory, and Practice*. Springer Science.

Nuñez, A. M., Ramalho, E. M., & Cuero, K. K. (2010). Pedagogy for equity: Teaching in a Hispanic-Serving Institution. *Innovative Higher Education*, *35*(3), 177–190. doi:10.1007/s10755-010-9139-7

Orozco, M., & Furszyer, J. (2022). *State of Latino entrepreneurship*. Standford Graduate School of Business.

Padilla, R., & Chavez, R. (1995). *The Leaning Ivory Tower: Latino Professors in American Universities*. State University of New York Press.

Peyton, J. K. (2017). Spanish for Native Speakers Education. In O. E. Kagan, M. H. Carrera, & C. H. Chick (Eds.), *Heritage Language Education*. Routledge. doi:10.4324/9781315092997-18

Polkinghome, D., Bauman, G., & Vallejo Peña, E. (2013). Doing research that makes a difference. *The Journal of Higher Education*, *75*(1), 104–126. doi:10.1353/jhe.2013.00485

Scherer, Z., & Mayol García, Y. (2022). *Hardships and disjunctives across Hispanic Groups*. US Census Bureau.

Shorris, E. (2015). *Latinos: A Biography of the People*. Norton & Co.

Smith, D. G., & Wolf-Wendel, L. (2007). *The challenge of diversity: Involvement or alienation in the academy?* Jossey-Bass.

Smith, J. W., & Calasanti, T. (2005). The Influences of Gender, Race, Ethnicity on Workplace Experiences of Institutional and Social Isolation: An Exploratory Study of University Faculty. *Sociological Spectrum*, *25*(3), 307–334. doi:10.1080/027321790518735

Snyder, T. D., & de Brey, C. (2016). [National Center for Education Statistics.]. *Digest of Educational Statistics*, ●●●, 2015.

Snyder, T. D., & Dillow, S. A. (2011). [National Center for Education Statistics Institute of Education Sciences.]. *Digest of Educational Statistics*, ●●●, 2010.

Sorcinelli, M. D., Austin, A. E., Eddy, P. L., & Beach, A. L. (2016). *Creating the Future of Faculty Development*. Anker Publishing.

Takami, M. (2022). AASCU president discusses her leadership journey. *Dean and Provost*, *23*(10), 12–22. doi:10.1002/dap.31047

Urrieta, L., & Chavez, R. (2010). *Latino Faculty in Academelandia*. Routledge.

KEY TERMS AND DEFINITIONS

Higher Education: In the U.S., 'higher education' refers to postsecondary education, which is offered at institutions such as colleges, universities, community colleges, and vocational-technical schools.

Hispanic: Hispanic refers to a person with ancestry from a country whose primary language is Spanish. Latino and its variations refer to a person with origins from anywhere in Latin America (Mexico, South and Central America) and the Caribbean.

President (of university): The President is the chief officer of the university and is responsible for the operation of the entire university within the framework of general policies provided by the Board of Trustees in keeping with the laws of the state.

Social Recognition: Social recognition, or peer-to-peer recognition, is the act of employees empowering and acknowledging one another for great work. It is a meaningful source of motivation and, when it's a company habit, it becomes the backbone to an inclusive and collaborative working environment.

UTEP: The University of Texas at El Paso (UTEP) is one of the largest and most successful Hispanic-serving institutions in the country, with a student body that is 84% Hispanic. UTEP enrolls nearly 24,000 students in 169 bachelor's, master's, and doctoral programs in eight colleges and schools.

Chapter 9
The Western Gaze and African Feminism:
Twin Peaks in the Global Higher Education Workforce

Catherine Hayes
University of Sunderland, UK

ABSTRACT

This chapter serves as a mechanism of recognizing and acknowledging the illegitimacy of historic and traditional western approaches to narratives of African feminist epistemology. These approaches have engendered lenses of perspective which are irrefutably skewed by colonialism and whose address is warranted in ensuring both a means of learning about the end of an era and the prospect of a more authentically framed future framed, shaped, and determined from within African culture and context by those. To undertake this acknowledgement and recognition is one of the first and much belated to framing steps in ensuring that the articulation of truth lies best with those whose lived truths they are, rather than any tokenistic perceptions of them, consequently articulated through Western lenses of perspective.

INTRODUCTION

'In the consciousness of the truth he has perceived man now sees everywhere only the awfulness or the absurdity of existence and loathing seizes him.' (Friedrich Nietzsche, 1844-1900)

DOI: 10.4018/979-8-3693-0102-9.ch009

Copyright © 2024, IGI Global. Copying or distributing in print or electronic forms without written permission of IGI Global is prohibited.

Hermeneutical injustice via interpretive harm has been recognised as a longstanding impact of colonialism and has been directly attributed to structural oppression (Berenstain, 2016). Traditionalist approaches to Social Constructivist methodologies have become a mechanism by which this oppression can be actively perpetuated (Falola, 2022). This results in contention within the context of African feminist epistemology since this too relies on an interpretivist lens within which, acknowledgement of the epistemic position of the researcher is made (Adebayo & Njoku, 2023). The outcome is that this acknowledgement of positionality still uses a one dimensional concept to make meaning of a three dimensional intersectional lived experience. The impact of this has been that both African men and women's capacity for knowing in the field of African feminist epistemology has only actually been visible through the lens of white feminist methodology (Mellor, 2022).

The integration of the epistemologies and conceptual bases of domination have the effect of being hidden within traditional white feminist research, which predominantly serve to place the source of challenges and issues within black female populations with little or no regard for the structural inequalities of oppression which actively pervade African lives (Wielanga, 2022). The impact of this is to further entrench perceptions of the West within conceptual foundations now tarnished by ideologies that neither serve to represent or interpret the concept of hermeneutical justice (Akoleowo, 2022). In the context of the paradigmatic sufficiency of social research, epistemology remains an integral component in the relationship between ontology, philosophy, methodology and methods (Jackson et al, 2022). This chapter will provide an overview of how African feminist epistemology in the context of knowledge and knowledge acquisition has largely become the preserve of white feminists whose portrayal of cause and effect within an interpretive lens continue to impact on the capacity of African feminists to identify, acknowledge and address the structural inequalities which constrain efforts to engender authentic change. An insight will be gained into the relative differences that can exist between different types of knowledge and how this then influences how knowledge is established, articulated, and regarded in the wider context of research (Jensen et al, 2007). For the purposes of this chapter epistemology, is operationally defined as the nature and form of knowledge in relation to how this relationship is articulated in feminist praxis. Underpinning this definition is the assumption that the basis of all human knowledge is subjective and is rooted in the socially constructed meaning-making that underpins human curiosity, inquiry and subsequently assumption (Hester, 2020). The issue of contention is not this assumption but rather the assumption that an interpretive lens as applied to African feminist epistemology can refract a vision which is not in any way authentic and remains void of the truth of experience lived within structural oppression (Ossome, 2023). As a white western author myself, I seek not to challenge this but rather acknowledge it so that it can be accounted for and acknowledged by my Western and Eurocentric counterparts who seek to wholly interpret and represent the voices of those who live lives still dominated by the structural oppression imposed upon them (Hurlbut, 2021). The context of social science presents an ideal arena from a disciplinary perspective to consider the relationship between what it is possible to know and the knower. What this relationship constitutes is a prevailing dilemma in the study of epistemology that has been continually extended to incorporate the concept of the personal in epistemic cognition (Chinn & Rinehart, 2016). What that dilemma actually constitutes, is the fundamental difference between truth and verisimilitude and the contention of whether a re-examination of the constructive alignment of methodological approaches to Western social research methodologies in relation to what they make possible to interpret are required (Bernecka, 2022).

CONSIDERING VISUAL EPISTEMOLOGY

The acquisition of knowledge in relation to sensory engagement with specific artefacts, such as art, or media, such as music, presents an alternative insight into what knowledge is, especially in contrast to the study of propositional knowledge or truth in African feminist epistemology, regardless of geographical context (Simba and Davids, 2020). It is here that it can be posited that the relative inseparability of cognitive skill and affective impact are evident and where the concept of aesthetic knowledge is open to question in terms of the internalisation of perceived reality (DeNora, 2014). In turn this raises questions of what constitutes knowledge or whether knowledge itself can be perceived in the context of sensory engagement, a process of critical reflection which can potentially lead to critical reflexivity in action (Bleich, 1975; Nzegwu, 2019). Academic researchers doubtlessly use reflection to challenge their personally held assumptions and translate this into deliberate action in the real world – as with seminal academic texts, such as the work of Shakespeare, the universality of creative practice has the potential to transcend generations and become an embedded part of historical knowledge, capturing an insight into our cultural heritage and ancestry (Stupples, 2017; Varela, Thompson & Rosch, 2017).

Whilst art does not seek or necessitate propositional truth in the same sense, as evidence-based approaches to health and social care, it has historically been posited that it provides a metaphorical anchor for the recognition that all interpretation is essentially subjective, when perceived and reported by humankind (Jahn & Dunne, 2007). Ultimately all ways of knowing, regardless of discipline, have the capacity to shape how sense is made of the world within which humankind exists (Van Veeren, 2019). As such it can be stated that all epistemological stances are beyond disciplinarity, and it is methodological approaches that define our signature and traditionally adopted methods to the acquisition of knowledge in practice (Hayes et al, 2020).

Providing an insight into the liminal space between what is the basis of 'knowing' and the knower is essential to deconstructing meaning in the context of perception (Fox, 2017; Grene & Grene, 1974). This insight can then be used to consider how personal epistemology influences choice of philosophical underpinnings in processes of research design and methodology (Hofer & Pintrich, 2012). Facilitating the consideration of both traditional and contemporary epistemological lenses, using recognised philosophical perspectives it is possible to raise awareness of a wider range of epistemological stances (Tirri, Husu, & Kansanen, 1999). Making sense is an integral part of being human (Eisner, 2017). It lies at the heart of the fundamental understanding explanation and comprehension (Park, 2017). In terms of human need, control of extraneous environments and the emotions that regulate interaction with them are the pivotal basis of the need to 'make sure' (Pekrun, 2011). This has now also become a core characteristic in how tacit knowledge can become 'transferrable knowledge' in the context of gamification (ter Vrugte and de Jong, 2017). Basically, it implies the relationship between the human mind and the universe in which it is acknowledged to exist is pivotal to knowledge and subsequent understanding (Nicolelis, 2020).

CONTEXTUALISING AND FRAMING AFRICAN FEMINIST EPISTEMOLOGY

Epistemology extends beyond the scope of purist philosophy, which is significant in how it effectively reaches beyond the context of individual and collective identities in social research settings (Lahroodi, 2018). Epistemology is not only an academic endeavour or pursuit, but also pivotal in the transgenerational sharing of knowledge from one to the next where knowledge rather than perception ultimately underpins belief (Kane, Ragsdell, & Oppenheim, 2006; Kaplan, Sanchez and Hoffman, 2017). For any sustainable change in culture for women and their advocates to occur beyond the here and now, the difference between truth and verisimilitude is pivotal to acknowledge and embed in societal structures (Tonkin, 2021).

Justifying or providing an evidence base for knowledge is now a fundamental part of any sociological research (Lemos, 2020). It is the basis of rationalism, empiricism, and the fundamental structure of knowledge (Szigeti, 2024). The concept of perceived versus actual reality is important in differentiating what we perceive knowledge to be from what it is (Inkpin, 2021). The differentiation between what knowledge is and what knowledge constitutes is also paramount since it impacts on the capacity humankind has to react to it in practice (Carter, 2017). The lens of perspective that white Western and Eurocentric epistemologies have placed upon African epistemology can be revealed as a deficit model, in the progression of equality, equity and the acknowledgement for the necessity of each in any democratic global society (Ndofirepi & Gwaravanda, 2020). It ought to be acknowledged, too, that many individuals embody or espouse an absolutist perspective and that a more evaluative perspective of different domains of knowledge in sociological research is necessary in practice (Markauskaite and Goodyear, 2017). Within this chapter the contemplation of both theory and practice in applied research design and methodology is considered alongside the contextual significance of African feminist epistemology, as perceived through that Western and Eurocentric lens and then the skewed implications of this to the lives of millions (Matiluko, 2020).

BINDING TIES OF IMPOSED ONTOLOGY AND EPISTEMOLOGY

Where theoretical positioning illuminates the whole rationale for social research, the significance of ontology and epistemology to framing and contextualising African feminist epistemology is irrefutable (Cunliffe and Scaratti, 2017). An understanding of both ontology and epistemology and their symbiotic relationship is essential in subsequently understanding the connection between the origins and foundations of post-colonial research (R'Boul, 2022). The morphologic design of research is dependent on the ontological and epistemological stance underpinning it and then supporting the adoption of specific methodologies and methods which serve to advocate question led rather than methods driven research approaches (Akanle & Shittu, 2020). Certain ontological and epistemological stances offer the opportunity for African Feminist researchers to acknowledge their own embedded stance or philosophical assumptions which can potentially influence their interpretive capacity and ability to disseminate findings in the context of social research methods (Okech, 2020). Within the context of African feminist epistemology, the resonance of colonialism and post-colonial perspectives still pervade into the 21st Century (Andrews, 2021).

The term ontology can be operationally defined in relation to its relationship with epistemology (Al-Ababneh, 2020). Essentially, two distinct ontological positions exist, foundationalism and anti-foundationalism (Jong, 2023). Both deal with the nature of being, truth and reality. It is the theoretical significance of ontology that embeds it into the very being of an epistemological stance (Arenhart & Arroyo, 2021). The longstanding issue is exactly where the origins of imposed epistemologies have stemmed from, indeed raising the question of why African feminist perspectives have not been articulated as such and why a clouded lens of post-Colonialism still pervade despite Western allusions to the contrary (Thomas, 2020). Of greater relevance is the notion of Foundationalism. Foundationalism posits that the reality of the world exists in the form of a mosaic, composed of the material substances of a physical world. These materials are extraneous and independent of the human experience. Anti-foundationalism in contrast posits that there can be nothing independent of knowledge since social construction of the world by human actors is what gives them their meaning, sense-making and ultimately their reality (Spiegel, 2017). It is here that by speaking through a lens of perception unknown and only assumed, that Western and Eurocentric approaches to African feminist epistemologies have skewed knowledge in this disciplinary field (Moyo, 2020).

Foundationalism and anti-foundationalism as the two most prominent ontological stances frame and determine epistemological stance or 'ways of knowing' (Moreira, 2022). Most associated with the two distinctions in ontological stance are (a) empirical or positivist epistemology (the notion that world reality exists value free and independently of man's knowledge of it) and (b) subjective or interpretivist epistemology, which posits that there is a social construction of the work that has engendered meaning and subjectivity, (Connell, 2020).

The illumination of subjective interpretation of African feminist epistemology can therefore be regarded as a double hermeneutic, which negates the need for objectivity in the construction of new theoretical perspectives (Jimoh, 2017). The objective entity represented by the world means it is possible to generate specific questions or hypotheses which can be tested by direct observation. In this sense there is an evidently parallel position with natural science which also uses theoretical perspectives to generate new hypotheses that can also be tested by direct observation. In an ideal world, who undertakes this research ought to be an integral part of stating researcher positionality and epistemic stance.

If these suppositions hold, it is possible to state that the world itself represents an objective entity, which can subsequently be subject to verification and further investigation. Differentiating the aim of explaining action rather than the meaning of it is what characterises positivist inquiry. The interpretivist stance stands in contrast to this, positing that without perceived reality, things cannot exist. It is from this stance that interpretivist research seeks the multiple subjective realities of those experiencing specific phenomena i.e.) perspectives on African feminist epistemology from the perspective of men and women of African origin, whose own authentic experiences are most representative of this.

METHODOLOGICAL AUTHENTICITY AND TRUSTWORTHINESS

There is an evident and frequently reported constructive alignment between ontology, epistemology, philosophy, methodology and methods (Choi and Richards, 2017).

With this alignment, it is possible to see the assumed precedence of each in the context of African feminist research. There is inevitably an assumed resultant methodological stance that results as a direct consequence of differing ontological or epistemological origin. The collective consideration of all is essential in the context of African feminist research if there is to be an authentic degree of systematisation of emergent theoretical perspectives.

Since a dichotomy can exist between ontological and epistemological stance then it is possible to have alternative resultant views of the same phenomena in research. There is a functional dependence rather than a hierarchical sense of precedence between ontology, epistemology, philosophy, methodology and methods and it is this which provides an overarching means of knowing the world and developing universal understanding of it.

Within a different signature discipline, African feminist epistemology provides an opportunity for new knowledge development and the making of the essential beliefs and values people hold into tangible objects or phenomena that act as central foci for the development of cognition and epistemological understanding. The trustworthiness and authenticity of findings ultimately lie in the transparency of how knowledge is created and by whom, with the epistemic stance of the researcher lying at the crux of their coherence.

In terms of operationally defining philosophical standpoint, it can be posited that this is where Interpretivist stances align with knowledge in the context of praxis. The resultant impact of it is to move epistemology or ways of knowing from a process of transactional gain to one of the facilitation of being able to articulate inherent experience alongside personal and collective belief (Russell and Martin, 2017). The epistemology of perception is such that the psychological or cognitive impact of sociology is permitted visibility and authentic resonance. Linked to this is the evocation of cognitive capacity, the potential for experience to add to epistemic cognition and the foundation of the debate as to whether cognitive and affective capacity is truly inseparable. These affective / emotive standpoints are pivotal to any consideration of applied sociological practice and understanding since they facilitate the theoretical embedding of social constructionism or situate it in broader contexts of contextualised human thought, which hold particular resonance in relation to African feminist epistemology (Akoleowu, 2022).

Approaches to epistemological relativism across the interpretivist research paradigm illustrate this, they can provide an alternative reflexive lens for examining the subtle difference between the production rather than the discovery of 'truth' in empirical inquiry (Latour, 1986). These approaches have the potential to be a mechanism of recognizing and segregating epistemic cognition since they permit research participants to define the world 'in their own terms' (Latour, 1999). Whittle and Spicer's (2008) insight into knowledge acquisition highlights that, whether intentional or not, ethnocentrism within qualitative research methods, as highlighted by Bloomfield and Vurdubakis, (1999), implies that participant explanations are at best naïve or at their worst wrong, which can potentially frame some approaches as simply a series of grand narratives (Lee and Brown 1994). To be truly reflexive, though, necessitates a value laden approach to all perceived realities having a degree of intrinsic truth. Where Western researchers have regularly fallen short, is in their willingness to acknowledge their role in the establishment of this. The conceptual common denominator in this process is cognition and it is at this point that the question of where human epistemology sits relative to human cognition is significant, certainly in the context of African feminist epistemology. Rand's (1990) response to this was to note that man's cognitive faculty is conceptual, which again stems back to the original nature of truth and knowledge (ontology).

Metaphysics embraces this context and is embedded in metacognition to form what is commonly termed epistemic cognition. From a metaphysical perspective, representation or meaning making posits or evokes emotion and hence authentically posited African feminist epistemology becomes a means of making tangible metaphysics in the form of specific phenomena (Kitchner, 1983).

INTEGRATING CONCEPTUAL KNOWLEDGE AND PERCEIVED REALITY

History points towards the issues of African feminism being rooted in the raising of social consciousness of the injustice women experience on both a personal and collective level. It is the intersectional divide between their individual lives and the context of economics, sexual politics and identity framing which framed the context of what was commonly termed as a feminist revolution in the 1970's Western and Eurocentric societies. A key driver for this were the visual aesthetics of the era via art, which provided a nexus between politicised issues and the embodiment that women in contemporary society at the time were experiencing. Belying this was the initiation of early ethnographic studies where story making for storytelling became an initial anchor for the mimetic representation of lived experience. Since works of art became central to this, then interpretation and meaning making remained the power preserve of Western and Eurocentric influence and development. The notion of progress narratives not only illuminated lived experience; it also further enabled the clouding of authentic meaning by the Western and Eurocentric lenses of perspective placed upon it. As trajectories of time entailed, the global power dimensions inflicted by the Western and Eurocentric world have gradually and rightly started to be more critically regarded in terms of their relevance to contextually positioned political and sociocultural narratives. The whole concept of legitimate peripheral participation has now been framed and identified as a potential barrier to the construction of new, authentic and embodied, subjective knowledge. It is here that not only illuminates a void between truth and verisimilitude but which on a more positive note provides a platform for the renegotiation and reworking of what the future of African feminist epistemology may become and what it might one day authentically represent within and between global sociocultural boundaries. On a positive note this may lead to the future eminence of question led rather than methods driven approaches to African feminist research which can ultimately be hinged around the concept of situated cognition and the notion of embodied agentic enquiry. It is here that there is an evident opportunity for the constraints of Westernised and Eurocentric imperialism with historical origins in the extent of power held by major global geopolitical players to become a key consideration in any interrogation of where power lies and, in the identification, and approaches to new knowledge creation. Deconstruction of these inequities can only be made possible by handing back and acknowledging the authentic ownership of epistemology to spatial and temporal domains of embodied knowledge and understanding.

VISUAL REPRESENTATIONS OF AFRICAN FEMINIST EPISTEMOLOGY

The integration of conceptual knowledge with sense data facilitates how visual abstractions can be linked to cognition. This is framed in the conceptual designation or delivery of cognate mechanisms where sensory perception begins and ends, for example via the eyes, touch sensors in the skin, the ears or the nose in relation to our ability to smell (Eisner, 2017). It can be posited that every living individual possesses their own perceived reality of the world, which can be regarded as subjective truth (Bruce and Young, 1998). Essentially there are four aspects of human experience which are of significance to the epistemic cognition, namely:

- Corporeality, which alludes to the notion of lived bodily experiences.
- Spatiality, which considers the concept of lived space.
- Relationality, which is directly concerned with lived human relationships.
- Temporality which is an engagement with the concept of lived time.

Because of these four aspects, methodologically speaking, the only credible, valid and authentic person to disseminate the reality of lived experience is the subject themselves but these aspects can also become a relational element of acknowledged epistemic cognition by the researcher. Considering their interrelationship provides an insight into how Western and Eurocentric researchers, however well intentioned, add the additional level of complexity of a post-colonial lens, in terms of their epistemic positionality and consequent epistemic bias. Understanding human behaviour and experience requires that the person must interpret the action or experience from the researcher and then the researcher must interpret the explanation provided by the person (Miščević, 2017). It is the most significant emotionally charged aspects of reality concept formation that ought to characterise question led research, since all inquiry, however empirical still must stem from human inquiry and human curiosity (Jiménez et al, 2017). The significance of the phenomena is also important since it entails the selective recreation of objective reality rather than the metaphysical assumptions surrounding it at an epistemic level (Pollner, 1975). It is here that the authenticity of Western and Eurocentric led research of African feminist epistemology can be contested and challenged within social science research both in terms of ethical responsibility and the morality of Western and Eurocentric research approaches.

Critical reflection and the capacity for reflexivity in the context of decision making now characterises the majority of social science investigations (Kinsella, 2010). This has entrenched the notion of an ethical stance as an integral part of professional practice in research. This lies in stark contrast to romantic epistemology, which advocated that imagination in conjunction and often in preference to rationalising ways of knowing was the greatest stance. It stems from the notion that accountability in terms of 'being' in the world belies the contextual and situational basis of how we might begin 'know' in practice. From this perspective it can be posited that epistemic reflexivity differs distinctly in terms of context specificity and that it is this which provides a mechanism of embedding what is epistemically and creatively derived back into processes of institutional approach, polemics, or technicality (Eisner, 2017).

Whilst creative practice offers no mechanism of addressing any empirical basis of truth, in relation to the seeking of propositional knowledge, the opportunity to be at one with a representational object offers a means by which the transience of self-legitimised inner thoughts can be examined. As such it necessitates a re-examination of the pre-suppositions we make about the manner in which we 'know' and gain knowledge from anything non-propositional in nature and presentation.

The concept of a visual epistemology has its origins in the notion of a constructed and idealised mental imagery, which in turn is reflective of the cognitive processes involved in its making. African feminist epistemology is characterised by this across the various media by which it is presented. Once translated into a mimetic object, depiction via abstraction is possible, at the heart of which is thinking and creation. As such, the representation of worldviews and life worlds through images remains a contentious debate in the field of visual epistemology and one which can never be confined purely to the discipline of arts and creative practice and which has consequently occupied an intersectional space between them and social sciences. This leads clearly into what has been termed 'the epistemic potential of pictures' via visual thinking and perception and which still has direct relevance to African feminist truth today (Klinke, 2014).

INTENTIONALITY AND WAYS OF KNOWING

Capacity for human reasoning and defence lies at the heart of propositional knowledge, the debate remains as to the relative impact of misrepresentation can potentially serve to skew processes and outcomes of knowledge creation. Klinke highlighted how Plato's "Allegory of the Cave" describes a system of epistemology in which there are three stages of understanding—from interpreting mere shadows to understanding that these are shadows only and grasping the ideas behind the apparent world. For Plato, those ideas, not the material world, are the highest forms of reality and constitute 'real knowledge' (Klinke, 2014). When applied to the context of African feminist epistemology, the resonance of needing to represent knowledge through experience rather than Western and Eurocentric perception of that experience is evident. It is here that the notion of Hermeneutical ignorance can be differentiated from many of the intentional Colonial perspectives that preceded it. Whereas current Western and Eurocentric approaches now seek to acknowledge the epistemic injustice that cultures and contexts have been subjected to over centuries of disempowerment, epistemic responsibility is still relatively misunderstood, misrepresented and misplaced in tokenistic attempts to right historical wrongs which still echo in the lives of African populations today (Ndofirepi & Gwaravanda, 2019). Only a clear differentiation between truth, verisimilitude and the doxastic injustice inflicted by Western and Eurocentric researchers, despite how well intentioned can begin to instill a sense of perspective transformation for those committed to authentic African feminism (Tobi, 2020).

Hermeneutical ignorance and doxastic injustice both impact on the potential interactions from a moral political and ethical perspective for those whose lives have been historically misrepresented. Not only does misrepresentation of new knowledge impact on the authenticity and trustworthiness of research undertaken, it also has a broader impact in terms of the potential for intersectional epistemic injustice within and between cultural contexts (Jiménez et al, 2017). The perpetuation of colonialist perspectives on the articulation of experience through a Eurocentric lens only contributes further to the epistemic injustice inflicted within the context of African feminist epistemology. Traditionally approaches to hermeneutics have not permitted cognisance of the contextually situated values and beliefs of marginalised communities and this causes further damage to authentic accounts of cultural heritage (Horn, 2020). It can be contested stances adopted to the foundations of cultural heritage by Western and Eurocentric social science researchers and politicians whose focus remains in abstraction from the salient issues that these marginalised communities face on a daily basis (ibid, 2020). The resultant epistemic injustice can go on to influence whole cultures and their heritage not simply the individual people for whom African Feminism is an issue of fundamental significance (Agra, 2020).

Counterbalancing debates of doxastic injustice versus hermeneutical injustice in relation to African feminist epistemology also warrants a consideration of how efforts to decolonise traditionally labelled geographical contexts have failed. Whilst this has been far more apparent in South Africa versus the context of Sub-Saharan Africa, the need for a sense of epistemic decoloniality has long been posited. Harms research indicated that Western and Eurocentric approaches to philosophy and theorising had engendered a series of professional identities which caused contradictory stances in terms of how the knowledge of those with greatest authentic experience has often been posited as indigenous and peripheral to central political issues. Whilst the context of Harm's work is social work, the potential for transferability to similar contexts and settings is apparent where, for example in contexts of African feminist epistemology still heavily influenced or overshadowed by Coloniality characterised by power, the creation of new knowledge and existentialism, which frames future projected philosophical perspectives (Harms, 2019). African feminist epistemology ought also to be challenged in terms of its ideology and tradition. Understanding and embracing both provides a means of truly understanding the impact of power dynamics, the legacy of colonisation, despite repeated attempts to decolonise, and the acknowledgement of centuries of white supremacy. If a new template of individual and undiluted expression is to characterise the future of African feminist epistemology, then this rich history will serve to benchmark the socio-political landscape which is now a starting point for progressive change and authenticity (Akinkunmi, 2021).

CONCLUSION

This chapter has explored some of the intersectional bases of African feminist epistemology, such as race, gender, culture and the polemic debates which serve to recognise and acknowledge the tensions that arise by theorizing from the perspective of post-colonial legacies and influences. Whilst, in theory, Feminism stemmed from the Enlightenment Period's ideologies of emancipation and social justice, the application of African feminist epistemology represents a contradiction where tokenistic efforts at co-construction and co-creation of truth are questionable in terms of their trustworthiness and authenticity with regard to the concept of post-colonialism in Western and Eurocentric approaches. It is clear from the chapter that debates regarding the accuracy of representation are central to this and whereas historically debates lay at the heart of whether male voices could accurately interpret and articulate feminist perspectives on behalf of females, the whole narrative surrounding the subordination of women, intentional or unintentional is continuing to progress and develop.

REFERENCES

Adebayo, K. O., & Njoku, E. T. (2023). Local and transnational identity, positionality and knowledge production in Africa and the African diaspora. *Field Methods*, *35*(1), 18–32. doi:10.1177/1525822X211051574

Agra, K. L. R. P. (2020). Epistemic Injustice, Epistemic Paralysis, and Epistemic Resistance: A (Feminist) Liberatory Approach to Epistemology. *Kritike: An Online. The Journal of Philosophy*, *14*(1).

Akanle, O., & Shittu, O. S. (2020). Study justification in social research. *Contemporary issues in social research*, *1*, 93-104.

Akinkunmi, K. (2021). An Analysis of "Encountering Development: The Making and Unmaking of the Third World" by Arturo Escobar. *Sustinere—The University of Toronto's Journal of Sustainable Development*, *1*(1), 64-71.

Akoleowo, V. O. O. (2022). African feminism, activism and decolonisation: The case of Alimotu Pelewura. *African Identities*, 1–16. doi:10.1080/14725843.2022.2157246

Al-Ababneh, M. (2020). Linking ontology, epistemology and research methodology. *Science & Philosophy*, *8*(1), 75–91.

Andrews, K. (2021). *The new age of empire: How racism and colonialism still rule the world.* Penguin UK.

Arenhart, J. R. B., & Arroyo, R. W. (2021). Back to the question of ontology (and metaphysics). *Manuscrito*, *44*, 01-51.

Berenstain, N. (2016). Epistemic exploitation.

Bernecker, S. (2022). Knowledge from Falsehood and Truth-Closeness. *Philosophia*, *50*(4), 1623–1638. doi:10.1007/s11406-022-00479-y

Bloomfield, B. P., & Vurdubakis, T. (1999). The outer limits: Monsters, actor networks and the writing of displacement. *Organization*, *6*(4), 625–647. doi:10.1177/135050849964004

Bruce, V., & Young, A. (1998). *In the eye of the beholder: The science of face perception.* Oxford university press.

Carter, J. A. (2017). Epistemological Implications of Relativism. In J. J. Ichikawa (Ed.), *The Routledge Handbook of Epistemic Contextualism*. Routledge. doi:10.4324/9781315745275-24

Chinn, C. A., & Rinehart, R. W. (2016). Epistemic cognition and philosophy: Developing a new framework for epistemic cognition. In *Handbook of epistemic cognition* (pp. 460–478). Routledge.

Choi, S., & Richards, K. (2017). *Interdisciplinary discourse: Communicating across disciplines*. Springer. doi:10.1057/978-1-137-47040-9

Connell, R. (2020). The social organization of masculinity. In *Feminist theory reader* (pp. 192–200). Routledge.

Cunliffe, A. L., & Scaratti, G. (2017). Embedding Impact in Engaged Research: Developing Socially Useful Knowledge through Dialogical Sensemaking. *British Journal of Management*, 28(1), 29–44. doi:10.1111/1467-8551.12204

DeNora, T. (2014). Making sense of reality: Culture and perception in everyday life. *Making Sense of Reality*, 1-200.

Eisner, E. W. (2017). *The enlightened eye: Qualitative inquiry and the enhancement of educational practice*. Teachers College Press.

Falola, T. (2022). *Decolonizing African Knowledge: Autoethnography and African Epistemologies*. Cambridge University Press. doi:10.1017/9781009049634

Fox, H. M. (2017). A way of knowing in search of our true identity. *Self and Society*, 45(1), 72–75. doi:10.1080/03060497.2017.1290453

Grene, M., & Grene, M. G. (1974). *The knower and the known* (Vol. 130). Univ of California Press.

Harms Smith, L. (2019). *Epistemic decoloniality as a pedagogical movement: a turn to anticolonial theorists such as Fanon, Biko and Freire*. Taylor & Francis. Routledge.

Hayes, C., Fulton, J., Livingstone, A., Todd, C., Capper, S., & Smith, P. (2020). *Beyond Disciplinarity: Historical Evolutions of Research Epistemology*. Routledge. doi:10.4324/9781315108377

Hester, J. P. (2020). The Subjective Import of Moral Knowledge. *Humanities Bulletin*, 3(2), 140–156.

Hofer, B. K., & Pintrich, P. R. (2012). *Personal epistemology: The psychology of beliefs about knowledge and knowing*. Routledge. doi:10.4324/9780203424964

Horn, J. (2020). Decolonising emotional well-being and mental health in development: African feminist innovations. *Gender and Development*, *28*(1), 85–98. doi:10.1080/13552074.2020.1717177

Hurlbut, C. D. (2021). *Crit: A Mixed Methods Examination of Epistemic Cognition During Source Evaluations*. McGill University.

Inkpin, A. (2021). Merleau-Ponty's 'sensible ideas' and embodied-embedded practice. *Phenomenology and the Cognitive Sciences*, 1–24.

Jackson, I., Watson, D. L., White, C. D., & Gallo, M. (2022). Research as (re)vision: Laying claim to oral history as a just-us research methodology. *International Journal of Research & Method in Education*, *45*(4), 330–342. doi:10.1080/1743727X.2022.2076827

Jahn, R. G., & Dunne, B. J. (2007). Science of the subjective. *Explore (New York, N.Y.)*, *3*(3), 295–305. doi:10.1016/j.explore.2007.03.014 PMID:17560358

Jensen, M. B., Johnson, B., Lorenz, E., Lundvall, B. Å., & Lundvall, B. A. (2007). Forms of knowledge and modes of innovation. *The learning economy and the economics of hope*, 155.

Jiménez, A. C., Galilei, G., Strathern, M., & Serres, M. (2017). How knowledge grows: an anthropological anamorphosis. *Cosmopolitics*, 227.

Jimoh, A. K. (2017). An African theory of knowledge. *Themes, issues and problems in African philosophy*, 121-136.

Jong, A. (2023). Social configurations in the moment of post-foundationalism. *Frontiers in Sociology*, *7*, 1078011. doi:10.3389/fsoc.2022.1078011 PMID:36779169

Kane, H., Ragsdell, G., & Oppenheim, C. (2006). Knowledge management methodologies. *Electronic Journal of Knowledge Management*, *4*(2), 141–152.

Kaplan, M., Sanchez, M., & Hoffman, J. (2017). Intergenerational Strategies for Establishing Sustainable Work Environments. In *Intergenerational Pathways to a Sustainable Society* (pp. 141–162). Springer International Publishing. doi:10.1007/978-3-319-47019-1_7

Kinsella, E. A. (2010). Professional knowledge and the epistemology of reflective practice. *Nursing Philosophy*, *11*(1), 3–14. doi:10.1111/j.1466-769X.2009.00428.x PMID:20017878

Kitchner, K. S. (1983). Cognition, metacognition, and epistemic cognition. *Human Development*, *26*(4), 222–232. doi:10.1159/000272885

Klinke, H. (Ed.). (2014). *Art theory as visual epistemology*. Cambridge Scholars Publishing.

Lahroodi, R. (2018). Virtue epistemology and collective epistemology. In *The Routledge handbook of virtue epistemology* (pp. 407–419). Routledge. doi:10.4324/9781315712550-34

Latour, B. (1986). Visualization and cognition. *Knowledge in Society*, *6*(6), 1–40.

Latour, B. (1999). *Pandora's hope: Essays on the reality of science studies*. Harvard university press.

Lemos, N. (2020). *An introduction to the theory of knowledge*. Cambridge University Press. doi:10.1017/9781108595162

Markauskaite, L., & Goodyear, P. (2017). Professional Epistemic Games. In *Epistemic Fluency and Professional Education* (pp. 395–434). Springer Netherlands. doi:10.1007/978-94-007-4369-4_14

Matiluko, O. (2020). Decolonising the master's house: How Black Feminist epistemologies can be and are used in decolonial strategy. *The Law Teacher*, *54*(4), 547–561. doi:10.1080/03069400.2020.1827839

Mellor, K. (2022). Developing a decolonial gaze: Articulating research/er positionality and relationship to colonial power. *Access: Critical explorations of equity in higher education, 10*(1), 26-41.

Miščević, N. (2017). Thought experiments in political philosophy. In *The Routledge companion to thought experiments* (pp. 153–170). Routledge. doi:10.4324/9781315175027-9

Moyo, Z. (2020). Moving toward indigenisation of knowledge: Understanding African women's experiences. In Curriculum Theory, Curriculum Theorising, and the Theoriser (pp. 92-105). Brill.

Ndofirepi, A. P., & Gwaravanda, E. T. (2019). Epistemic (in) justice in African universities: A perspective of the politics of knowledge. *Educational Review*, *71*(5), 581–594. doi:10.1080/00131911.2018.1459477

Ndofirepi, A. P., & Gwaravanda, E. T. (2020). Inclusion and social justice: Creating space for African epistemologies in the African university. In *Inclusion as Social Justice* (pp. 90–110). Brill. doi:10.1163/9789004434486_008

Nicolelis, M. (2020). *The true creator of everything: How the human brain shaped the universe as we know it*. Yale University Press.

Nzegwu, N. (2019). African Art in Deep Time: De-race-ing Aesthetics and De-racializing Visual Art: Nzegwu African Art in Deep Time. *The Journal of Aesthetics and Art Criticism, 77*(4), 367–378. doi:10.1111/jaac.12674

Okech, A. (2020). African feminist epistemic communities and decoloniality. *Critical African Studies, 12*(3), 313–329. doi:10.1080/21681392.2020.1810086

Ossome, L. (2020). African feminism. In *Routledge Handbook of Pan-Africanism* (pp. 159–170). Routledge. doi:10.4324/9780429020193-11

Park, C. L. (2017). Distinctions to promote an integrated perspective on meaning: Global meaning and meaning-making processes. *Journal of Constructivist Psychology, 30*(1), 14–19. doi:10.1080/10720537.2015.1119082

Pekrun, R. (2011). Emotions as drivers of learning and cognitive development. In *New perspectives on affect and learning technologies* (pp. 23–39). Springer New York. doi:10.1007/978-1-4419-9625-1_3

Pollner, M. (1975). 'The very coinage of your brain': The anatomy of reality disjunctures. *Philosophy of the Social Sciences, 5*(3), 411–430. doi:10.1177/004839317500500304

R'boul, H. (2022). Postcolonial interventions in intercultural communication knowledge: Meta-intercultural ontologies, decolonial knowledges and epistemological polylogue. *Journal of International and Intercultural Communication, 15*(1), 75–93. doi:10.1080/17513057.2020.1829676

Rand, A. (1990). *Introduction to Objectivist Epistemology: Expanded* (2nd ed.). Penguin.

Russell, T., & Martin, A. K. (2017). Reflective practice: Epistemological perspectives on learning from experience in teacher education. *Reflective theory and practice in teacher education*, 27-47.

Simba, P., & Davids, N. (2020). Cultivating Third Space thinking in ('African') feminism through the works of Nandipha Mntambo. *Agenda (Durban, South Africa), 34*(3), 87–99. doi:10.1080/10130950.2020.1790302

Spiegel, T. J. (2017). 2 Naturalism, Quietism. *On What It Is: Perspectives on Metaphilosophy*, 47.

Stupples, P. (2017). Beyond the predicted: Expanding our understanding of creative agency in international development through practice and policy. *International Journal of Cultural Policy, 23*(1), 52–67. doi:10.1080/10286632.2015.1035264

Szigeti, A. (2024). The heuristics theory of emotions and moderate rationalism. *Philosophical Psychology*, *37*(4), 861–884. doi:10.1080/09515089.2022.2094232

ter Vrugte, J., & de Jong, T. (2017). Self-Explanations in Game-Based Learning: From Tacit to Transferable Knowledge. In Instructional Techniques to Facilitate Learning and Motivation of Serious Games (pp. 141-159). Springer International Publishing.

Thomas, K. B. (2020). Intersectionality and epistemic erasure: A caution to decolonial feminism. *Hypatia*, *35*(3), 509–523. doi:10.1017/hyp.2020.22

Tirri, K., Husu, J., & Kansanen, P. (1999). The epistemological stance between the knower and the known. *Teaching and Teacher Education*, *15*(8), 911–922. doi:10.1016/S0742-051X(99)00034-7

Tobi, A. T. (2020). Towards a plausible account of epistemic decolonisation. *Philosophical Papers*, *49*(2), 253–278. doi:10.1080/05568641.2020.1779602

Tonkin, E. (2021). History and the Myth of Realism. In *The myths we live by* (pp. 25–35). Routledge. doi:10.4324/9781003174714-3

Van Veeren, E. (2019). Layered wanderings: Epistemic justice through the art of Wangechi Mutu and Njideka Akunyili Crosby. *International Feminist Journal of Politics*, *21*(3), 488–498. doi:10.1080/14616742.2019.1619468

Varela, F. J., Thompson, E., & Rosch, E. (2017). The embodied mind, revised edition: Cognitive science and human experience. MIT press. doi:10.7551/mitpress/9780262529365.001.0001

Whittle, A., & Spicer, A. (2008). Is actor network theory critique? *Organization Studies*, *29*(4), 611–629. doi:10.1177/0170840607082223

Wielenga, C. (2022). African Feminisms and Justice on the Ground. *African Feminisms and Women in the Context of Justice in Southern Africa*, 19-39.

ADDITIONAL READING

Ahikire, J. (2014). African feminism in context: Reflections on the legitimation battles, victories and reversals. *Feminist Africa*, *19*(7), 7–23.

Bayu, E. K. (2019). A comparative analysis on the perspectives of African Feminism Vs Western Feminism: Philosophical debate with their criticism and its implication for womens rights in Ethiopia context. *International Journal of Sociology and Anthropology*, *11*(4), 54–58.

Bleich, D. (1975). The subjective character of critical interpretation. *College English*, *36*(7), 739–755. doi:10.2307/375172

Dillard, C. B. (2000). The substance of things hoped for, the evidence of things not seen: Examining an endarkened feminist epistemology in educational research and leadership. *International Journal of Qualitative Studies in Education : QSE*, *13*(6), 661–681. doi:10.1080/09518390050211565

du Toit, L., & Coetzee, A. (2017). Gendering African philosophy, or: African feminism as decolonizing force. The Palgrave handbook of African philosophy, 333-347.

Griffiths, D. (2022). Decoloniality and the (im) possibility of an African feminist philosophy. *South African Journal of Philosophy*, *41*(3), 240–252. doi:10.1080/02580136.2022.2087144

Kwachou, M. (2022). In response to Acker: Black and African feminist theories on gender and education. *Comparative Education*, 1–24.

Lenine, E., & Alves, J. A. D. A. (2022). African feminisms and feminist political theory: Conceptual and epistemological encounters. *Revista Brasileira de Ciências Sociais*, 37. doi:10.1590/3711002/2022

Okech, A. (2020). African feminist epistemic communities and decoloniality. *Critical African Studies*, *12*(3), 313–329. doi:10.1080/21681392.2020.1810086

Oyewumi, O. (2000). Family bonds/conceptual binds: African notes on feminist epistemologies. *Signs (Chicago, Ill.)*, *25*(4), 1093–1098. doi:10.1086/495526

Segalo, P., & Fine, M. (2020). Under lying conditions of gender-based violence—Decolonial feminism meets epistemic ignorance: Critical transnational conversations. *Social and Personality Psychology Compass*, *14*(10), 1–10. doi:10.1111/spc3.12568

KEY TERMS AND DEFINITIONS

Authenticity: The quality or condition of being authentic, trustworthy, or genuine.
Colonialism: The operational policy or practice of the acquisition of full or partial political control over other countries, occupying them with people who seek to exploit it both economically and socially.

Doxastic Injustice: Doxastic injustice serves to underpin the assumption that what is used to represent others can essentially be damaging to them in terms of what others believe as a consequence.

Epistemic Injustice: Epistemic injustice is pertains to knowledge which is used to misrepresent, exclude or silence authentic meaning. Often this can emanate from inequity in terms of power relations which has the potential to diminish value of the perceptions and opinions of underrepresented or marginalised individuals or communities.

Epistemic Responsibility: Epistemic responsibility is the that despite not having been able, as researchers to directly experience or reason with a specific positional stance that it is still worthy of belief and accurate articulation.

Hermeneutical Ignorance: Hermeneutical ignorance stems from dominantly positioned or situated creators of knowledge who refuse to acknowledge their own sense of epistemic bias in relation to those who are directly experienced in terms of credibility and dependability.

Intersectionality: Pertains to the interconnected nature of identifiable classifications such as gender, class, and race as applied to collective or individual groups, which contribute to a distinct overlap in terms of the emergence of discrimination and active disadvantage.

Perspective Transformation: A key seminal theory of Jack Mezirow (1978), Perspective Transformation pertains to a structural change in terms of self-perception. The process reformulates the process of critical reflexivity, resulting in new and much developed attitudes and behaviour.

Verisimilitude: Is the appearance of truth or reality rather than actual truth or reality.

Chapter 10
Examining Women Leaders' Role in Broadening Participation in STEM at HBCUs

Kimarie Engerman
https://orcid.org/0000-0002-7845-9116
Center for the Advancement of STEM Leadership, University of the Virgin Islands, US Virgin Islands

Angelicque Tucker Blackmon
https://orcid.org/0000-0001-9429-9936
Center for the Advancement of STEM Leadership, University of the Virgin Islands, US Virgin Islands

Camille A. McKayle
Center for the Advancement of STEM Leadership, University of the Virgin Islands, US Virgin Islands

Elizabeth Jaeger
Center for the Advancement of STEM Leadership, University of the Virgin Islands, US Virgin Islands

ABSTRACT

This research examines women academic leaders' role in broadening participation in science technology, engineering, and mathematics (STEM) disciplines at Historically Black Colleges and Universities (HBCUs). HBCUs produce a high percentage of Black STEM graduates which contributes to the nation's diverse STEM workforce. Additionally, women are known to be transformative leaders. Interpretative phenomenological analysis (IPA) was used in this study to understand

DOI: 10.4018/979-8-3693-0102-9.ch010

Copyright © 2024, IGI Global. Copying or distributing in print or electronic forms without written permission of IGI Global is prohibited.

the academic women leaders' role. A semi-structured interview was administered to obtain information on the women's leadership style or characteristics, STEM success as a leader, and the relationship between women's leadership and STEM success at their respective institution. The study findings have implications for institutions to capitalize on the significant role women leaders play in the success of students, faculty, and the institution overall.

INTRODUCTION

In the United States, women outnumber men on college campuses in receiving undergraduate and master's degrees (National Center for Education Statistics, 2023). Although more women receive college degrees, data shows that fewer women ascend through academic ranks to become university leaders with only around 30% of university presidents were women (Gasman, 2023; Schaeffer; 2023). The American Association of University Women (2018) reported that the percentage of women holding tenure-track positions in four-year institutions increased from 40.5% in 2007 to 44.6% in 2017. However, despite this progress, women in science, technology, engineering, and mathematics (STEM) account for only 28% of tenure-track positions and 18% of full professors (American Association of University Women, 2018).

According to Mey (2022), systematic and societal barriers exist that prevent women from rising to the top positions at institutions of higher learning. Zgodic and Small (2021) addressed four challenges women face in higher education. The first challenge was that women were underrepresented, and that bias existed among search committees and governing boards. The second challenge was that women were reluctant to promote their professional accomplishments. The third challenge was that women were loyal to their institutions and lacked geographic mobility because they prioritized their partners' careers. The fourth challenge was the lack of leadership experience in fundraising and finance.

Kiral and Başara (2019) defined leadership as attaining goals through influence. They further noted that academic leaders are those individuals who possess a vision and can implement desired change through power. Barnard et al. (2022) clarified that higher education leaders are not limited to individuals in senior management positions. Higher education leadership is reflected in various roles within the institution, such as department chairs and deans. Women in leadership roles contribute to the advancement of higher education as institutions. Novotney (2023) found that when women lead, everyone benefits. Therefore, women are needed in senior-level higher education and academic leadership positions.

Based on the research conducted by Novotney (2023), productivity is increased, collaboration is enhanced, organizational dedication is inspired, and fairness is improved when women lead. Empirical data shows women's leadership styles were related to their transformational leadership style. According to Cherry (2023), transformational leaders are energetic, involved in the process, and help others on the team succeed. More importantly, transformational leaders envision the group's goals.

Choi et al. (2016) explored the characteristics of transformational leaders. These characteristics are exemplified in women leaders. One of the characteristics is inspirational motivation. In this characteristic, leaders ensure subordinates understand the purpose of the tasks. Clarity is gained through using effective communication strategies. According to Choi et al., women leaders hold high expectations, and subordinates focus on accomplishing stated goals. Because women leaders are clear in articulating their vision, subordinates are passionate and motivated to achieve goals (Cherry, 2023). Another characteristic of women leaders noted by Choi et al. (2016) is individualized consideration. This characteristic entails leaders supporting the skills of their subordinates. A supportive, nurturing relationship is developed, and subordinates freely share their ideas. Leaders provide advice and are seen as coaches. Intellectual stimulation is another characteristic of transformational leaders. Subordinates are encouraged to do things in a new way and think with reason and facts. This results in independent problem-solving. The final characteristic is that transformational leaders are charismatic leaders. Their subordinates trust and respect them, and there is a visible display of pride in the organization.

Furthermore, Ayers (2022) explored women's positive impact in higher education roles. One such benefit is diversity. With a diverse leadership team, the variety of perspectives and experiences at institutions of higher learning allow for more innovative and inclusive decision-making processes (Dezso & Ross, 2011). Diverse teams are better equipped to problem-solve and make more informed decisions, which are crucial skills needed in higher education leadership roles (Amar, 2023; Toke, 2023). Moreover, Ashcraft et al. (2016) concluded that teams with equal numbers of women and men were likelier than other compositions to complete tasks, be creative, experiment, and share information. Additionally, teams with more women had a higher level of collective intelligence than teams with more men and less women. Collective intelligence was the combination of the intelligence of individual members on the team.

Another benefit of women in leadership roles in higher education is that women serve as role models for students. Serving as role models is especially beneficial for young women who aspire to pursue a career in academia. Seeing women in positions of power and influence sends the message that women can be successful in leadership roles within any field they choose.

The representation of women can significantly impact the confidence and aspirations of young women, encouraging them to pursue various majors and leadership careers in higher education. Improved confidence was confirmed in the qualitative phenomenological study of 12 women conducted by Stewart (2021). Women in various science, technology, engineering, and mathematics (STEM) fields, including secondary educators, university professors, and STEM professionals, were participants in the study. The participants consistently reported that their development, academic pathway, and career choices resulted from positive contributions made by a woman role model and/or mentor.

Additionally, Latu et al. (2019) explored how women leaders empower other women through mimicry. The participants consisted of 86 women college students. In the study, body posture men and women role models were manipulated. Latu et al. proposed "that women will mimic female role models during a novel, stressful task, given that learning the nonverbal signals produced by these successful role models may help women respond appropriately to the stressful situation" (p. 13). The findings revealed that female role models, rather than male role models, empowered female participants to perform better on public speaking tasks. Their research highlighted the need for more women leaders, especially since the evidence shows they can inspire the advancement of other women.

Regarding the advancement of women leaders, the study conducted by Engerman et al. (2022) addressed strategies that can be implemented to assist women in obtaining leadership roles. Engerman et al. studied four mid-career women at Historically Black Colleges and Universities (HBCUs) who were in STEM academic leadership positions. A key finding from the study was for women to purposefully seek career advancement. One recommendation was for women to capitalize on leadership opportunities presented to them. Another suggestion was for women to participate in leadership development programs. Other recommendations included building internal and external networks, collaborating with colleagues, and getting a mentor.

In summary, women in varying leadership roles within higher education, especially in STEM leadership roles, generate significant advantages for the institutions where they serve. Most notable is the transformation, inspiration, and motivation women in leadership roles create. Further, women in leadership roles serve as important role models, bolstering the confidence of women students who aspire to obtain future leadership roles in higher education. Having women in leadership positions is especially beneficial in science, technology, engineering, and mathematics (STEM) fields.

Role of HBCUs in Broadening Participation in STEM

HBCUs offer educational opportunities to students of all ages, races, and economic backgrounds and afford this opportunity to students who may have never been able to attend an institution of higher learning. Despite serving a wide array of student backgrounds and levels of academic preparation, HBCUs are credited with producing most of the nation's Black STEM professionals (Esters & Strayhorn, 2013, Owens et al., 2012; Williams & Palmer, 2019; Willliams & Taylor, 2022) and contribute to the improvement of students' self-efficacy, cultural connectedness, psychological wellness, and social uplift (Palmer & Strayhorn, 2008; Preston & Palmer, 2018). Furthermore, Jaeger et al. (2021) noted that HBCUs support and affirm students and promote their success in STEM through institutional and leadership characteristics. Such characteristics included leaders' commitment to STEM education, strategies to support students, STEM education funding, and a STEM focused mission.

To gain a deeper understanding of academic leaders' role in broadening participation in STEM, Boncana et al. (2021) explored the role of the president. A case study on four presidents at HBCUs was conducted to examine their role in producing STEM graduates. Findings from the study revealed that the presidents' leadership characteristics included competence that was directed by vision, experience with challenges, strategic hiring, and bold actions.

Overall, students at HBCUs are also more likely to report a sense of belonging on their campuses and express feelings of being supported by their peers (Toldson, 2019). Within STEM education, African American students attending HBCUs and majoring in STEM disciplines have more positive perceptions of their educational experiences, higher self-efficacy, and more post-baccalaureate educational aspirations than African American students attending non-HBCUs (Palmer & Strayhorn, 2008; Toldson, 2019).

RESEARCH STUDY

Methodology

To understand the role of women leaders in broadening participation in STEM at HBCUs, an interpretative phenomenological analysis (IPA) was conducted. According to Alase (2017), IPA allows researchers to develop rich, deep insights into the livid experience of their research participants. Through the sharing of stories by research participants, the research findings are strengthened and reflect the lived experiences of women. Themes are extracted to make sense of participants' experiences. The participants are deans and chairs at their respective institutions. Collectively, they had over 15 years of leadership experience.

Participants

The participants in this study were selected from a study conducted by the Center for the Advancement of STEM Leadership (CASL). Funded by the National Science Foundation, CASL is a collaboration among the University of the Virgin Islands, Fielding Graduate University, North Carolina A&T State University, and the Association of American Colleges and Universities. The Center for the Advancement of STEM Leadership aims to examine the correlation between leadership and broadening participation in STEM at Historically Black Colleges and Universities (HBCUs). As such, CASL only focuses on leaders.

There are 66 HBCUs that serve as CASL Affiliate Institutions. HBCUs selected as Affiliate Institutions must have a record of producing a high number of STEM graduates, including those who earned post-baccalaureate degrees. Also, the criteria for being selected as a CASL Affiliate Institution were:

- Large (>1000) vs. Small (<1000) total enrollment over last 3 years;
- (b)Land Grant vs. non-Land Grant
- Public vs. private
- Offers baccalaureate only vs. undergraduate and graduate programs
- Many vs. few STEM degrees offered
- Total STEM degree enrollment over last 3 years, by gender
- Level of external funding for STEM
- Accreditations related to STEM
- Number of STEM baccalaureate graduates proceeding to masters, doctoral programs
- Graduate school destinations of STEM students
- Number of graduates employed in a STEM field

A snowballing approach was used to identify individuals to participate in the broader CASL study. The executive director for CASL sent a letter to institutional leaders asking to identify a campus representative. The role of the campus representative was to identify and schedule semi-structured interviews with STEM leaders (provosts, vice presidents/vice provosts, deans, chairs, and directors).

For this paper, a convenient sample was drawn from the broader CASL study. The criteria for participating in this study were (a) knowledgeable about or had demonstrated a legacy of leadership that was associated with the advancement of STEM at their respective HBCU institution; (b) serving as a dean or chair of the department; and (c) working at a small or large HBCU. The data collection was done through semi-structured interviews. The analysis was shaped through data description rather than theory building. Codes were formed from responses to open-ended questions to create themes.

The paper focuses on four women leaders at four HBCUs. According to Subedi (2021), a small sample size allows for an in-depth exploration of the study phenomenon. Also, Young and Casey (2018) found that sufficient themes could be extracted for studies with sample sizes ranging from 4-6 participants. Young and Casey further noted that small sample sizes can produce meaningful and thorough findings. Malterud et al. (2016) stated that the size of the sample is determined by the purpose of the study.

Pseudonyms are given to protect the women's identity. Again, the selection criteria were women serving as dean or chair, working at small or large HBCU, and knowledgeable about or had demonstrated a legacy of leadership that was associated with the advancement of STEM at their respective HBCU institution.

- Amy was at a small, public HBCU. She was in the dean's position for seven years. Her academic background was in a non-STEM discipline.
- Paige was at a small, public HBCU. She was in the dean's position for three years. Her academic background is in a STEM discipline.
- Pamela was at a small, private HBCU. She was in the department chair position for one year. Her academic background was in a STEM discipline.
- Brenda was at a large, public HBCU. She was in the department chair position for four years. Her academic background was in a STEM discipline.

Instrument

A demographic sheet and 12-question semi-structured interview protocol were administered to the women leaders with IRB approvals in place. The purpose was to obtain information on their success in STEM and their role in broadening participation in STEM. According to Blackmon et al. (2021), broadening participation involves helping STEM students be successful in higher education. This study focused on the following three questions:

1. How would you describe your leadership style or characteristics?
2. What has been your greatest success as a leader, with particular reference to STEM?
3. What do you think is the relationship between your leadership and STEM success at your college/university?

Methods

After receiving Institutional Review Board approval, participants were recruited via telephone and email. Participants completed consent forms prior to the interview. The interviews were conducted electronically via Zoom, recorded, and transcribed. Identifying information was removed from the interview transcripts prior to analysis.

Interpretive Phenomenological Analysis (IPA) was used for this study. IPA is an approach to qualitative research that focuses on discovering insights into how a person makes sense of a given phenomenon within a particular context (Alase, 2017; Smith, Flowers & Larkins, 2022; Smith & Nizza, 2022). According to Smith and Nizza (2022), IPA is an approach developed to examine participants' experiences closely. Usually, these phenomena relate to personally significant experiences, such as an important life event or a meaningful relationship development. In this study, the phenomenon of interest was perceptions of leadership characteristics, leadership success in STEM, and perceptions on the relationship between leadership success and broadening participation in STEM.

FINDINGS

To understand women leaders' role in broadening participation in STEM at HBCUs, the findings for the three interview questions are presented below. Information is presented individually for each question. Diagrams are included to provide a visual representation of the findings. Additionally, quotes from participants are given to bring the text to life.

Leadership Style or Characteristics

All the participants described their leadership style or characteristic as one that is people-oriented. The concern for people was at the center of how they led. This entailed leading by example, being a team player, and being inclusive. The people-oriented leadership style or characteristic described is reflected below in Figure 1.

Amy acknowledged that she led by example and said, "*I believe in allowing individuals to be themselves but yet provide direction and guidance.*" Pamela said her leadership style was collaborative and that she was a team player. Paige stated that she works closely with the group to collectively accomplish goals. She further added that she invests in her staff and faculty to make sure they have what they need to reach those goals. Additionally, Brenda said, "*I am all inclusive. I believe in shared governance. Everybody has a word. . . I believe in nurturing. I also believe in exposure, giving everybody an opportunity to be exposed to different things.*"

Figure 1. Leadership characteristic themes

Greatest Success as a Leader in STEM

The women in this study were asked to share their greatest success related to STEM. The greatest success for Amy was getting a program accredited within a two-year period. However, the other three participants' greatest success pertained to people such as students, and faculty (see Figure 2).

Figure 2. Greatest success with people

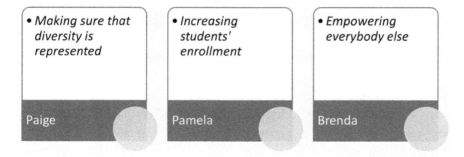

For instance, Paige was proud of her ability to diversify the faculty. Paige stated,

Probably one of the things that I would be most proud of is actually focusing more on bringing women and underrepresented minorities into faculty positions where they are underrepresented. And so, focusing on making sure that diversity is represented among the faculty in STEM continues to be really very important to me. . . [A]s a person who studied diversity, [I] also know how important it is for people to see themselves in those positions. Important to women to see women for African Americans to see African Americans and so also recruiting . . . faculty [that] reflects that diversity and reflects the people that they're teaching has been important to me . . .

Furthermore, Pamela felt that her greatest success was empowering students to obtain terminal degrees. She said,

Our greatest success under my leadership is increasing students' enrollment into medical school, into graduate programs. I have students who have terminal degrees now. It's something when I came to [Name redacted], it was one or two. . . One of the things I realized when I first got to [Name redacted], that there were average performance students that had great potential. They just needed someone to help mold them, get them into class, and focused. And they have been my greatest success in taking an average student that have gone on and gotten terminal degrees.

Brenda added,

My greatest success is empowering everybody else, that includes faculty and students, to make them think that STEM is reachable. It's not intangible and I tell my students all the time, I'm not the brightest star in the sky but I'm a star and you are too. So, I just encourage my faculty to realize that we can be wrong and it's okay. . . I think my biggest contribution to STEM has been the empowerment of others including women that are younger, to include African American women, to include all women...

Relationship between Leadership and STEM Success

As figure 3 shows, faculty relationship and faculty development were the overarching themes for what participants perceived to be the relationship between their leadership and STEM success at their respective institutions.

Amy was intentional in building a collegial relationship with chairpersons and faculty. She provided feedback on research ideas. As a result of her efforts, they invited her to meetings and professional conferences. Amy stated,

Figure 3. Important factors for STEM success

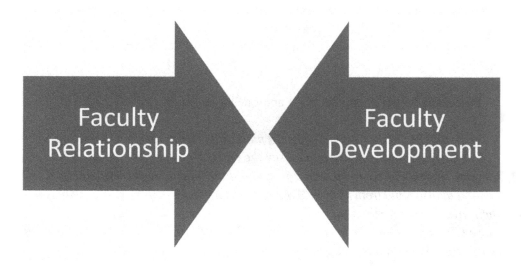

I think the relationship with success is my ability to communicate effectively with our chairpersons. And to really promote the mission of our school, as well as the mission of the university and staying in line with that mission. And, faculty know, that if they have a research idea, they can come to me and, and I think I'm fortunate that people know my abilities to write. And I think that's a strength, you know, if you can write well, and you can communicate that, what you're thinking and writing, and you can help the chairs to really come together and collaborate. I've been able to communicate across disciplines and to assist, if necessary, because I am available, I started going to departmental meetings.

Paige on the other hand reinvested in the Sponsored Program Office by hiring a new director and invested in the Office of Undergraduate Research. The staff in the Sponsored Program Office worked with faculty on writing grants. A noticeable difference in faculty's motivation to pursue grants was seen within two years. According to Paige, in the past, her institution used to have great grants which led to a lot of their historical STEM performances. Therefore, the relationship between leadership and STEM success was,

The investment to make in faculty's ability to develop themselves, which I see through investments in sponsored programs but also investments in our own faculty development. And then the investments that you make in creating the ability for students to engage in research. And so, when you have those two things go on, faculty development and research, and then outlet for students. I think we start to make a real impact on your student's ability to, you know, get ready to go on to graduate school, especially to, to go on and do whatever they want in STEM. And so, I've really been trying to focus back on that because I believe you can't have strong STEM unless you have strong faculty, you can't have strong faculty unless they're engaged in their own research.

Pamela had a collaborative, team approach. She stated,

It's the ability to act as a good coach in pulling this team together. Knowing when to pull the reins, knowing when to loosen the reins. It's a lot of trial and error along the way in trying to come up with this model to be able to work with people. I also have tried to expand from us in STEM to give others an idea of how they can promote their areas and move the areas into another arena so that they can be successful with those too. Some of them have been successful with the model. But that relationship of having that collaborative effort allows us to flourish and grow.

However, Brenda discussed using her voice to encourage others. She said,

I think that STEM is a vehicle, but I don't think it's my reason. It just so happens I'm in STEM. It just so happens that it is a field that is not as populated for blacks and black women, but I think that my voice is bigger than my degree. What I've been through is much more of a pathway to lead and a testimony to others of what they can do . . .I have girls who come up to me that I've seen over the years. [T]hey say, "Do you remember when you told me that I was the smartest thing in the room? I got a doctorate degree because of that. [D]o you remember when you asked me why did I get up at 8 o'clock in the morning to put makeup on and you told me I was beautiful to look at in an 8 o'clock class?" She said, "I got a doctorate degree." So, that had nothing to do with STEM. It's the respect of the STEM degree and . . .encouraging [students].

CONCLUSION

The existing literature on the role of women leaders in higher education describes them as transformers of their institutions (Novotney, 2023). They help advance other women leaders and serve as role models for their students (Stewart, 2021; Latu et al., 2019). This study examined the leadership styles and success of women leaders in STEM at HBCUs. It also analyzed the relationship between leadership style and STEM success. In terms of leadership styles, women described being people centered, leading by example, working closely with faculty to accomplish, promoting inclusive leadership, believing in nurturing others and using their voice to empower and encourage both students and faculty.

Women leaders in STEM at HBCUs described their greatest STEM successes as hiring diverse faculty that would work to ensure students' STEM success, investing in faculty so they could win grant awards that would support the preparation of students for STEM graduate and professional degree programs. One leader described her greatest success as taking an average student and providing academic support to a student that eventually received a terminal degree in a STEM discipline.

In terms of the relationship between leadership styles and STEM success, the people centered aspect shows how these women leaders' styles results in STEM success for students and faculty. They focused on the success of others as evident in the persistent theme showing their people centered style of leadership. The women's leadership style results in success for students, faculty, and their institution overall.

ACKNOWLEDGMENT

This work was supported by the National Science Foundation through the Center for the Advancement of STEM Leadership (CASL) under NSF Grant No. 1818424, 1818425, 1818447, and 1818459. Any opinions, findings, conclusions, or recommendations expressed in this report are those of the authors and do not necessarily reflect the views of the National Science Foundation.

REFERENCES

Alase, A. (2017). The interpretative phenomenological analysis (IPA): A guide to a good qualitative research approach. *International Journal of Education and Literacy Studies*, *5*(2), 9–19. doi:10.7575/aiac.ijels.v.5n.2p.9

Amar, S. (2023). Why everyone wins with more women in leadership. Forbes. Retrieved from https://www.forbes.com/sites/forbesbusinesscouncil/2023/02/07/why-everyone-wins-with-more-women-in-leadership/?sh=2c7dfb3f3cdd

Ashcraft, C., McLain, B., & Eger, E. (2016). Women in tech: The facts. National Center for Women & Technology (NCWIT). Retrieved from: https://www.ncwit.org/resources/women-tech-facts-2016-update

Barnard, S., Arnolda, J., Bosleya, S., & Munir, F. (2022). The personal and institutional impacts of a mass participation leadership programme for women working in Higher Education: A longitudinal analysis. *Studies in Higher Education*, *47*(7), 1372–1385. doi:10.1080/03075079.2021.1894117

Blackmon, A. T., Askew, K., McKayle, C., Engerman, K., & Clavier, N. (2021). "I see the potential in you": Provosts' purposeful perspective-taking on HBCU students to promote broadening STEM participation. *The Journal of Negro Education*, *90*(3), 322–333.

Boncana, M., McKayle, C., Engerman, K., & Askew, K. (2021). What is going on here? Exploring why HBCU presidents are successful in producing STEM graduates. *The Journal of Negro Education*, *90*(3), 277–287.

Cherry, K. (2023). How transformational leadership can inspire others. Retrieved from https://www.verywellmind.com/what-is-transformational-leadership-2795313

Choi, S. L., Goh, C. F., Adam, M. B., & Tan, O. K. (2016). Transformational leadership, empowerment, and job satisfaction: The mediating role of employee empowerment. *Human Resources for Health*, *14*(1), 73. doi:10.1186/s12960-016-0171-2 PMID:27903294

Dezso C. L. Ross D. G. (2011). Does female representation in top management improve firm performance? A panel data investigation. Robert H. Smith School Research Paper No. RHS 06-104. Retrieved from: https://ssrn.com/abstract=1088182

Engerman, K., McKayle, C., Blackmon Tucker, A., & Askew, K. (2022). Elevating the voice of mid-career academic women leaders in broadening participation in STEM. In H. Schnackenberg (Ed.), *Women in Higher Education and the Journey to Mid-Career: Challenges and Opportunities*. IGI Global., doi:10.4018/978-1-6684-4451-1.ch005

Engerman, K., McKayle, C., & Tucker Blackmon, A. (2021). Presidents' role in broadening participation in STEM. In M. T. Miller & G. D. Gearhart (Eds.), *Handbook of research on the changing role of college and university leadership*. IGI Global., doi:10.4018/978-1-7998-6560-5.ch012

Esters, L. L., & Strayhorn, T. L. (2013). Demystifying the contributions of public land-grant historically Black colleges and universities: Voices of HBCU presidents. *Negro Educational Review*, *64*(1-4), 119–134.

Gasman, M. (2023). Women are on the rise as leaders of top research universities. Forbes. Retrieved from https://www.forbes.com/sites/marybethgasman/2023/06/05/women-are-on-the-rise-as-leaders-of-top-research-universities/?sh=3c6e93a49c80

Jaeger, E., McKayle, C., Engerman, K., Boncana, M., Joseph, C., & Askew, K. (2021). Institutional and Leadership Predictors of HBCU Success in Broadening Participation in STEM. *The Journal of Negro Education*, *90*(3), 371–382.

Latu, I. M., Mast, M. S., Bombari, D., Lammers, J., & Hoyt, C. L. (2019). Empowering mimicry: Female leader role models empower women in leadership tasks through body posture mimicry. *Sex Roles*, *80*(1/2), 11–24. doi:10.1007/s11199-018-0911-y PMID:30651662

Malterud, K., Siersma, V. D., & Guassora, A. D. (2016). Sample size in qualitative interview studies: Guided by information power. *Qualitative Health Research*, *26*(13), 1753–1760. doi:10.1177/1049732315617444 PMID:26613970

Mey, K. (2022). More than just a matter of style: female leadership in higher education. European University Association. Retrieved from https://eua.eu/resources/expert-voices/285:more-than-just-a-matter-of-style-female-leadership-in-higher-education.html

National Center for Education Statistics. (2023)... *Digest of Educational Statistics*, *2021*, •••. https://nces.ed.gov/programs/digest/d21/

Novotney, A. (2023). Women leaders make work better. Here's the science behind how to promote them. American Psychological Association. Retrieved from https://www.apa.org/topics/women-girls/female-leaders-make-work-better

Owens, E. W., Shelton, A. J., Bloom, C. M., & Cavil, J. K. (2012). The significance of HBCUs to the production of STEM graduates: Answering the call. *Educational Foundations*, *26*, 33–47.

Palmer, R. T., & Strayhorn, T. L. (2008). Mastering one's own Fate: Non-cognitive factors associated with the success of African American males at an HBCU. *NASAP Journal*, *11*, 126–143.

Preston, D. C., & Palmer, R. T. (2018). When relevance is no longer the question. *Journal of Black Studies*, *49*(8), 782–800. doi:10.1177/0021934718798088

Schaeffer, K. (2023). The data on women leaders. Pew Research Center. Retrieved from https://www.pewresearch.org/social-trends/fact-sheet/the-data-on-women-leaders/

Smith, J. A., Flowers, P., & Larkin, M. (2022). *Interpretative phenomenological analysis: theory, method, and research* (2nd ed.). SAGE Publications Ltd. doi:10.1037/0000259-000

Smith, J. A., & Nizza, I. E. (2022). *Essentials of interpretative phenomenological analysis*. American Psychological Association. doi:10.1037/0000259-000

Stewart, C. A. (2021). Underrepresentation of women STEM leaders: Twelve women on different journeys using their voices to shape the world through science. *European Journal of STEM Education, 6*(1), 16. doi:10.20897/ejsteme/11387

Subedi, K. R. (2021). Determining the sample in qualitative research. *Scholars'. Journal, 4*, 1–13.

Toke, N. (2023). Empowering women in leadership. Diversity for Social Impact. Retrieved from https://diversity.social/empowering-women-in-leadership/

Toldson, I. A. (2019). Cultivating STEM Talent at Minority Serving Institutions: Challenges and Opportunities To Broaden Participation in STEM at Historically Black Colleges and Universities. In Growing Diverse STEM Communities: Methodology, Impact, and Evidence (Vol. 1328, pp. 1–8). American Chemical Society. doi:10.1021/bk-2019-1328.ch001

Williams, J. L., & Palmer, R. T. (2019). A response to racism: How HBCU enrollment grew in the face of hatred. Retrieved from https://cmsi.gse.rutgers.edu/content/response-to-racism

Williams, K. L., & Taylor, L. D. (2022). The Black cultural student STEM success model: A framework for Black students' STEM success informed by HBCU environments and Black educational logics. *Journal of Women and Minorities in Science and Engineering, 28*(6), 81–108. doi:10.1615/JWomenMinorScienEng.2022036596

Young, D. S., & Casey, E. A. (2018). An examination of the sufficiency of small qualitative samples. *Social Work & Criminal Justice Publications, 500*, https://digitalcommons.tacoma.uw.edu/socialwork_pub/500

Zgodic, A., & Small, L. (2021). Increasing representation of women in leadership positions at the University of South Carolina. Retrieved from https://sc.edu/about/offices_and_divisions/provost/docs/pacwi_policy_brief_final_october_19_2021.pdf

KEY TERMS AND DEFINITIONS

Academic Leaders: Individuals in senior level positions such as president, vice president, provost, dean, and chair at an institution of higher learning.

Academic Leadership: The implement change through influence and power.

Broadening Participation: Students from underrepresented groups being successful in STEM (Engerman et al, 2021).

CASL: Center for the Advancement of STEM Leadership.

HBCUS: Historically Black Colleges and Universities that predominantly serve minority students. These institutions were founded before the Civil Rights Act of 1964.

STEM: Science, technology, engineering, and mathematics fields.

Chapter 11
Micro-Enterprises, Performance Factors, and the Role of Gender

Chelo Durante
Cebu Technological University, Philippines

Michel Plaisent
Université du Québec à Montréal, Canada

Cataldo Zuccaro
Université du Québec à Montréal, Canada

Jean-Pierre Gueyie
Université du Québec à Montréal, Canada

Prosper Bernard
Université du Québec à Montréal, Canada

ABSTRACT

Life in developing countries often relies on informal economy and micro-enterprises, often created and managed by women. Their performance has been studied in the literature of management and world development and factors of success have been suggested among which the access to micro-financing organizations, being member of network, having an innovative spirit and accepting the related risk and being able to overcome hostile business conditions. The difficulties are reported as being worst for women who suffers from stereotypes about their abilities and negative cultural factors. This chapter reports on a cross-sectional study among 200 entrepreneurs and test those hypothesis.

DOI: 10.4018/979-8-3693-0102-9.ch011

1. INTRODUCTION

1.1 Entrepreneurship, Startups and Women

Research on entrepreneurship often overlooks or minimizes women's roles in the innovation process and may even perpetuate gender bias (Chávez-Rivera et al., 2024). Despite these challenges, women entrepreneurs play a vital role in job creation and economic growth (Bullough et al., 2019). Studies suggest that women entrepreneurs excel in communication and often outperform men in business ventures (Gorbatai and Nelson, 2017). For instance, Neumeyer and Santos (2020) found that teams with a higher proportion of women tend to perform better in entrepreneurial endeavors, highlighting women's qualities such as controlled audacity, self-discipline, and effective communication skills.

Hughes (2017) found that only 10% of startups were founded by women, with many operating in sectors traditionally dominated by women and often opting for non-profit ventures over profit-seeking enterprises. Moreover, transformational leadership in charitable organizations is predominantly led by women in Canada (Alonzo et al., 2024). Gender disparities persist in science-related entrepreneurship, with women entrepreneurs facing significant challenges compared to their male counterparts (Poggesi et al., 2020). Personal characteristics influence women's career choices and entrepreneurial success (Kuschel et al., 2020), with studies showing fewer women commercializing their research and opting for less lucrative sectors compared to men (Abreu and Grinevich, 2017).

Entrepreneurial orientation significantly impacts enterprise growth and performance, as evidenced by research across multiple countries (Khadhraoui et al., 2019). However, women entrepreneurs face various constraints, including family responsibilities, low education levels, limited access to finance, and legal and policy barriers (Nyangarika, 2016). Addressing these challenges requires education and financial access for women, improvements in the business environment, and equitable distribution of household responsibilities. Politicians are increasingly recognizing the importance of female entrepreneurship and are allocating resources to support and promote it, particularly in Canada (Bosma, 2020). In Tanzania, women entrepreneurs face numerous constraints related to personal characteristics, lack of information, finance, and unfavorable legal and policy frameworks (Nyangarika, 2016). Overcoming these barriers requires interventions such as education, financial access, and improvements in the business environment.

Micro, Small, and Medium Enterprises (MSMEs) play a critical role in the Philippine economy, contributing significantly to employment generation and national wealth (Anoos et al., 2020). These enterprises are vital for economic development, enhancing purchasing power, and contributing to tax revenue.

1.2 Objective of This Chapter

The role of culture in women's entrepreneurship remains largely unexplored, despite its recognized influence on success or failure due to societal barriers such as values, beliefs, and local behaviors (Bullough et al., 2022). This chapter seeks to address this gap by examining the impact of gender, stereotypes, and cultural factors on women's entrepreneurship, particularly in the context of microfinance.

Firstly, it aims to enhance understanding of the challenges women face in entrepreneurship due to cultural norms and gender biases. Secondly, it intends to compare the performance of women entrepreneurs with that of men, focusing on informal economic activities. This approach draws inspiration from Tossou, Gueyie, & Couchoro's (2022) study on "Female Managers, Informal Enterprises, and Their Perceived Financial Performance in Togo," which explores similar themes in a different context.

2. THEORETICAL BACKGROUND AND HYPOTHESES DEVELOPMENT

2.1 Financial Performance of Women

Financial performance serves as a crucial metric for assessing an organization's current status and potential for growth (Kim et al., 2021), providing insights into the effectiveness of its leadership (Collazos & Botero, 2024). By evaluating financial performance, management can gauge whether the company has met its profitability objectives (Azizah, Manik, & Sumarni, 2023) and conduct necessary monitoring and analysis for decision-making purposes (Tossou et al., 2022). Developing a robust performance measurement system is a priority for modern businesses (Waśniewski, 2021). Business success hinges on various factors, including trade expertise, access to capital, networking capabilities (both personal and professional), family support, understanding customer needs, and investing additional time and effort into work (Kamau, 2023).

Studies by Akintimehin et al. (2021) and Mansur & Djaelani (2023) shed light on additional factors influencing business performance. Akintimehin et al. (2021) found that social capital significantly impacts business performance, particularly internal social capital affecting non-financial performance. Mansur & Djaelani (2023) identified standard entrepreneurial orientations, such as a lack of market expertise and government support, as contributors to the low success rates of informal small firms.

Moreover, research by Pagaddut (2021) highlighted key variables influencing the financial performance of Philippine MSMEs, with tax policies, credit availability, and financial literacy emerging as statistically significant factors affecting SME performance (Benedict et al., 2021).

These findings lead to the main hypothesis of this chapter:

H1: The performance of women-led businesses surpasses that of men-led ones.

2.2 The Perceived Financial Performance and the Stereotypes Toward Females' Managerial Abilities

Gender stereotypes encompass societal perceptions regarding the typical traits associated with men and women, exerting influence on individuals' entrepreneurial intentions and motivations based on their gender role orientation (Liñán et al., 2024). Women's participation in management or board positions and their ownership of companies can significantly impact the financial performance of these entities (Collazos et al., 2024).

A study conducted by Emon and Nepa (2024) delves into the multifaceted aspects of social empowerment stemming from women's entrepreneurial pursuits, highlighting entrepreneurship's potential to drive broader societal transformations. Similarly, findings from research by Trần et al. (2024) indicate that Asian companies operating in the transportation and logistics sector could experience enhanced financial performance with greater female representation on their boards of directors. Women bring unique values and skills to corporate boards, bolstering board effectiveness and influencing organizational outcomes for stakeholders and shareholders (Pérez, 2022). Recognizing women's contributions to business is paramount given their significant impact.

However, prevailing attitudes toward female leaders often erect barriers hindering women's leadership aspirations and impeding their success in leadership roles (Bullough et al., 2022). Hence, hypothesis 2 posits that:

H2: The relationship between PFP and stereotypes regarding females' managerial abilities varies for women.

2.3 The PFP and the Cultural Factors

Culture in business refers to the collective norms and practices that shape how management and staff conduct business operations. An organization's culture can foster an environment where employees adhere to principles of honesty, fairness, and morality when making decisions that impact stakeholders (Ahsan, 2023). Collazos et al. (2024) suggest that testing their hypotheses across diverse cultural contexts would provide valuable insights into how culture influences the impact of women on firm performance.

Research findings highlight the influence of Tanzanian culture on entrepreneurial risk-taking behavior, which in turn shapes decisions related to seizing business opportunities (Liu et al., 2018). Similarly, a study by Khan et al. (2021) conducted in Pakistan reveals that women's success is influenced by socio-cultural factors, including religious barriers and family business history.

Therefore, hypothesis 3 posits that:

H3: The relationship between PFP and cultural factors varies for women.

2.4 Other Factors

2.4.1 The Business Environment and the PFP

In contemporary times, the technological landscape is deemed pivotal in enhancing the performance of SMEs in Malaysia, particularly concerning networking (Yeoh, 2023). Establishing a conducive business environment is imperative for fostering business growth, a principle that applies to both formal and informal economies. The business environment significantly influences firm performance through various channels, including government policies and regulations, institutional frameworks, infrastructure, and macroeconomic dynamics (Orjiakor, 2022).

Research conducted by Mawejje and Sebudde (2018) identifies several business constraints that exert the most significant impact on firm performance, including macroeconomic instability, demand volatility, limited financial accessibility, corruption, and weather variability. Similarly, studies by et al. (2016) focus on taxation, regulatory frameworks, judicial efficiency, and infrastructure deficiencies, highlighting these aspects as primary constraints on firm growth.

Estevão et al. (2022) underscore the challenges faced by economies with high levels of informality, such as difficulty in accessing financing, inefficient tax systems, inadequate investor protection, and deficient licensing mechanisms. To cultivate a business-friendly environment, measures must be implemented, including infrastructural development, robust legal frameworks, and supportive government policies (Tossou et al., 2022).

Thus, hypothesis 4 posits that:

H4: The relationship between PFP and constraints in the business environment varies for women.

2.4.2 The Difficulty to Access Financing and Perceived Financial Performance

Microfinance has emerged as a tool to combat poverty by extending credit to underprivileged and marginalized economic groups (Chikwira et al., 2022). Operating within the formal environment confers significant advantages, providing access to government programs, subsidies, incentives, and technology upgrade funding, including collateral-free loans (Koshy, 2019). However, informal MSMEs encounter numerous challenges. Access to finance and credit plays a pivotal role in sustaining livelihoods, improving living standards, and nurturing small businesses (Olugbenga & Mashigo, 2017).

In the Philippines, social enterprises, particularly startups, grapple with various challenges, from securing capital to managing finances and finding markets for their products and services (Habaradas, 2022). Despite the potential of women-led startups, Kuschel and Lepeley (2016) highlight investor reluctance to finance them, fearing disruptions such as sudden pregnancies that could impact company performance. However, post-global economic crisis studies indicate that women tend to repay loans more expeditiously, prompting financial institutions to view them as less risky (Cowling et al., 2019).

Contrarily, Aristei and Gallo (2021) found that female-led businesses are more likely than their male counterparts to encounter financing challenges and refrain from seeking credit. Rudhumbu (2020) outlines several challenges faced by women entrepreneurs, including limited access to financing, lack of technical skills, and inadequate information about financing options and marketing techniques. Despite these hurdles, the legal and regulatory environment in Botswana is viewed as conducive to women's entrepreneurship due to available training opportunities.

Thus, hypothesis 5 posits that:

H5: The relationship between PFP and accessibility to financing varies for women.

2.4.3 The Perceived Financial Performance and the Entrepreneur's Network

Networking plays a pivotal role in business, fostering close relationships among members who support each other and bridge gaps. A well-functioning network, characterized by continuous communication, significantly enhances innovation performance in women-owned businesses (Rivera et al., 2023). Various forms of interaction occur within networks, facilitating relationship-building and collaboration among like-minded individuals.

Social networks and media platforms have emerged as crucial tools for global communication and collaboration, enabling individuals to connect and engage with others who share similar interests (Ruël et al., 2014). Utilizing diverse entrepreneurial networks, including strategically positioned and effective structural holes, network structures, densities, linkages, and centrality, has been found to positively impact overall performance in medium-sized businesses (Gatwiri, 2021). Moreover, social media serves as a valuable co-creation technique, enhancing organizational performance through structural, cognitive, and relational linkages (Donga & Wu, 2015), thereby fostering the creation of more networks that can enhance business performance.

In Canada, a research community was established to encourage the creation of spin-outs by graduate students in engineering and sciences, with successful entrepreneurs mentoring aspiring individuals contemplating launching a business from their research. The results revealed that newcomers benefit from the guidance of experienced and successful women entrepreneurs, highlighting the importance of networks in navigating this challenging journey (Plaisent et al., 2021).

Thus, hypothesis 6 posits that:

H6: The relationship between PFP and network affiliation varies for women.

2.4.4 The PFP and the Risk Appetite

The concept of risk appetite is widely acknowledged as a guiding principle for strategic risk management (Marshall et al., 2018). Research by Mat et al. (2020) revealed that risk-taking propensity serves as a complete mediator of the effect of personality variables on the success of female entrepreneurs.

In Pakistan, Khan et al. (2021) identified several factors that significantly impact women's success, including personal characteristics like the need for achievement, risk-taking propensity, and self-confidence, as well as economic factors such as access to finance and manpower availability, and socio-cultural factors like religious barriers and family business history. Various factors, including socioeconomic status, capital availability, firm type, industry, financial literacy, and cultural beliefs, contribute significantly to explaining the gender gap in risk aversion. Risk tolerance is prevalent among entrepreneurs, with gender cited as one of the factors influencing entrepreneurs' risk attitudes in Ghana (Asravor & Vera, 2021).

Thus, hypothesis 7 posits that:

H7: The relationship between PFP and the propensity to take risks (risk appetite) varies for women.

2.4.5 The Perceived Financial Performance and the Innovative Spirit of the Entrepreneur

An entrepreneur is characterized by possessing a strong aptitude for information and skills, a drive to continuously learn, and innovative ideas that enable them to remain competitive in today's dynamic business landscape (Harini et al., 2024). For female entrepreneurs, spiritual capital can serve as a valuable tool for enhancing performance, creativity, and innovation in the business realm (Juliana et al., 2023). The transformative potential of innovation is exemplified by women entrepreneurs. According to Cho et al. (2020, p.3), entrepreneurs are defined as "those who initiate, own, and manage startups and small-medium enterprises (SMEs), focusing on innovation in products, processes, or markets."

Thus, hypothesis 8 posits that:

H8: The relationship between PFP and the innovative spirit varies for women.

2.5 The Microfinance in the Philippines and Users' Satisfaction

Microfinance refers to financial services tailored for individuals from lower socioeconomic backgrounds or those lacking access to traditional financial services, encompassing savings accounts, checking accounts, fund transfers, micro-insurance, and microcredit (Corporate Finance Institute). The Philippines stands out globally as a leader in utilizing microcredit to alleviate poverty, with a particular focus on women (Parmanand, 2021). Microcredit institutions allocate significant funds toward providing small loans, primarily to female entrepreneurs, as part of poverty alleviation efforts (Karlan & J Zinman, 2011). Layaoen and Takahashi (2021) indicated that microfinance tends to supplant informal lending from moneylenders, friends, and family. According to the Bangko Sentral ng Pilipinas report, informal lenders accounted for 10% of outstanding loans in 2019, with microfinance NGOs being the preferred choice among formal lenders (Bangko Sentral ng Pilipinas [BSP], 2019).

In the Philippines, microfinance is recognized not only as a pivotal tool for poverty reduction but also for empowering marginalized populations lacking access to traditional financial services (Gabriel et al., 2021). This study identified financial security, health concerns, and educational needs as key motivators for household clients to utilize microfinance services. Assessing the quality of services provided by microfinance institutions is crucial for governmental agencies seeking to promote entrepreneurship. Conducting surveys among microfinance members to gauge their satisfaction levels with these services is one approach.

Microfinance institutions offer a diverse range of services to meet the financial and non-financial needs of micro, small, and medium-sized enterprises (MSMEs), including credit, savings, leasing, insurance facilities, and training programs (Shah & Hingu, 2022). Microfinance has historically been hailed as an inclusive financial tool, ensuring that credit flows to low-income families without stringent collateral requirements (Das, 2022). The primary social objective of microfinance is to uplift the lives of the impoverished (Ofori & Kashiwagi, 2022).

A study evaluating the impact of microfinance products and services in the Philippines revealed that microfinance institutions provided high-quality loans and products, leading to high member satisfaction levels and positively influencing economic growth among members (Irorita et al., 2023). To achieve financial inclusion, it is imperative to design microfinance schemes tailored to encompass the entire population.

Thus, hypothesis 9 posits that:

H9: The satisfaction of women entrepreneurs with microfinance organizations differs.

2.6 Research Model

The research objectives and hypotheses can be summarized in the following conceptual diagram.

Figure 1. Conceptual diagram of the research

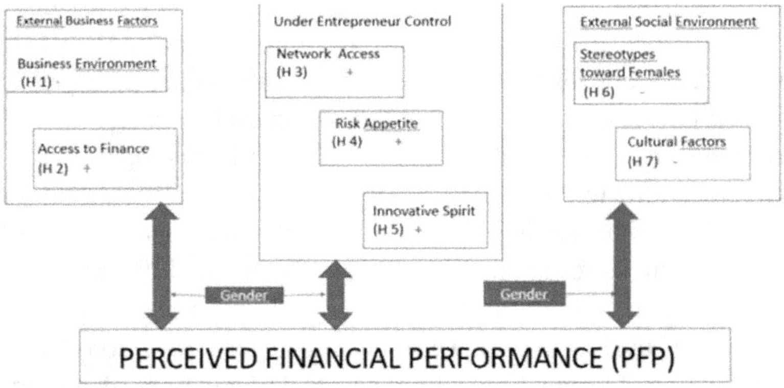

3. METHODOLOGY

The researchers utilized an instrument developed by Tossou et al. (2021) in a similar study involving women entrepreneurs in Togo. The questionnaire was administered through the SurveyMonkey website and comprised X sections. These sections included a description of the enterprise and the entrepreneur, 32 Likert-style questions (rated on a 5-point scale) related to the hypotheses on performance and the constraints faced, particularly cultural factors and stereotypes, and a question regarding satisfaction with the microfinance institution.

The study involved a sample of entrepreneurs and members of a local microfinance organization. Data were collected through convenience sampling, with research assistants stationed at the microfinance organization building, inviting entrepreneurs visiting the institution to participate. Participants were asked to complete the questionnaire either directly on their smartphone, on a tablet provided by research assistants, or on their own device at home.

4. DATA ANALYSIS

4.1 Data Examination

Out of the 210 responses collected, several records had to be removed for various reasons, such as outliers or a high percentage of incomplete forms. This resulted in 179 valid questionnaires available for data analysis.

4.2 Socio-Demographic Characteristics of Respondents

The respondents are unequally divided between men (n=49, i.e., 27.4%) and women (n=130, i.e., 72.6%). In the Philippines, the percentage of MSMEs owned by women is 38 percent or fewer, and they tend to be smaller, more informal, and home-based (Qasim, 2018). However, women generally show more openness to answering questionnaires. Nevertheless, there are enough men to perform gender comparisons. Almost 48% live alone, either single or divorced, while 52% are in a couple. Additionally, 39.3% have no or undergraduate scholarship, while 60.7% have a bachelor's or master's degree.

4.3 Examination of the Potential Role of Gender

a) Role of Gender on the Perceived Financial Performance (PFP)

A t-test was conducted to determine whether gender has an effect on PFP. The results are presented in Figure 2.

The t-test yielded a value of -1.777, with a significance level of .077. Therefore, the hypothesis suggesting a difference in perceived performance based on gender is not statistically significant.

Figure 2. T-test statistics of the difference between genders regarding PFP

Group Statistics					
	Q03. Gender	N	Mean	Std. Deviation	Std. Error Mean
q30 performance (C5)	Male	49	17,3265	3,57298	,51043
	Female	129	18,3256	3,26239	,28724

Independent Samples Test							
		Levene's Test for Equality of Variances		t-test		Significance	
		F	Sig.	t	df	One-Sided p	Two-Sided p
q30 performance (C5)	Equal variances assumed	,474	,492	-1,777	176	,039	,077
	Equal variances not assumed			-1,706	80,199	,046	,092

b) Role of Gender as a Moderator of the Relationships Between PCP and Other Variables

A t-test was conducted to examine whether gender can account for variations in PFP in comparison to other potentially associated variables. The results are presented below:

Table 1. Summary of t-tests to examine gender role

topic	t-test, p 2-sided	conclusion
stereotypes	t=.612 p=.541	no difference
cultural factors	t=-.316 p=.752	no difference
business environment	t=.927 p=.355	no difference
access to financing	t=1.036 p=.302	no difference
innovative spirit	t=-1.228 p= .224	no difference
risk appetite	t=-.950 p=.343	no difference
satisfaction with micro-finance organism	t=-2.289, sig=.026	difference

The analysis indicates that there is no significant difference in the perception of the primary potential performance determinants between men and women. However, women exhibit significantly higher satisfaction levels with the microfinance organization compared to men (female = 3.85/5 while male = 3.35/5).

As a consequence of these tests, the hypothesis about the role of gender is rejected.

Figure 3. Model summary

Model Summary

Model	R	R Square	Adjusted R Square	Std. Error of the Estimate
1	,133[a]	,018	,012	3,34995

a. Predictors: (Constant), Q03. Gender

ANOVA[a]

Model		Sum of Squares	df	Mean Square	F	Sig.
1	Regression	35,444	1	35,444	3,158	,077[b]
	Residual	1975,101	176	11,222		
	Total	2010,545	177			

a. Dependent Variable: q30 performance (C5)
b. Predictors: (Constant), Q03. Gender

5. CONCLUSION

5.1 Findings and Limitations

This chapter aims to enhance understanding of micro-enterprises, drawing data from a developing country where many women manage micro-businesses to support their families. While existing literature, predominantly from Western sources, identifies determinants of perceived financial performance, only three have been empirically linked to performance in this research context: positive risk appetite, innovation spirit, and negative cultural factors. Generally, entrepreneurs who have secured loans from micro-finance organizations express satisfaction. Analyses reveal no discernible differences between men and women. This study suggests focusing on beneficial variables to assist micro-entrepreneurs.

However, this study has limitations, including the convenience-based data collection approach, a relatively small sample size, and potential misunderstandings of questionnaire items by self-reporting respondents. Further research in this area is warranted.

5.2 Recommendations

Adequate training: According to Rudhumbu (2020), women entrepreneurs often face challenges such as a lack of technical skills and information regarding financing possibilities and marketing techniques. Building on Nyangarika's (2016) concept, chambers of commerce and micro-finance providers are urged to implement specific technical training programs covering operations, marketing, and finance. Understanding the distinction between cash flow and the owner's wealth is crucial for maintaining business liquidity despite emergency family financial needs. Banks and financing institutions should establish necessary controls to ensure that loan applicants utilize funds for their intended purpose, with loan objectives serving as the basis for determining loan amounts. This could be achieved through appropriate borrower training.

Finance access: Given that women-led MSMEs are vital for the economy, policymakers should review the lending policies of all microfinance institutions to ensure impartial loan approvals regardless of the borrower's gender. Additionally, the government could introduce a policy requiring banks and financial institutions to allocate a percentage of their loans specifically for financing women entrepreneurs. This would enhance women's financial capacity at a lower cost than direct funding. Regular evaluation of accredited microfinance institutions' services should ensure compliance with the aforementioned policy, particularly regarding quotas for loans granted to women entrepreneurs.

Fostering a favorable business environment: Telecommunications and electricity are essential for business operations. Governments could provide subsidies to partially offset the costs of these infrastructure needs, especially for women entrepreneurs contributing to family income. Such subsidies could be provided in the form of loans for a specified period. Simplifying administrative procedures, at least for the initial years, could reduce bureaucratic hurdles and promote sustainable business growth.

Targeting sustainability: Local government units should mandate MSMEs to register with the Barangay and the Department of Trade and Industry (DTI) to receive proper assistance and access government programs and support initiatives, including credit management workshops, financial literacy programs, and home-based business opportunities. Simplifying the registration process is crucial for its success. To protect consumers, DTI and other government agencies should require MSMEs to adopt Business Continuity Plans, enhancing their resilience and sustainability.

Shared familial responsibilities: Women often bear the burden of household chores and children's education. Encouraging a shift towards shared responsibilities between parents is necessary. Media outlets should promote alternative family dynamics and diverse perspectives in their content, while web influencers should be encouraged to endorse this new family model. Local celebrities could advocate for this shift in family roles to promote wider acceptance and adoption.

5.3 Future Research Directions

- This research was conducted through a cross-sectional quantitative study in a single province of the Philippines. Expanding the scope of the research to other developing countries in South Asia and Africa would enhance our

understanding of the cultural factors' significance and facilitate broader generalization of the findings.
- Additionally, employing a more qualitative approach would yield more nuanced insights into women's perceptions of the drivers and barriers to their business expansion.
- What are the expectations placed on women by microfinance institutions, and how are these expectations formalized in their internal regulations and policies?
- How do stereotypes impact enterprises managed by women when engaging with suppliers or buyers, and how can women be empowered to assert their value despite prevailing stereotypes, especially in situations requiring a continuous flow of transactions?
- Many women entrepreneurs have achieved notable success and expanded their businesses. Do these successful women entrepreneurs alter public perceptions, particularly among lenders, or do entrenched perceptions remain unchanged? How can these perceptions evolve over time, and which communication channels are most effective for catalyzing this "image revolution"?
- Historically, women have tended to start very small businesses catering to local needs, such as sari-sari stores, ukay-ukay shops, eateries, and handmade folk art. How can women leverage the digitalization of the economy to promote their products, streamline delivery processes, and transform their supply and value chains?

REFERENCES

Abreu, M., and Grinevich, V. (2017). "Gender patterns in academic entrepreneurship," *Journal of Technology Transfer* (42:4), pp. 763-794.

Ahsan, M. J. (2023). Unlocking sustainable success: Exploring the impact of transformational leadership, organizational culture, and CSR performance on financial performance in the Italian manufacturing sector. *Social Responsibility Journal.* Advance online publication. doi:10.1108/SRJ-06-2023-0332

Akintimehin, O. O., Eniolaa, A. A., Eluyelac, Felix, D., Okered, Wisdom, & Ozordie, E. (2021). Social capital and its effect on business performance in the Nigeria's informal sector. doi:10.1016/j.heliyon.2019.e02024

Alonzo, M. L. M., Zuccaro, C., Plaisent, M., & Bernard, P. (2024). Examination of the Relationship Between Organizational Effectiveness and Transformational Leadership: The Case of Registered Charities. In Trends, Challenges, and Practices in Contemporary Strategic Management (pp. 194-212). IGI Global.

Anoos, J. M., Gimena, J. A., Etcuban, J. O., Dinauanao, A. M., Macugay, P., & Velita, L. V. (2020). Financial management of micro, small, and medium enterprises in Cebu, Philippines. *International Journal of Small Business and Entrepreneurship Research*, 53–76.

Aristei, D., & Gallo, M. (2021). Are female-led firms disadvantaged in accessing bank credit? Evidence from transition economies. *International Journal of Emerging Markets*, *17*(6), 1484–1521. doi:10.1108/IJOEM-03-2020-0286

Armuña, C., Ramos, S., Ruiz, J. J., Feijoo, C., and Arenal, A. 2020. "From stand-up to start-up: exploring entrepreneurship competencies and STEM women's intention," *International Entrepreneurship and Management Journal* (16:1), pp. 69-92.

Asravor, R. K., & Acheampong, V. (2021). Factors influencing risk attitudes of entrepreneurs in Ghana: The role of gender. *Journal of Small Business and Entrepreneurship*, *36*(1), 29–52. doi:10.1080/08276331.2021.1980838

Azizah, N., Manik, M. B., & Ilham, R. N. (2023). Analysis of Financial Performance in the Home Industry of Kerupuk Tempe in Matang Munye, Syamtalira Aron Sub-district. *Journal of Accounting Research. Utility Finance and Digital Assets*, *1*(3), 304–311.

Bangko Sentral ng Pilipinas, (2019) Financial Inclusion Survey. BSP. Retrieved from https://www.bsp.gov.ph › 2019FISToplineReport.

Benedict, A., Gitongab, J. K., Agyemanc, A. S., & Kyeid, B. T. (2021). Financial determinants of SMEs performance. Evidence from Kenya leather industry.

Bosma, N., (2020). Global Entrepreneurship Monitor 2019/2020.

Bullough, A., Guelich, U., Manolova, T. S., & Schjoedt, L. (2022). Women's entrepreneurship and culture: Gender role expectations and identities, societal culture, and the entrepreneurial environment. *Small Business Economics*, *58*(2), 985–996. doi:10.1007/s11187-020-00429-6 PMID:38624690

Bullough, A., Hechavarria, D., Brush, C., & Edelman, L. (Eds.). (2019). *High-growth women's entrepreneurship programs, policies and practices*. Edward Elgar Publishing. doi:10.4337/9781788118712

Chávez-Rivera, M. E., Ruíz-Jiménez, J. M., & Fuentes-Fuentes, M. D. M. (2024). The effects of context and characteristics of women entrepreneurs on innovation performance. *Business Research Quarterly*, *27*(1), 73–90. doi:10.1177/23409444231220951

Chikwira, C., Vengesai, E., & Mandude, P. (2022). The Impact of Microfinance Institutions on Poverty Alleviation. *Journal of Risk and Financial Management*, *15*(9), 393. Advance online publication. doi:10.3390/jrfm15090393

Cho, Y., Li, J., & Chaudhuri, S. (2020). Women entrepreneurs in Asia: Eight country studies. *Advances in Developing Human Resources*, *22*(2), 115–123. doi:10.1177/1523422320907042

Collazos, L. E. O., & Botero, I. C. (2024). *Women ownership as a form of leadership: The role of context in understanding its effects on financial performance.* BRQ Business Research Quarterly., doi:10.1177/23409444231222503

Cowling, M., Marlow, S., & Liu, W. C. (2019). Gender and bank lending after the global financial crisis: Are women entrepreneurs safer bets? *Small Business Economics*, •••. Advance online publication. doi:10.1007/s11187-019-00168-3

Das, R. C. (2022). *Microfinance to Combat Global Recession and Social Exclusion: An Empirical Investigation.* doi:10.1007/978-981-16-4329-3

Donga, o. Q., & Wu, W. (2015). Business value of social media technologies: Evidence from online user innovation communities. *24*(2), 113-227. doi:10.1016/j.jsis.2015.04.003

Emon, M. H., & Nipa, M. N. (2024). Exploring the gender dimension in entrepreneurship Development: A Systematic Literature Review in the context of Bangladesh. *Westcliff International Journal of Applied Research*, *8*(1), 34–49. doi:10.47670/wuwijar202481mhemnn

Estevão, J., Lopes, J. D., & Penela, D. (2022). The importance of the business environment for the informal economy: Evidence from the Doing Business ranking. *Technological Forecasting and Social Change*, *174*, 121288. doi:10.1016/j.techfore.2021.121288

GabrielA. G.SuyuJ. B.FrondaJ. G.RamosV. (2021). The impact of microfinance to borrowers, business, personal and financial status and the mediating role of service satisfaction: evidence from the Philippines. doi:10.21203/rs.3.rs-182720/v1

Gatwiri, K. D. (2021). *Influence of Entrepreneurial Networks on Financial Performance of Medium-Sized Enterprises in Kenya*. Retrieved from http://localhost/xmlui/handle/123456789/5552

Gorbatai, A., & Nelson, L. (2015). The narrative advantage: Gender and the language of crowdfunding. *Haas School of Business UC Berkeley. Research Papers*, 1-32.

Habaradas, R. B. (2022). *Social Entrepreneurship: Conceptual Definition, Bried literature Review and some Examples from the Philippines*. Asian Development Bank. Retrieved December 23, 2022, from https://www.adb.org › files › institutional-document

Harini, S., Yuningsih, E., & Latipah, I. (2024). The influence of competence, business motivation, and entrepreneurial spirit on business success in Ciawi District, Bogor Regency (Case Study of Snack Food MSMEs). *INTERNATIONAL JOURNAL OF SOCIAL SCIENCE AND EDUCATION RESEARCH STUDIES*, *04*(01). Advance online publication. doi:10.55677/ijssers/V04I1Y2024-07

Hughes, K. D. 2017. "GEM Canada 2015/16 Report on Women's Entrepreneurship". Available online at: www.gemcanada.org

Juliana, S. M., & Simatupang, P. (2023). The Empowering Church Members in the Implementation of the Creative Economy: An Interpretative Approach to the Concept of Missionary Congregation Development. *Asian Journal of Management. Entrepreneurship and Social Science*, *3*(04), 1395–1410.

KamauC. G. (2023). *Availability of Finance, Finance Costs, and Business Success in Kenya: Focus on the Small and Micro Enterprises*. SSRN.

Karlan, D., & J Zinman, J. (2011). Microcredit in Theory and Practice: Using Randomized Credit Scoring for Impact Evaluation. doi:10.1126/science.1200138

Khadhraoui, M., Plaisent, M., Lakhal, L., & Prosper, B. (2019). The impact of entrepreneurial orientation on spin-offs' performance: A cross-cultural study. *SAGE Open*, *9*(3), 2158244019865817. doi:10.1177/2158244019865817

Khan, R. U., Salamzadeh, Y., Shah, S. Z. A., & Hussain, M. (2021). Factors affecting women entrepreneurs' success: A study of small and medium-sized enterprises in the emerging market of Pakistan. *Journal of Innovation and Entrepreneurship*, *10*(1), 1–21. doi:10.1186/s13731-021-00145-9 PMID:33686362

Kim, C. Y., Seo, E. H., Booranabanyat, C., & Kim, K. (2021). Effects of emerging-economy firms' knowledge acquisition from an advanced international joint venture partner on their financial performance based on the open innovation perspective. *Journal of Open Innovation, 7*(1), 67. doi:10.3390/joitmc7010067

Koshy, P. (2019). Integration into formal enterprise space: Challenges and opportunities for informal sector entrepreneurs. Retrieved from https://mpra.ub.uni-muenchen.de/95346/

Kuschel, K., Kerstin, E., Díaz-García, C., and Alsos, G. A. 2020. "Stemming the gender gap in STEM entrepreneurship – insights into women's entrepreneurship in science, technology, engineering, and mathematics," *International Entrepreneurship and Management Journal* (16:1), pp. 1-15.

Kuschel, K., & Lepeley, M. T. (2016). Copreneurial women in start-ups: Growth-oriented or lifestyle? An aid for technology industry investors. *Academia (Caracas), 29*(2), 181–197. doi:10.1108/ARLA-08-2015-0231

Layaoen, C. W. G., & Takahashi, K. (2021b). Can microfinance lending crowd out informal lenders? Evidence from the Philippines. *Journal of International Development, 34*(2), 379–414. doi:10.1002/jid.3604

Liñán, F., Jaén, I., & Rodríguez, M. J. (2024). Gender and sex in starting up: A social stereotype approach. *Entrepreneurship and Regional Development, 36*(3–4), 243–265. doi:10.1080/08985626.2023.2295266

Liu, J., Thomas, P. F., & Xuhui, W. (2018). The influence of culture in entrepreneurs' opportunity exploitation decision in Tanzania. *Journal of Entrepreneurship in Emerging Economies, 11*(1), 22–43. doi:10.1108/JEEE-02-2017-0014

Mansur, M., & Djaelani, A. Q. (2023). Business Strategy Approach to Informal Small Businesses in Increasing Productivity and Competitiveness. doi:10.52970/grmapb.v3i1.206

Marshall, A., Ojiako, U., & Chipulu, M. (2018). A futility, perversity, and jeopardy critique of "risk appetite". *The International Journal of Organizational Analysis, 27*(1), 51–73. Advance online publication. doi:10.1108/IJOA-06-2017-1175

Mat, Z. C., Hakimin, M. N., & Zaino Anwar, A. A. (2020). It was discovered that risk-taking. doi:10.31838/jcr.07.06.217

Mawejje, J., & Sebudde, R. K. (2018). Constraints or Complaints? Business Climate and Firm Performance Perceptions in Uganda. *The Journal of Development Studies*. Advance online publication. doi:10.1080/00220388.2018.1502878

Neumeyer, X., & Santos, S. C. (2020). A lot of different flowers make a bouquet: The effect of gender composition on technology-based entrepreneurial student teams. *The International Entrepreneurship and Management Journal, 16*(1), 93–114. doi:10.1007/s11365-019-00603-7

Nyangarika, A. (2016). Social-economic constraints towards women business growth in Tanzania.

Ofori, E., & Kashiwagi, K. (2022). Impact of Microfinance on the Social Performance of Local Households: Evidence from the Kassena Nankana East District of Ghana. doi:10.3390/su14106002

Olugbenga, S., & Mashigo, P. (2017). *The impact of microfinance on microenterprises.* Investment Management and Financial Innovations. doi: (3).2017.08 doi:10.21511/imfi.14

Orjiakor, E. C. (2022). Business climate and firm exit in developing countries: Evidence from Nigeria. *Future Business Journal, 8*(1), 51. doi:10.1186/s43093-022-00160-6

Pagaddut, J. G. (2021). The financial factors affecting the financial performance of Philippines msmes. *Universal Journal of Accounting and Finance, 9*(6), 1524–1532. doi:10.13189/ujaf.2021.090629

Parmanand, S. (2021). Regulating motherhood through markets: Filipino women's engagement with microcredit. 129(1), 32–47. doi:10.1177/01417789211040506

Pérez, M. (2022). Gender diversity on corporate boards: Does it really make a difference. *International Journal of Governance and Financial Intermediation, 1*(3), 219. doi:10.1504/IJGFI.2022.123898

Petruzzelli, E. 2020. "Empowering women and girls in engineering," *Chemical Engineering Progress* (116:1), pp. 3.

Plaisent, M., Lafranchise, N., Tomiuk, D., Zuccaro, C., Mondesir, S., Khadhraoui, M. & Bernard, P. (2021). Networking to Support Spin-out Decision: the Case of Women in Engineering.

Poggesi, S., Mari, M., De Vita, L., and Foss, L. 2020. "Women entrepreneurship in STEM fields: Literature review and future research avenues," *International Entrepreneurship and Management Journal* (16:1), pp. 17-41.

Qasim, Q. (2018). *Access to Finance for Female-led Micro, Small and Medium-sized Enterprises in Bosnia and Herzegovina.* World Bank Group IBRD-IDA. Retrieved from https://openknowledge.worldbank.org/handle/10986/29530

Respicio, M. T. L., Irorita, E. S., Corpuz, J. S., & Abad, K. A. (2023). Effects of the Products and Services of Microfinance Institutions on the Economic Development of Their Members in Vintar, Ilocos Norte, Philippines. *Divine Word International Journal of Management and Humanities*, *2*(3), 565752. doi:10.62025/dwijmh.v2i3.37

Rivera, M. E. C., Jiménez, J. M. R., & Del Mar Fuentes, M. (2023). *The effects of context and characteristics of women entrepreneurs on innovation performance*. BRQ Business Research Quarterly., doi:10.1177/23409444231220951

Rudhumbu, N., Du Plessis, E. C., & Maphosa, C. (2020). Challenges and opportunities for women entrepreneurs in Botswana: Revisiting the role of entrepreneurship education. *Journal of International Education in Business*, *13*(2), 183–201. doi:10.1108/JIEB-12-2019-0058

Ruël, H., Bondarouk, T., & Dresselhaus, L. (2014). *Global Talent Management in Multinational Corporations and the Role of Social Networks*. Social Media in Strategic Management., doi:10.1108/S1877-6361(2013)0000011015

Shah, S., & Hingu, J. (2022). The Impact of Microfinance on the MSMES Sector. *International Journal of Management. Public Policy Research*, *1*(3), 67–71. doi:10.55829/ijmpr.v1i3.69

Tossou, A. G., Bodjona, C. P. H., Aboudou, M. T., & Gueyie, J. P. (2021). The influence of CSR practices on the financial performance of microfinance institutions in Togo. *International Journal of Economics and Finance*, *13*(2), 52. doi:10.5539/ijef.v13n2p52

Tossou, A. G., Gueyie, J.-P., & Couchoro, M. K. (2022). Female Managers, Informal Enterprises, and Their Perceived Financial Performance in Togo. *Journal of African Business*. Advance online publication. doi:10.1080/15228916.2022.2070387

Trần, T. H., Nguyen, T. S., & Lien, M. L. T. (2024). Women on corporate boards and firm financial performance: Empirical evidence from a multi-country in Asia. *Business Strategy & Development*, *7*(1), e340. Advance online publication. doi:10.1002/bsd2.340

Waśniewski, P. (2021). Informal performance measurement in small enterprises. doi:10.1016/j.procs.2021.09.104

Yeoh, K. (2023, July). Effect of Serene Business Environment on the Performance of Small and Medium Enterprises in Malaysia. *Malaysian Management Journal, 27*.

ADDITIONAL READINGS

Abuhussein, T., & Koburtay, T. (2021). Opportunities and constraints of women entrepreneurs in Jordan: An update of the 5Ms framework. *International Journal of Entrepreneurial Behaviour & Research*, 27(6), 1448–1475. doi:10.1108/IJEBR-06-2020-0428

Alonso-Población, E., & Siar, S. V. (2018). Women's participation and leadership in fisherfolk organizations and collective action in fisheries: A review of evidence on enablers, drivers and barriers. *FAO Fisheries and Aquaculture Circular*, (C1159), I-48.

Austin, M. J., & Nauta, M. M. (2016). Entrepreneurial role-model exposure, self-efficacy, and women's entrepreneurial intentions. *Journal of Career Development*, 43(3), 260–272. doi:10.1177/0894845315597475

Badura, K. L., Grijalva, E., Newman, D. A., Yan, T. T., & Jeon, G. (2018). Gender and leadership emergence: A meta-analysis and explanatory model. *Personnel Psychology*, 71(3), 335–367. doi:10.1111/peps.12266

Bianchi, M., Parisi, V., & Salvatore, R. (2016). Female entrepreneurs: Motivations and constraints. An Italian regional study. *International Journal of Gender and Entrepreneurship*, 8(3), 198–220. doi:10.1108/IJGE-08-2015-0029

Braun, P. (2010). Going green: Women entrepreneurs and the environment. *International Journal of Gender and Entrepreneurship*, 2(3), 245–259. doi:10.1108/17566261011079233

Brush, C. G., De Bruin, A., Gatewood, E. J., & Henry, C. (Eds.). (2010). *Women entrepreneurs and the global environment for growth: a research perspective.* doi:10.4337/9781849806633

Khadhraoui, M., Plaisent, M., Lakhal, L., & Bernard, P. (2016). The impact of entrepreneurial culture dimensions on entrepreneurial intention: A cross cultural study. *Universal Journal of Management*, 4(12), 685–693. doi:10.13189/ujm.2016.041205

Khadhraoui, M., Plaisent, M., Lakhal, L., & Prosper, B. (2019). The impact of entrepreneurial orientation on spin-offs' performance: A cross-cultural study. *SAGE Open*, 9(3). doi:10.1177/2158244019865817

McKinsey Global Institute. (2018). The power of parity: Advancing women's equality in Asia Pacific [Report]. https://www.mckinsey.com/featured-insights/gender-equality/the-power-of-parity-advancing-womens-equality-in-asia-pacific

Rosca, E., Agarwal, N., & Brem, A. (2020). Women entrepreneurs as agents of change: A comparative analysis of social entrepreneurship processes in emerging markets. *Technological Forecasting and Social Change, 157*, 120067. doi:10.1016/j.techfore.2020.120067

Rudhumbu, N., Du Plessis, E. C., & Maphosa, C. (2020). Challenges and opportunities for women entrepreneurs in Botswana: Revisiting the role of entrepreneurship education. *Journal of International Education in Business, 13*(2), 183–201. doi:10.1108/JIEB-12-2019-0058

Toh, S. M., & Leonardelli, G. J. (2012). Cultural constraints on the emergence of women as leaders. *Journal of World Business, 47*(4), 604–611. doi:10.1016/j.jwb.2012.01.013

Wadhwa, S., & Retnakaran, D. (2020). Barriers and Enablers to Women's Participation in the Workforce: A Case Study from India. *Review of Market Integration, 12*(3), 114–138. doi:10.1177/09749292211013680

World Bank. (2019). *Making Inroads for Women: A Qualitative Study on Constraints and Opportunities of Women's Equal Participation in the Roads Sector in Malawi.* World Bank.

KEY TERMS AND DEFINITIONS

Barrier: A barrier is an obstacle that can hinder physical movement or intellectual progress. Physical barriers, such as walls or pedestrian obstructions, impede physical movement, while intellectual barriers can stem from authoritative censorship or ignorance of fundamental principles. In the economic context, barriers may arise from a lack of funding or technological expertise, hindering entry into a particular industry. In the business realm, barriers may include shortages of skilled labor, permits, equipment, or bureaucratic hurdles. A primary cause of barriers for extremely small enterprises is often a lack of resources, particularly financial.

Constraint: In contrast to a barrier, a constraint is essentially a limitation on action imposed by circumstances (e.g., winter weather) or regulations (e.g., minimum wage laws), alleviated by resources, expertise, legal or bureaucratic decisions, or appropriate action. When used to coerce someone against their will, constraints can range from moral or physical coercion to outright violence.

Cultural Factor: A cultural factor encompasses the values, beliefs, attitudes, traditions, and behaviors inherent in a group or nation that shape its way of thinking, expressing, and reacting, consistent with the reference group. This can range from a small administrative unit within a company to an entire nation. These factors may not be consciously recognized by members of the community and may only manifest when encountering foreigners or unexpected situations. They are often more readily apparent to third parties.

Driver: A driver is a factor that promotes progression and development in a project, relationship, or activity. Analogous to its meaning in vehicle operation, this concept refers to an organized method for achieving or succeeding in something. In business, drivers can be personal motivations (such as desire, hard work, perseverance), skills (self-confidence, interpersonal skills, leadership ability), or economic, political, and managerial factors more or less under the entrepreneur's control.

Entrepreneurship: Entrepreneurship refers to the process of establishing a business, primarily for growth and profit, although it can also apply to social enterprises aimed at serving beneficiaries rather than generating profit. Entrepreneurs possess specific qualities such as opportunism, sound judgment, the ability to discern opportunities from scams and trends, resilience in the face of uncertainty and risk, and proficiency in acquiring and allocating resources—material, financial, and human—to achieve their business objectives.

Startup: A startup is a newly established company that leverages a competitive advantage in the market, whether through location, knowledge, product, or service. It may be founded by an individual, a group of individuals, or a more formal entity such as a cooperative or corporation. Some women gravitate towards low-capital startups such as sari-sari shops, artisanal crafts sales, house cleaning services, or childcare.

Stereotype: A stereotype is a widely held, unfounded belief about a person or group, often portraying "others" who are not members of the group in a negative light. Stereotypes are challenging to dispel and often revolve around factors such as gender, physical appearance, or religion. They are perpetuated by influential figures navigating conflicts. Recognizing and challenging stereotypes is essential, as they lack evidence and should not be accepted as truth.

Chapter 12
Inclusive Practices in Higher Education and Workplaces Strategies for Empowering Women

Mustafa Kayyali
https://orcid.org/0000-0003-3300-262X
HE Higher Education Ranking, Syria

ABSTRACT

This book chapter addresses the shifting landscape of inclusive practices in both higher education and workplace contexts, with a specific focus on strategies targeted at empowering women. It looks into the multiple facets of gender equality, covering the historical context of gender inequality, contemporary issues encountered by women, cross-cultural viewpoints, success stories, and best practices. The chapter underlines the crucial importance of intersectionality and mental health support in establishing an inclusive and equal environment for women. By studying and praising these inclusive traditions, this chapter strives to provide a thorough knowledge of the challenging journey towards gender equality and the empowerment of women in many cultural contexts.

DOI: 10.4018/979-8-3693-0102-9.ch012

INTRODUCTION

In the ever-shifting terrain of the contemporary world, the goal of gender equality and inclusivity has crossed geographical, cultural, and socioeconomic boundaries to become a thundering imperative. This quest strives to overcome historical injustices and establish a global reality in which individuals, regardless of their gender, are able to contribute fully to the intricate fabric of society. Despite remarkable improvements in recent years, women continue to contend with persisting hurdles that prevent their full empowerment and involvement in educational and professional domains. This chapter strives to engage in a comprehensive examination, digging deep into the various facets of inclusive practices within the realms of higher education and businesses. It is vital to stress that this attempt is genuinely anchored in a profound commitment to empowering women on a worldwide basis. Over the years, the roles and achievements of women in education and employment have experienced profound and astonishing alterations (Bartels et al, 2021). With persistent tenacity, they have destroyed barriers and busted through glass ceilings in sectors that were formerly entirely male-dominated. These outstanding feats not only deserve recognition but also serve as sources of inspiration for future generations. Yet, the longevity of certain hurdles underlines the importance of a more comprehensive examination, a more in-depth analysis, and a joint effort to destroy the remaining barriers. At the heart of this book chapter is the awareness that gender equality is not a set destination but an ongoing, dynamic journey. To reach its ultimate vision, we must cross a multidimensional maze of hurdles, prejudices, and structural inequities that continue to cast shadows on the path of women's advancement. This trip is not linear but packed with twists and turns, and it is within the subtleties of these complexities that our exploration finds its purpose.

The foundation of our investigation is profoundly entrenched in a profound dedication to unraveling the numerous layers of inclusive practices. These practices are not monolithic but ever-evolving and diverse in their forms. They offer a key conduit through which the empowerment of women is not just an abstract concept but an actual reality. Our purpose is to unearth these practices, illuminate their subtleties, and systematically analyze their usefulness as transforming agents in the unrelenting pursuit of gender equality. Higher education serves as a significant battleground where the battle for gender equality unfolds (Rose, 2018). Women's access to quality education and their engagement in academic pursuits have made considerable progress, however, various barriers exist. Women suffer discrepancies in enrolment, graduation rates, and fields of study, underscoring the need for gender-inclusive procedures. While it is exciting to watch more women pursuing degrees in traditionally male-dominated professions such as science, technology, engineering, and mathematics (STEM), a gender gap still looms large in these areas (García-

Holgado & García-Peñalvo, 2022). This chapter tries to study the numerous elements of inclusive practices in higher education, attempting to analyse the barriers that limit women's advancement, and putting light on measures that might be applied to bridge this disparity. The workplace, like higher education, is a crucial battleground for achieving gender equality (Kandrichina et al, 2016). Women have made great breakthroughs in different professions and businesses, displaying their aptitude and talents. However, discrepancies in salary, representation in leadership roles, and the continuation of workplace harassment remain topics of considerable concern. In the aftermath of the #MeToo movement and increased focus on gender diversity in corporate settings (Alaggia et al, 2020), the globe is witnessing a growing awareness of the importance of inclusive practices in the workforce. The issues experienced by women in higher education and the workforce are not isolated to a specific nation or region but resound across borders. Achieving gender equality is not just an issue of justice but also a driver of economic and social growth. Empowering women internationally is not simply an ethical commitment but a practical need for creating a wealthier and equal world.

This chapter goes on a journey that is enormous, profound, and naturally interwoven. Our purpose is to deepen our understanding of the numerous problems involved in achieving gender equality, with a special emphasis on the advancement of women in higher education and the workforce. We set sail for a more inclusive society where women are not only participants but leaders, and makers of their own destinies. This adventure is defined by rigorous examination, insightful analysis, and an unshakable adherence to global viewpoints. It is our earnest desire that this inquiry would serve as a guiding lighthouse, directing us toward the fulfillment of a society where the potential of every woman is fully acknowledged, harnessed, and cherished, independent of the cultural tapestry that surrounds her. As we navigate the difficult and ever-evolving landscape of gender equality and inclusivity, we must remember that this path is not just about women—it is about creating a more equitable, just, and prosperous society for all.

THE HISTORICAL CONTEXT OF GENDER INEQUALITY

To properly appreciate the modern difficulties of gender disparity in higher education and workplaces, it is important to engage in a detailed investigation of the historical backdrop that has sculpted these persisting discrepancies. Gender inequality, deeply ingrained in society conventions, economic institutions, and cultural traditions, has been an ongoing issue, often sustained across generations (Anderson, 1983). This historical analysis will provide critical insights into the emergence of gender inequities and set the foundation for a deeper and more nuanced exploration of inclusive practices as methods for empowering women. The seeds of gender inequity can be traced back to the dawn of human society (Wiesner-Hanks, 2021). In innumerable early communities, gender roles were thoroughly ingrained in the fabric of daily life, with men primarily tasked with physical work, defense, and governance, while women were committed to the realms of domestic responsibilities and child-rearing (Raukar & Mishkin, 2020). These differences were frequently rationalized through religious, philosophical, or cultural views, thus strengthening and sustaining gender inequities. The epic narratives of goddesses and heroines in mythology often stood in sharp contrast to the stark reality of women's constrained status in many ancient societies (Sen, A. 2001).

During the medieval and early modern epochs in Europe, women's rights were severely constrained (Kabeer, 2020). The notion of "coverture" was the dominant legal norm, wherein a woman's legal rights and possessions were subsumed by her husband upon marriage. Women were mostly excluded from school, politics, and the labor field, confined to the shadows of men's desires and successes. This time provided the foundation for the persisting gender inequities that still echo today (Smith, 2010). The 19th and early 20th centuries marked a turning point in the global campaign against gender discrimination (Glazebrook et al, 2020). Suffragettes and feminists worked vigorously for women's right to vote, access to education, and the ability to join the labor sector. The heroic and tireless efforts of leaders like Susan B. Anthony, Elizabeth Cady Stanton, and Emmeline Pankhurst, among many others, culminated in major victories, including the suffrage movement that led to women's ability to vote (deVries, 2020). These fights radically impacted society's standards and gave birth to a budding wave of feminism, setting the way for important legal changes and greater possibilities for women.

The devastating events of the World Wars in the 20th century accelerated a profound transition in women's position in society (Delap, 2020). With men abroad at war, women stepped into positions previously designated for their male colleagues, displaying their ability and capacities on a worldwide stage. Rosie the Riveter became a symbol of women's contributions to the war effort, indicating that they were more than capable of doing traditionally "men-only" jobs (Matthews et al, 2021). The post-war era witnessed an increased awareness of women's achievements, and this impetus translated into key legislation reforms that provided women more rights and access to higher education and professional prospects. While tremendous progress has clearly been accomplished in the late 20th and early 21st centuries, gender inequality has not been totally erased. Women still encounter inequities in salary, underrepresentation in leadership roles, and gender-based discrimination in both school and the workplace. The historical legacy of gender inequity continues to impact present attitudes and practices, needing a determined effort to challenge and change deeply rooted societal standards (Scott, 1986).

Understanding the historical backdrop of gender discrimination is vital for appreciating the multiple issues that women continue to encounter in higher education and workplaces. It shows the lengthy and nuanced road women have made in their quest for gender equality, underlining the battles won and those still underway. In the chapters that follow, we will delve into the methods and inclusive practices that have been established to solve these difficulties, empower women, and create a more equitable and inclusive society (Kabeer, N., 2005). By acknowledging the historical background, we may better appreciate the progress that has been accomplished and acknowledge the work that remains to be done to establish enduring and meaningful gender equality, ensuring that the sacrifices and triumphs of women throughout history are not in vain.

CONTEMPORARY CHALLENGES FACED BY WOMEN

In the 21st century, women have made amazing gains in numerous sectors of life, from politics to business, science to the arts. Yet, it would be naïve to think that gender inequity is a relic of the past. Despite major achievements, modern issues exist, creating hurdles that continue to restrict women's full participation and empowerment in higher education and workplaces.

Gender Pay Gap

One of the most persistent contemporary difficulties faced by women is the gender wage gap (Hoff, 2021). While the difference has lessened in many nations, women still earn less on average than their male colleagues. This discrepancy is impacted by a complex interaction of factors, including occupational segregation, limited access to women in higher-paying positions, and the impact of parenthood on earnings (Crenshaw, 1989). The gender wage gap not only undermines women's financial stability but also fosters a cycle of economic inequity. Women are typically forced into lower-paying industries, where they meet a double-edged sword. They not only face the glass ceiling in these areas but also receive disproportionately lower compensation for the same responsibilities as their male counterparts. Occupational segregation, where women are commonly found in caregiving professions or roles that have traditionally been underestimated, further exacerbates this issue. Moreover, parenting can worsen income gaps, as women commonly face the "motherhood penalty," incurring wage losses after having children. These salary differences contribute to long-term financial inequality, hurting women's ability to save, invest, and achieve economic stability. The financial ramifications extend beyond individual women to affect entire families and communities (Mason, 2013).

Underrepresentation in Leadership Roles

Women remain underrepresented in leadership positions across numerous industries. The "glass ceiling" is a figurative barrier that stops women from reaching the upper levels of organizations (Begeny et al, 2021). This underrepresentation in leadership promotes a lack of diversity and can contribute to a workplace culture that does not fully reflect the viewpoints and experiences of women. The underrepresentation of women in leadership posts is a multidimensional issue with strong cultural origins. Women often confront hurdles such as gender bias, preconceptions, and limited networking opportunities that inhibit their success. Stereotypes that link leadership with male attributes might limit women's job success, as they may not match the traditional pattern of a leader (United Nations, 2020). Additionally, women generally lack the same access to mentoring and networking opportunities that might catapult males into leadership roles. The absence of female role models in top positions can prevent young women from pursuing ambitious career objectives (O'Leary, 1974). When young women do not witness women in leadership, they may be discouraged from aspiring for these positions, as they might regard it as unachievable. Representation in leadership is not just about numbers; it's about establishing an example for the next generation of women. Furthermore, the burden of family responsibilities generally falls more heavily on women, resulting in a difficult choice between career success and home life. This difficulty, sometimes referred to as the "second shift," is the additional workload women undertake in terms of domestic and childcare tasks. The idea that women should be the primary caregivers poses a severe constraint on their capacity to take on leadership responsibilities, which often entail long hours and high levels of dedication. The ramifications of women's underrepresentation in leadership posts are far-reaching. A lack of diversity in leadership results in decision-making processes that do not take into consideration the whole range of opinions and experiences, sustaining a culture that may unwittingly favor one group over another (Hill, 2007). This not only limits women's individual success but also inhibits the growth and innovation of businesses as a whole.

Discrimination and Harassment

Discrimination and harassment, both overt and subtle, continue to plague the workplace and educational institutions (Bell et al, 2002). Women often face biases based on their gender, leading to unequal opportunities and career advancement. Sexual harassment is also a pressing issue that affects women in both educational and professional settings, creating hostile environments and mental distress. Gender-based discrimination manifests in a multitude of ways, from subtle microaggressions to overt acts of bias. These behaviors are deeply ingrained in societal norms and are sometimes perpetuated unconsciously. Stereotypes about women's competence or leadership abilities can hinder their career progression. Women are frequently subjected to doubts about their qualifications, which can manifest as a lack of mentorship and growth opportunities. This discrimination takes a toll on women's self-confidence and professional growth, undermining their full potential. Moreover, the issue of sexual harassment remains an alarming concern (Murrell et al, 1995). It ranges from inappropriate comments to more severe forms of harassment and abuse. Such incidents create hostile work and educational environments, where women often fear speaking out due to the potential backlash or lack of support. Addressing this challenge requires a comprehensive effort to establish safe reporting mechanisms, raise awareness, and change the culture of organizations and educational institutions to ensure that they are respectful and inclusive spaces for women.

Work-Life Balance

Balancing work and family life is a challenge many women confront (World Economic Forum. 2020). Societal expectations often place a disproportionate burden on women to manage household responsibilities and caregiving. This challenge is further compounded by limited access to affordable childcare and family-friendly workplace policies, which can hinder career progression. The struggle to achieve work-life balance is not just a personal challenge but also a systemic issue deeply embedded in societal norms. The expectations placed on women to manage household and caregiving responsibilities can be overwhelming. Often referred to as the "second shift," women not only bear the responsibilities of their careers but also assume the lion's share of work within the home. This dual role can lead to exhaustion and burnout, affecting women's physical and mental health. Many women are faced with the difficult choice between pursuing their career ambitions and taking on more domestic responsibilities. The pressure to conform to traditional gender roles creates an unnecessary constraint on women's professional development. This challenge extends beyond women and impacts the broader society by perpetuating outdated gender norms. It calls for systemic changes, including affordable and accessible childcare, family-friendly workplace policies, and equal sharing of household responsibilities within partnerships and families (United Nations, 2015).

STEM Gender Gap

In fields relating to science, technology, engineering, and mathematics (STEM), a considerable gender gap continues. Women are underrepresented in STEM disciplines, both in education and the workforce. This disparity is reinforced by preconceptions, a lack of female role models, and an unwelcoming environment in many STEM disciplines. The gender discrepancy in STEM areas has deep-rooted foundations that begin in childhood (Wang, 2023). From a young age, girls may be discouraged or directed away from STEM pursuits due to societal prejudices that associate these disciplines with masculinity. The paucity of female role models in STEM jobs can make it challenging for young women to envisage themselves in these roles (Sassler et al, 2017). Moreover, the male-dominated atmosphere in many STEM workplaces can lead to feelings of isolation and exclusion. The ramifications of the STEM gender gap extend to the fields themselves. The lack of diversity in STEM leads to missed chances for innovation and problem-solving. Research demonstrates that diverse teams are more creative and efficient, making it vital to solve this dilemma for the sake of both women and the growth of these critical disciplines.

Access to Education

While tremendous progress has been achieved in improving educational opportunities for women globally, discrepancies in access to education exist, especially in developing nations. This dilemma shows the persisting constraints that impede women and girls from acquiring a proper education. These impediments might be varied and include poverty, cultural norms, and discrimination. Access to decent education is considered a fundamental right, although it remains elusive for many girls and women in diverse regions of the world. In various underdeveloped nations, girls are more likely to be denied educational chances due to cultural traditions that promote boys' education (Jayachandran, 2015). Deeply rooted preconceptions and traditions reinforce the belief that girls are better suited for household labour and childcare, while boys are encouraged to pursue academic interests. This gender bias within schooling hinders girls' possibilities for intellectual and personal growth, robbing them of the capacity to fulfill their full potential. Furthermore, many girls and women encounter gaps in educational access due to economic circumstances. Families in underprivileged communities typically struggle to afford school fees, uniforms, and other educational expenses. This economic obstacle can force families to prioritize the education of their sons over their daughters, leading to increased gender inequity. In some regions, societal expectations have a substantial effect in limiting women's access to higher education. Girls may be pressured to marry at an early age or comply with traditional gender norms, which can impede their educational chances. The repercussions of these hurdles are severe, as education is a crucial driver of economic and social empowerment, enabling women to pursue rewarding occupations, make educated decisions, and actively participate in the advancement of their communities and nations.

Intersectionality

Contemporary issues experienced by women are sometimes worsened by overlapping characteristics, such as race, ethnicity, sexual orientation, and financial background (Boni & Circelli, 2002). Women from underprivileged groups may suffer additional hurdles and prejudice that aggravate the obstacles they face in education and employment. The notion of intersectionality recognizes that women's experiences of discrimination and inequality are influenced not only by their gender but also by their other identities and circumstances. For women of color, women with disabilities, and women from lower socioeconomic origins, the obstacles they encounter are often compounded by a network of intersecting oppressions. These intersecting identities determine the type and degree of discrimination people encounter. For example, women of color may experience both gender and racial discrimination concurrently, making their journey to education and career progression even more onerous (Turner & González, 2011). Women from lower socioeconomic origins may encounter extra financial and societal challenges that restrict their access to quality education and professional prospects. Understanding these intersecting issues is vital for building inclusive solutions to meet the different challenges encountered by women. By acknowledging the intricacies of women's experiences, society may design more fair policies and programs that encourage the advancement of all women, regardless of their particular circumstances.

Mental Health Implications

The cumulative effects of these contemporary difficulties on women's mental health are significant. The ongoing battle against discrimination, the endeavor to establish work-life balance, and the stress of tackling many challenges can take a toll on women's emotional and psychological well-being. The mental health ramifications of contemporary concerns are far-reaching. Women often find themselves navigating a high-stress atmosphere in both their personal and professional lives. Constantly confronting bias and discrimination can lead to feelings of anger and helplessness (Swim & Thomas, 2006). Striving to attain work-life balance can produce a tremendous sense of pressure and stress, as women strive to meet the demands placed on them in numerous positions, such as caretakers, professionals, and community leaders. In addition to these problems, the fear and experience of harassment, whether in the workplace, educational institutions, or elsewhere, can contribute to anxiety and trauma. The impact of discrimination and harassment on women's mental health is significant and can result in stress-related disorders, depression, and other emotional issues. Recognizing the need for mental health support is vital in managing the emotional and psychological impact of these contemporary difficulties. Creating supportive work environments, educational institutions, and community networks is crucial to helping women negotiate the unique problems they encounter. Moreover, decreasing the stigma associated with seeking mental health assistance is crucial in ensuring that women can obtain the required support to cope with the emotional toll of these issues.

While great progress has been made in promoting gender equality, current issues continue to restrict women's full involvement and empowerment in higher education and workplaces (Subrahmanian, 2003). Recognizing and tackling these difficulties is vital for developing a more inclusive and fair society. In the subsequent sections of this chapter, we will explore the strategies and inclusive practices that have been developed to confront these challenges, empower women, and pave the way for a more equitable future where women can fully realize their potential and contribute to the betterment of society. It is through these efforts that we can gradually demolish the ongoing barriers that women encounter and establish a society where gender equality is not only a goal but a reality for all. By embracing the interconnectedness of women's experiences and prioritizing their mental health and well-being, we can construct a more just and equitable world where women can thrive in every part of their lives. In conclusion, current obstacles facing women are varied, persistent, and deeply rooted in societal norms and structures. Discrimination and harassment, work-life balance concerns, and the STEM gender gap continue to hamper women's full involvement and empowerment. Recognizing and tackling these difficulties is vital for developing a more inclusive and fair society. In the subsequent sections of this chapter, we will explore the strategies and inclusive practices that have been developed to confront these challenges, empower women, and pave the way for a more equitable future where women can fully realize their potential and contribute to the betterment of society. It is through these efforts that we can gradually eliminate the ongoing barriers that women confront and establish a world where gender equality is not only a goal but a reality for all.

INCLUSIVE PRACTICES: A CROSS-CULTURAL PERSPECTIVE

In an era marked by increased globalization and interconnectedness, the goal of gender equality transcends geographical boundaries, cultural nuances, and entrenched traditions (Cox, T., 1994). The issues women confront and the strategies adopted to empower them are deeply impacted by the specific cultural environments in which they reside. A cross-cultural perspective not only offers a deeper understanding of the intricate interplay between societal norms, cultural values, and inclusive practices but also underscores the importance of adopting flexible, context-specific approaches to address the diverse challenges women encounter worldwide. It is a perspective that simultaneously appreciates and embraces the rich tapestry of human difference while maintaining a strong dedication to the universal values of equality and empowerment.

Diverse Cultural Landscapes: The Global Mosaic of Experience

Across the globe, varied cultural landscapes define and impact the experiences of women as they navigate the domains of higher education and workplaces. These cultural roots closely influence gender conventions, societal expectations, and the role of women within their different communities. The realisation of this immense diversity is not simply an acceptance of cultural distinctions but also a celebration of the varied global community we live (Jackson, S. E., 2018). In certain countries, conventional gender roles are thoroughly engrained, promoting the assumption that women should primarily prioritize family and domestic chores. These roles, entrenched in centuries-old norms, often impose certain gender-related expectations and tasks. The continuance of these conventional roles can create strong barriers to women's access to education and engagement in the workforce, especially in countries where deviations from these standards are met with opposition (Kabeer, 2005). In some cultural contexts, more progressive attitudes have taken root, enabling women greater opportunities to pursue education, jobs, and positions that were traditionally exclusively for men. These countries have undergone a substantial shift in attitudes toward gender roles and have, in many cases, accepted the principles of gender equality and women's empowerment. Such improvements have enabled women to excel in previously male-dominated areas, breaking down barriers and creating important examples for future generations (Mojab, 2000).

Gender Roles and Expectations: Navigating Traditional and Progressive Contexts

The cross-cultural perspective on gender equality places a magnifying glass on the intricate issue of gender roles and expectations. Understanding the interplay between traditional and progressive attitudes is paramount to the development of effective strategies for empowerment.

In cultures where traditional gender roles persist, women often find themselves torn between familial obligations and personal aspirations. The expectation to fulfill the roles of caregiver, homemaker, and mother can significantly impede their access to higher education and their participation in the workforce (Inglehart, 2003). Addressing these challenges necessitates a sensitive approach that respects cultural traditions while advocating for change. Such initiatives should aim to gradually shift the balance, ensuring that women are not confined by gender roles but are free to choose their own path. Conversely, in cultures where progressive attitudes prevail, women enjoy more equitable opportunities. However, they may still encounter subtle gender biases and stereotypes that persist even in forward-thinking societies. Overcoming these ingrained prejudices requires continued awareness and education to ensure that women can fully harness their potential without being held back by subtle biases.

The Power of Intersectionality and Cultural Context

The notion of intersectionality, which acknowledges the overlapping and crossing components of identity, is of particular value within the cross-cultural viewpoint on gender equality. The convergence of gender with other characteristics such as race, ethnicity, sexual orientation, religion, and financial background can present particular obstacles for women. Recognizing these connections and their impact on women's lives is vital for establishing holistic, context-specific tactics for empowerment. For instance, a woman's experience in a culture that promotes racial or ethnic homogeneity may differ dramatically from that of a woman in a more diversified cultural setting. Understanding the complexities of these experiences is crucial for designing targeted and effective inclusive strategies that identify and accommodate these intersecting identities (Crenshaw, 1991).

Inclusive Practices within Cultural Contexts: Fostering Empowerment Through Diversity

To empower women across diverse cultural contexts, it is essential to adopt inclusive practices that are sensitive to local cultures. These inclusive practices may include tailored educational programs that address cultural barriers, mentorship initiatives that respect and incorporate cultural traditions, and workplace policies that accommodate cultural norms while fostering gender equality. These initiatives recognize and celebrate the value of cultural diversity in inclusive practices. Rather than imposing a one-size-fits-all approach, they adapt and integrate cultural nuances, fostering empowerment while respecting the cultural tapestry of each society.

Celebrating Diversity, Forging Equality

A cross-cultural perspective on inclusive practices in higher education and workplaces offers a lens through which we can comprehend the complexities of gender equality within the rich mosaic of our world (Bhavnani, R. 2009). While the challenges women face and the strategies employed may differ across cultures, the fundamental principles of equality and inclusion are universal. By respecting and understanding cultural contexts, we can develop strategies that effectively address the unique challenges women encounter, regardless of where they are in the world. This perspective underscores the importance of celebrating cultural diversity while remaining committed to the global pursuit of gender equality and empowerment. In the following sections of this chapter, we will delve deeper into specific examples of inclusive practices in various cultural contexts, showcasing how these practices can be adapted and implemented to empower women worldwide (Sen, 1997).

Inclusive Practices: A Cross-Cultural Perspective: Unlocking Paths to Gender Equality

The examination of gender equality transcends national borders, crossing cultural frontiers to encompass the vast, complicated tapestry of human society. In an era marked by globalization and interconnection, it is vital to realize that women's experiences and the techniques adopted to empower them are significantly molded by the cultural contexts in which they navigate higher education and workplaces. A cross-cultural view on this journey offers a window into the interplay of societal norms, cultural values, and the vital role of inclusive behaviors (de Castro Salgado et al, 2014). It reiterates the need for adaptive, context-specific measures to meet the numerous issues women experience across the globe while respecting the universal principles of equality and empowerment (World Bank, 2009).

Diverse Cultural Landscapes: A Global Montage

The world is a canvas adorned with a multitude of diverse cultural landscapes that influence and define the experiences of women in their pursuit of higher education and professional endeavors. These cultural backdrops intricately shape gender norms, societal expectations, and the roles attributed to women. Recognizing and appreciating the diversity of these cultural contexts is not merely an act of acknowledgment but a celebration of the multifaceted global community which we coexist within. In various cultures, traditional gender roles remain deeply entrenched, rigidly prescribing the duties and responsibilities assigned to women. In these societies, women are often expected to prioritize family and domestic obligations, and their career aspirations are frequently stifled by the weight of age-old customs (Maume, 2006). The persistence of these traditional roles poses substantial challenges to women's access to education and their participation in the workforce. The balancing act between fulfilling family duties and pursuing personal and professional growth is often an intricate dance that women must perform. Conversely, progressive attitudes prevalent in some cultures have paved the way for women to embrace broader roles, affording them the freedom to pursue education and careers on a more equal footing with their male counterparts. In such societies, the liberation of women from traditional norms and the recognition of their potential have become central tenets. This shift in mindset has opened the doors to various fields and industries previously dominated by men, enabling women to shatter barriers and set a powerful example for future generations (Chen, 2019).

Gender Roles and Expectations: Navigating the Spectrum

In the cross-cultural perspective on gender equality, an essential focus is on the examination of the fluid spectrum of gender roles and expectations. Grasping the intricate interplay between traditional and progressive attitudes becomes critical to crafting effective strategies for empowerment. In societies where traditional gender roles are steadfast, women often find themselves caught in the crosshairs of familial obligations and personal aspirations. The role of caregiver, homemaker, and mother is impressed upon them, often restraining their access to higher education and participation in the workforce. Tackling these ingrained norms calls for a nuanced approach that respects cultural traditions while advocating for change, thus striving to shift the balance away from prescribed gender roles and toward freedom of choice. In contrast, cultures where progressive attitudes prevail still experience subtle gender biases and stereotypes, even when they have broken free from the more rigid traditional norms. These deeply ingrained prejudices can manifest as obstacles on the path to women's empowerment. Overcoming these biases necessitates continual awareness and education to ensure that women can unleash their full potential without being encumbered by societal preconceptions.

The Power of Intersectionality and Cultural Context: Unveiling Unique Challenges

The notion of intersectionality assumes a particularly salient role when contemplating gender equality within diverse cultural contexts. The intersection of gender with other identity factors such as race, ethnicity, sexual orientation, religion, and socioeconomic status can introduce unique layers of complexity to women's experiences. This cross-cultural perspective compels us to fathom how these multifaceted identities intersect and intertwine, creating distinct challenges for women in various settings. For instance, the experience of a woman in a culture that emphasizes racial or ethnic homogeneity may differ significantly from that of a woman in a more diverse cultural environment. Recognizing these intricate layers is crucial to forging comprehensive, context-specific strategies for empowerment.

Inclusive Practices within Cultural Contexts: Nurturing Empowerment Through Diversity

Empowering women in diverse cultural contexts necessitates the adoption of inclusive practices that are not only sensitive to local cultures but also respectful of the rich diversity within these settings. These practices may encompass tailored educational programs designed to address cultural barriers, mentorship initiatives rooted in cultural traditions, and workplace policies that accommodate cultural norms while remaining committed to the principles of gender equality. These initiatives not only respect and celebrate cultural diversity within the inclusive practices but also seek to ensure women's empowerment while honoring the cultural tapestry of each society.

A Global Kaleidoscope of Gender Equality

The cross-cultural perspective on inclusive practices in higher education and workplaces provides a multifaceted lens through which we can contemplate the intricacies of gender equality (Valentine et al, 2019). While the challenges and strategies for empowering women may shift across the varied cultural landscapes, the fundamental values of equality and inclusion are universal. By respecting and embracing cultural contexts, we can formulate strategies that effectively address the unique challenges women face, wherever they may be. This perspective underscores the significance of celebrating cultural diversity while standing united in the worldwide endeavor for gender equality and empowerment. In the subsequent sections of this chapter, we will delve deeper into specific examples of inclusive practices across various cultural contexts, revealing how these practices can be adapted and implemented to empower women across the globe.

SUCCESS STORIES AND BEST PRACTICES: PAVING THE WAY FOR GENDER EQUALITY

In the constant and continual quest for gender equality within the realms of higher education and workplaces, it is vital to cast a spotlight on the success stories and best practices that serve as beacons of inspiration, guiding us toward a better, more equitable future (Eagly, 1995). This chapter offers a deep dive into a captivating array of anecdotes and behaviours that stand as testimonials to the progress accomplished in empowering women, encouraging inclusivity, and deconstructing the hurdles that have long inhibited their success. These success stories and best practices provide a map for traversing the challenging terrain of gender equality, illustrating that with the appropriate tools and a collective commitment to change, an equitable future is indeed within reach (Grant, 2010).

Pioneering Women in Leadership: Breaking the Glass Ceiling

In recent years, companies and educational institutions have embarked on a revolutionary journey towards promoting women to leadership roles. These success stories concentrate on institutions that have taken deliberate steps to select women for high-ranking positions, consequently building diverse leadership teams that better reflect the society they serve. The women who have broken through the glass ceiling in these institutions serve as live testaments to the notion that not only do women rightfully belong in the upper echelons of power, but they also add unique perspectives and insights to the decision-making process. Institutional transformation generally starts with visionary leaders who are unafraid to confront the established quo (UN Women, 2015). These executives know that gender diversity at the top is not simply a moral requirement but a strategic benefit. By promoting women to leadership posts, they convey a powerful message that women can not only participate in leadership but excel in it. These success stories indicate that women executives not only contribute to the success of their organizations but also encourage future generations of women to aspire to leadership posts. Moreover, they expose persistent prejudices and preconceptions that have held women back from leadership roles for far too long. These trailblazing women executives don't merely lead for the sake of gender diversity; they lead with excellence, creativity, and inclusivity as their guiding principles. Their presence at the top echelons of enterprises reveals the practical benefits of diverse leadership, leading to better decision-making, greater problem-solving, and an enhanced corporate culture. These success stories remind us that promoting women to leadership roles is not just about parity; it's about improving the quality and effectiveness of leadership itself (Catalyst, 2019).

Mentorship and Sponsorship Programs: Nurturing Talent and Fostering Success

Mentorship and sponsorship programs have emerged as indispensable tools for empowering women in the spheres of education and the workplace. These initiatives pair experienced professionals, often both women and men, with emerging female talent, providing a nurturing environment where guidance, support, and opportunities for career growth flourish. Successful mentorship and sponsorship initiatives have played a pivotal role in helping women navigate the challenges they inevitably encounter along their journeys, offering them the invaluable support of a trusted ally who is there to guide them through the labyrinth of career progression. Mentorship, in particular, focuses on providing guidance, advice, and a listening ear to women as they navigate the intricate terrain of their careers. These relationships often transcend professional guidance and evolve into deeply meaningful personal connections. Experienced mentors offer insights that can only come from years of experience, helping their mentees make informed decisions, set achievable goals, and develop essential skills. The impact of mentorship extends far beyond the individual; it ripples through organizations and industries, fostering a culture of learning and growth (Cook, 2014). Sponsorship, on the other hand, entails influential individuals within organizations advocating for the advancement of women. Sponsors use their clout and influence to ensure that talented women are given opportunities to showcase their abilities and excel. By placing their professional reputations on the line to support and vouch for women, sponsors act as powerful catalysts for career advancement. They help women secure critical roles, responsibilities, and recognition, enabling them to thrive in their careers. The success stories born from mentorship and sponsorship programs are replete with women who have risen to prominent positions, thanks to the guidance and support they received. These women are proof that mentorship and sponsorship are not merely feel-good initiatives but rather dynamic, transformative practices that drive progress and bolster the advancement of women (UN Women, 2011).

Success Stories and Best Practices: Shaping a More Inclusive and Equal Future

In the unceasing quest for gender equality, certain initiatives and best practices stand as compelling evidence of progress and hope. This chapter delves into a collection of these stories and practices that exemplify the significant headway made in empowering women, fostering inclusivity, and dismantling the structural barriers that have perpetuated gender disparities. These narratives not only serve as beacons of inspiration but also as concrete roadmaps guiding us toward a future defined by equity and inclusiveness.

Equal Pay Initiatives: Bridging the Gender Pay Gap

Several countries and organizations worldwide have taken resolute steps to address the persistent gender pay gap. These initiatives have resulted in tangible and encouraging progress toward wage equality (World Economic Forum, 2020). Legal measures, such as pay equity laws and salary transparency regulations, have played a crucial role in leveling the compensation landscape. These measures have compelled organizations to critically evaluate their salary structures and make necessary adjustments to ensure that gender-based wage disparities are rectified. As a result, we witness more equitable compensation structures, closing the pay gap incrementally. In tandem with these legal measures, numerous companies and institutions have proactively embraced the practice of conducting regular pay audits and making adjustments accordingly. This approach not only reflects a commitment to transparency but also demonstrates a dedication to rectifying disparities that may have accumulated over time. These success stories serve as powerful reminders that with a concerted and comprehensive effort, the gender pay gap is not an insurmountable challenge (Lean In, 2019). Rather, it is a problem that can be effectively addressed through diligent and systematic measures. The initiatives to bridge the gender pay gap offer critical lessons for other entities striving to rectify wage disparities. They underscore the importance of combining legal mandates with organizational commitment to effect lasting change. The success stories in this regard are instrumental in demonstrating the positive impact of such initiatives, motivating others to follow suit and tackle the pay gap head-on (United Nations, 2015).

Inclusive Policies and Family Support: The Family-Friendly Workplace

Organizations that appreciate the value of family-friendly workplace policies have experienced the many benefits of a contented and productive workforce. Initiatives like as flexible work hours, paid parental leave, and on-site daycare services have created conditions where employees may efficiently balance their jobs with family responsibilities. Flexible work hours allow employees to customise their work schedules to their family needs, resulting in higher job satisfaction and productivity (Scandura & Lankau, 1997). Employees can better balance their personal and professional lives, lowering stress and boosting general well-being. Paid parental leave is another key component of having a family-friendly company. It allows new parents to bond with their children, minimizing turnover and attracting brilliant employees who respect work-life balance (National Women's Law Center, 2020). On-site childcare facilities reduce one of the greatest challenges for working parents – the necessity to acquire reliable childcare. This not only decreases stress for employees but also ensures that they may remain completely engaged and productive at work. The success stories of firms that prioritize family-friendly workplace policies offer a compelling template for other workplaces aiming to build cultures where employees may thrive both professionally and personally. These rules are not simply helpful for women but for all employees, fostering more inclusive and supportive workplaces.

Intersectional Approaches: Addressing the Complexity of Identity

In the constant fight for gender equality, the use of intersectional approaches has emerged as a critical best practice. Organizations and institutions that understand and address intersectionality have proved the significant impact of such efforts. Intersectionality underlines the idea that an individual's experiences of discrimination can be magnified when they belong to many marginalized groups. The strength of intersectional methods resides in their ability to adjust strategies to address these compounded kinds of prejudice. By realizing that gender inequality is not a one-size-fits-all issue, these businesses have established more inclusive and egalitarian settings for all women (Chuang, 2019). They have recognized that the difficulties encountered by diverse groups of women are not isolated but interconnected, and by addressing these intersections, they develop an environment that allows every woman to thrive. These organizations and institutions acknowledge that the one-size-fits-all approach to gender equality is inadequate and that a nuanced understanding of individual experiences is necessary. By addressing the unique obstacles encountered by women at the intersections of gender, race, sexual orientation, and socioeconomic position, they pave the way for a more just and equitable future.

Mental Health Support: A Foundation for Empowerment

Creating an atmosphere that prioritizes mental health and provides solid support networks for employees and students has emerged as a characteristic of success for many organizations and institutions. Mental health assistance comprises a range of measures, from counseling services to stress management programs and the promotion of mental health awareness.

These groups acknowledge that the contemporary issues women confront can exact a considerable emotional toll. Balancing employment, school, family duties, and societal expectations can be daunting. By giving access to counseling services, they give a secure space for individuals to discuss their mental health difficulties. This support not only supports women in coping with the difficulties they confront but also contributes to their overall success and empowerment. Stress management programs have evolved as a crucial aspect of mental health support (Macy, 2004). These programs empower women with the tools to manage stress, build resilience, and negotiate the pressures of higher education and the job. Stress management activities encourage emotional well-being, boosting women's ability to overcome hurdles and prosper in their chosen industries. Moreover, these groups actively encourage mental health awareness. By removing the stigma surrounding mental health disorders, they create an environment where individuals feel safe getting treatment when they need it. This greater openness surrounding mental health has considerably benefited the general mental well-being of women, paving the road for their empowerment.

Learning from Success, Shaping a Brighter Future

The success stories and best practices in gender equality are beacons of inspiration, offering significant lessons and guiding principles for individuals, organizations, and societies at large (Scheffer, 2020). They remind us that progress is possible, that equity is attainable, and that inclusivity is not just a goal but an obligation. As we explore deeper into these stories and tactics, we get not only insights but also motivation. These examples of success highlight the possibility for change and underscore the transformative effect of gender equality programmes. They offer a path for constructing a more inclusive, equitable, and successful society where the potential of all, regardless of their gender, is fully acknowledged and tapped. In the chapters that follow, we will explore additional specific examples, new trends, and innovative initiatives that continue to illuminate the route forward on this incredible journey toward gender equality in higher education and workplaces.

CONCLUSION

In traversing the pages of this book chapter, we have embarked on an illuminating journey through the intricate landscape of gender disparities in higher education and workplaces. As we draw this discourse to a close, it is imperative to reiterate the profound importance of addressing these disparities through the lens of inclusive practices. Our comprehensive exploration, spanning historical foundations, contemporary challenges, cross-cultural perspectives, and tales of triumph, serves as a clarion call to action. It beckons us to recognize the complexities woven into the fabric of gender equality, embrace diversity, and empower women on a global scale. The historical context that we have unraveled has illuminated the shadows of antiquity, casting a revealing light on the origins of gender disparities. We have seen how centuries of systemic biases, institutionalized discrimination, and societal expectations have created a formidable barrier to women's advancement. Understanding this historical trajectory is not merely an exercise of historical curiosity but an essential foundation for appreciating the urgency of change. Contemporary challenges, as we have explored, continue to shape the experiences of women in educational and professional spheres. Gender bias, stereotypes, unequal pay, and limited access to leadership positions persist as formidable obstacles, impacting women from all walks of life. Our examination has underscored the critical need for sustained efforts to dismantle these barriers, fostering environments that celebrate the potential of all individuals, regardless of gender. Yet, in the face of these challenges, there is hope. Hope that emanates from the myriad inclusive practices that have emerged worldwide to address these disparities. As we have ventured into diverse cultural contexts, we have uncovered a rich tapestry of strategies. Mentorship programs, diversity initiatives, policy changes, and more have illuminated a path toward empowerment. These practices represent a collective commitment to inclusivity, demonstrating that change is not only possible but achievable when we unite our efforts.

The concluding spotlight on success stories and best practices resonates as a beacon of inspiration. It reminds us that the quest for gender equality is not a quixotic endeavor but an attainable goal. These stories of triumph—whether they stem from educational institutions, corporations, or grassroots movements—showcase the tangible benefits of inclusive practices. They dispel any doubts that may cloud our vision and propel us toward action. As this chapter comes to a close, it is critical to recognise a fundamental truth: inclusive practices do not apply to all situations. Each cultural setting, community, and person has particular requirements and nuances. We must adapt our tactics to account for these subtleties if we are to truly empower women. Our collective power is found in this variety of strategies, which helps to create a global tapestry of empowerment. This chapter's conclusion isn't just a call to action; it also acknowledges that gender equality is a universal responsibility that transcends cultures and boundaries. This declaration advocates for a future in which women are not only equal participants but also leaders and visionaries, in which their potential is infinite, and in which their contributions strengthen every facet of society. We truly hope that this presentation advances the continuing dialogue on women's emancipation and ushers in a period in which all women, regardless of their cultural origins, are given equal opportunities to succeed in higher education and the workforce. Work together to make gender equality a reality that we can all proudly claim in the future, not just a pipe dream.

REFERENCES

Alaggia, R., & Wang, S. (2020). "I never told anyone until the# metoo movement": What can we learn from sexual abuse and sexual assault disclosures made through social media? *Child Abuse & Neglect, 103*, 104312. doi:10.1016/j.chiabu.2019.104312 PMID:32200194

Anderson, B. (1983). *Imagined communities: Reflections on the origin and spread of nationalism*. Verso.

Bartels, L. K., Weissinger, S. E., O'Brien, L. C., Ball, J. C., Cobb, P. D., Harris, J., ... Feldmann, M. L. (2021). Developing a system to support the advancement of women in higher education. *Journal of Faculty Development*, *35*(1), 34–42.

Begeny, C., Wong, C. Y. E., Kirby, T. A., & Rink, F. (2021). Gender, Race & Leadership. In Oxford research encyclopedia of psychology.

Bell, M. P., McLaughlin, M. E., & Sequeira, J. M. (2002). Discrimination, harassment, and the glass ceiling: Women executives as change agents. *Journal of Business Ethics*, *37*(1), 65–76. doi:10.1023/A:1014730102063

Bhavnani, R. (2009). *Women, 'culture' and development: A critical analysis*. Taylor & Francis.

Boni, N., & Circelli, M. (2002). *Contemporary issues facing women in policing*. Australasian Centre for Policing Research.

. Catalyst. (2019). Getting to the corporate boardroom: Progress of women corporate board directors. Catalyst.

Chen, M. A., & Duflo, E. (2019). The economic lives of the poor. *The Journal of Economic Perspectives*, *33*(1), 3–34.

Chuang, S. (2019). Exploring women-only training program for gender equality and women's continuous professional development in the workplace. Higher Education. *Skills and Work-Based Learning*, *9*(3), 359–373. doi:10.1108/HESWBL-01-2018-0001

Cook, A., & Glass, C. (2014). Above the glass ceiling: When are women and racial/ethnic minorities promoted to CEO? *Strategic Management Journal*, *35*(7), 1080–1089. doi:10.1002/smj.2161

Cox, T. (1994). *Cultural diversity in organizations: Theory, research, and practice*. Berrett-Koehler.

Crenshaw, K. (1989). Demarginalizing the intersection of race and sex: A black feminist critique of antidiscrimination doctrine, feminist theory, and antiracist politics. *University of Chicago Legal Forum*, *140*, 139–167.

Crenshaw, K. (1991). Mapping the margins: Intersectionality, identity politics, and violence against women of color. *Stanford Law Review*, *43*(6), 1241–1299. doi:10.2307/1229039 de Castro Salgado, L. C., Leitão, C. F., & Souza, C. S. (2014). *A Journey Through Cultures Metaphors for Guiding the Design of Cross-Cultural Interactive Systems.* Springer Publishing Company, Incorporated.

Delap, L. (2020). *Feminisms: A global history.* University of Chicago Press. doi:10.7208/chicago/9780226754123.001.0001

deVries, J. R. (2020). Those Who Came from Curiosity Remained from Interest. *Minnesota History, 67*(3), 146–152.

Eagly, A. H., Karau, S. J., & Makhijani, M. G. (1995). Gender and the effectiveness of leaders: A meta-analysis. *Psychological Bulletin, 117*(1), 125–145. doi:10.1037/0033-2909.117.1.125 PMID:7870858

García-Holgado, A., & García-Peñalvo, F. J. (2022). A model for bridging the gender gap in STEM in higher education institutions. In *Women in STEM in Higher Education: Good Practices of Attraction, Access and Retainment in Higher Education* (pp. 1–19). Springer Nature Singapore. doi:10.1007/978-981-19-1552-9_1

Glazebrook, T., Noll, S., & Opoku, E. (2020). Gender matters: Climate change, gender bias, and women's farming in the global South and North. *Agriculture, 10*(7), 267. doi:10.3390/agriculture10070267

Grant, A. M., & Gino, F. (2010). A little thanks goes a long way: Explaining why gratitude expressions motivate prosocial behavior. *Journal of Personality and Social Psychology, 98*(6), 946–955. doi:10.1037/a0017935 PMID:20515249

Hill, C., & McGinn, K. (2007). Global business case for corporate gender diversity. *Harvard Business Review, 85*(2), 129–137. PMID:17345686

Hoff, T., & Lee, D. R. (2021). The gender pay gap in medicine: A systematic review. *Health Care Management Review, 46*(3), E37–E49. doi:10.1097/HMR.0000000000000290 PMID:33534271

Inglehart, R., & Norris, P. (2003). *Rising tide: Gender equality and cultural change around the world.* Cambridge University Press. doi:10.1017/CBO9780511550362

Jackson, S. E., Ruderman, M., & Ehrhart, M. (2018). Diversity policies and practices. In *The Oxford Handbook of Organizational Psychology* (pp. 295–314). Oxford University Press.

. Jayachandran, S. (2015). The roots of gender inequality in developing countries. economics, 7(1), 63-88.

Kabeer, N. (2005). Gender equality and women's empowerment: A critical analysis of the third Millennium Development Goal 1. *Gender and Development, 13*(1), 13–24. doi:10.1080/13552070512331332273

Kabeer, N. (2020). Women's empowerment and economic development: A feminist critique of storytelling practices in "randomista" economics. *Feminist Economics, 26*(2), 1–26. doi:10.1080/13545701.2020.1743338

. Kandrichina, I. N., Yakimovich, E. V., Haurylenka, A. V., Saskevich, V. V., Zinchenka, Y. B., Bezbozhna, O. M., ... & Shadurski, V. G. (2016). Gender equality in higher education system: ways and means of achievement.

Lean, In. (2019). Women in the Workplace Study. Retrieved from https://leanin.org/women-in-the-workplace

Macy, R. D., Behar, L., Paulson, R., Delman, J., Schmid, L., & Smith, S. F. (2004). Community-based, acute posttraumatic stress management: A description and evaluation of a psychosocial-intervention continuum. *Harvard Review of Psychiatry, 12*(4), 217–228. doi:10.1080/10673220490509589 PMID:15371064

Mason, M. A., Wolfinger, N. H., & Goulden, M. (2013). Do babies matter? The effect of family formation on the lifelong careers of academic men and women. *Academe, 99*(2), 10–15.

Matthews, T. A., Robbins, W., Preisig, M., von Känel, R., & Li, J. (2021). Associations of job strain and family strain with risk of major depressive episode: A prospective cohort study in US working men and women. *Journal of Psychosomatic Research, 147*, 110541. doi:10.1016/j.jpsychores.2021.110541 PMID:34130004

Maume, D. J. (2006). Gender differences in restricting work efforts because of family responsibilities. *Journal of Marriage and Family, 68*(4), 859–869. doi:10.1111/j.1741-3737.2006.00300.x

Mojab, S. (2000). Theorizing the politics of 'veiling' in contemporary Western societies. *Feminist Review, 64*(1), 20–58.

Murrell, A. J., Olson, J. E., & Frieze, I. H. (1995). Sexual harassment and gender discrimination: A longitudinal study of women managers. *The Journal of Social Issues, 51*(1), 139–149. doi:10.1111/j.1540-4560.1995.tb01313.x

National Women's Law Center. (2020). The Wage Gap: The Who, How, Why, and What to Do. Retrieved from https://nwlc.org/resources/the-wage-gap-the-who-how-why-and-what-to-do/

O'Leary, V. E. (1974). Some attitudinal barriers to occupational aspirations in women. *Psychological Bulletin, 81*(11), 809–826. doi:10.1037/h0037267

. Raukar, N. P., & Mishkin, H. M. (2020). Domestic responsibilities and career advancement. Burnout in women physicians: prevention, treatment, and management, 69-76.

Rose, D. (2018). *Citizens by degree: Higher education policy and the changing gender dynamics of American citizenship.* Oxford University Press.

Sassler, S., Glass, J., Levitte, Y., & Michelmore, K. M. (2017). The missing women in STEM? Assessing gender differentials in the factors associated with transition to first jobs. *Social Science Research, 63,* 192–208. doi:10.1016/j.ssresearch.2016.09.014 PMID:28202143

Scandura, T. A., & Lankau, M. J. (1997). Relationships of gender, family responsibility and flexible work hours to organizational commitment and job satisfaction. Journal of Organizational Behavior: The International Journal of Industrial. *Journal of Organizational Behavior, 18*(4), 377–391. doi:10.1002/(SICI)1099-1379(199707)18:4<377::AID-JOB807>3.0.CO;2-1

. Scheffer, R. (2020). Engineering a Brighter Future: Increasing the Representation of Women of Color in Engineering.

Scott, J. W. (1986). Gender: A Useful Category of Historical Analysis. *The American Historical Review, 91*(5), 1053–1075. doi:10.2307/1864376

Sen, A. (1997). Human capital and human capability. *World Development, 25*(12), 1959–1961. doi:10.1016/S0305-750X(97)10014-6

Sen, A. (2001). The many faces of gender inequality. *New Republic (New York, N.Y.), 215*(22), 35–39.

Smith, J. (2010). *Women and Gender in Early Modern Europe.* Cambridge University Press.

Subrahmanian, R. (2003). Promoting gender equality. In *Targeting Development* (pp. 208–232). Routledge. doi:10.4324/9780203403235.ch9

Swim, J. K., & Thomas, M. A. (2006). Responding to everyday discrimination: A synthesis of research on goal-directed, self-regulatory coping behaviors. In *Stigma and group inequality* (pp. 119–140). Psychology Press.

Turner, C. S. V., & González, J. C. (2011). Faculty women of color: The critical nexus of race and gender. *Journal of Diversity in Higher Education*, 4(4), 199. doi:10.1037/a0024630

United Nations. (2015). HeForShe Campaign. Retrieved from https://www.heforshe.org/

United Nations. (2015). Transforming our world: The 2030 Agenda for Sustainable Development. Retrieved from https://sustainabledevelopment.un.org/post2015/transformingourworld

United Nations. (2020). *Progress of the world's women 2019-2020: Families in a changing world*. UN Women.

Valentine, C. G., Trautner, M. N., & Spade, J. Z. (Eds.). (2019). *The kaleidoscope of gender: Prisms, patterns, and possibilities*. Sage Publications.

Wang, S. (2023). Exploring Early Childhood Educators' Perceptions and Practices Towards Gender Differences in STEM Play: A Multiple-Case Study in China. *Early Childhood Education Journal*, 1–14. doi:10.1007/s10643-023-01499-3 PMID:37360596

Wiesner-Hanks, M. E. (2021). *Gender in history: Global perspectives*. John Wiley & Sons.

Women, U. N. (2011). *Progress of the world's women 2011-2012: In pursuit of justice*. UN Women. doi:10.18356/9789210550307

Women, U. N. (2015). *Progress of the world's women 2015-2016: Transforming economies, realizing rights*. UN Women. doi:10.18356/2d5f74e3-en

World Bank. (2009). *Gender and Development in the Middle East and North Africa: Women in the Public Sphere*. World Bank.

World Economic Forum. (2020). Global Gender Gap Report. Retrieved from https://www.weforum.org/reports/gender-gap-2020-report-100-years-pay-equality

Conclusion

To understand the active roles of women in society and appreciate their advancements in higher education and the workplace, it is essential to explore their historical foundations. Throughout history, women have played a vital role in society, advocating for equality, and combatting gender biases at different societal levels. This is further evidenced in today's global movements aimed at advancing women.

In ancient times, women had the opportunity to play different roles in their societies and become influential in their political authority and rulings. For instance, in ancient Mesopotamia, women were nurturers and priestesses, and Pharaohs and rulers in ancient Egypt. In ancient Greece, women like Sappho used their poetry to challenge societal norms and perceptions of women throughout intellectual and cultural spheres. In Rome, women assumed roles of matrons and empresses, showcasing their political influence. Another notable example of a powerful woman is Cleopatra, the last Pharaoh of Egypt, who was able to maintain Egypt's independence through her intelligence and political power.

Speaking out on women's rights and attitudes toward women's inferior status to men is as old as 14th-and early 15th Century, emphasized through the works of French philosopher, Christine de Pisan. Her writings challenged intellectual pursuits to advocate for gender equality and challenge the status quo, that women's work should be confined to the home and caretaking for family members. During the Enlightenment era, women intellectuals such as Mary Wollstonecraft argued for women's education and political representation. This, and others, later set the stage for feminist movements that focused on women's education, better working conditions, voting rights, and abolishing gender stereotypes.

It is important to note that, as societies progressed, so did the status of women and the advocacy for their active roles across various societies and cultures. The 19th century, for example, marked a *turning point* in women's history, particularly with the suffrage movement gaining momentum. Women like Susan B. Anthony fought for women's right to vote, paving the way for the 19th Amendment to the U.S. Constitution, which was not ratified until the early 20th century (1920).

Following this period, and the beginning of a transformative 20th century, issues such as employment discrimination and educational opportunities were making an impact on societies at large. Particularly important were women entering the workforce following the two world wars, replacing male workers who had gone to fight, partly instigating the women's liberation movements in the 1960s and 1970s which demanded, among other things, equal pay.

In conclusion, it is important to note that the history of women is a very important subject that spans over centuries and encompasses diverse cultures across many civilizations. From their traditional roles in caretaking for their families and fighting against societal stereotypes of what women can and should do to their advancements across various fields of study, women have proven resilience and progress in challenging social norms. Their advocacy for gender equality in higher education and the workplace reflects their power to break through the glass ceiling and move beyond sticky floors in reaching leadership positions. It is our duty then, as educators, to critically examine the historical underpinnings and contributions of women throughout history to the modern-day global efforts made toward a more equitable and inclusive society for all.

Compilation of References

. Catalyst. (2019). Getting to the corporate boardroom: Progress of women corporate board directors. Catalyst.

. Jayachandran, S. (2015). The roots of gender inequality in developing countries. economics, 7(1), 63-88.

. Kandrichina, I. N., Yakimovich, E. V., Haurylenka, A. V., Saskevich, V. V., Zinchenka, Y. B., Bezbozhna, O. M., ... & Shadurski, V. G. (2016). Gender equality in higher education system: ways and means of achievement.

. Raukar, N. P., & Mishkin, H. M. (2020). Domestic responsibilities and career advancement. Burnout in women physicians: prevention, treatment, and management, 69-76.

. Scheffer, R. (2020). Engineering a Brighter Future: Increasing the Representation of Women of Color in Engineering.

Abreu, M., and Grinevich, V. (2017). "Gender patterns in academic entrepreneurship," *Journal of Technology Transfer* (42:4), pp. 763-794.

Adebayo, K. O., & Njoku, E. T. (2023). Local and transnational identity, positionality and knowledge production in Africa and the African diaspora. *Field Methods*, *35*(1), 18–32. doi:10.1177/1525822X211051574

Agra, K. L. R. P. (2020). Epistemic Injustice, Epistemic Paralysis, and Epistemic Resistance: A (Feminist) Liberatory Approach to Epistemology. *Kritike: An Online. The Journal of Philosophy*, *14*(1).

Aguirre, A. (2000). *Women and Minority Faculty in the Academic Workplace: Recruitment, Retention and Academic Culture*. ASHE-ERIC.

Aguirre, A., & Martinez, R. (2006). *Diversity leadership in higher education*. Jossey-Bass.

Ahsan, M. J. (2023). Unlocking sustainable success: Exploring the impact of transformational leadership, organizational culture, and CSR performance on financial performance in the Italian manufacturing sector. *Social Responsibility Journal*. Advance online publication. doi:10.1108/SRJ-06-2023-0332

Ajogbeje, T. O. (2016). Women political participation and decision-making in Nigeria: The case of Edo State House of Assembly. *African Journal of Political Science and International Relations, 10*(9), 234–245.

Akanle, O., & Shittu, O. S. (2020). Study justification in social research. *Contemporary issues in social research, 1*, 93-104.

Akinkunmi, K. (2021). An Analysis of "Encountering Development: The Making and Unmaking of the Third World" by Arturo Escobar. *Sustinere—The University of Toronto's Journal of Sustainable Development, 1*(1), 64-71.

Akintimehin, O. O., Eniolaa, A. A., Eluyelac, Felix, D., Okered, Wisdom, & Ozordie, E. (2021). Social capital and its effect on business performance in the Nigeria's informal sector. doi:10.1016/j.heliyon.2019.e02024

Akkari, A. (2004). Education in the Middle East and North Africa: The Current Situation and Future Challenges. *International Education Journal*.

Akoleowo, V. O. O. (2022). African feminism, activism and decolonisation: The case of Alimotu Pelewura. *African Identities*, 1–16. doi:10.1080/14725843.2022.2157246

Al Khatib, M. (2020). Facilitating female employment in Jordan: Key Issues and Trends. *UNESCO*. Retrieved August 14, 2020, from https://unevoc.unesco.org/yem/Female+unemployment+in+Jordan+YEM+Blog&context

Al-Ababneh, M. (2020). Linking ontology, epistemology and research methodology. *Science & Philosophy, 8*(1), 75–91.

Alaggia, R., & Wang, S. (2020). "I never told anyone until the# metoo movement": What can we learn from sexual abuse and sexual assault disclosures made through social media? *Child Abuse & Neglect, 103*, 104312. doi:10.1016/j.chiabu.2019.104312 PMID:32200194

Alase, A. (2017). The interpretative phenomenological analysis (IPA): A guide to a good qualitative research approach. *International Journal of Education and Literacy Studies, 5*(2), 9–19. doi:10.7575/aiac.ijels.v.5n.2p.9

Aldrich, A. S., & Lotito, N. J. (2020). Pandemic Performance: Women Leaders in the Covid-19 Crisis. *Politics & Gender, 16*(4), 1–9. doi:10.1017/S1743923X20000549

Al-Faham, H., Davis, A. M., & Ernst, R. (2019). Intersectionality: From theory to practice. *Annual Review of Law and Social Science, 15*(1), 247–265. doi:10.1146/annurev-lawsocsci-101518-042942

Allen, T. G., & Flood, C. T. (2018). The Experiences of Women in Higher Education: Who Knew There Wasn't a Sisterhood? *Leadership and Research in Education, 4*, 10–27.

Alleyne, L. K. (2021) "You Is Kind, You Is Smart, You Is Important: The] Black Female Professor as 'the Help.'" Teaching Black: The Craft of Teaching on Black Life and Literature, edited by Ana-Maurine Lara and Drea Brown, University of Pittsburgh Press, pp. 172–77. JSTOR, https://doi.org/. Accessed 17 Jan. 2024. doi:10.2307/j.ctv22tnmhk.23

Compilation of References

Allison, D. C. (2008). Free to Be Me? Black Professors, White Institutions. *Journal of Black Studies*, *38*(4), 641–662. https://doi-org.proxyhu.wrlc.org/10.1177/0021934706289175. doi:10.1177/0021934706289175

Alonzo, M. L. M., Zuccaro, C., Plaisent, M., & Bernard, P. (2024). Examination of the Relationship Between Organizational Effectiveness and Transformational Leadership: The Case of Registered Charities. In Trends, Challenges, and Practices in Contemporary Strategic Management (pp. 194-212). IGI Global.

Amar, S. (2023). Why everyone wins with more women in leadership. Forbes. Retrieved from https://www.forbes.com/sites/forbesbusinesscouncil/2023/02/07/why-everyone-wins-with-more-women-in-leadership/?sh=2c7dfb3f3cdd

American Association of University Professors. (2023). *Faculty child care*. https://www.aaup.org/report/faculty-child-care

American Community Survey (2023). *U.S. Census Bureau.* Census.gov

American Council on Education (2017). Minority presidents. *American Council on Education.* aceacps.org

American Federation of Teachers (2020). *Report reveals grave plight of contingent college faculty*. aft.org

American Federation of Teachers, Higher Education. (2011). Promoting gender diversity in the faculty: What higher education unions can do. *American Federation of Teachers. Higher Education.*

Anderson, B. (1983). *Imagined communities: Reflections on the origin and spread of nationalism.* Verso.

Andrews, K. (2021). *The new age of empire: How racism and colonialism still rule the world.* Penguin UK.

Anoos, J. M., Gimena, J. A., Etcuban, J. O., Dinauanao, A. M., Macugay, P., & Velita, L. V. (2020). Financial management of micro, small, and medium enterprises in Cebu, Philippines. *International Journal of Small Business and Entrepreneurship Research*, 53–76.

Antecol, H., Bedard, K., & Stearns, J. (2018). Equal but inequitable: Who benefits from gender-neutral tenure clock stopping policies? *The American Economic Review*, *108*(9), 2420–2441. doi:10.1257/aer.20160613

Arciniega, T. A. (2012). The Crucial Role of Hispanic-Serving Institutions in the Education of Latino/a Youth. *Journal of Latinos and Education*, *11*(3), 150–156. doi:10.1080/15348431.2012.686348

Arenhart, J. R. B., & Arroyo, R. W. (2021). Back to the question of ontology (and metaphysics). *Manuscrito, 44*, 01-51.

Aristei, D., & Gallo, M. (2021). Are female-led firms disadvantaged in accessing bank credit? Evidence from transition economies. *International Journal of Emerging Markets*, *17*(6), 1484–1521. doi:10.1108/IJOEM-03-2020-0286

Armuña, C., Ramos, S., Ruiz, J. J., Feijoo, C., and Arenal, A. 2020. "From stand-up to start-up: exploring entrepreneurship competencies and STEM women's intention," *International Entrepreneurship and Management Journal* (16:1), pp. 69-92.

Arriaga, T. T., Stanley, S. L., & Lindsey, D. B. (2020). *Leading While Female: A Culturally Proficient Response for Gender Equity*. Corwin.

Artz, B., & Welsch, D. M. (2014) "The Effect of Peer and Professor Gender on College Student Performance." *Southern Economic Journal*, vol. 80, no. 3, pp. 816 38. JSTOR, https://www.jstor.org/stable/23809653. Accessed 17 Jan. 2024.

Ashcraft, C., McLain, B., & Eger, E. (2016). Women in tech: The facts. National Center for Women & Technology (NCWIT). Retrieved from: https://www.ncwit.org/resources/women-tech-facts-2016-update

Asravor, R. K., & Acheampong, V. (2021). Factors influencing risk attitudes of entrepreneurs in Ghana: The role of gender. *Journal of Small Business and Entrepreneurship*, *36*(1), 29–52. doi:10.1080/08276331.2021.1980838

Association of American Colleges and Universities. (2015). *Committing to equity and inclusive excellence: A campus guide for self-study and planning*. ERIC Clearinghouse.

Austin, A. E. (2012). Preparing the next generation of faculty: Graduate school as socialization to the academic career. *Journal of Higher Education (Columbus, Ohio)*, *73*(1), 94–122. doi:10.1353/jhe.2002.0001

Azizah, N., Manik, M. B., & Ilham, R. N. (2023). Analysis of Financial Performance in the Home Industry of Kerupuk Tempe in Matang Munye, Syamtalira Aron Sub-district. *Journal of Accounting Research. Utility Finance and Digital Assets*, *1*(3), 304–311.

Bagilhole, B. (2019). Against the odds: Women academics' research opportunities. In *Gender, teaching and research in higher education* (pp. 46–56). Routledge. doi:10.4324/9781315254548-5

Bailes, L. P., & Guthery, S. (2020). Held Down and Held Back: Systematically Delayed Principal Promotions by Race and Gender. *AERA Open*, *6*(2), 2332858420929298. doi:10.1177/2332858420929298

Bailey, M.Moya Bailey & Trudy. (2018). On misogynoir: Citation, erasure, and plagiarism. *Feminist Media Studies*, *18*(4), 762–768. doi:10.1080/14680777.2018.1447395

Baker, V. L., & Manning, C. (2021). A mid-career faculty agenda: A review of four decades of research and practice. Higher education: Handbook of theory and research, 36, 1-66. doi:10.1007/978-3-030-43030-6_10-1

Baker, V. L. (2020). *Charting your path to full*. Rutgers University Press. doi:10.36019/9781978805972

Compilation of References

Baldwin, J. (1955). "Stranger in the Village." Notes of a Native Son. Beacon.

Bangko Sentral ng Pilipinas, (2019) Financial Inclusion Survey. BSP. Retrieved from https://www.bsp.gov.ph › 2019FISToplineReport.

Barba, I., & Iraizoz, B. (2020). Effect of the Great Crisis on Sectoral Female Employment in Europe: A Structural Decomposition Analysis. *Economies*, *8*(3), 64. doi:10.3390/economies8030064

Barnard, S., Arnolda, J., Bosleya, S., & Munir, F. (2022). The personal and institutional impacts of a mass participation leadership programme for women working in Higher Education: A longitudinal analysis. *Studies in Higher Education*, *47*(7), 1372–1385. doi:10.1080/03075079.2021.1894117

Barnett, R. (1990). *The idea of higher education*. McGraw-Hill Education.

Bartel, S. (2018). *Leadership barriers for women in higher education.* https://bized.aacsb.edu/articles/2018/12/leadership-barriers-for-women-in-higher- education.

Bartels, L. K., Weissinger, S. E., O'Brien, L. C., Ball, J. C., Cobb, D., Harris, J., Morgan, S. M., Love, E., Moody, S. B., & Feldman, M. L. (2021). Developing a system to support the advancement of women in higher education. *Journal of Faculty Development*, *35*(1), 34–42.

Bauer, N. M., & Taylor, T. (2022). Selling them short? Differences in news coverage of female and male candidate qualifications. *Political Research Quarterly*.

Begeny, C., Wong, C. Y. E., Kirby, T. A., & Rink, F. (2021). Gender, Race & Leadership. In Oxford research encyclopedia of psychology.

Belkin, L. (2003). The opt-out revolution. *New York Times Magazine*, *26*, 42–47.

Bellini, M. I., Graham, Y., Hayes, C., Zakeri, R., Parks, R., & Papalois, V. (2019). A woman's place is in theatre: Women's perceptions and experiences of working in surgery from the Association of Surgeons of Great Britain and Ireland women in surgery working group. *BMJ Open*, *9*(1), e024349. doi:10.1136/bmjopen-2018-024349 PMID:30617103

Bell, M. P., McLaughlin, M. E., & Sequeira, J. M. (2002). Discrimination, harassment, and the glass ceiling: Women executives as change agents. *Journal of Business Ethics*, *37*(1), 65–76. doi:10.1023/A:1014730102063

Benedict, A., Gitongab, J. K., Agyemanc, A. S., & Kyeid, B. T. (2021). Financial determinants of SMEs performance. Evidence from Kenya leather industry.

Benokraitis, N. V., & Feagin, J. R. (1978). *Affirmative Action and Equal Opportunity: Action. Inaction and Reaction.*

Benslimane, M., & Moustaghfir, K. (2020). Career development practices and gender equity in higher education. *International Journal of Management Education*, *14*(2), 183–211.

Benziman, Y. (2020). "Winning" the "battle" and "beating" the COVID-19 "enemy": Leaders' use of war frames to define the pandemic. *Peace and Conflict*, *26*(3), 247–256. doi:10.1037/pac0000494

Berenstain, N. (2016). Epistemic exploitation.

Bernecker, S. (2022). Knowledge from Falsehood and Truth-Closeness. *Philosophia*, *50*(4), 1623–1638. doi:10.1007/s11406-022-00479-y

Bhavnani, R. (2009). *Women, 'culture' and development: A critical analysis*. Taylor & Francis.

Bilmoria, D., Joy, S., & Liang, X. (2008). Breaking barriers and creating inclusiveness: Lessons of organizational transformation to advance women faculty in academic science and engineering. *Human Resource Management*, *47*(3), 423–441. doi:10.1002/hrm.20225

Blackmon, A. T., Askew, K., McKayle, C., Engerman, K., & Clavier, N. (2021). "I see the potential in you": Provosts' purposeful perspective-taking on HBCU students to promote broadening STEM participation. *The Journal of Negro Education*, *90*(3), 322–333.

Blake, D. J. (2022). Gendered and racialized career sacrifices of women faculty accepting dual-career offers. *Journal of Women and Gender in Higher Education*, *15*(2), 113–133. doi:10.1080/26379112.2022.2067168

Bloomfield, B. P., & Vurdubakis, T. (1999). The outer limits: Monsters, actor networks and the writing of displacement. *Organization*, *6*(4), 625–647. doi:10.1177/135050849964004

Boice, B. (2010). *Advice for new faculty members*. Allyn Bacon.

Boncana, M., McKayle, C., Engerman, K., & Askew, K. (2021). What is going on here? Exploring why HBCU presidents are successful in producing STEM graduates. *The Journal of Negro Education*, *90*(3), 277–287.

Boni, N., & Circelli, M. (2002). *Contemporary issues facing women in policing*. Australasian Centre for Policing Research.

Bosma, N., (2020). Global Entrepreneurship Monitor 2019/2020.

Boutwell, B. B., Nedelec, J. L., Winegard, B., Shackelford, T., Beaver, K. M., Vaughn, M., Barnes, J. C., & Wright, J. P. (2017). The prevalence of discrimination across racial groups in contemporary America: Results from a nationally representative sample of adults. *PLoS One*, *12*(8), e0183356. doi:10.1371/journal.pone.0183356 PMID:28837680

Boyer, E. L. (1990). *Scholarship Reconsidered: Priorities of the Professoriate*. The Carnegie Foundation for the Advancement of Teaching.

Bright, A., Acosta, S., & Parker, B. (2020). Humility Matters: Interrogating Our Positionality, Power, and Privilege Through Collaboration. In Handbook of Research on Diversity and Social Justice in Higher Education (pp. 19-40). IGI Global.

Bruce, V., & Young, A. (1998). *In the eye of the beholder: The science of face perception*. Oxford university press.

Bruckmuller, S., Ryan, M. K., Rink, F., & Haslam, S. A. (2014). Beyond the glass ceiling: The glass cliff and its lessons for organizational policy. *Social Issues and Policy Review*, *8*(1), 202–232. doi:10.1111/sipr.12006

Bullough, A., Guelich, U., Manolova, T. S., & Schjoedt, L. (2022). Women's entrepreneurship and culture: Gender role expectations and identities, societal culture, and the entrepreneurial environment. *Small Business Economics*, *58*(2), 985–996. doi:10.1007/s11187-020-00429-6 PMID:38624690

Bullough, A., Hechavarria, D., Brush, C., & Edelman, L. (Eds.). (2019). *High-growth women's entrepreneurship programs, policies and practices*. Edward Elgar Publishing. doi:10.4337/9781788118712

Burgess, P. (2007). *Women Empowered: Inspiring Change in the Emerging World*. Rizzoli.

Burke, P. J., & Crozier, G. (2014). Higher education pedagogies: Gendered formations, mis/recognition and emotion. *Journal of Research in Gender Studies*, *4*(2), 52.

Burke, R. J. (1984). Mentors in organizations. *Group & Organization Studies*, *9*(3), 195–207. doi:10.1177/105960118400900304

Cahdriyana, R. A., Richardo, R., Fahmi, S., & Setyawan, F. (2019, March). Pseudo-thinking process in solving logic problem. *Journal of Physics: Conference Series*, *1188*(1), 012090. doi:10.1088/1742-6596/1188/1/012090

Cahn, P. S., Gona, C. M., Naidoo, K., & Truong, K. A. (2022). Disrupting bias without trainings: The effect of equity advocates on faculty search committees. *Innovative Higher Education*, *47*(2), 253–272. doi:10.1007/s10755-021-09575-5 PMID:34456457

Campante, F. R., & Chor, D. (2012). Why was the Arab World Poised for Revolution? Schooling, Economic Opportunities, and the Arab Spring. *The Journal of Economic Perspectives*, *26*(2), 167–188. doi:10.1257/jep.26.2.167

Canaan, J. E., & Shumar, W. (Eds.). (2008). *Structure and agency in the neoliberal university* (Vol. 15). Routledge. doi:10.4324/9780203927687

Cardel, M. I., Dhurandhar, E., Yarar-Fisher, C., Foster, M., Hidalgo, B., McClure, L. A., ... Willig, A. L. (2020). Turning chutes into ladders for women faculty: A review and roadmap for equity in academia. *Journal of Women's Health*, *29*(5), 721–733. doi:10.1089/jwh.2019.8027 PMID:32043918

Carrigan, C., Quinn, K., & Riskin, E. A. (2011). The gendered division of labor among STEM faculty and the effects of critical mass. *Journal of Diversity in Higher Education*, *4*(3), 131–146. doi:10.1037/a0021831

Carter, J. A. (2017). Epistemological Implications of Relativism. In J. J. Ichikawa (Ed.), *The Routledge Handbook of Epistemic Contextualism*. Routledge. doi:10.4324/9781315745275-24

Casad, B. J., Franks, J. E., Garasky, C. E., Kittleman, M. M., Roesler, A. C., Hall, D. Y., & Petzel, Z. W. (2020). Gender inequality in academia: Problems and solutions for women faculty in STEM. *Journal of Neuroscience Research*, *99*(1), 13–23. doi:10.1002/jnr.24631 PMID:33103281

Cassola, A., Raub, A., Foley, D., & Heymann, J. (2014). Where do Women Stand? New Evidence on the Presence and Absence of Gender Equality in the World's Constitutions. *Politics & Gender*, *10*(2), 200–235. doi:10.1017/S1743923X1400004X

Castellanos, J., Gloria, A. M., & Kamimura, M. (2003). The Latino Pathway to the PhD. *Stylus (Rio de Janeiro)*.

Castellanos, J., & Jones, L. (2003). The Majority in the Minority: Expanding the Representation of Latino Faculty, Administrators and Students in Higher Education. *Stylus (Rio de Janeiro)*.

Catalyst. (2005). *Catalyst census of women corporate officers and top earners of the Fortune 500*. www.catalyst.org/system/files/2005_Census_Fortune_500_Women_Corporate_Officers.pdf

Catalyst. (2014). *Statistical overview of women in the workplace*. http://www.catalyst.org/knowledge/statistical-overview-women-workplace

Center of Arab Women for Training and Research (CAWTAR). (2007). https://cawtar.org/en/nged-network

Chambers, C. (2023). *African American Women Leaders in Higher Education: An Examination of Job Satisfaction* (Doctoral dissertation, St. John's University (New York)).

Chance, N. L. (2020). *"Nevertheless, She Persisted": Exploring the Influence of Adversity on Black Women in Higher Education Senior Leadership* (Doctoral dissertation, Indiana Institute of Technology).

Chance, N. L. (2021). A phenomenological inquiry into the influence of crucible experiences on the leadership development of Black women in higher education senior leadership. *Educational Management Administration & Leadership*, *49*(4), 601–623. doi:10.1177/17411432211019417

Chance, N. L. (2022). Resilient leadership: A phenomenological exploration into how black women in higher education leadership navigate cultural adversity. *Journal of Humanistic Psychology*, *62*(1), 44–78. doi:10.1177/00221678211003000

Chance, S. (2010). Strategic by design: Iterative approaches to educational planning. *Planning for Higher Education*, *38*(2), 40–54.

Chávez-Rivera, M. E., Ruíz-Jiménez, J. M., & Fuentes-Fuentes, M. D. M. (2024). The effects of context and characteristics of women entrepreneurs on innovation performance. *Business Research Quarterly*, *27*(1), 73–90. doi:10.1177/23409444231220951

Cha, Y. (2013). Overwork and the persistence of gender segregation in occupations. *Gender & Society*, *27*(2), 158–184. doi:10.1177/0891243212470510

Compilation of References

Chen, M. A., & Duflo, E. (2019). The economic lives of the poor. *The Journal of Economic Perspectives*, *33*(1), 3–34.

Cherry, K. (2023). How transformational leadership can inspire others. Retrieved from https://www.verywellmind.com/what-is-transformational-leadership-2795313

Chikwira, C., Vengesai, E., & Mandude, P. (2022). The Impact of Microfinance Institutions on Poverty Alleviation. *Journal of Risk and Financial Management*, *15*(9), 393. Advance online publication. doi:10.3390/jrfm15090393

Chinn, C. A., & Rinehart, R. W. (2016). Epistemic cognition and philosophy: Developing a new framework for epistemic cognition. In *Handbook of epistemic cognition* (pp. 460–478). Routledge.

Chinowaita, M. (undated). Does affirmative action benefit women? *Standard Online,* <www.samara.co.zw/standard>

Chinowaita, M. (undated). Organisation aims to politically empower women, Standard *Online,* <http:// www.samara.co.zw/standard/index>

Choi, S. L., Goh, C. F., Adam, M. B., & Tan, O. K. (2016). Transformational leadership, empowerment, and job satisfaction: The mediating role of employee empowerment. *Human Resources for Health*, *14*(1), 73. doi:10.1186/s12960-016-0171-2 PMID:27903294

Choi, S., & Richards, K. (2017). *Interdisciplinary discourse: Communicating across disciplines*. Springer. doi:10.1057/978-1-137-47040-9

Cho, S. (2002). Understanding white women's ambivalence towards affirmative action: Theorizing political accountability in coalitions. *UMKC Law Review*, *71*, 399.

Cho, Y., Li, J., & Chaudhuri, S. (2020). Women entrepreneurs in Asia: Eight country studies. *Advances in Developing Human Resources*, *22*(2), 115–123. doi:10.1177/1523422320907042

Chuang, S. (2019). Exploring women-only training program for gender equality and women's continuous professional development in the workplace. Higher Education. *Skills and Work-Based Learning*, *9*(3), 359–373. doi:10.1108/HESWBL-01-2018-0001

Clance, P. R., & Imes, S. A. (1978). The imposter phenomenon in high achieving women: Dynamics and therapeutic intervention. *Psychotherapy (Chicago, Ill.)*, *15*(3), 241–247. doi:10.1037/h0086006

Clark, R. L., & D'Ambrosio, M. B. (2015). *Recruitment, Retention and Retirement in Higher Education: Building and Managing the Faculty of the Future*. Edward Edgar.

Colby, G., & Fowler, C. (2020). *Data snapshot: IPEDS data on full-time women faculty and faculty of color*. American Association of University Professors.

Coleman, M. (2010). Women-only (homophilous) networks supporting women leaders in education. *Journal of Educational Administration*, *48*(6), 769–781. doi:10.1108/09578231011079610

Collazos, L. E. O., & Botero, I. C. (2024). *Women ownership as a form of leadership: The role of context in understanding its effects on financial performance*. BRQ Business Research Quarterly., doi:10.1177/23409444231222503

Collins, P. H. (2000). *Black Feminist Thought: Knowledge, Consciousness, and the Politics of Empowerment*. Routledge.

Colon-Alverio, I. D., & Flowers, T. D. (2022). The Racial Battle Fatigue of Black Graduate Women in the Academy. In Black Women Navigating Historically White Higher Education Institutions and the Journey Toward Liberation (pp. 69-87). IGI Global. doi:10.4018/978-1-6684-4626-3.ch004

Columbia University. (2016). Guide to best practices in faculty search and hiring.

Connell, R. (2020). The social organization of masculinity. In *Feminist theory reader* (pp. 192–200). Routledge.

Contreras, F. E., Malcom, L. E., & Bensimon, E. M. (2018). *Hispanic-Serving Institutions*. State University of New York Press.

Cook, A., & Glass, C. (2014). Above the glass ceiling: When are women and racial/ethnic minorities promoted to CEO? *Strategic Management Journal*, 35(7), 1080–1089. doi:10.1002/smj.2161

Cowling, M., Marlow, S., & Liu, W. C. (2019). Gender and bank lending after the global financial crisis: Are women entrepreneurs safer bets? *Small Business Economics*, •••. Advance online publication. doi:10.1007/s11187-019-00168-3

Cox, T. (1994). *Cultural diversity in organizations: Theory, research, and practice*. Berrett-Koehler.

Crenshaw, K. (1989). Demarginalizing the intersection of race and sex: A black feminist critique of antidiscrimination doctrine, feminist theory and antiracist politics. University of Chicago Legal Forum, Volume 1989, Article 8.

Crenshaw, K. (1989). Demarginalizing the intersection of race and sex: A black feminist critique of antidiscrimination doctrine, feminist theory, and antiracist politics. *University of Chicago Legal Forum*, 140, 139–167.

Crenshaw, K. (1991). Mapping the margins: Intersectionality, identity politics, and violence against women of color. *Stanford Law Review*, 43(6), 1241–1299. doi:10.2307/1229039

Culpepper, D., Kilmer, S., O'Meara, K., Misra, J. & Jaeger, A. J. (2020. The Terrapin time initiative: A workshop to enhance alignment between faculty work priorities and time- use. *Innovative Higher Education, 45,* 165-179. https://doi.org/ 09490-w DesRoches, C. M. & Zinner, D. E., Rao, S. R., Lezzoni, L. I., & Campbell, E.G. (April 2010). Activities, productivity, and compensation of men and women in the life sciences. *Academic Medicine, 85*(4), 631-639. https:// doi.org/ doi:10/1007/s10755-019-

Cunliffe, A. L., & Scaratti, G. (2017). Embedding Impact in Engaged Research: Developing Socially Useful Knowledge through Dialogical Sensemaking. *British Journal of Management*, 28(1), 29–44. doi:10.1111/1467-8551.12204

Compilation of References

Damaske, S. (2011). *For the Family? How Class and Gender Shape Women's Work*. Oxford University Press.

Dandan, M. M., & Marques, A. P. (2017). Education, Employment and Gender Gap in Mena Region. *Asian Economic and Financial Review*, 7(6), 573–588. doi:10.18488/journal.aefr.2017.76.573.588

Das, R. C. (2022). *Microfinance to Combat Global Recession and Social Exclusion: An Empirical Investigation*. doi:10.1007/978-981-16-4329-3

Daun, H., & Arjmand, R. (2002). Arab Countries: Oil Boom, Religious Revival and Non Reform. In H. Daun (Ed.), *Educational Restructuring in the Context of Globalization and National Policy*. Routledge.

Davey, T. L., Johnson, K. F., Webb, L., & White, E. (2021). Recruitment inclusive champions: Supporting university diversity and inclusion goals. *Journal of Faculty Development*, 35(2), 50–57.

de Castro Salgado, L. C., Leitão, C. F., & Souza, C. S. (2014). *A Journey Through Cultures Metaphors for Guiding the Design of Cross-Cultural Interactive Systems*. Springer Publishing Company, Incorporated.

De los Santos, A. G. Jr, & De los Santos, G. E. (2013). Hispanic-Serving Institutions in the 21st century: Overview, challenges, and opportunities. *Journal of Hispanic Higher Education*, 2(4), 377–391. doi:10.1177/1538192703256734

Delap, L. (2020). *Feminisms: A global history*. University of Chicago Press. doi:10.7208/chicago/9780226754123.001.0001

Delgado-Romero, E. A., Manlove, A. N., Manlove, J. D., & Hernandez, C. E. (2007). Controversial Issues in the Recruitment and Retention of Latino Faculty. *Journal of Hispanic Higher Education*, 6(1), 34–51. doi:10.1177/1538192706294903

Deniz, Z., & Dogruel, A. (2008). Disaggregated Education Data And Growth: Some Facts From Turkey And Mena Countries. Topics. In *Middle Eastern & North African Economies*. Proceedings Of The Middle East Economic Association.

DeNora, T. (2014). Making sense of reality: Culture and perception in everyday life. *Making Sense of Reality*, 1-200.

Devine, P. G., Forscher, P. S., Austin, A. J., & Cox, W. T. L. (2012). Long-term reduction in implicit race bias: A prejudice habit-breaking intervention. *Journal of Experimental Social Psychology*, 48(6), 1267–1278. doi:10.1016/j.jesp.2012.06.003 PMID:23524616

deVries, J. R. (2020). Those Who Came from Curiosity Remained from Interest. *Minnesota History*, 67(3), 146–152.

Dewey, J. (1933). *How We Think A Restatement of the Relation of Reflective Thinking to the Educative Process*. Heath & Co Publishers.

DezsoC. L.RossD. G. (2011). Does female representation in top management improve firm performance? A panel data investigation. Robert H. Smith School Research Paper No. RHS 06-104. Retrieved from: https://ssrn.com/abstract=1088182

DiAngelo, R. (2011). White fragility. *The International Journal of Critical Pedagogy*, *3*(3), 54–70.

Dilnot, C. (2018). The relationship between A-level subject choice and league table score of university attended: The 'facilitating', the 'less suitable', and the counter-intuitive. *Oxford Review of Education*, *44*(1), 118–137. doi:10.1080/03054985.2018.1409976

Donga, o. Q., & Wu, W. (2015). Business value of social media technologies: Evidence from online user innovation communities. *24*(2), 113-227. doi:10.1016/j.jsis.2015.04.003

Doucet, A. (2006). Estrogen-filled worlds: Fathers as primary caregivers and embodiment. *The Sociological Review*, *54*(4), 696–716. doi:10.1111/j.1467-954X.2006.00667.x

Dreher, G. F., & Ash, R. A. (1990). A comparative study of mentoring among men and women in managerial, professional, and technical positions. *The Journal of Applied Psychology*, *75*(5), 539–546. doi:10.1037/0021-9010.75.5.539

Drozdowski, M. J. (2022, February). The plight of adjunct faculty on America's campuses. *Best Colleges*. bestcolleges.com

Eagly, A. H., Karau, S. J., & Makhijani, M. G. (1995). Gender and the effectiveness of leaders: A meta-analysis. *Psychological Bulletin*, *117*(1), 125–145. doi:10.1037/0033-2909.117.1.125 PMID:7870858

Eisner, E. W. (2017). *The enlightened eye: Qualitative inquiry and the enhancement of educational practice*. Teachers College Press.

El-Besomey, D. A. M. (2020). The Contemporary Vision of Universal Strategic Planning for Facing (COVID-19) Crisis in the Field of Higher Education Via Virtual Learning-Training. *European Journal of Education*, *3*(2), 151–164. doi:10.26417/869dvb85y

Ellsworth, D., Harding, E., Law, J., & Pinder, D. (2022). *Racial and ethnic equity in US higher education*. McKinsey and Company.

Ely, R. J., Stone, P., & Ammerman, C. (2014). Rethink what you know about high-achieving women. *Harvard Business Review*, *92*, 101–109.

Emerson, J. (2017). Don't give up on unconscious bias training – Make it better. *Harvard Business Review*. https://publicsector.sa.gov.au/modern-manager-series-making-better-decisions-unconscious-bias-at-work/

Emon, M. H., & Nipa, M. N. (2024). Exploring the gender dimension in entrepreneurship Development: A Systematic Literature Review in the context of Bangladesh. *Westcliff International Journal of Applied Research*, *8*(1), 34–49. doi:10.47670/wuwijar202481mhemnn

Compilation of References

Engerman, K., McKayle, C., Blackmon Tucker, A., & Askew, K. (2022). Elevating the voice of mid-career academic women leaders in broadening participation in STEM. In H. Schnackenberg (Ed.), *Women in Higher Education and the Journey to Mid-Career: Challenges and Opportunities*. IGI Global., doi:10.4018/978-1-6684-4451-1.ch005

Engerman, K., McKayle, C., & Tucker Blackmon, A. (2021). Presidents' role in broadening participation in STEM. In M. T. Miller & G. D. Gearhart (Eds.), *Handbook of research on the changing role of college and university leadership*. IGI Global., doi:10.4018/978-1-7998-6560-5.ch012

Equal Employment Opportunity Commission. (1981). Affirmative action appropriate under title vii of the civil rights act of 1964, as amended. Code of Federal Regulations, vol. 29, sec. 1608. Retrieved from CM-607 Affirmative Action | U.S. Equal Employment Opportunity Commission (eeoc.gov).

Esters, L. L., & Strayhorn, T. L. (2013). Demystifying the contributions of public land-grant historically Black colleges and universities: Voices of HBCU presidents. *Negro Educational Review*, *64*(1-4), 119–134.

Estevão, J., Lopes, J. D., & Penela, D. (2022). The importance of the business environment for the informal economy: Evidence from the Doing Business ranking. *Technological Forecasting and Social Change*, *174*, 121288. doi:10.1016/j.techfore.2021.121288

Evans, A., & Chun, E. B. (2007). Are the Walls Really Down? Behavioral and Organizational Barriers to Faculty and Staff Diversity. *ASHE Higher Education Report*, *33*, 1–139.

Fadia, B. (2014). *Gender politics in global governance*. Routledge.

Falola, T. (2022). *Decolonizing African Knowledge: Autoethnography and African Epistemologies*. Cambridge University Press. doi:10.1017/9781009049634

Farmer, P. (1999). *Pathologies of Power: Health, Human Rights, and the New War on the Poor*. University of California Press.

Ferrant, G. (2010). *A New Way to Measure Gender Inequalities in Developing Countries: The Gender Inequalities Index. CES working Report*. The University of Paris, the Sorbonne.

Fitzgerald, T. (2008). The continued politics of mistrust: Performance management and the erosion of professional work. *Journal of Educational Administration and History*, *40*(2), 113–128. doi:10.1080/00220620802210871

Fitzgerald, T. (2014). *Women leaders in higher education: Shattering the myths*. Routledge.

Fitzgerald, T. (2020). Mapping the terrain of leadership: Gender and leadership in higher education. *Irish Educational Studies*, *39*(2), 1–12. doi:10.1080/03323315.2020.1729222

Flaherty, C. (2020, April). Barely getting by: New report on adjuncts says many make less than $3500 per course and live in poverty. Inside Higher Ed. insidehighered.com

Foley, M., & Williamson, S. (2018). Managerial perspectives on implicit bias, affirmative action and merit. *Public Administration Review*, *79*(1), 35–45. doi:10.1111/puar.12955

Fontein, J. (2006). *The Silence of Great Zimbabwe*. Weaver Press.

Fox, H. M. (2017). A way of knowing in search of our true identity. *Self and Society*, *45*(1), 72–75. doi:10.1080/03060497.2017.1290453

Francis, L., & Stulz, V. (2020). Barriers and facilitators for women academics seeking promotion. *Australian Universities Review*, *62*(2), 47–60.

Frantell, K. A., Miles, J. R., & Ruwe, A. M. (2019). Intergroup dialogue: A review of recent empirical research and its implications for research and practice. *Small Group Research*, *50*(5), 654–695. doi:10.1177/1046496419835923

Fry, R. (2012). *Latinos in higher education: Many enroll, too few graduate*. Pew Hispanic Center.

GabrielA. G.SuyuJ. B.FrondaJ. G.RamosV. (2021). The impact of microfinance to borrowers, business, personal and financial status and the mediating role of service satisfaction: evidence from the Philippines. doi:10.21203/rs.3.rs-182720/v1

Galinsky, E., Saka, K., Eby, S., Bond, J. T., & Wigton, T. (2010). Employer-provided workplace flexibility. In K. Christensen & B. Schneider (Eds.), Workplace Flexibility: Realigning 20th-century Jobs for a 21st-century Workforce. Ithaca, NY: Cornell University Press.

Galtung, J. (1969). Violence, peace, and peace research. *Journal of Peace Research*, *6*(3), 167–191. doi:10.1177/002234336900600301

Gandara, P., & Contreras, F. (2009). *The Latino education crisis*. Harvard University Press. doi:10.4159/9780674056367

Gapminder. (2024). www.gapminder.org/data/

García-Holgado, A., & García-Peñalvo, F. J. (2022). A model for bridging the gender gap in STEM in higher education institutions. In *Women in STEM in Higher Education: Good Practices of Attraction, Access and Retainment in Higher Education* (pp. 1–19). Springer Nature Singapore. doi:10.1007/978-981-19-1552-9_1

Gardner, H. (1995). *Leading Minds*. Harper Collins.

Garrison-Wade, D. F., & Lewis, C. W. (2004). Affirmative action: History and analysis. *Journal of College Admission*, *184*, 23–26.

Garza, H. (1993). *Second Class Academics: Chicana/Latino Faculty in US Universities*. Jossey-Bass.

Gasman, M. (2023). Women are on the rise as leaders of top research universities. Forbes. Retrieved from https://www.forbes.com/sites/marybethgasman/2023/06/05/women-are-on-the-rise-as-leaders-of-top-research-universities/?sh=3c6e93a49c80

Compilation of References

Gatwiri, K. D. (2021). *Influence of Entrepreneurial Networks on Financial Performance of Medium-Sized Enterprises in Kenya*. Retrieved from http://localhost/xmlui/handle/123456789/5552

Gaucher, D., Friesen, J., & Kay, A. C. (2011). Evidence that gendered wording in job advertisements exists and sustains gender inequality. *Journal of Personality and Social Psychology, 101*(1), 109–128. doi:10.1037/a0022530 PMID:21381851

Gause, S. A. (2021). White privilege, Black resilience: Women of color leading the academy. *Leadership, 17*(1), 74–80. doi:10.1177/1742715020977370

Gayles, J. G. (2022). Does Anyone See Us? Disposability of Black Women Faculty in the Academy. *Diverse*. https://www.diverseeducation.com/opinion/article/15295726/doesanyone-see-us-disposability-of-black-women-faculty-in-the-academy

Geisler, G. (1995). Troubled sisterhood: women and politics in Southern Africa: case studies from Zambia, Zimbabwe and Botswana. *African Affairs, 94*(377), 545–578. doi:10.1093/oxfordjournals.afraf.a098873

Geyton, T., Johnson, N., & Ross, K. (2022). 'I'm good': Examining the internalization of the strong Black woman archetype. *Journal of Human Behavior in the Social Environment, 32*(1), 1–16. doi:10.1080/10911359.2020.1844838

Gisselquist, R. M., Schotte, S., & Kim, M. J. (2023). *Affirmative action around the world: insights from a new dataset* (No. 2023/59). WIDER Working Paper.

Glazebrook, T., Noll, S., & Opoku, E. (2020). Gender matters: Climate change, gender bias, and women's farming in the global South and North. *Agriculture, 10*(7), 267. doi:10.3390/agriculture10070267

Global Gender Gap Report. (2020). World Economic Forum. https://www3.weforum.org/docs/WEF_GGGR_2020.pdf

Göransson, K. E., Ehnfors, M., Fonteyn, M. E., & Ehrenberg, A. (2008). Thinking strategies used by Registered Nurses during emergency department triage. *Journal of Advanced Nursing, 61*(2), 163–172. doi:10.1111/j.1365-2648.2007.04473.x PMID:18186908

Gorbatai, A., & Nelson, L. (2015). The narrative advantage: Gender and the language of crowdfunding. *Haas School of Business UC Berkeley. Research Papers*, 1-32.

Gorman, E. (2005). Gender stereotypes, same-gender preferences, and organizational variation in hiring women. *American Sociological Review, 70*(4), 702–728. doi:10.1177/000312240507000408

Goulden, M., Mason, M. A., & Frasch, K. (2011). Keeping women in the science pipeline. *The Annals of the American Academy of Political and Social Science, 638*(1), 141–162. Advance online publication. doi:10.1177/0002716211416925

Gracia, J. (2008). *Latinos in America: Philosophy and social identity*. Blackwell. doi:10.1002/9780470696484

Grant, A. M., & Gino, F. (2010). A little thanks goes a long way: Explaining why gratitude expressions motivate prosocial behavior. *Journal of Personality and Social Psychology*, *98*(6), 946–955. doi:10.1037/a0017935 PMID:20515249

Grene, M., & Grene, M. G. (1974). *The knower and the known* (Vol. 130). Univ of California Press.

Griffin, K. A. (2019). Institutional barriers, strategies, and benefits to increasing the representation of women and men of color in the professoriate: Looking beyond the pipeline. Higher Education: Handbook of Theory and Research: Volume 35, 1-73.

Griffin, K. A., & Reddick, R. J. (2015). Surveillance and Sacrifice. *American Educational Research Journal*, *48*(5), 1032–1057. doi:10.3102/0002831211405025

Griffin, R. A. (2016). Black female faculty, resilient grit, and determined grace or "Just because everything is different doesn't mean anything has changed". *The Journal of Negro Education*, *85*(3), 365–379.

Grimson, J., & Grimson, W. (2019). Eliminating gender inequality in engineering, industry, and academia. In *The Engineering-Business Nexus* (pp. 315–339). Springer. doi:10.1007/978-3-319-99636-3_15

Gudhlanga, E. (2013). Shutting them out: Opportunities and challenges of women's participation in Zimbabwean politics-a historical perspective. *Journal of Third World Studies*, *30*(1), 151–170.

Gururaj, S., Somers, P., Fry, J., Watson, D., Cicero, F., Morosini, M., & Zamora, J. (2021). Affirmative action policy: Inclusion, exclusion, and the global public good. *Policy Futures in Education*, *19*(1), 63–83. doi:10.1177/1478210320940139

Gutierrez, M., Castañeda, C., & Katsinas, S. G. (2012). Latino Leadership in Community Colleges: Issues and Challenges. *Community College Journal of Research and Practice*, *26*(4), 297–314. doi:10.1080/106689202753546457

Gvozdanovic, J., & Maes, K. (2018). Implicit bias in academia: A challenge to meritocratic principle and to women's careers—And what to do about it. League of European Research Universities (LERU). Leuven.

Gvozdanovic, J., & Bailey, J. (2020). Unconscious bias in academia: A threat to meritocracy and what to do about it. In E. Drew & S. Canavan (Eds.), *The gender-sensitive university* (pp. 110–123). Routledge. doi:10.4324/9781003001348-9

Haan, H. H. (2014). Where is the gap between internationalisation strategic planning and its implementation? A study of 16 Dutch universities' internationalisation plans. *Tertiary Education and Management*, *20*(2), 135–150. doi:10.1080/13583883.2014.896407

Habaradas, R. B. (2022). *Social Entrepreneurship: Conceptual Definition, Bried literature Review and some Examples from the Philippines*. Asian Development Bank. Retrieved December 23, 2022, from https://www.adb.org › files › institutional-document

Hall, P. D. (2016). White fragility and affirmative action. *The Journal of Race & Policy*, *12*(2), 7.

Hamandishe, A. (2018). Rethinking women's political participation in Zimbabwe's elections. *Democracy (New York, N.Y.)*, *27*(4).

Hamandishe, T. (2018). Equitable participation in democratic governance: The role of women. *Journal of Democracy and Human Rights*, *15*(2), 78–89.

Hamilton, R. (2013). After Quarter-Century on the Job, UTEP President is Still Making Waves. *The Texas Tribune*, 11th March.

Hardy, A., McDonald, J., Guijt, R., Leane, E., Martin, A., James, A., Jones, M., Corban, M., & Green, B. (2016, June). Academic parenting: Work–family conflict and strategies across child age, disciplines and career level. *Studies in Higher Education*, *43*(4), 625–643. doi:10.1080/03075079.2016.1185777

Harini, S., Yuningsih, E., & Latipah, I. (2024). The influence of competence, business motivation, and entrepreneurial spirit on business success in Ciawi District, Bogor Regency (Case Study of Snack Food MSMEs). *INTERNATIONAL JOURNAL OF SOCIAL SCIENCE AND EDUCATION RESEARCH STUDIES*, *04*(01). Advance online publication. doi:10.55677/ijssers/V04I1Y2024-07

Harms Smith, L. (2019). *Epistemic decoloniality as a pedagogical movement: a turn to anticolonial theorists such as Fanon, Biko and Freire. Taylor & Francis*. Routledge.

Harris, A. (2019, April). The death of an adjunct. *Atlantic (Boston, Mass.)*.

Hart, J. (2008). Mobilization among women academics: The interplay between feminism and professionalization. *National Women's Studies Association (NWSA). Journal*, *20*(1), 184–208.

Harvey, W. B. (2013). *Minorities in Higher Education: Annual Status Report*. American Council on Education.

Hassim, S. (2019). Women's representation in South Africa's national and provincial legislatures: Lessons from the African National Congress' voluntary party quotas. *Women's Studies International Forum*, *73*, 130–137.

Hatem, M. (1995). Political Liberalization, Gender and the State. Political Liberalization and Democratization in the Arab World, 187–205.

Hayes, C., & Graham, Y. N. (2020). Prophylaxis in Action:# MeToo for Women of Medical and Surgical Disciplines. In Gender Equity in the Medical Profession (pp. 270-279). IGI Global.

Hayes, C., Fulton, J., Livingstone, A., Todd, C., Capper, S., & Smith, P. (2020). *Beyond Disciplinarity: Historical Evolutions of Research Epistemology*. Routledge. doi:10.4324/9781315108377

Henderson, M., Sullivan, A., Anders, J., & Moulton, V. (2018). Social class, gender and ethnic differences in subjects taken at age 14. *Curriculum Journal*, *29*(3), 298–318. doi:10.1080/09585176.2017.1406810

Hendrix, K. G. (2021). Disrupting institutional erasure: Organizational exit, remembrance, value, and the need to matter. *Gender, Work and Organization*, *28*(4), 1323–1336. https://doi-org.proxyhu.wrlc.org/10.1111/gwao.12609. doi:10.1111/gwao.12609

Henley, J., & Roy, E. A. (2020). Are female leaders more successful at managing the coronavirus crisis. *Guardian.* https://www.theguardian.com/world/2020/apr/25/why-do-female-leadersseem-to-be-more-successful-at-managing-the-coronavirus-crisis

Henry, F., Dua, E., Kobayashi, A., James, C., Li, P., Ramos, H., & Smith, M. S. (2016). Race, rationalization and indigeneity in Canadian universities. *Race, Ethnicity and Education*, *20*(3), 300–314. doi:10.1080/13613324.2016.1260226

Hester, J. P. (2020). The Subjective Import of Moral Knowledge. *Humanities Bulletin*, *3*(2), 140–156.

Heymann, J., Levy, J. K., Bose, B., Ríos-Salas, V., Mekonen, Y., Swaminathan, H., ... Darmstadt, G. L. (2019). Improving health with programmatic, legal, and policy approaches to reduce gender inequality and change restrictive gender norms. *Lancet*, *393*(10190), 2522–2534. doi:10.1016/S0140-6736(19)30656-7 PMID:31155271

Higginbotham, A., Bellisari, A., Poston, M., Treichler, P., West, M., & Levy, A. (2011). Recommendations on partner accommodation and dual-career appointments (September 2010). *Academic Bulletin of the American Association of University Professors*, *97*(5), 81–87.

Hill, C., Miller, K., Benson, K., & Handley, G. (2016). *Barriers and bias: The status of women in leadership*. American Association of University Women. https://www.aauw.org/resources/research/barrier-bias/

Hill, C., & McGinn, K. (2007). Global business case for corporate gender diversity. *Harvard Business Review*, *85*(2), 129–137. PMID:17345686

Hills, D. D. W. (2019). "Admirable or Ridiculous?": The Burdens of Black Women Scholars and Dialogue in the Work of Solidarity. *Journal of Feminist Studies in Religion*, *35*(2), 5–21.

Ho, C. (2007). Understanding Structural Violence: A Social Structural Analysis. *Peace Review*, *19*(3), 331–337.

Hofer, B. K., & Pintrich, P. R. (2012). *Personal epistemology: The psychology of beliefs about knowledge and knowing*. Routledge. doi:10.4324/9780203424964

Hoff, T., & Lee, D. R. (2021). The gender pay gap in medicine: A systematic review. *Health Care Management Review*, *46*(3), E37–E49. doi:10.1097/HMR.0000000000000290 PMID:33534271

Ho, K. (2007). Structural violence as a human rights violation. *Essex Human Rights Review*, *4*(2), 1–17.

Horn, J. (2020). Decolonising emotional well-being and mental health in development: African feminist innovations. *Gender and Development*, *28*(1), 85–98. doi:10.1080/13552074.2020.1717177

Compilation of References

Hubbard, S., & Stage, F. (2009). Attitudes, perceptions, and preferences of faculty at Hispanic serving institutions. *The Journal of Higher Education, 80*(3), 270–289. doi:10.1080/00221546.2009.11779013

Hudson, J. B. (1999). Affirmative action and American racism in historical perspective. *The Journal of Negro History, 84*(3), 260–274. doi:10.2307/2649005

Hughes, K. D. 2017. "GEM Canada 2015/16 Report on Women's Entrepreneurship". Available online at: www.gemcanada.org

Hungwe, B. 2000. Women's League threatens to boycott congress, *Zimbabwe Independent*, 19 November 2000, <http://www.samara.co.zw/zimin/index>

Hunt, C. M., Oosting, K. W., Stevens, R., Loudon, D., & Migliore, R. H. (1997). *Strategic Planning for Higher Education*. Haworth Press.

Hunt, M. O., & Smith, R. A. (2022). White Americans' Opposition to Affirmative Action, Revisited: New Racism, Principled Objections, or Both? *Social Currents, 9*(2), 107–117. doi:10.1177/23294965211024679

Hurlbut, C. D. (2021). *Crit: A Mixed Methods Examination of Epistemic Cognition During Source Evaluations*. McGill University.

Hurtado, S. (2001). *Linking Diversity and Educational Purpose: How Diversity Affects the Classroom Environment and Student Development*. Harvard Educational Publishing Group.

Ibarra, R. (2003). Latino Faculty and the Tenure Process in Cultural Content. *Stylus (Rio de Janeiro)*.

Information and Research Center – King Hussein Foundation (IRCKHF). (2019). *Gender Discrimination in Jordan*. Retrieved August 14, 2020, from http://irckhf.org/en/project/gender-discrimination/jordan

Inglehart, R., & Norris, P. (2003). *Rising tide: Gender equality and cultural change around the world*. Cambridge University Press. doi:10.1017/CBO9780511550362

Inkpin, A. (2021). Merleau-Ponty's 'sensible ideas' and embodied-embedded practice. *Phenomenology and the Cognitive Sciences*, 1–24.

Inman, A. G. (2020). Culture and Positionality: Academy and Mentorship. *Women & Therapy, 43*(1-2), 112–124. doi:10.1080/02703149.2019.1684678

International Labour Office (ILO). (2017). *Jordan: Young women's employment and empowerment in the rural economy*. Retrieved August 14, 2020, from https://www.ilo.org/wcmsp5/groups/public/---ed_emp/documents/publication/wcms_622766.pdf

International Labour Organization. (n.d.). *ILO Modelled Estimates and Projections database*. ILOSTAT. Accessed September 05, 2023. Ilostat.ilo.org/data.

International Ombuds Association (2023). Ombursassociation.org/

IPEDS. (2013). *Full-time instructional staff, by faculty and tenure status, academic rank, race/ethnicity, and gender (degree-granting institutions): Fall staff 2013 Survey*. Washington, D.C.: National Center for Education Statistics, IPEDS (The Integrated Postsecondary Education Data System).

Jackson, I., Watson, D. L., White, C. D., & Gallo, M. (2022). Research as (re) vision: Laying claim to oral history as a just-us research methodology. *International Journal of Research & Method in Education*, *45*(4), 330–342. doi:10.1080/1743727X.2022.2076827

Jackson, S. E., Ruderman, M., & Ehrhart, M. (2018). Diversity policies and practices. In *The Oxford Handbook of Organizational Psychology* (pp. 295–314). Oxford University Press.

Jaeger, E., McKayle, C., Engerman, K., Boncana, M., Joseph, C., & Askew, K. (2021). Institutional and Leadership Predictors of HBCU Success in Broadening Participation in STEM. *The Journal of Negro Education*, *90*(3), 371–382.

Jahn, R. G., & Dunne, B. J. (2007). Science of the subjective. *Explore (New York, N.Y.)*, *3*(3), 295–305. doi:10.1016/j.explore.2007.03.014 PMID:17560358

Jalal, A., & Murray, A. (2019). Strategic planning for higher education: A novel model for strategic planning process for higher education. *Journal of Higher Education Service Science and Management*, *2*(2), 1–10.

Jamali, A., Bhutto, A., Khaskhely, M., & Sethar, W. (2022). Impact of leadership styles on faculty performance: Moderating role of organizational culture in higher education. *Management Science Letters*, *12*(1), 1–20. doi:10.5267/j.msl.2021.8.005

Jameson, J. (Ed.). (2019). *International perspectives on leadership in higher education: Critical thinking for global challenges*. Routledge. doi:10.4324/9781315122410

Jandrić, P., Hayes, D., Truelove, I., Levinson, P., Mayo, P., Ryberg, T., ... & Jackson, L. (2020). Teaching in the Age of Covid-19. *Postdigital Science and Education*, 1-162.

Jaramillo, A., Ruby, A., Henard, F., & Zaafrane, H. (2011). *Internationalization of Higher Education in MENA: Policy Issues Associated with Skills Formation and Mobility*. World Bank.

Jenkins, L. D., & Moses, M. S. (2014). *Affirmative Action Matters*. Routledge. doi:10.4324/9781315795744

Jensen, M. B., Johnson, B., Lorenz, E., Lundvall, B. Å., & Lundvall, B. A. (2007). Forms of knowledge and modes of innovation. *The learning economy and the economics of hope, 155*.

Jephias, M. (2013). The feminist discourse and the development of a civic virtue in Zimbabwe: Case of Women of Zimbabwe Arise (WOZA). *Journal of African Studies and Development*, *5*(8), 261–270.

Jiménez, A. C., Galilei, G., Strathern, M., & Serres, M. (2017). How knowledge grows: an anthropological anamorphosis. *Cosmopolitics*, 227.

Jimoh, A. K. (2017). An African theory of knowledge. *Themes, issues and problems in African philosophy*, 121-136.

Jones, T. B., ... (2013). "*Employing a Black Feminist Approach to Doctoral Advising: Preparing Black Women for the Professoriate.*" *The Journal of Negro Education*, vol. 82, no. 3, pp. 326-38. *JSTOR*, . Accessed 3 Feb. 2024.

Jong, A. (2023). Social configurations in the moment of post-foundationalism. *Frontiers in Sociology*, 7, 1078011. doi:10.3389/fsoc.2022.1078011 PMID:36779169

Juliana, S. M., & Simatupang, P. (2023). The Empowering Church Members in the Implementation of the Creative Economy: An Interpretative Approach to the Concept of Missionary Congregation Development. *Asian Journal of Management. Entrepreneurship and Social Science*, 3(04), 1395–1410.

Juraqulova, Z. H., McCluskey, J. J., & Mittelhammer, R. C. (2019). Work-life policies and female faculty representation in US doctoral-granting economics departments. *Industrial Relations Journal*, 50(2), 168–196. Advance online publication. doi:10.1111/irj.12246

Kabeer, N. (2005). Gender equality and women's empowerment: A critical analysis of the third Millennium Development Goal 1. *Gender and Development*, 13(1), 13–24. doi:10.1080/13552070512331332273

Kabeer, N. (2020). Women's empowerment and economic development: A feminist critique of storytelling practices in "randomista" economics. *Feminist Economics*, 26(2), 1–26. doi:10.1080/13545701.2020.1743338

Kachchaf, R., Ko, L., Hodari, A., & Ong, M. (2015). Career-life balance for women of color: Experiences in science and engineering academia. *Journal of Diversity in Higher Education*, 8(3), 175–191. doi:10.1037/a0039068

KamauC. G. (2023). *Availability of Finance, Finance Costs, and Business Success in Kenya: Focus on the Small and Micro Enterprises*. SSRN.

Kane, H., Ragsdell, G., & Oppenheim, C. (2006). Knowledge management methodologies. *Electronic Journal of Knowledge Management*, 4(2), 141–152.

Kaplan, M., Sanchez, M., & Hoffman, J. (2017). Intergenerational Strategies for Establishing Sustainable Work Environments. In *Intergenerational Pathways to a Sustainable Society* (pp. 141–162). Springer International Publishing. doi:10.1007/978-3-319-47019-1_7

Karlan, D., & J Zinman, J. (2011). Microcredit in Theory and Practice: Using Randomized Credit Scoring for Impact Evaluation. doi:10.1126/science.1200138

Kena, G., Hussan, W., McFarland, J., De Brey, C., & Musu-Gillette, L. (2016). [National Center for Education Statistics.]. *The Condition of Education*, 2016.

Kezar, A. (2014). Higher education and social networks: A review of research. *The Journal of Higher Education*, 85(1), 91–124. doi:10.1080/00221546.2014.11777320

Kezar, A. (2018). *How colleges change: Understanding, leading, and enacting change*. Routledge. doi:10.4324/9781315121178

Khadhraoui, M., Plaisent, M., Lakhal, L., & Prosper, B. (2019). The impact of entrepreneurial orientation on spin-offs' performance: A cross-cultural study. *SAGE Open, 9*(3), 2158244019865817. doi:10.1177/2158244019865817

Khan, R. U., Salamzadeh, Y., Shah, S. Z. A., & Hussain, M. (2021). Factors affecting women entrepreneurs' success: A study of small and medium-sized enterprises in the emerging market of Pakistan. *Journal of Innovation and Entrepreneurship, 10*(1), 1–21. doi:10.1186/s13731-021-00145-9 PMID:33686362

Kim, C. Y., Seo, E. H., Booranabanyat, C., & Kim, K. (2021). Effects of emerging-economy firms' knowledge acquisition from an advanced international joint venture partner on their financial performance based on the open innovation perspective. *Journal of Open Innovation, 7*(1), 67. doi:10.3390/joitmc7010067

Kincade, L. L. (2023). At the Crossroads: A Social-Ecological Model of Support for Women of Color in Higher Education Leadership. In Stabilizing and Empowering Women in Higher Education: Realigning, Recentering, and Rebuilding (pp. 87-105). IGI Global. Doi:10.4018/978-1-6684-8597-2.ch006

King, P. M., & Kitchener, K. S. (2004). Reflective judgment: Theory and research on the development of epistemic assumptions through adulthood. *Educational Psychologist, 39*(1), 5–18. doi:10.1207/s15326985ep3901_2

Kinsella, E. A. (2010). Professional knowledge and the epistemology of reflective practice. *Nursing Philosophy, 11*(1), 3–14. doi:10.1111/j.1466-769X.2009.00428.x PMID:20017878

Kitchner, K. S. (1983). Cognition, metacognition, and epistemic cognition. *Human Development, 26*(4), 222–232. doi:10.1159/000272885

Klinke, H. (Ed.). (2014). *Art theory as visual epistemology*. Cambridge Scholars Publishing.

Kobakhidze, N. (2020). *Pandemic Changes Global Dynamics in Education*. Academic Press.

Koenig, A., Eagly, A., Mitchell, A., & Ristikari, T. (2011). *Are Leader Stereotypes Masculine? A meta-analysis of three research paradigms*. National Library of Medicine. National Center for Biotechnology Information.

Koshy, P. (2019). Integration into formal enterprise space: Challenges and opportunities for informal sector entrepreneurs. Retrieved from https://mpra.ub.uni-muenchen.de/95346/

Krogstad, J. M. (2016). *5 Facts about Latinos and education*. Pew Research Center.

Krogtad, J., Passel, J. S., & Noe Bustamante, L. (2022). *Key facts about U.S. Latinos for national Hispanic Heritage month*. Pew Research Center.

Compilation of References

Kuradusenge-McLeod, C. (2021). Multiple Identities and Scholarship: Black Scholars' Struggles for Acceptance and Recognition in the United States of America. *International Studies Review*, *23*(2), 346–369. https://doi-org.proxyhu.wrlc.org/10.1093/isr/viaa098. doi:10.1093/isr/viaa098

Kuschel, K., Kerstin, E., Díaz-García, C., and Alsos, G. A. 2020. "Stemming the gender gap in STEM entrepreneurship – insights into women's entrepreneurship in science, technology, engineering, and mathematics," *International Entrepreneurship and Management Journal* (16:1), pp. 1-15.

Kuschel, K., & Lepeley, M. T. (2016). Copreneurial women in start-ups: Growth-oriented or lifestyle? An aid for technology industry investors. *Academia (Caracas)*, *29*(2), 181–197. doi:10.1108/ARLA-08-2015-0231

LacombaC. (2022). Hispanic Map of the United States. *Observatorio Cervantes*, 1-126. https://doi.org/ doi:10.15457/OR084-02/2023EN

Laden, B. V. (2014). Hispanic Serving Institutions: What are they? Where are they? *Community College Journal of Research and Practice*, *28*(3), 181–198. doi:10.1080/10668920490256381

Lahroodi, R. (2018). Virtue epistemology and collective epistemology. In *The Routledge handbook of virtue epistemology* (pp. 407–419). Routledge. doi:10.4324/9781315712550-34

Lange, A. C., & Lee, J. A. (2024). Centering our Humanity: Responding to Anti-DEI Efforts Across Higher Education. *Journal of College Student Development*, *65*(1), 113–116. doi:10.1353/csd.2024.a919356

Lannelli, C., & Duta, A. (2018). Inequalities in school leavers' labour market outcomes: Do school subject choices matter? *Oxford Review of Education*, *44*(1), 56–74. doi:10.1080/03054985.2018.1409970

Latour, B. (1986). Visualization and cognition. *Knowledge in Society*, *6*(6), 1–40.

Latour, B. (1999). *Pandora's hope: Essays on the reality of science studies*. Harvard university press.

Latu, I. M., Mast, M. S., Bombari, D., Lammers, J., & Hoyt, C. L. (2019). Empowering mimicry: Female leader role models empower women in leadership tasks through body posture mimicry. *Sex Roles*, *80*(1/2), 11–24. doi:10.1007/s11199-018-0911-y PMID:30651662

Layaoen, C. W. G., & Takahashi, K. (2021b). Can microfinance lending crowd out informal lenders? Evidence from the Philippines. *Journal of International Development*, *34*(2), 379–414. doi:10.1002/jid.3604

Lean, In. (2019). Women in the Workplace Study. Retrieved from https://leanin.org/women-in-the-workplace

Ledford, H. (2017). US postdocs face steep challenges when starting families. *Nature*. Advance online publication. doi:10.1038/nature.2017.22200

Lee, R. T., Perez, A. D., Boykin, C. M., & Mendoza-Denton, R. (2019). On the prevalence of racial discrimination in the United States. *PLoS One*, *14*(1), e0210698. doi:10.1371/journal.pone.0210698 PMID:30629706

Lemos, N. (2020). *An introduction to the theory of knowledge*. Cambridge University Press. doi:10.1017/9781108595162

Lester, J. (2008). Performing gender in the workplace: Gender socialization, power, and identity among women faculty members. *Community College Review*, *35*(4), 227–305. doi:10.1177/0091552108314756

Liben, L. S., & Coyle, E. F. (2014). Developmental interventions to address the STEM gender gap: Exploring intended and unintended consequences. In L. S. Liben & R. S. Bigler (Eds.), Advances in child development and behavior, Vol. 47. The role of gender in educational contexts and outcomes (pp. 77–115). Elsevier Academic Press. doi:10.1016/bs.acdb.2014.06.001

Liñán, F., Jaén, I., & Rodríguez, M. J. (2024). Gender and sex in starting up: A social stereotype approach. *Entrepreneurship and Regional Development*, *36*(3–4), 243–265. doi:10.1080/08985626.2023.2295266

Lipton, B. (2015). A New" ERA" of Women and Leadership: The Gendered Impact of Quality Assurance in Australian Higher Education. *Australian Universities Review*, *57*(2), 60–70.

Liu, J., Thomas, P. F., & Xuhui, W. (2018). The influence of culture in entrepreneurs' opportunity exploitation decision in Tanzania. *Journal of Entrepreneurship in Emerging Economies*, *11*(1), 22–43. doi:10.1108/JEEE-02-2017-0014

Looney, D., & Lusin, N. (2019). *Enrollments in languages other than English in United States institutions of higher education*. Modern Language Association.

Lopez, M. H. (2013). *Three-Fourths of Hispanics say their community needs leader*. Pew Research Center.

Lorde, A. (2007). *"The Transformation of Silence into Language and Action." Sister Outsider*. Crossing.

Love, B. H., Templeton, E., Ault, S., & Johnson, O. (2021). Bruised, not broken: Scholarly personal narratives of Black women in the academy. *International Journal of Qualitative Studies in Education : QSE*, 1–23.

Lundine, J., Bourgeault, I. L., Clark, J., Heidari, S., & Balabanova, D. (2018, May 5). The gendered system of academic publishing. *Lancet*, *391*(10132), 1754–1756. doi:10.1016/S0140-6736(18)30950-4 PMID:29739551

Maas, B., Grogan, K. E., Chirango, Y., Harris, N., Liévano-Latorre, L. F., McGuire, K. L., ... Primack, R. B. (2020). Academic leaders must support inclusive scientific communities during COVID-19. *Nature Ecology & Evolution*, *4*(8), 1–2. doi:10.1038/s41559-020-1233-3 PMID:32493950

Mactezuma, P., & Navarro, A. (2011). Internacionalización de la educación superior: Aprendizaje institucional en Baja California. *Revista de la Educación Superior*, *40*(59), 47–66.

Macy, R. D., Behar, L., Paulson, R., Delman, J., Schmid, L., & Smith, S. F. (2004). Community-based, acute posttraumatic stress management: A description and evaluation of a psychosocial-intervention continuum. *Harvard Review of Psychiatry*, *12*(4), 217–228. doi:10.1080/10673220490509589 PMID:15371064

Madera, J. M., Hebl, M. R., Dial, H., Martin, R., & Valian, V. (2018). Raising doubt in letters of recommendation for academia: Gender differences and their impact. *Journal of Business and Psychology*, 1–17. doi:10.1007/s10869-018-9541-1

Madera, J., Hebl, M., & Marn, R. (2009). Gender and letters of recommendation for academia: Agents and communal differences. *The Journal of Applied Psychology*, *94*(6), 1591–1599. doi:10.1037/a0016539 PMID:19916666

Magua, W., Zhu, X., Battacharya, A., Filut, A., Potvien, A., Leatherberry, R., ... Kaatz, A. (2017). Are female applicants disadvantaged in National Institutes of Health peer review? Combining algorithmic text mining and qualitative methods to detect evaluative differences in R01 reviewers' critiques. *Journal of Women's Health*, *26*(5), 560–570. doi:10.1089/jwh.2016.6021 PMID:28281870

Malterud, K., Siersma, V. D., & Guassora, A. D. (2016). Sample size in qualitative interview studies: Guided by information power. *Qualitative Health Research*, *26*(13), 1753–1760. doi:10.1177/1049732315617444 PMID:26613970

Mansur, M., & Djaelani, A. Q. (2023). Business Strategy Approach to Informal Small Businesses in Increasing Productivity and Competitiveness. doi:10.52970/grmapb.v3i1.206

Mapuva, J. (2013). Women in politics: Zimbabwean perspective. In *Conference Paper of the Women's Global Leadership in Africa: Expanding the African Women's Voice and Visibility in Global Leadership*, Victoria Falls, Zimbabwe.

Markauskaite, L., & Goodyear, P. (2017). Professional Epistemic Games. In *Epistemic Fluency and Professional Education* (pp. 395–434). Springer Netherlands. doi:10.1007/978-94-007-4369-4_14

Marshall, A., Ojiako, U., & Chipulu, M. (2018). A futility, perversity, and jeopardy critique of "risk appetite". *The International Journal of Organizational Analysis*, *27*(1), 51–73. Advance online publication. doi:10.1108/IJOA-06-2017-1175

Martínez Riera, J. R., Ferrer, L., Cassiani, S. H., & Laverde, M. C. (2015). Envejecimiento: Retos y oportunidades para la investigación. *Revista Iberoamericana de Saúde e Envelhecimiento*, *1*(1), 100–119. doi:10.24902/r.riase.2015.1(1).119

Mason, M. A., Wolfinger, N. H., & Goulden, M. (2013). Do babies matter? The effect of family formation on the lifelong careers of academic men and women. *Academe*, *99*(2), 10–15.

Mat, Z. C., Hakimin, M. N., & Zaino Anwar, A. A. (2020). It was discovered that risk-taking. doi:10.31838/jcr.07.06.217

Mathieu-Frasier, L. (2021). An outsider looking in: Advocating a sense of community for adjunct faculty. *Faculty Focus.* facultyfocus.com

Matiluko, O. (2020). Decolonising the master's house: How Black Feminist epistemologies can be and are used in decolonial strategy. *The Law Teacher, 54*(4), 547–561. doi:10.1080/03069400.2020.1827839

Matthews, T. A., Robbins, W., Preisig, M., von Känel, R., & Li, J. (2021). Associations of job strain and family strain with risk of major depressive episode: A prospective cohort study in US working men and women. *Journal of Psychosomatic Research, 147*, 110541. doi:10.1016/j.jpsychores.2021.110541 PMID:34130004

Maume, D. J. (2006). Gender differences in restricting work efforts because of family responsibilities. *Journal of Marriage and Family, 68*(4), 859–869. doi:10.1111/j.1741-3737.2006.00300.x

Mawejje, J., & Sebudde, R. K. (2018). Constraints or Complaints? Business Climate and Firm Performance Perceptions in Uganda. *The Journal of Development Studies.* Advance online publication. doi:10.1080/00220388.2018.1502878

McDermott, M., Gelb, D. J., Wilson, K., Pawloski, M., Burke, J. F., Shelgikar, A. V., & London, Z. N. (2018). Sex differences in academic rank and publication rate at top-ranked U.S. neurology programs. *JAMA Neurology, 75*(8), 956–961. doi:10.1001/jamaneurol.2018.0275 PMID:29610899

McEarcharn, M., Boswell, K., Chauhan, K., & Siereveld, S. O. (2019). Tenure clock policy transparency for biological clock (family friendly) events. *Administrative Issues Journal: Connecting Education, Practice, and Research, 9*(2), 28–41. doi:10.5929/9.2.4

McNair, T. B., Bensimon, E. M., & Malcom-Piqueux, L. (2020). *From equity talk to equity walk: Expanding practitioner knowledge for racial justice in higher education.* John Wiley & Sons. doi:10.1002/9781119428725

McNeil, L., & Sher, M. (1999). The dual-career-couple problem. *Physics Today, 52*(7), 32–37. doi:10.1063/1.882719

Medina, C., & Luna, G. (2000). Narratives from Latina Professors in Higher Education. *Anthropology & Education Quarterly, 31*(1), 47 66. https://www.jstor.org/stable/3196270

Meletiadou, E. (2022). The lived experiences of female educational leaders in higher education in the UK: Academic resilience and gender. In *Handbook of Research on Practices for Advancing Diversity and Inclusion in Higher Education* (pp. 1–19). IGI Global. doi:10.4018/978-1-7998-9628-9.ch001

Melidona D. Cassell A. Chessman H. Cecil B. G. (2023). The American College President: 2023 Edition. *Available at* SSRN 4689236.

Mellor, K. (2022). Developing a decolonial gaze: Articulating research/er positionality and relationship to colonial power. *Access: Critical explorations of equity in higher education, 10*(1), 26-41.

Compilation of References

Mey, K. (2022). More than just a matter of style: female leadership in higher education. European University Association. Retrieved from https://eua.eu/resources/expert-voices/285:more-than-just-a-matter-of-style-female-leadership-in-higher-education.html

Meyers, M. (2013). The war on academic women: Reflections on post-feminism in the neoliberal academy. *The Journal of Communication Inquiry*, *37*(4), 274–283. doi:10.1177/0196859913505619

Mezirow, J. (2009). Transformative learning theory. In J. Mezirow & E. W. Taylor (Eds.), *Transformative Learning in Practise: Insights from Community, 39 Workplace, and Higher Education* (pp. 18–32). Jossey Bass.

Milem, J. F., Chang, M. J., & Antonio, A. L. (2005). *Making diversity work on campus: A research-based perspective*. Association American Colleges and Universities.

Miller, D., Eagly, A., & Linn, M. (2015). Women's representation in science predicts national gender-science stereotypes: Evidence from 66 nations. *Journal of Educational Psychology*, *107*(3), 631–644. doi:10.1037/edu0000005

Milovanović, A., Kostić, M., Zorić, A., Đorđević, A., Pešić, M., Bugarski, J., Todorović, D., Sokolović, N., & Josifovski, A. (2020). Transferring COVID-19 Challenges into Learning Potentials: Online Workshops in Architectural Education. *Sustainability (Basel)*, *12*(17), 7024. doi:10.3390/su12177024

Miščević, N. (2017). Thought experiments in political philosophy. In *The Routledge companion to thought experiments* (pp. 153–170). Routledge. doi:10.4324/9781315175027-9

Modern Diplomacy. (n.d.). Retrieved from https://moderndiplomacy.eu/2023/05/04/the-covid-19-pandemicchanges-global-dynamics-in-education/

Moghadam, V. M. (2005). Women's Economic Participation in the Middle East: What Difference Had the Neoliberal Policy Turn Made? *Journal of Middle East Women's Studies*, *1*(1), 110–146. doi:10.2979/MEW.2005.1.1.110

Mohr, T.S. (2014, August). Why women don't apply for jobs unless they're 100% qualified. *Harvard Business Review*. hbr.org

Mojab, S. (2000). Theorizing the politics of 'veiling' in contemporary Western societies. *Feminist Review*, *64*(1), 20–58.

Mojab, S. (2022). *Women and Education in the Middle East and North Africa*. Oxford Research Encyclopedias. doi:10.1093/acrefore/9780190264093.013.1544

Montemayor, R., & Mendoza, H. (2004). *Right before our eyes: Latinos past, present and future*. Scholarly Publishing.

Moody, A. T., & Lewis, J. A. (2019). Gendered racial microaggressions and traumatic stress symptoms among Black women. *Psychology of Women Quarterly*, *43*(2), 201–214. doi:10.1177/0361684319828288

Mora, L. (2022). *Hispanic enrollment reaches new high at four-year colleges in the U.S. but affordability remains an obstacle*. Pew Research Center.

Morrison, Toni. (1977). *Song of Solomon. Vintage. Oxford Languages*. (2013). 7th ed.). Oxford English Dictionary.

Morson, J. (2016). A delicate balance: The role of the ombuds in resolving campus conflict. *Advice and News*. https://www.higheredjobs.com/

Moyo, Z. (2020). Moving toward indigenisation of knowledge: Understanding African women's experiences. In Curriculum Theory, Curriculum Theorising, and the Theoriser (pp. 92-105). Brill.

Moyo, S. (2017). Gender quotas, empowerment, and women's political participation in Zimbabwe. *Journal of African Elections*, *16*(1), 123–139.

Murrell, A. J., Olson, J. E., & Frieze, I. H. (1995). Sexual harassment and gender discrimination: A longitudinal study of women managers. *The Journal of Social Issues*, *51*(1), 139–149. doi:10.1111/j.1540-4560.1995.tb01313.x

Musendekwa, M. 2011. *Messianic expectations as prophetic responses to crises: a Zimbabwean perspective*. MTh Thesis, University of Stellenbosch, Stellenbosch.

Musendekwa, M. 2018. Messianic characterisation of Mugabe as rhetorical propaganda to legitimise his authority in crisis situations. *SHE* 44/3, 1-17. https://upjournals.co.za/index.php/SHE/ index.

Myerchin, A. D. (2014). Experiences of female faculty with maternity leave at four-year universities in an upper mid-west state. *Journal of the Communication. Speech & Theatre Association of North Dakota*, *26*, 1–13.

Myers, S. S. (2023). Building Bridges. In L. M. Pipe & J. T. Stephens (Eds.), *Ignite* (pp. 57–80). Vernon Press.

National Center for Educational Statistics. (May 2019). Characteristics of post-secondary faculty. https://nces.ed.gov/programs/coe/indicator_csc.asp

National Democratic Institute for International Affairs. (2010). *Democracy and the Challenge of Change: A Guide to Increasing Women's Political Participation*. Washington: National Democratic Institute National Democratic Institute for International Affairs. (2010). *The role of women in political parties*. https://www.ndi.org/sites/default/files/The_Role_of_Women_in_Political_Parties.pdf

National Women's Law Center. (2020). The Wage Gap: The Who, How, Why, and What to Do. Retrieved from https://nwlc.org/resources/the-wage-gap-the-who-how-why-and-what-to-do/

Nazier, H. (2019). *Women's Economic Empowerment: An Overview for the MENA Region. Strategic Sectors*. Economy and Territory.

Compilation of References

Nazier, H., & Ramadan, R. (2018). What empowers Egyptian women: Resources versus social constraints? *Review of Economics and Political Science*, *3*(3/4), 153–175. doi:10.1108/REPS-10-2018-015

Ndofirepi, A. P., & Gwaravanda, E. T. (2019). Epistemic (in) justice in African universities: A perspective of the politics of knowledge. *Educational Review*, *71*(5), 581–594. doi:10.1080/00131911.2018.1459477

Ndofirepi, A. P., & Gwaravanda, E. T. (2020). Inclusion and social justice: Creating space for African epistemologies in the African university. In *Inclusion as Social Justice* (pp. 90–110). Brill. doi:10.1163/9789004434486_008

Nelson, D. L., & Quick, J. C. (1985, April). Professional women: Are distress and disease inevitable? *Academy of Management Review*, *10*(2), 206–218. doi:10.2307/257963 PMID:10300087

Neumeyer, X., & Santos, S. C. (2020). A lot of different flowers make a bouquet: The effect of gender composition on technology-based entrepreneurial student teams. *The International Entrepreneurship and Management Journal*, *16*(1), 93–114. doi:10.1007/s11365-019-00603-7

Newman, C. B., Tran, M. C., & Chang, M. (2015). Improving the rate of success for underrepresented racial minorities in STEM fails. *New Directions for Institutional Research*, *148*, 5–15. doi:10.1002/ir.357

Nicolelis, M. (2020). *The true creator of everything: How the human brain shaped the universe as we know it*. Yale University Press.

Nielson, M. (2016). Limits to meritocracy? Gender in academic recruitment and promotion policies. *Science & Public Policy*, *43*(3), 386–399. doi:10.1093/scipol/scv052

Niemann, Y. F., & Maruyama, G. (2005). Inequities in higher education: Issues and promising practices in a world ambivalent about affirmative action. *The Journal of Social Issues*, *61*(3), 407–426. doi:10.1111/j.1540-4560.2005.00414.x

Nora, A., & Crisp, G. (2019). *Hispanics and Higher Education: An Overview of Research, Theory, and Practice*. Springer Science.

Nosek, B. A., & Smyth, F. L. (2007). A multitrait-multimethod validation of the Implicit Association Test: Implicit and explicit attitudes are related but distinct constructs. *Experimental Psychology*, *54*(1), 14–29. doi:10.1027/1618-3169.54.1.14 PMID:17341011

Novotney, A. (2023). Women leaders make work better. Here's the science behind how to promote them. American Psychological Association. Retrieved from https://www.apa.org/topics/women-girls/female-leaders-make-work-better

Nuñez, A. M., Ramalho, E. M., & Cuero, K. K. (2010). Pedagogy for equity: Teaching in a Hispanic-Serving Institution. *Innovative Higher Education*, *35*(3), 177–190. doi:10.1007/s10755-010-9139-7

Nyangarika, A. (2016). Social-economic constraints towards women business growth in Tanzania.

Nzegwu, N. (2019). African Art in Deep Time: De-race-ing Aesthetics and De-racializing Visual Art: Nzegwu African Art in Deep Time. *The Journal of Aesthetics and Art Criticism, 77*(4), 367–378. doi:10.1111/jaac.12674

O'Connor, P. (2011). Irish universities: Male dominated? Limits and possibilities for change? *Equality, Diversity and Inclusion, 31*(1), 83–96. doi:10.1108/02610151211199236

O'Connor, P. (2019). Gender imbalance in senior positions in higher education: What is the problem? What can be done? *Policy Reviews in Higher Education, 3*(1), 28–50. doi:10.1080/23322969.2018.1552084

O'Connor, P. (2020). Creating gendered change in Irish higher education: Is managerial leadership up to the task? *Irish Educational Studies, 39*(2), 139–155. doi:10.1080/03323315.2019.1697951

O'Connor, P. J., Jimmieson, N. L., Bergin, A. J., Wiewiora, A., & McColl, L. (2022). Leader tolerance of ambiguity: Implications for follower performance outcomes in high and low ambiguous work situations. *The Journal of Applied Behavioral Science, 58*(1), 65–96. doi:10.1177/00218863211053676

O'Leary, V. E. (1974). Some attitudinal barriers to occupational aspirations in women. *Psychological Bulletin, 81*(11), 809–826. doi:10.1037/h0037267

O'Meara, K. & Stromquist, N.P. (2015). Faculty peer networks: Role and relevance in advancing agency and gender equity. *Gender and Education, 27*(3)m 338-358. doi:10.1080/09540253.2015.1027668

O'Meara, K., Culpepper, D., Misra, J., & Jaeger, A. (2021). Equity-minded faculty work-loads: What we can and should do now. ACE. https://www.acenet.edu/Documents/Equity-Minded-Faculty-Workloads.pdf

Oates, M. (2023, March). How it works: Gender equity in higher education. *Academic Diversity Search.* academicdiversitysearch.com

Ofori, E., & Kashiwagi, K. (2022). Impact of Microfinance on the Social Performance of Local Households: Evidence from the Kassena Nankana East District of Ghana. doi:10.3390/su14106002

Okech, A. (2020). African feminist epistemic communities and decoloniality. *Critical African Studies, 12*(3), 313–329. doi:10.1080/21681392.2020.1810086

Okoli, G. N., Moore, T. A., Thomas, S. L., & Allen, T. T. (2020). Minority Women in Educational Leadership. *Handbook on Promoting Social Justice in Education*, 1711-1727.

Olugbenga, S., & Mashigo, P. (2017). *The impact of microfinance on microenterprises.* Investment Management and Financial Innovations. doi: (3).2017.08 doi:10.21511/imfi.14

Orjiakor, E. C. (2022). Business climate and firm exit in developing countries: Evidence from Nigeria. *Future Business Journal, 8*(1), 51. doi:10.1186/s43093-022-00160-6

Orozco, M., & Furszyer, J. (2022). *State of Latino entrepreneurship*. Standford Graduate School of Business.

Orr, C. J., Raphael, J. L., Klein, M., Corley, A. M., Tatem, A., Li, S. T. T., Pitt, M. B., Gustafson, S., & Lopez, M. A. (2023). Moving toward diversity, equity, and inclusion: Barriers, consequences, and solutions. *Academic Pediatrics*, *23*(8), 1524–1525. doi:10.1016/j.acap.2023.07.019 PMID:37543084

Ossome, L. (2020). African feminism. In *Routledge Handbook of Pan-Africanism* (pp. 159–170). Routledge. doi:10.4324/9780429020193-11

Owens, E. W., Shelton, A. J., Bloom, C. M., & Cavil, J. K. (2012). The significance of HBCUs to the production of STEM graduates: Answering the call. *Educational Foundations*, *26*, 33–47.

Padavic, I., Ely, R., & Reid, E. (2020). Explaining the Persistence of Gender Inequality: The Work-family Narrative as a Social Defense against the 24/7 Work Culture. *Administrative Science Quarterly*, *65*(1), 61–111. doi:10.1177/0001839219832310

Padilla, R., & Chavez, R. (1995). *The Leaning Ivory Tower: Latino Professors in American Universities*. State University of New York Press.

Pagaddut, J. G. (2021). The financial factors affecting the financial performance of Philippines msmes. *Universal Journal of Accounting and Finance*, *9*(6), 1524–1532. doi:10.13189/ujaf.2021.090629

Palmer, R. T., & Strayhorn, T. L. (2008). Mastering one's own Fate: Non-cognitive factors associated with the success of African American males at an HBCU. *NASAP Journal*, *11*, 126–143.

Park, C. L. (2017). Distinctions to promote an integrated perspective on meaning: Global meaning and meaning-making processes. *Journal of Constructivist Psychology*, *30*(1), 14–19. doi:10.1080/10720537.2015.1119082

Parmanand, S. (2021). Regulating motherhood through markets: Filipino women's engagement with microcredit. 129(1), 32–47. doi:10.1177/01417789211040506

Pekrun, R. (2011). Emotions as drivers of learning and cognitive development. In *New perspectives on affect and learning technologies* (pp. 23–39). Springer New York. doi:10.1007/978-1-4419-9625-1_3

Pellegrini, M., Uskov, V., & Casalino, N. (2020). Reimagining and Re-Designing the Post-COVID-19 Higher Education Organizations to Address New Challenges and Responses for Safe and Effective Teaching Activities. Law and Economics Yearly Review Journal, 9(part 1), 219-248.

Pérez, M. (2022). Gender diversity on corporate boards: Does it really make a difference. *International Journal of Governance and Financial Intermediation*, *1*(3), 219. doi:10.1504/IJGFI.2022.123898

Perlow, L., & Kelly, E. L. (2014). Toward a model of work redesign for better work and better life. *Work and Occupations*, *41*(1), 111–134. doi:10.1177/0730888413516473

Peters, M. A., Rizvi, F., McCulloch, G., Gibbs, P., Gorur, R., Hong, M., ... Quay, J. (2020). Reimagining the new pedagogical possibilities for universities post-Covid-19: An EPAT Collective Project. *Educational Philosophy and Theory*, 1–44.

Petruzzelli, E. 2020. "Empowering women and girls in engineering," *Chemical Engineering Progress* (116:1), pp. 3.

Peyton, J. K. (2017). Spanish for Native Speakers Education. In O. E. Kagan, M. H. Carrera, & C. H. Chick (Eds.), *Heritage Language Education*. Routledge. doi:10.4324/9781315092997-18

Pincus, F. L. (2003). *Reverse discrimination: Dismantling the myth*. Lynne Rienner Publishers. doi:10.1515/9781626374874

Pittman, C. T. (2010). Race and Gender Oppression in the Classroom: The Experiences of Women Faculty of Color with White Male Students. *Teaching Sociology*, *38*(3), 183–196. https://www.jstor.org/stable/27896528. doi:10.1177/0092055X10370120

Plaisent, M., Lafranchise, N., Tomiuk, D., Zuccaro, C., Mondesir, S., Khadhraoui, M. & Bernard, P. (2021). Networking to Support Spin-out Decision: the Case of Women in Engineering.

Poggesi, S., Mari, M., De Vita, L., and Foss, L. 2020. "Women entrepreneurship in STEM fields: Literature review and future research avenues," *International Entrepreneurship and Management Journal* (16:1), pp. 17-41.

Polkinghome, D., Bauman, G., & Vallejo Peña, E. (2013). Doing research that makes a difference. *The Journal of Higher Education*, *75*(1), 104–126. doi:10.1353/jhe.2013.00485

Pollner, M. (1975). 'The very coinage of your brain': The anatomy of reality disjunctures. *Philosophy of the Social Sciences*, *5*(3), 411–430. doi:10.1177/004839317500500304

Porter, J., & Oliver, R. (2015). Rethinking lactation space: Working mothers, working bodies, and the politics of inclusion. *Space and Culture*, *19*(1), 80–93. doi:10.1177/1206331215596488

Power, K. (2020). The COVID-19 pandemic has increased the care burden of women and families. *Sustainability: Science. Practice and Policy*, *16*(1), 67–73.

Preston, D. C., & Palmer, R. T. (2018). When relevance is no longer the question. *Journal of Black Studies*, *49*(8), 782–800. doi:10.1177/0021934718798088

Prime, J., & Moss-Racusin, C. A. (2009). Engaging men in gender initiatives: What change agents need to know. *Catalyst : Feminism, Theory, Technoscience*.

Prime, J., Moss-Racusin, C. A., & Foust-Cummings, H. (2009). Engaging men in gender initiatives: Stacking the deck for success. *Catalyst : Feminism, Theory, Technoscience*.

Putnam, R. (1995a). Bowling Alone: America's Declining Social Capital. *Journal of Democracy*, *6*(1), 65–78. doi:10.1353/jod.1995.0002

Pyke, J. (2013). Women, choice and promotion or why women are still a minority in the professoriate. *Journal of Higher Education Policy and Management, 35*(4), 444–454. doi:10.1080/1360080X.2013.812179

Qasim, Q. (2018). *Access to Finance for Female-led Micro, Small and Medium-sized Enterprises in Bosnia and Herzegovina.* World Bank Group IBRD-IDA. Retrieved from https://openknowledge.worldbank.org/handle/10986/29530

Quillian, L., Pager, D., Hexel, O., & Midtbøen, A. H. (2017). Meta-analysis of field experiments shows no change in racial discrimination in hiring over time. *Proceedings of the National Academy of Sciences of the United States of America, 114*(41), 10870–10875. doi:10.1073/pnas.1706255114 PMID:28900012

R'boul, H. (2022). Postcolonial interventions in intercultural communication knowledge: Meta-intercultural ontologies, decolonial knowledges and epistemological polylogue. *Journal of International and Intercultural Communication, 15*(1), 75–93. doi:10.1080/17513057.2020.1829676

Rai, K. B., & Critzer, J. W. (2000). *Affirmative action and the university: Race, ethnicity, and gender in higher education employment.* U of Nebraska Press.

Ramarajan, L., McGinn, K., & Kolb, D. (2012). *An outside–inside evolution in gender and professional work.* Harvard Business School Working Paper, 13–051.

Rand, A. (1990). *Introduction to Objectivist Epistemology: Expanded* (2nd ed.). Penguin.

Rapanta, C., Botturi, L., Goodyear, P., Guàrdia, L., & Koole, M. (2020). Online university teaching during and after the Covid-19 crisis: Refocusing teacher presence and learning activity. *Postdigital Science and Education*, 1-23.

Resmini, M. (2016). The "leaky pipeline.". *Chemistry (Weinheim an der Bergstrasse, Germany), 22*(11), 3533–3534. doi:10.1002/chem.201600292 PMID:26878818

Respicio, M. T. L., Irorita, E. S., Corpuz, J. S., & Abad, K. A. (2023). Effects of the Products and Services of Microfinance Institutions on the Economic Development of Their Members in Vintar, Ilocos Norte, Philippines. *Divine Word International Journal of Management and Humanities, 2*(3), 565752. doi:10.62025/dwijmh.v2i3.37

Rhoades, G. (2013). Adjunct professors are the new working poor. *CNN.* cnn.com

Rice, C. (2012). Why women leave academia and why universities should be worried. *The Guardian.* theguardian.com

Riley, S., & Wrench, D. (1985). Mentoring among women lawyers. *Journal of Applied Social Psychology, 15*(4), 374–386. doi:10.1111/j.1559-1816.1985.tb00913.x

Rose, D. (2018). *Citizens by degree: Higher education policy and the changing gender dynamics of American citizenship.* Oxford University Press.

Rosenfeld, M. (1991). *Affirmative action and justice: a philosophical and constitutional inquiry.* Yale University Press. doi:10.12987/9780300159547

Roudi-Fahimi, F., & Moghadam, V. (2003). *Empowering Women, Developing Society: Female Education in the Middle East and North Africa. From.* Population Reference Bureau.

Roudi-Fahimi, F., & Moghadam, V. (2006). Empowering Women, Developing Society: Female Education. In *The Middle East And North Africa. Women's Studies* International.

Royal Society. (2015) *Unconscious bias briefing (Prof Uta Frith).* https:// royalsociety.org/~/media/policy/Publications/2015/unconscious-bias-briefing-2015.pdf

Ruben, B., Mahon, G., & Shapiro, K. (2022). Academic Leader Selection, Development, Evaluation, and Recognition: Four Critical Higher Education Challenges. In International Perspectives on Leadership in Higher Education (Vol. 15, pp. 115-138). Emerald Publishing Limited.

Rubin, L. (2023). Faculty ombudsperson: Mission statement. Texas Woman's University. twu.edu

Rubio, P. F. (2009). *A history of affirmative action, 1619-2000.* Univ. Press of Mississippi.

Rudhumbu, N., Du Plessis, E. C., & Maphosa, C. (2020). Challenges and opportunities for women entrepreneurs in Botswana: Revisiting the role of entrepreneurship education. *Journal of International Education in Business, 13*(2), 183–201. doi:10.1108/JIEB-12-2019-0058

Ruël, H., Bondarouk, T., & Dresselhaus, L. (2014). *Global Talent Management in Multinational Corporations and the Role of Social Networks.* Social Media in Strategic Management., doi:10.1108/S1877-6361(2013)0000011015

Russell, T., & Martin, A. K. (2017). Reflective practice: Epistemological perspectives on learning from experience in teacher education. *Reflective theory and practice in teacher education,* 27-47.

Ryan, M. (2022). Addressing Workplace Gender Inequality: Using the Evidence to Avoid Common Pitfalls. *British Journal of Social Psychology.* PMID:36415906

Sassler, S., Glass, J., Levitte, Y., & Michelmore, K. M. (2017). The missing women in STEM? Assessing gender differentials in the factors associated with transition to first jobs. *Social Science Research, 63,* 192–208. doi:10.1016/j.ssresearch.2016.09.014 PMID:28202143

Savigny, H. (2014). Women, know your limits: Cultural sexism in academia. *Gender and Education, 26*(7), 794–809. doi:10.1080/09540253.2014.970977

Scandura, T. A., & Lankau, M. J. (1997). Relationships of gender, family responsibility and flexible work hours to organizational commitment and job satisfaction. Journal of Organizational Behavior: The International Journal of Industrial. *Journal of Organizational Behavior, 18*(4), 377–391. doi:10.1002/(SICI)1099-1379(199707)18:4<377::AID-JOB807>3.0.CO;2-1

Schaeffer, K. (2023). The data on women leaders. Pew Research Center. Retrieved from https://www.pewresearch.org/social-trends/fact-sheet/the-data-on-women-leaders/

Schell, E. E. (1997). Gypsy academics and mother-teachers: Gender, contingent labor, and writing instruction. *Cross Currents*.

Scherer, Z., & Mayol García, Y. (2022). *Hardships and disjunctives across Hispanic Groups*. US Census Bureau.

Schiebinger, L. L., Henderson, A. D., & Gilmarting, S. K. (2008). Dual-career academic couples: What universities need to know. Michelle R. Clayman Institute for Gender Research, Stanford University.

Scott, J. W. (1986). Gender: A Useful Category of Historical Analysis. *The American Historical Review*, *91*(5), 1053–1075. doi:10.2307/1864376

Seider, S., El-Amin, A., & Kelly, L. L. (2020). The development of critical consciousness. The Oxford handbook of moral development: An interdisciplinary perspective, 203-221.

Seidman, G. W. (1984). Women in Zimbabwe: Postindependence Struggles. *Feminist Studies*, *10*(3), 419–440. doi:10.2307/3178033

Sen, A. (1997). Human capital and human capability. *World Development*, *25*(12), 1959–1961. doi:10.1016/S0305-750X(97)10014-6

Sen, A. (2001). The many faces of gender inequality. *New Republic (New York, N.Y.)*, *215*(22), 35–39.

Shaheen, K. (2020). First Mars Mission from UAE Aims to Inspire a New Generation of Space Scientists. *National Geographic*. https://www.nationalgeographic.com/science/article/uae-mars-mission-hope-aims-inspire-new-generation-space-scientists

Shah, S., & Hingu, J. (2022). The Impact of Microfinance on the MSMES Sector. *International Journal of Management. Public Policy Research*, *1*(3), 67–71. doi:10.55829/ijmpr.v1i3.69

Sharpe, C. (2016). *In the Wake: On Being and Blackness*. Duke.

Shorris, E. (2015). *Latinos: A Biography of the People*. Norton & Co.

Shulman, L. S. (2005). Signature pedagogies in the professions. *Daedalus*, *134*(3), 52–59. doi:10.1162/0011526054622015

Simba, P., & Davids, N. (2020). Cultivating Third Space thinking in ('African') feminism through the works of Nandipha Mntambo. *Agenda (Durban, South Africa)*, *34*(3), 87–99. doi:10.1080/10130950.2020.1790302

Smith, M. (2016). Adjunct faculty union advocates for rights. *New York University*. nyunews.com

Smith, D. G., & Wolf-Wendel, L. (2007). *The challenge of diversity: Involvement or alienation in the academy?* Jossey-Bass.

Smith, J. (2010). *Women and Gender in Early Modern Europe*. Cambridge University Press.

Smith, J. A., Flowers, P., & Larkin, M. (2022). *Interpretative phenomenological analysis: theory, method, and research* (2nd ed.). SAGE Publications Ltd. doi:10.1037/0000259-000

Smith, J. W., & Calasanti, T. (2005). The Influences of Gender, Race, Ethnicity on Workplace Experiences of Institutional and Social Isolation: An Exploratory Study of University Faculty. *Sociological Spectrum, 25*(3), 307–334. doi:10.1080/027321790518735

Snyder, T. D., & de Brey, C. (2016). [National Center for Education Statistics.]. *Digest of Educational Statistics,* 2015.

Soni, V. (1999). Morality vs. mandate: Affirmative action in employment. *Public Personnel Management, 28*(4), 577–594. doi:10.1177/009102609902800407

Sorcinelli, M. D., Austin, A. E., Eddy, P. L., & Beach, A. L. (2016). *Creating the Future of Faculty Development*. Anker Publishing.

Spiegel, T. J. (2017). 2 Naturalism, Quietism. *On What It Is: Perspectives on Metaphilosophy, 47*.

Spillers, H. J. (1987). Mama's Baby, Papa's Maybe: An American Grammar Book. *Diacritics, 17*(2), 65–81. doi:10.2307/464747

Stainback, K., & Tomaskovic-Devey, D. (2012). *Documenting Desegregation: Racial and Gender Segregation in Private Sector Employment since the Civil Rights Act*. Russell Sage Foundation.

Stanley, C. A. (2006). Coloring the Academic Landscape: Faculty of Color Breaking the Silence in Predominantly White Colleges and Universities. *American Educational Research Journal, 43*(4), 701–736. https://www.jstor.org/stable/4121775. doi:10.3102/00028312043004701

Stepan-Norris, J., & Kerrissey, J. (2016). Enhancing gender equity in academia: Lessons from the ADVANCE program. *Sociological Perspectives, 59*(2), 225–245. doi:10.1177/0731121415582103

Stewart, C. A. (2021). Underrepresentation of women STEM leaders: Twelve women on different journeys using their voices to shape the world through science. *European Journal of STEM Education, 6*(1), 16. doi:10.20897/ejsteme/11387

Stone, P. (2007). *Opting Out? Why Women Really Quit Careers and Head Home*. University of California Press. doi:10.1525/9780520941793

Stupples, P. (2017). Beyond the predicted: Expanding our understanding of creative agency in international development through practice and policy. *International Journal of Cultural Policy, 23*(1), 52–67. doi:10.1080/10286632.2015.1035264

Subedi, K. R. (2021). Determining the sample in qualitative research. *Scholars'. Journal, 4*, 1–13.

Subrahmanian, R. (2003). Promoting gender equality. In *Targeting Development* (pp. 208–232). Routledge. doi:10.4324/9780203403235.ch9

Sue, D. W. (2010). *Microaggressions in everyday life: Race, gender, and sexual orientation*. John Wiley & Sons.

Compilation of References

Swim, J. K., & Thomas, M. A. (2006). Responding to everyday discrimination: A synthesis of research on goal-directed, self-regulatory coping behaviors. In *Stigma and group inequality* (pp. 119–140). Psychology Press.

Syed, M. (2019). Rebel Ideas: The power of diverse thinking. Hachette UK.

Szigeti, A. (2024). The heuristics theory of emotions and moderate rationalism. *Philosophical Psychology*, *37*(4), 861–884. doi:10.1080/09515089.2022.2094232

Takami, M. (2022). AASCU president discusses her leadership journey. *Dean and Provost*, *23*(10), 12–22. doi:10.1002/dap.31047

Tamtik, M., & Guenter, M. (2019). Policy analysis of equity, diversity and inclusion strategies in Canadian universities – How far have we come? *Canadian Journal of Higher Education*, *49*(3), 41–56. doi:10.47678/cjhe.v49i3.188529

Taylor, M., Turk, J. M., Chessman, H. M., & Espinosa, L. L. (2020). Race and ethnicity in higher education: 2020 supplement. American Council on Education (ACE).

Taylor, L. L., Beck, M. I., Lahey, J. N., & Froyd, J. E. (2017). Reducing inequality in higher education: The link between faculty empowerment and climate and retention. *Innovative Higher Education*, *42*(5-6), 391–405. doi:10.1007/s10755-017-9391-1

Teelken, C., & Deem, R. (2013). All are equal, but some are more equal than others: Managerialism and gender equality in higher education in comparative perspective. *Comparative Education*, *49*(4), 520–535. doi:10.1080/03050068.2013.807642

ter Vrugte, J., & de Jong, T. (2017). Self-Explanations in Game-Based Learning: From Tacit to Transferable Knowledge. In Instructional Techniques to Facilitate Learning and Motivation of Serious Games (pp. 141-159). Springer International Publishing.

Thomas, K. B. (2020). Intersectionality and epistemic erasure: A caution to decolonial feminism. *Hypatia*, *35*(3), 509–523. doi:10.1017/hyp.2020.22

Thomas, S. (2020). Women in Higher Education Administration Leadership and the Role of Institutional Support. In *Accessibility and Diversity in the 21st Century University* (pp. 234–249). IGI Global. doi:10.4018/978-1-7998-2783-2.ch012

Tichagwa, W. 1998. in P Maramba (ed) Beyond inequalities: Women in Zimbabwe. Waldahl, R. 2004. Politics and persuasion: Media coverage of Zimbabwe's 2000 election. Avondale: Weaver Press.

Tirri, K., Husu, J., & Kansanen, P. (1999). The epistemological stance between the knower and the known. *Teaching and Teacher Education*, *15*(8), 911–922. doi:10.1016/S0742-051X(99)00034-7

Tiwary, A. R., & Gupta, T. (2022). Stereotypical Barriers Affecting Women Aspiring High-ranking Leadership Role in Higher Education. In *Role of Leaders in Managing Higher Education* (Vol. 48, pp. 99–116). Emerald Publishing Limited. doi:10.1108/S2055-364120220000048007

Tobi, A. T. (2020). Towards a plausible account of epistemic decolonisation. *Philosophical Papers*, *49*(2), 253–278. doi:10.1080/05568641.2020.1779602

Toke, N. (2023). Empowering women in leadership. Diversity for Social Impact. Retrieved from https://diversity.social/empowering-women-in-leadership/

Toldson, I. A. (2019). Cultivating STEM Talent at Minority Serving Institutions: Challenges and Opportunities To Broaden Participation in STEM at Historically Black Colleges and Universities. In Growing Diverse STEM Communities: Methodology, Impact, and Evidence (Vol. 1328, pp. 1–8). American Chemical Society. doi:10.1021/bk-2019-1328.ch001

Tolley, K. (2018). Why we should care about the unionization of adjunct faculty in higher ed. *Johns Hopkins University Press*. press.jhu.edu

Tonkin, E. (2021). History and the Myth of Realism. In *The myths we live by* (pp. 25–35). Routledge. doi:10.4324/9781003174714-3

Tossou, A. G., Bodjona, C. P. H., Aboudou, M. T., & Gueyie, J. P. (2021). The influence of CSR practices on the financial performance of microfinance institutions in Togo. *International Journal of Economics and Finance*, *13*(2), 52. doi:10.5539/ijef.v13n2p52

Tossou, A. G., Gueyie, J.-P., & Couchoro, M. K. (2022). Female Managers, Informal Enterprises, and Their Perceived Financial Performance in Togo. *Journal of African Business*. Advance online publication. doi:10.1080/15228916.2022.2070387

Trần, T. H., Nguyen, T. S., & Lien, M. L. T. (2024). Women on corporate boards and firm financial performance: Empirical evidence from a multi-country in Asia. *Business Strategy & Development*, *7*(1), e340. Advance online publication. doi:10.1002/bsd2.340

Trent, R. J. (2020). *Women's Perspectives on the Role of Organizational Culture in Their Career Advancement to Leadership Positions: A Generic Inquiry* (Doctoral dissertation, Capella University).

Tripp, A. M. (2015). Rwanda: Women in post-genocide politics. In Women and Power in Postconflict Africa. Cambridge University Press.

Tshivhase, M. (2020). Personhood: Implications for Moral Status and Uniqueness of Women. Handbook of African Philosophy of Difference, 347-360.

Tufekci, O., & Hashiru, I. (2019). The Convention on the Elimination of All Forms of Discrimination against Women: A shift towards the empowerment of women in Africa. *Journal of Women's Empowerment*, *3*(2), 98–115.

Tufekci, O., & Hashiru, M. (2019). Women Empowerment through Political Participation in Rising Powers: Comparison of Turkey and Nigeria. In M. İnce Yenilmez & O. B. Çelik (Eds.), *A Comparative Perspective of Women's Economic Empowerment* (pp. 219–233). Routledge. doi:10.4324/9780429053146-13

Compilation of References

Turner, C. S. V., & González, J. C. (2011). Faculty women of color: The critical nexus of race and gender. *Journal of Diversity in Higher Education*, *4*(4), 199. doi:10.1037/a0024630

Tversky, A., & Kahneman, D. (1974). Judgment under uncertainty: Heuristics and biases. *Science*, *185*(4157), 1124-1131.

U.S. Department of Education, National Center for Education Statistics, IPEDS, 2020, HR Survey component (provisional data).

U.S. Department of Education. (2017). Integrated Postsecondary Education. *Data Systems*.

UNESCO. (n.d.). *Education for All: Regional Synthesis Report of the 2015 National Reviews in the Arab States Region*. https://www.unesco.org/new/fileadmin/MULTIMEDIA/FIELD/Doha/pdf/UNESCOEFAReviewArabStatesENG.pdf

United National Children's Fund (UNICEF). (2019a). *Syria Crisis Fast Facts*. Available at: https://www.unicef.org/mena/reports/syria-crisis-fast-facts

United Nations Children's Fund (UNICEF). (2019b). *To keep children in education, UNICEF starts incentives for school-based staff in Yemen*. Available at: https://www.unicef.org/press-releases/keep-children-education-unicef-starts-incentives-school-based-staff-yemen

United Nations Organization for Education, Science and Culture (UNESCO). (2020). *UIS Institute for Statistics*. Available at: http://data.uis.unesco.org/#

United Nations. (2015). HeForShe Campaign. Retrieved from https://www.heforshe.org/

United Nations. (2015). Transforming our world: The 2030 Agenda for Sustainable Development. Retrieved from https://sustainabledevelopment.un.org/post2015/transformingourworld

United Nations. (2020). *Progress of the world's women 2019-2020: Families in a changing world*. UN Women.

Urrieta, L., & Chavez, R. (2010). *Latino Faculty in Academelandia*. Routledge.

US Bureau of Labor Statistics. (2023). Labor force characteristics by race and ethnicity, 2023. *BLS Report no. 1100*.

Valentine, C. G., Trautner, M. N., & Spade, J. Z. (Eds.). (2019). *The kaleidoscope of gender: Prisms, patterns, and possibilities*. Sage Publications.

Van Veeren, E. (2019). Layered wanderings: Epistemic justice through the art of Wangechi Mutu and Njideka Akunyili Crosby. *International Feminist Journal of Politics*, *21*(3), 488–498. doi:10.1080/14616742.2019.1619468

Varela, F. J., Thompson, E., & Rosch, E. (2017). The embodied mind, revised edition: Cognitive science and human experience. MIT press. doi:10.7551/mitpress/9780262529365.001.0001

Vilar-Compte, M., Hernandez-Cordero, S., Ancira-Moreno, M., Burrola-Mendez, S., Ferre-Eguiluz, I., Omaña, I., & Pérez Navarro, C. (2021). Breastfeeding at the workplace: A systematic review of interventions to improve workplace environments to facilitate breastfeeding among working women. *International Journal for Equity in Health*, *20*(1), 110. doi:10.1186/s12939-021-01432-3 PMID:33926471

Villiers, C. (2019). Boardroom Culture: An Argument for Compassionate Leadership. *European Business Law Review*, *30*(2), 253–278. doi:10.54648/EULR2019012

Walkington, L. (2017). How Far Have We Really Come? Black Women Faculty and Graduate Students' Experiences in Higher Education. *Humboldt Journal of Social Relations*, *39*(39), 51–65. https://www.jstor.org/stable/90007871. doi:10.55671/0160-4341.1022

Wang, S. (2023). Exploring Early Childhood Educators' Perceptions and Practices Towards Gender Differences in STEM Play: A Multiple-Case Study in China. *Early Childhood Education Journal*, 1–14. doi:10.1007/s10643-023-01499-3 PMID:37360596

Waśniewski, P. (2021). Informal performance measurement in small enterprises. doi:10.1016/j.procs.2021.09.104

Weeks, K. (2011). *The Problem with Work: Feminism, Marxism, Antiwork Politics, and Postwork Imaginaries*. Duke University Press.

Wenham, C., Smith, J., & Morgan, R. (2020). COVID-19: The gendered impacts of the outbreak. *Lancet*, *395*(10227), 846–848. doi:10.1016/S0140-6736(20)30526-2 PMID:32151325

Wheaton, M. M., & Kezar, A. (2019). Interlocking systems of oppression: Women navigating higher education leadership. In *Challenges and opportunities for women in higher education leadership* (pp. 61–83). IGI Global. doi:10.4018/978-1-5225-7056-1.ch005

Wheeler, E. M., & Freeman, S. Jr. (2018). "Scholaring" While Black: Discourses on Race, Gender, and the Tenure Track. *Journal of the Professoriate*, *9*(2), 57–86.

White, D. G. (2007). "Matter out of Place": Ar'n't I a Woman? Black Female Scholars and the Academy. *Journal of African American History*, *92*(1), 5–12. https://www.jstor.org/stable/20064150. doi:10.1086/JAAHv92n1p5

Whittle, A., & Spicer, A. (2008). Is actor network theory critique? *Organization Studies*, *29*(4), 611–629. doi:10.1177/0170840607082223

Whitty-Collins, G. (2020). *Why Men Win at Work:...and How to Make Inequality History*. Luath Press Ltd.

Wielenga, C. (2022). African Feminisms and Justice on the Ground. *African Feminisms and Women in the Context of Justice in Southern Africa*, 19-39.

Wiesner-Hanks, M. E. (2021). *Gender in history: Global perspectives*. John Wiley & Sons.

Compilation of References

Wilder, C. S. (2013). *Ebony and Ivy: Race, Slavery, and the Troubled History of America's Universities*. Bloomsbury.

Williams, J. L., & Palmer, R. T. (2019). A response to racism: How HBCU enrollment grew in the face of hatred. Retrieved from https://cmsi.gse.rutgers.edu/content/response-to-racism

Williams, D. A. (2021). Strategic planning in higher education: A simplified B-VAR model. *International Journal of Educational Management*, *35*(6), 1205–1220. doi:10.1108/IJEM-08-2020-0382

Williams, K. L., & Taylor, L. D. (2022). The Black cultural student STEM success model: A framework for Black students' STEM success informed by HBCU environments and Black educational logics. *Journal of Women and Minorities in Science and Engineering*, *28*(6), 81–108. doi:10.1615/JWomenMinorScienEng.2022036596

Williams, M. G., & Lewis, J. A. (2019). Gendered racial microaggressions and depressive symptoms among Black women: A moderated mediation model. *Psychology of Women Quarterly*, *43*(3), 368–380. doi:10.1177/0361684319832511

Wilson Center. (2021). *Education in the Arab World: A Legacy of Coming Up Short. Part of the Viewpoints Series*. Author.

Wilson, R. (2003). Baby, baby, baby. *The Chronicle of Higher Education*, *49*(25), A10.

Winter, J., & Pauwels, A. (2006). Men staying at home looking after their children: Feminist linguistic reform and social change. *International Journal of Applied Linguistics*, *16*(1), 16–36. doi:10.1111/j.1473-4192.2006.00104.x

Women, U. N. (2011). *Progress of the world's women 2011-2012: In pursuit of justice*. UN Women. doi:10.18356/9789210550307

Women, U. N. (2015). *Progress of the world's women 2015-2016: Transforming economies, realizing rights*. UN Women. doi:10.18356/2d5f74e3-en

World Bank. (2001). *Engendering Development: Through Gender Equality in Rights, Resources, and Voice*. Author.

World Bank. (2005). *Introduction to poverty analysis*. http://siteresources.worldbank.org/PGLP/Resources/PovertyManual.pdf

World Bank. (2009). *Gender and Development in the Middle East and North Africa: Women in the Public Sphere*. World Bank.

World Bank. (2012). *Capabilities, Opportunities and Participation: Gender Equality and Development in the Middle East and North Africa Region, A companion to the World Development Report*. http://siteresources.worldbank.org/INTMENA/Resources/World_Development_Report_2012_Gender_Equality _ Development_Overview_MENA.pdf

World Bank. (2020). *COVID-19 Could Lead to Permanent Loss in Learning and Trillions of Dollars in Lost Earnings*. Retrieved from https://www.worldbank.org/en/news/press-release/2020/06/18/covid-19-could-lead-to-permanent-loss-in-learning-and-trillions-of-dollars-in-lost-earnings

World Bank. (2021). *Labor Force Participation Rate, female (% of female population ages 15+) (modeled ILO estimate)-Middle East & North Africa*. Author.

World Economic Forum. (2020). Global Gender Gap Report. Retrieved from https://www.weforum.org/reports/gender-gap-2020-report-100-years-pay-equality

World Economic Forum. (2020). *The Global Gender Gap Report*. Available at: http://www3.weforum.org/docs/WEF_GGGR_2020.pdf

World Health Organization. (2020). COVID-19 and violence against women: what the health sector/system can do, 7 April 2020 (No. WHO/SRH/20.04). World Health Organization.

Wright, C. A., & Wright, S. D. (1987). The role of mentors in the career development of young professionals. *Family Relations*, *36*(2), 204–208. doi:10.2307/583955

Wynter, S. (1989). Beyond the Word of Man: Glissant and the New Discourse of the Antilles. *World Literature Today*, *63*(4), 637–648. doi:10.2307/40145557

Yeoh, K. (2023, July). Effect of Serene Business Environment on the Performance of Small and Medium Enterprises in Malaysia. *Malaysian Management Journal, 27*.

Young, D. S., & Casey, E. A. (2018). An examination of the sufficiency of small qualitative samples. *Social Work & Criminal Justice Publications, 500,* https://digitalcommons.tacoma.uw.edu/socialwork_pub/500

Young, C. J., MacKenzie, D. L., & Sherif, C. W. (1982). In search of token women in academia: Some definitions and clarifications. *Psychology of Women Quarterly*, *7*(2), 166–169.

Young, J. L., & Hines, D. E. (2018). Killing my spirit, renewing my soul: Black female professors' critical reflections on spirit killings while teaching. *Women, Gender, and Families of Color*, *6*(1), 18–25.

Ysseldyk, R., Greenaway, K. H., Hassinger, E., Zutrauen, S., Lintz, J., Bhatia, M. P., Frye, M., Starkenburg, E., & Tai, V. (2019). A leak in the academic pipeline: Identity and health among postdoctoral women. *Frontiers in Psychology*, *10*, 1297. Advance online publication. doi:10.3389/fpsyg.2019.01297 PMID:31231285

Zgodic, A., & Small, L. (2021). Increasing representation of women in leadership positions at the University of South Carolina. Retrieved from https://sc.edu/about/offices_and_divisions/provost/docs/pacwi_policy_brief_final_october_19_2021.pdf

Zikhali, A. (2018). Women's representation in African politics: A review post-CEDAW. *Journal of African Politics*, *20*(3), 45–56.

About the Contributors

Reem Ali Abu-Lughod is a Professor of Criminal Justice at the California State University Bakersfield and has recently joined the Royal University for Women (RUW) in Bahrain as the Fulbright U.S. Scholar for the 2023-2024 academic year. Dr. Abu-Lughod's professorship extends for almost two decades, holding various teaching and administrative positions, engaging in community outreach, and working at local, national, and international levels. Dr. Abu-Lughod was actively involved with the U.S. State Department, conducting cultural and religious sensitivity training workshops to troops being deployed to the MENA region. Furthermore, Dr. Abu-Lughod has facilitated workshops on leadership to female employees at her local law enforcement agency. At the international level, Dr. Abu-Lughod was a faculty member at the National Defense College (NDC) in Abu-Dhabi-UAE; facilitating graduate level course workshops and developed graduate level courses as part of the Strategic and Security Studies program at NDC. In her research experience, Dr. Abu-Lughod has published on various issues of conflict and is currently collaborating on research projects with the Ministry of Interior-Bahrain, focusing on raising awareness among school children about online exploitation. Away from her teaching and research, Dr. Abu-Lughod enjoys spending time and traveling with her husband and three children; Ghazal, Rama, and Ameer; exploring new learning activities and helping them discover their inner interests and hobbies.

***

Prosper Bernard is a professor of management at the University of Quebec in Montréal where he was previously vice-rector and member of the BOARD of TRUSTEES of the university. He is also Chairman of the Board of the University Consortium of the Americas in Florida. He holds several degrees including a PhD from City University of New York. He has served successively as Director of the PHD program in management, and managed a PHD consortium including McGill university,Director of the department of management and technology, Director of the MBA program locally and abroad, namely in China, the only one Executive

MBA officially recognized by the Chinese government. Lately, China's Jiangsu Province presented him with the prestigious Friendship Medal and the Labor Prize for his contribution to university education. He has published numerous books and articles in academic conferences and scopus, IEEE and other prestigious journals.

Rosalynne E. Duff (She/ Her/ Hers) is an international educator, leader, and healer with over a decade of experience in urban education. She is a teacher educator of professional learning, serving in a predominantly Black university and school district in Atlanta, GA. She is also a doctoral student at Georgia State University's College of Education and Human Development, examining Teaching and Teacher Education. Black Women's holistic, healing, and liberatory practices are at the heart of her dissertation. She aims to develop a holistic framework for teacher education utilizing critical contemplative pedagogy, integrating educational equity, SEL, and academics. Duff authored "My Freedom Framework," a chapter in the book Black Women Navigating Historically White Higher Education Institutions and the Journey Toward Liberation (2022). She has co-authored three book chapters on innovative methods of (re)centering well-being, equity, and social justice in teacher-educator professional development and programs. Nationally, she has studied social and emotional learning (SEL), mindfulness, equity, and leadership through the Transformative Educational Leadership (TEL) program at the Omega Institute in Rhinebeck, NY. She was a facilitator with Millennium Forum, a platform for educator well-being. Internationally, she contributed to creating an innovative social and emotional curriculum with the SEE (Social, Emotional, and Ethical) Learning program and traveled to India to speak on a global teaching panel about the impact of SEE Learning in the urban classroom.

Chelo C. Durante is a faculty member in the College of Management and Entrepreneurship at Cebu Technological University-Danao Campus, Cebu Province Philippines. She is teaching Management, Marketing, and Fundamentals of Accounting. She obtained her Baccalaureate Degree in Bachelor of Science in Commerce, majoring in Accounting at the University of San Carlos, earned a Bachelor of Laws at the University of the Visayas, finished her Master in Business Administration at the Cebu Institute of Technology University, and is currently pursuing in Doctor in Management at the University of the Visayas. A recipient of the CANADA-ASEAN SEED Scholarship, she has undergone a research internship in Canada. After acting as an expert for the Philippine government, Chelo was recruited by CTU to share her great knowledge in finances and management. She is a recognized author and speaker.

About the Contributors

Kimarie Engerman is Dean of the College of Liberal Arts and Social Sciences, and Professor of Psychology at the University of the Virgin Islands. She is Associate Director on her campus for the Center for the Advancement of STEM Leadership (CASL) funded by the National Science Foundation.

Gueyie Jean-Pierre is a full professor of finance at the School of Management, University of Quebec in Montréal (Canada). He hold a Ph.D. in business administration for Laval University, Canada. His research interests are on financial institutions management (including banks, financial cooperatives and microfinance institutions), financial risk management, corporate governance, development economics and alternative investments. He has published several articles in Journal such as Journal of Banking and Finance, Energy Economics, Applied Economics, Journal of Small Business and Entrepreneurship, to name few, and has edited books in several areas in finance.

Catherine Hayes is Professor of Health Professions Pedagogy and Scholarship at the University of Sunderland, UK. She is a UK National Teaching Fellow and Principal Fellow of the UK Higher Education Academy. As a graduate of Podiatric Medicine in 1992, Catherine was a Founding Fellow of the Faculty of Podiatric Medicine at the Royal College of Physicians and Surgeons (Glasgow) in 2012 and was awarded Fellowship of the Royal College of Podiatry (London) in 2010. She is currently Programme Leader of the University of Sunderland's Professional Doctorate pathways for the DBA, EdD, DPM and DProf.

Elizabeth Jaeger is Associate Professor of Social Sciences and Chair of the Social Sciences Department at the University of the Virgin Islands. She is a Researcher at the Center for the Advancement of STEM Leadership (CASL) funded by the National Science Foundation.

Antonio D. Juan has a degree in English Studies from the University of Murcia and a PhD from the National University of Distance Education (UNED) with the positive accreditation by the ANECA body, being given the Extraordinary Doctorate Award. He is currently working as a professor at the University of Granada. He has been awarded a scholarship by University College (Cork, Ireland), the Franklin Institute (University of Alcala de Henares, Spain) and the Radcliffe Institute for Advanced Study (Harvard University, USA), where he conducted a pre-doctoral research visit in the year 2012. He is currently a member of the scientific committee of several national and international journals as well as a member of the editorial board of several international journals. He also belongs to the organizing and scientific committee of several conferences organized by the Athens Institute for Education and Research (Greece). Among his main lines of research we can emphasize the following aspects: cultural studies in the United States; gender issues associated with the role of women in the Anglo-American literature; or the teaching practice and process of English.

Mustafa Kayyali is an ardent advocate for excellence in higher education, driven by a relentless pursuit of quality, recognition, and innovation. My journey in academia started with a Master's in Quality Management and Evaluation in Higher Education from Universitat Oberta de Catalunya, followed by a Ph.D. in Quality Management from Azteca University. These academic pursuits have laid a strong foundation for my expertise in Accreditation, Quality Assurance, and Higher Education Rankings. As an entrepreneur, researcher, translator, and publisher, I am deeply involved in various facets of the academic world. My diverse interests encompass Management, Translation, Interpretation, and Academic consulting, contributing to a well-rounded understanding of the industry. Throughout my career, I have made significant contributions to academic literature, with more than 20 published papers and 7 book chapters to my name. Additionally, I take pride in having translated 5 books, bridging language gaps, and promoting knowledge exchange on a global scale. I am committed to fostering positive change in higher education and contributing to its continuous improvement.

Lolita L. Kincade, Ph.D., CFLE, PPS, NCC, LPC, is an Associate Professor and Chair of the Human Development and Family Relations Department at the State University of New York Plattsburgh in Plattsburgh, New York. She is certified as a Family Life Educator through the National Council on Family Relations (NCFR) and is also a Licensed Professional Counselor. Her professional interests include improving quality and standards of individual and family life. Dr. Kincade has published research on diverse topics, including the intersection of race and gender, and social justice education and advocacy. She has worked with diverse populations in academic, hospital and community settings, and is experienced in research consultation, program development and planning, non-profit administration and policy advocacy. Dr. Kincade is motivated to impact and transform institutions of higher education in the interest of students, faculty, and leaders of color.

Camille A. McKayle (PhD) is Provost and Professor of Mathematics at the University of the Virgin Islands (US). Her research focuses on organizational creativity, creativity in higher education, creativity and self-efficacy in students, and higher education leadership focusing on Historically Black Colleges/Universities that. She is a lead investigator for the National Science Foundation-funded Center for the Advancement of STEM Leadership (CASL).

About the Contributors

Michel Plaisent is a full professor in the University of Québec in Montréal (Canada). After a bachelor in Information technology, a M.Sc. in project management and a Ph.D. in Information Technology Management, he joined the Business school in 1980 where he held different position while developing his research career, namely IT program director for 6 years. His doctoral research was pioneer as he studied the use of computer mediated communication systems by CEO. Since then, Dr. Plaisent's researches continue to focus human factors of IT, namely cognitive ergonomics, learning problems and personal productivity tools for managers. Among his new researches namely: Education 4.0 concepts and tools, and more broadly the impact of internet on life and society. He has published more than 25 books and more than one hundred of articles in international conferences and academic indexed journals. He is engaged in China EMBA program and he manages for UQAM research collaboration protocols with three South-Asia universities.

Catherine C. Saunders is a recent graduate of Howard University where she earned her PhD in English with a specialty in African American literature. Her scholarship focuses on Black interiority and her theoretical framework strives to contemplate Black people and Black culture beyond resistance and response. In the fall, she will join the faculty at Bates College as a Visiting Assistant Professor of Africana.

Angelicque Tucker Blackmon is the Director of Research at the Center for the Advancement of STEM Leadership (CASL), University of the Virgin Islands, funded by the National Science Foundation. Also, she is President, CEO and Chief Inspiration Officer at Innovative Learning Center, LLC.

Sandy Watson is an Associate Professor of Curriculum & Instruction at the University of Louisiana Monroe where she teaches undergraduate and graduate courses in multiculturalism and curriculum. Her research interests include science education, curriculum studies, multiculturalism and diversity, and teacher education. An educator for 26+ years, Dr. Watson has published many articles and has presented at multiple conferences across her research areas.

Cataldo Zuccaro obtained a Ph.D. in marketing at the University of Quebec in Montreal in 1999. He is a professor of marketing at the University of Quebec in Montreal. He had been a director of the MBA Research and the chair of the department of business strategies. Dr. Cataldo Zuccaro is a specialist in Data Analysis, Business Analytics and Marketing. His areas of research are marketing research methods, business modeling, customer scoring and segmentation, business analytics and research methods. He has taught and continues to teach in the university's Executive MBA program in such countries as Romania, Poland, France, Morocco, Algeria, Tunisia, Lebanon, Mexico and Peru. He has also consulted for large multinational corporations and government agencies. Dr. Zuccaro has published his research in such journals as Recherches sociologiques Revue des sciences administratives du Canada, Journal of the market research society Journal of social psychology, International journal of market research, Journal of modelling management, International journal of bank marketing, Social research indicators and the Journal of Economics and Economic Education Research. He is the winner, in 2010, of the silver medal for the best paper in the International Journal of Market Research.

Index

A

Academic Leaders 197-198, 201, 212
Academic Leadership 170, 198, 200, 212
Affirmative action 87, 90-95, 97-98, 101-107, 143
agentic qualities 20, 22-24, 32-34
Authenticity 141, 182-183, 186-188, 195

B

Black femininity 45
Black women professors 60-65, 70-71, 78-79
Broadening Participation 128, 197, 201-204, 212

C

Career Advancement 9, 120-121, 124, 200, 242, 253
career trajectories 20, 24, 26, 28, 31
CASL 202, 209, 213
civic progression 20, 34
collective commitment 252, 257
Colonialism 177-178, 181, 195
COVID-19 pandemic 6, 18-20, 23-24, 28
creative practice 179, 186
Critical Reflection 22, 42, 64, 179, 186
Critical Reflexivity 22, 30, 34, 42, 179, 196
Cultural factors 214, 216-217, 223, 225

D

democracy 5, 91, 138, 140
disciplinary perspectives 19, 31, 34
discriminatory practices 6-7
domestic roles 3, 6
dominated professions 24, 28
Doxastic Injustice 187-188, 196
Driver 184, 236, 239, 244

E

Economic Development 11-12, 161, 172, 215
educational attainment 2, 7
Emotional Labour 34, 42
Empowering Women 10, 12, 237-240, 251-253
empowerment 5, 7, 10-12, 91, 138, 143, 146, 206, 217, 237-238, 241, 244, 246-251, 255-257
Entrepreneurship 7, 11, 215-217, 219, 221, 236
epistemic cognition 21, 179, 183-185
Epistemic Injustice 187-188, 196
Epistemic Responsibility 187, 196
epistemological stance 181-183

F

family obligations 8, 116
feminist epistemology 177-188

G

Gender Equality 4-8, 10-12, 122, 127, 138, 140, 142-143, 145, 148, 237-239, 241, 246-251, 253, 255-257

Gender Norms 10, 243-244, 249
Gender Pay Gap 4, 26, 241, 253-254

H

HBCUS 197, 200-204, 208-209, 213
Healing 60-64, 66, 68-70, 72-79
Hermeneutical Ignorance 187, 196
Higher Education 1-8, 10, 18-22, 25-28, 33-34, 42, 46, 53, 61-67, 69, 71, 76-79, 87-88, 90-101, 104, 107, 113-117, 121, 123-124, 127-129, 151-156, 158-163, 165-168, 170, 176-177, 198-200, 203, 208, 237-241, 244, 246-251, 255-257
Hispanic female 151-152, 159
Hispanic population 151, 153
human capital 2-3, 5

I

Inclusive Practices 237-239, 241, 246, 248-249, 251, 256-257
Inclusivity 4, 11, 33, 238-239, 251-253, 256-257
Inequality 4, 6, 9, 18, 21, 28, 42, 90-93, 95, 126, 139, 141, 143, 163, 237, 239-241, 245, 255
institutional structure 46, 55-56
Institutional Transformation 117, 122, 127, 252
institutional wrath 47, 54
Intersectionality 25, 61, 64, 77, 79, 96, 196, 237, 245, 248, 250, 255

K

knowledge acquisition 178, 183

L

legislative reforms 3, 10
lived experience 178, 184-185

M

male counterparts 6, 18-19, 26, 33, 46, 55, 92, 116, 145-146, 158, 215, 219, 241, 250
MENA 1-9, 11-12
Micro-Enterprises 214, 225
Micro-Financing 214
mimetic ordering 48

N

Neoliberalism 27, 42

O

organisational culture 25, 28
organisational hierarchy 31-32

P

Perspective Transformation 21, 187, 196
Pipeline Initiatives 113, 117-118, 122, 127
politics 10, 50-51, 69, 137-140, 142-143, 145, 147-148, 184, 240-241
Positionality 19-20, 42, 44, 49, 66, 178, 182, 186
President (of university) 176
Professors 28, 44-45, 49-51, 53, 60-66, 70-71, 78-79, 113, 116, 118, 120, 123, 151-152, 154-158, 198, 200
propositional knowledge 179, 186-187

Q

Quota System 137, 139-140, 142, 144-146, 148

R

Research and Evaluation 99, 113, 117
Retainment 113-114, 116

S

Signature Pedagogy 29, 42
Social ecological model 106
Social Recognition 176
social science 155, 179, 186-187
societal expectations 6, 8, 243-244, 247, 249, 255-256

Index

Startup 236
STEM 3-4, 28, 115-116, 121-122, 127-128, 163, 186, 197-198, 200-209, 212-213, 235, 238, 243-244, 246, 257
STEM Leadership 200, 202, 209, 213
Stereotypes 3-5, 7-8, 10, 12, 96, 98, 115, 146, 214, 216-217, 223, 236, 242-243, 248, 250, 256
sustained commitment 152, 167
systemic power 53-54

T

Teacher education 60-63, 67, 70-71, 75, 77-79
teacher preparation 62-64, 71, 76, 78-79
transformative learning 21, 30, 32

U

US Higher Education 95, 156, 158
UTEP 152-153, 165-172, 176

V

Verisimilitude 179-180, 185, 187, 196

W

Well-being 60-67, 70-79, 93, 96, 120, 245-246, 254-256
Women of color 53, 66, 87-88, 90-91, 93-98, 101-107, 162, 245
women's rights 3, 5, 138, 240
Workforce diversity 98
work-life balance 8, 11, 120, 243, 245-246, 254

Publishing Tomorrow's Research Today

Uncover Current Insights and Future Trends in Education
with IGI Global's Cutting-Edge Recommended Books

Print Only, E-Book Only, or Print + E-Book.
Order direct through IGI Global's Online Bookstore at www.igi-global.com or through your preferred provider.

ISBN: 9781668493007
© 2023; 234 pp.
List Price: US$ 215

ISBN: 9798369300749
© 2024; 383 pp.
List Price: US$ 230

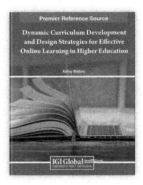

ISBN: 9781668486467
© 2023; 471 pp.
List Price: US$ 215

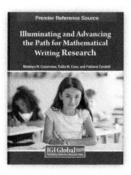

ISBN: 9781668465387
© 2024; 389 pp.
List Price: US$ 215

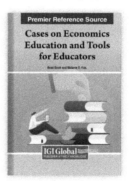

ISBN: 9781668475836
© 2024; 359 pp.
List Price: US$ 215

ISBN: 9781668444238
© 2023; 334 pp.
List Price: US$ 240

Do you want to stay current on the latest research trends, product announcements, news, and special offers?
Join IGI Global's mailing list to receive customized recommendations, exclusive discounts, and more.
Sign up at: www.igi-global.com/newsletters.

Scan the QR Code here to view more related titles in Education.

www.igi-global.com   Sign up at www.igi-global.com/newsletters   facebook.com/igiglobal   twitter.com/igiglobal   linkedin.com/igiglobal

Ensure Quality Research is Introduced to the Academic Community

Become a Reviewer for IGI Global Authored Book Projects

 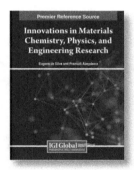 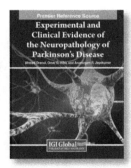 

The overall success of an authored book project is dependent on quality and timely manuscript evaluations.

Applications and Inquiries may be sent to:
development@igi-global.com

Applicants must have a doctorate (or equivalent degree) as well as publishing, research, and reviewing experience. Authored Book Evaluators are appointed for one-year terms and are expected to complete at least three evaluations per term. Upon successful completion of this term, evaluators can be considered for an additional term.

If you have a colleague that may be interested in this opportunity, we encourage you to share this information with them.

www.igi-global.com

IGI Global's Open Access Journal Program
Publishing Tomorrow's Research Today

Including Nearly 200 Peer-Reviewed, Gold (Full) Open Access Journals across IGI Global's Three Academic Subject Areas:
Business & Management; Scientific, Technical, and Medical (STM); and Education

Consider Submitting Your Manuscript to One of These Nearly 200 Open Access Journals for to Increase Their Discoverability & Citation Impact

Web of Science Impact Factor **6.5**	Web of Science Impact Factor **4.7**	Web of Science Impact Factor **3.2**	Web of Science Impact Factor **2.6**
JOURNAL OF **Organizational and End User Computing**	JOURNAL OF **Global Information Management**	INTERNATIONAL JOURNAL ON **Semantic Web and Information Systems**	JOURNAL OF **Database Management**

Choosing IGI Global's Open Access Journal Program Can Greatly Increase the Reach of Your Research

Higher Usage
Open access papers are 2-3 times more likely to be read than non-open access papers.

Higher Download Rates
Open access papers benefit from 89% higher download rates than non-open access papers.

Higher Citation Rates
Open access papers are 47% more likely to be cited than non-open access papers.

Submitting an article to a journal offers an invaluable opportunity for you to share your work with the broader academic community, fostering knowledge dissemination and constructive feedback.

Submit an Article and Browse the IGI Global Call for Papers Pages

We can work with you to find the journal most well-suited for your next research manuscript.
For open access publishing support, contact: journaleditor@igi-global.com

Are You Ready to Publish Your Research?

IGI Global
Publishing Tomorrow's Research Today

IGI Global offers book authorship and editorship opportunities across three major subject areas, including Business, STM, and Education.

Benefits of Publishing with IGI Global:

- Free one-on-one editorial and promotional support.
- Expedited publishing timelines that can take your book from start to finish in less than one (1) year.
- Choose from a variety of formats, including Edited and Authored References, Handbooks of Research, Encyclopedias, and Research Insights.
- Utilize IGI Global's eEditorial Discovery® submission system in support of conducting the submission and double-blind peer review process.
- IGI Global maintains a strict adherence to ethical practices due in part to our full membership with the Committee on Publication Ethics (COPE).
- Indexing potential in prestigious indices such as Scopus®, Web of Science™, PsycINFO®, and ERIC – Education Resources Information Center.
- Ability to connect your ORCID iD to your IGI Global publications.
- Earn honorariums and royalties on your full book publications as well as complimentary content and exclusive discounts.

Join Your Colleagues from Prestigious Institutions, Including:

Australian National University
Massachusetts Institute of Technology
Johns Hopkins University
Harvard University
Tsinghua University
Columbia University in the City of New York

Learn More at: www.igi-global.com/publish
or by Contacting the Acquisitions Department at: acquisition@igi-global.com

Individual Article & Chapter Downloads
US$ 37.50/each

Easily Identify, Acquire, and Utilize Published Peer-Reviewed Findings in Support of Your Current Research

- Browse Over **170,000+ Articles & Chapters**
- **Accurate & Advanced** Search
- Affordably Acquire **International Research**
- **Instantly Access** Your Content
- Benefit from the **InfoSci® Platform Features**

" *It really provides an excellent entry into the research literature of the field. It presents a manageable number of highly relevant sources on topics of interest to a wide range of researchers. The sources are scholarly, but also accessible to 'practitioners'.* "

- Ms. Lisa Stimatz, MLS, University of North Carolina at Chapel Hill, USA

Printed in the USA
CPSIA information can be obtained
at www.ICGtesting.com
LVHW081927041124
795688LV00041B/1299

9 798369 301036